SCHAUM'S OUTLINE OF

Theory and Problems of

INTRODUCTION TO

PSYCHOLOGY

Second Edition

ARNO F. WITTIG, Ph.D.

Professor Emeritus of Psychology and Former Dean
Honors College
Ball State University

Schaum's Outline Series

McGRAW-HILL

New York   San Francisco   Washington, D.C.   Auckland   Bogotá   Caracas
Lisbon   London   Madrid   Mexico City   Milan   Montreal   New Delhi
San Juan   Singapore   Sydney   Tokyo   Toronto

ARNO F. WITTIG is a Professor Emeritus of Psychology and Former Dean of the Honors College at Ball State University. He received his B.A. from Hobart College and an M.A. and Ph.D. from The Ohio State University. He has taught Introductory Psychology for forty years. He specializes in sport psychology research, concentrating on gender differences and psychological rehabilitation from injury. He has been elected as a Fellow in three divisions of the American Psychological Association. His doctorate was in Experimental Psychology, but over the years he moved from verbal learning investigations to sport behavior. The three APA divisons in which he holds a Fellow status are General Psychology, Teaching of Psychology, and Exercise and Sport Psychology. He is the author or coauthor of several books and numerous articles. One of the books he has coauthored is on the ethics of teaching.

Schaum's Outline of Theory and Problems of
INTRODUCTION TO PSYCHOLOGY

1 2 3 4 5 6 7 8 9 10 11 12 13 14 15 16 17 18 19 20 **PRS PRS** 0 9 8 7 6 5 4 3 2 1 0

ISBN 0-07-134709-7

Sponsoring Editor: Barbara Gilson
Production Supervisor: Tina Cameron
Editing Supervisor: Maureen B. Walker
Compositor: Keyword Publishing Services Ltd.

Library of Congress Cataloging-in-Publication Data applied for.

McGraw-Hill
A Division of The McGraw-Hill Companies

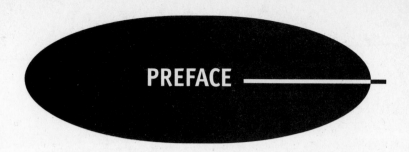

PREFACE

Psychology is defined as the scientific study of behavior and mental processes. As a scientific discipline, psychology attempts to provide an understanding of how and why organisms behave as they do. Therefore, as you begin to study this subject, you should keep in mind that psychology depends on the careful and objective consideration of evidence, not on what "common sense" tells us.

This outline is an overview of the most basic principles of psychology. The outline may be used as a self-teaching tool, in conjunction with a standard textbook, or as a supplement to classroom and laboratory instruction. Each chapter begins with a concise summary of *psychological principles*, many of which are illustrated with examples. Following the discussion of theory in each chapter is a group of *solved problems*, which are used to illustrate the principles and often contain refinements and extensions of, or exceptions to, the principles. Finally, each chapter contains a list of *key terms*; like other disciplines, psychology has a specialized vocabulary, and familiarity with it is essential for students who wish to have a firm grasp of the subject matter.

The outline also contains three examinations and a final examination. By taking each examination and comparing your answers with those provided, you should be able to estimate how well you have mastered the basic principles of psychology.

ARNO F. WITTIG

CONTENTS

CHAPTER 1

Psychology: Definition and History

We are all interested in how people act. Not only do we want to know what is happening; quite frequently we want to know why. Although these questions often are answered in a rather loose or undisciplined fashion, a more rigorous body of knowledge concerning behavior has developed. This body of knowledge is called *psychology*.

1.1 DEFINITION AND PURPOSE

Psychology is the *scientific study of behavior and cognitive processes*. As such, psychology describes thinking and behavior and looks at the relationships between them (the what) and tries to explain the causes for them (the why).

EXAMPLE 1.1. Why did you buy this book? What do you expect to accomplish? If you accomplish your goals, will you be likely to buy another, similar book in a different subject? Psychologists try to answer questions like these to determine how people think, how they act, and why they do.

The descriptions of behavior or thought that result from psychological study are not casual or without aim. The study of behavior and mental processes has as its purposes understanding, prediction, modification, or improvement of actions or thoughts. Basically, understanding and prediction occur when a psychologist anticipates events that will occur in natural or contrived situations, whereas modification and improvement mean the psychologist has somehow manipulated the situation and subsequently observed an expected result.

EXAMPLE 1.2. It is understandable and predictable that a child in the early stages of language development at first may call all beverages "pop." Manipulating the child's experiences will lead to learning different labels so that the child eventually correctly identifies "water," "milk," and "pop" as different drinks.

1.2 AREAS OF STUDY

Humans and Animals. *Behavior* is defined as any observable or measurable response by a person or animal. The definition of psychology includes the study of *all* behavior, including both animal and

1

human behavior. Although currently less than 10 percent of the studies conducted involve animals, animals sometimes are studied when the use of human subjects is prevented by specific ethical problems, the availability of subjects, the duration of the treatment, or special expenses.

Heredity and Environment.   One of the questions psychology attempts to answer is whether behavior occurs as a result of inherited characteristics (*hereditary influences*) or because of some effect of learning (*environmental influences*). A controversy regarding the relative importance of *heredity* and *environment* has continued in psychology for a long time and remains unresolved. The generally accepted finding is that both influences affect behavior—separately and as they interact. (See Chapter 3 for a more thorough discussion of this interaction.)

Conscious and Unconscious.   Behavior is often the product of a *conscious* choice. Some behaviors, however, may result from motives that are below a level of awareness. Many theorists refer to these motives as *unconscious*. Both conscious and unconscious motives may lead to responses, and psychology therefore studies both.

Normal and Abnormal.   Psychology studies both *normal* and *abnormal behavior*. It is often difficult to decide whether a behavior or thought pattern should be classified as normal or abnormal. The criteria used to make this decision include the level of distress or disability being experienced and how maladaptive, disruptive, or harmful the behavior is for the person or for society. Decisions of this nature may depend on the specific characteristics of the individual or the culture in which the individual resides.

Age Range.   Psychology studies behavior over the entire life span. Indeed, because behavior may depend on hereditary characteristics as well as learning, psychologists are concerned with the individual from the moment of conception until death. However, very few psychologists study the entire age range; most prefer to concentrate on a distinct span, such as early childhood, adolescence, or late adulthood.

Theory or Applied.   Finally, the breadth of psychological study is such that it includes both theoretical studies and the application of psychological principles to specific problems. Probably the majority of psychological specialties can be categorized as applied. (See Section 1.5.)

1.3   THE BACKGROUND AND BEGINNING OF PSYCHOLOGY

In the history of scientific endeavor, psychology is considered a relatively new discipline. While many other disciplines—such as biology, chemistry, and physics—have traditions dating back to ancient history, the usual date selected for the beginning of psychology is 1879. This date is chosen because in that year *Wilhelm Wundt* (1832–1920) started the first formal psychology research laboratory at the University of Leipzig, Germany. Other researchers had preceded Wundt in conducting psychological investigations, but Wundt was the first to call psychology an independent experimental science and describe his facility as a psychology laboratory. Wundt also started the first journal for psychology and wrote an early textbook of physiological psychology.

· Psychology did not spring suddenly onto the scientific scene. Concern with "psychological issues" extends back into antiquity. Some of the areas which contributed to the development of psychology as a separate discipline are philosophy, the natural sciences, and medicine.

Philosophy.   For thousands of years, philosophers have tried to understand thinking and behavior. Many of the basic areas of psychology, such as learning, motivation, personality, perception, and physiological influences on behavior, were first discussed by philosophers. Many departments of psychology in colleges and universities originated in departments of philosophy and only later gained independent status.

EXAMPLE 1.3.   Psychologists are concerned with questions of how the human mind develops from birth to adulthood. Philosophers also faced the same questions. For example, Plato, a Greek philosopher of the fourth century B.C., believed that a human was born with certain innate, or given, mental abilities and knowledge. By contrast, John Locke, a seventeenth-century English philosopher, believed that the human mind was at birth a *tabula rasa*, or "blank slate," on which impressions were made by experiences. Neither philosophers nor psychologists have concluded definitively which, if either, of these views is correct.

What made psychology separate from philosophy was a difference in approach. As philosophy in the eighteenth and nineteenth centuries began to change toward a greater emphasis on empirical values, the eventual rise of an independent psychology became possible. An attitude of scientific inquiry became the mainstay of psychology. (See Chapter 2.)

The Sciences.   Much of the methodology that accompanied the introduction of scientific inquiry into behavioral areas was borrowed or adapted from other sciences. Physics, chemistry, biology, and physiology were all important contributors to the start of psychology. The methodologies that developed are discussed in Chapter 2, but it is worthwhile to mention briefly some of the contributions that came from these sciences.

Both physics and chemistry provided concerns regarding sensations and perceptions. These concerns quickly became part of the physiology of the time. More recently, developments in chemistry have led to the vastly increased use of drugs in the treatment of behavioral problems.

The biological theory of evolution gave strong support for *comparative psychology*, in which the behavior of one species is compared with that of another. Biology also provided much of the information on genetics, heredity, and physiological structures and processes which has been used by psychologists in considering the effects of these factors on behavior and thought processes.

EXAMPLE 1.4.   Biopsychologists often study the nervous system in an attempt to relate physiological processes to observed behaviors or thoughts. The questions asked might include trying to determine which parts of the brain are involved when a child learns a new word and trying to determine what effect may occur when a person suffers brain damage in an accident.

Thus, methodology, areas for investigation, and justification for study were all taken from older scientific disciplines.

Medicine.   In a somewhat indirect manner, medicine made a major contribution to the beginning of psychology. Until the early 1800s, most people who exhibited abnormal personality patterns were thought to be possessed by the devil. In the early 1880s, medical interest brought treatment for physical illnesses that were thought to cause abnormal patterns of behavior or thinking.

By the late 1800s, the attitude had changed. These abnormal patterns were classified as *mental illnesses*, and treatment changed accordingly. This led to the development of what is now called *psychiatry* and had an important effect on the beginnings of *clinical psychology*. The concerns of psychiatry and clinical psychology began from a medical tradition.

EXAMPLE 1.5.   A person who wishes to become a psychiatrist must, after finishing undergraduate work, receive both a degree in medicine and subsequent specialized training. As a result, a strong orientation for psychiatrists has come to be called the *medical model*, in which the psychiatrist treats a client as a "sick" person. Many other practitioners do not accept this concept of "disease." They prefer terms such as "abnormal patterns of behavior" and "psychopathology" to describe the actions of the people they observe and treat.

Other Early Influences.   In the early 1900s, much of what was called *clinical psychology* was based in education or school endeavors. Psychological studies also were conducted as responses to nonscientific prompting. These investigations tried to determine the validity of claims made by groups such as *physiognomists*, who believed that the appearance of the face and head revealed personality characteristics, and *phrenologists*, who "mapped" areas of the skull, claiming knowledge of brain function and its effects on behavior. It is safe to say that psychology arose from the effects of numerous early influences.

1.4 EARLY DEVELOPMENT OF PSYCHOLOGY

Early psychology is characterized as a period of *systems of psychology*. These systems were attempts to explain all of behavior by using a single set of principles. Although none continues to be of major importance, all contributed significantly to present-day psychology.

Structuralism. The position developed by Wundt and later expanded by Edward Titchener (1867–1927) was called *Structuralism*. Psychology for the Structuralists was the study of the *introspective* reports of normal human adults. Trained subjects made descriptive reports of what they believed were the elements of stimuli presented to them. These reports were supposed to allow a psychologist to interpret the structure of the mind and how it worked. The work of the Structuralists paralleled that of scientists in other disciplines; for example, studies in chemistry focused on analyzing substances into their chemical elements.

EXAMPLE 1.6. In a Structuralist experiment, you might be asked to report how you sensed the weight, color, and texture of this book. You also might be asked to describe your feelings, if any, toward the book. Merely saying, "This is a psychology book," would not be sufficient as an introspective report.

As a system, Structuralism was very limited. However, the Structuralists did make important contributions to the early development of psychology by (a) testing the method of introspection, which ultimately failed because of disagreements regarding the properties of the experiences being reported and the inability to verify the accuracy of one report compared with another, (b) establishing psychology as a scientific endeavor and stressing appropriate scientific methodology, and (c) providing a starting point that was challenged and investigated by many of the later psychological systems.

Functionalism. One of the systems that developed as a reaction to Structuralism was called *Functionalism*, and was the first system to develop in the United States. Functionalists were concerned with the purposes of behavior rather than the structure of the mind. Influenced by Charles Darwin's theory of evolution, which stressed species survival and natural selection, Functionalism investigated the adaptation or adjustment the subject achieved in different environments.

Functionalists generally adopted a broader view of psychology than did Structuralists. This allowed them to study all age groups and a variety of subjects. Many new areas of investigation resulted, including the study of motivation and emotion, child psychology, animal experimentation, and various areas of *applied psychology*.

EXAMPLE 1.7. The Functionalists were not limited to the use of normal human adults as subjects for their experiments. (They did not rely exclusively on introspective reports, as did the Structuralists.) The Functionalists, for example, might investigate the ways in which very young children responded to novel problem-solving situations.

Behaviorism. John Watson (1878–1958) established a system for the study of behavior in which it was believed that only the observable responses made by the subject were relevant. That system came to be known as *Behaviorism* and was characterized by an interest in the muscular movements and glandular secretions of the subject. Behaviorists denied the concept of mind because a mind could not be observed. Their goal was to identify orderly, lawful stimulus-response relationships.

EXAMPLE 1.8. Behaviorists were interested only in observable phenomena. A strict Behaviorist would not describe a person as "happy," because happiness is a state of mind and mind is not observable. Instead, a Behaviorist might describe the person's smile or laugh, noting the observable response to a stimulus.

Although this system soon received much criticism, it did point out the possible futility of trying to describe unobservable activities of the subject and helped psychology confront the ideas of stimulus control and determinism of behavior. Direct concern with stimuli and the consequent responses became an important part of several psychological positions, although the recent growth of cognitive psychology has brought a greater focus on and understanding of how people think about, know, and understand their worlds.

Gestalt Psychology. *Gestalt psychology* developed in Germany with particular interest in perceptual problems and how they could be interpreted. In general, the Gestalt psychologists pointed out that previous attempts at explaining perception (and other types of behaviors) were simplistic because they fragmented behavior and failed to take into account the *whole* environment. The phrase frequently used to describe this holistic position is "the whole is greater than (different from) the sum of its parts."

EXAMPLE 1.9. The Gestaltists believed that other systematic positions were mistaken in their attempts to divide behavior (including mental activity) into discrete, or separate, functions. They believed that behavior, especially human mental behavior, was a creative process of synthesis that was more than or different from the sum of its constituent parts. Gestaltists might cite as an example a person watching a movie—instead of seeing a series of still pictures (the separate frames of the film), the viewer perceives or "sees" a continuous, moving image.

Psychodynamic Psychology. Sigmund Freud (1856–1939), a Viennese medical doctor, was the first person to practice *psychoanalysis*. Freud did not intend for psychoanalysis to become a system, but the theories he developed to support his therapeutic techniques came to be taken as one. His very extensive investigation of the development and maintenance of personality, with an emphasis on things such as early childhood experiences and unconscious sources of motivation, eventually was treated as a systematic position. This in turn generated much inquiry intended to evaluate psychodynamic theory and affected areas such as clinical psychology, counseling psychology, and developmental psychology.

EXAMPLE 1.10. One of Freud's great contributions to psychology was his suggestion that many behaviors arose from motives that were unconscious—that is, motives of which a person was unaware. For example, in treating some of his patients, Freud discovered phobias (fears) that had sources that were "hidden" from the patients yet influenced their behaviors.

1.5 CURRENT OUTLOOKS IN PSYCHOLOGY

Attempts to explain all of behavior by reference to only one systematic position did not work out. By itself, no system could account for all types of behavior, and systematic interpretations fell into disfavor. The trend in psychology has been to limit areas of study to particular aspects of behavior. Although there continue to be attempts to promote unifying perspectives of psychology, *theories* and models generally are far more specialized than were the broad claims of the psychological systems.

In recent years, several perspectives have emerged, housing within them several hundred psychological specialties. These specialties can be grouped into several broad approaches to the study of behavior.

Perspectives. Today's perspectives often reflect psychology's beginnings and influence many of the fields of psychology discussed below. Many psychologists combine several of these outlooks, adopting an eclectic position in their work.

A popular perspective is the *Psychodynamic* outlook. Based on the Freudian background described above, this outlook emphasizes unconscious drives and the resolution of conflicts. A *Behavioral* perspective also has long history tracing back to the work of Watson and the early Behaviorists. This emphasis stresses the acquisition and alteration of observable responses.

The emphasis of the *Humanistic* perspective is on achieving or maximizing human potential, often called *self-actualization*. The *Biological* perspective is based on physiological explanations of behavior, while an *Evolutionary* perspective has genes, evolution, and natural selection at its core.

The most recent perspectives to emerge are the *Cognitive* perspective and the *Sociocultural* perspective. The Cognitive outlook, which developed to a great extent because of the increased use of computers, stresses thinking or mental processes, information processing, and problem solving. Enhanced technology also made the Sociocultural perspective more likely, as comparisons of different ethnic or cultural groups became possible.

Fields of Psychology.   Regardless of the perspective adopted, the hundreds of specialties in psychology usually are categorized into several general fields. The following sections give a sense of where psychologists choose to work.

Clinical and Counseling Psychology.   Nearly 60 percent of all psychologists in the United States work as *clinical* or *counseling* psychologists. Although there is much overlap in what they do, in applying psychological principles to help people overcome problems, clinical psychologists are more likely to treat or conduct research into the causes of abnormal behaviors, while counseling psychologists more often work with mild social or emotional problems. Typically, the individuals who seek the help of a counselor are not classified as abnormal or mentally ill but are looking for help with problems such as vocational difficulties and interpersonal relationships.

EXAMPLE 1.11.   A college freshman may have difficulties with the first semester's studying because he cannot adjust to dormitory life, to teaching techniques that are new to him, or even to his roommate. A counseling psychologist may be called upon to help the freshman make the necessary adjustments. However, if the freshman repeatedly responds in ways that appear to be significantly out of touch with reality, he may be referred to a clinical psychologist.

Clinical and counseling psychology differ from *psychiatry* in the kind of schooling pursued at the graduate level. While psychologists typically obtain a Ph.D. (Doctor of Philosophy in Psychology) or Psy.D. (Doctor of Psychology), psychiatrists receive an M.D. (Doctor of Medicine). About 10 percent of all psychiatrists are also *psychoanalysts*. They have received training at psychoanalytic training institutes in the techniques developed by Freud and usually have undergone psychoanalysis. Psychologists, psychiatrists, and psychoanalysts often use the same diagnostic and treatment techniques when working with clients.

Educational and School Psychology.   Closely related to counseling psychology are *Educational* and *School* psychology. Educational psychology is concerned with the use of psychological principles to increase the effectiveness of the learning experience. This frequently includes the study of learning facilities, curricula, teaching techniques, and particular student problems. A psychologist who specifically tries to assess, counsel, or guide students who have emotional or academic problems is referred to as a school psychologist.

EXAMPLE 1.12.   In recent years, technological advances have revolutionized the presentation of materials in a classroom. Much of this work is done using computers, television, and other nonhuman devices. The integration of these techniques into the classroom might be a major concern for an educational psychologist, while the difficulty a particular student has in dealing with the equipment might require the counseling of a school psychologist.

Scientific Investigations in Psychology.   Although psychologists in almost all areas of psychology conduct research, certain areas within psychology are thought to use scientific investigations primarily to explore fundamental questions of behavior or cognition. Investigators in these areas—typically called *experimental psychology*—may study processes such as sensation, perception, learning, motivation, and memory, as well as the neurological or biological bases of these processes.

Experimental studies most frequently are conducted using the special approaches of the experimental or scientific method. (See Chapter 2.) Both human and animal subjects have been used in the wide variety of problems that have been investigated. Much of this research is conducted in college or university settings, often looking at principles of behavior without regard to practical applications.

Cognitive Psychology.   Growing out of experimental psychology, *Cognitive psychology* focuses on higher mental processes such as thinking, reasoning, and decision making. A major influence on cognitive approaches has been the development of *computer analogies* for learning and memory. Computer modeling of human mental processes allows an understanding of how the mind works and how thinking influences observable behaviors.

Developmental Psychology.   *Developmental psychology* studies how people mature and change from the moment of conception until death. Some developmental psychologists concentrate on all behaviors in one part of the life span, such as early childhood or adolescence. Others study only a particular aspect of behavior, such as learning, as it develops throughout life.

EXAMPLE 1.13.   Developmental psychologists have found that learning a second language is much easier to accomplish if the learner is fairly young, often pre-adolescent. This principle is applied in many countries during the early years of schooling but generally is ignored in the United States, where second-language learning is postponed until the high school years.

Social Psychology.   Psychology pertains to the behavior of individuals; sociology studies the behaviors of groups as groups. *Social psychology* investigates group influence on the behavior of individuals. The behaviors of people in crowds, work groups, recreational groups, subcultural or cultural groups, and many other types of groups are studied by social psychologists.

EXAMPLE 1.14.   Sitting in the audience attending a television game show, a person may applaud repeatedly even when she thinks that the activity of the participants is dumb. Her responses reflect the influence of those around her, as she feels she would look odd if she did not applaud. This "going along with the crowd" reaction is the type of behavior that interests social psychologists.

Other Applied Psychologies.   Modern psychology is broad and diverse enough to include many specialties, especially in applied psychology. A sample of these applied areas is given here:

Industrial/Organizational Psychology.   Often abbreviated as *I/O* Psychology, this area is concerned with psychology in the work environment. Issues such as improving that environment to increase productivity, increasing job satisfaction, and altering decision-making attempts are the ones often considered.

Consumer Psychology.   Understanding the motivation of consumers and applying this knowledge to influence their buying habits is the prime concern of consumer psychologists. These psychologists often work in the area of market research.

Engineering Psychology.   An engineering psychologist studies the relationships of people to machines, with the intent of improving such relationships. This may involve redesigning equipment, changing the way people use machines, or changing the location in which work takes place. Often, the work of an engineering psychologist is described as making the relationship more "user-friendly."

EXAMPLE 1.15.   With the rapid increase in the use of computers in the workplace, psychologists have become very much involved in creating the best possible setting for that use. Distress, such as carpal tunnel syndrome, has led to extensive investigations of how the positioning of the person and/or the machine can alleviate the difficulties experienced by many users.

Forensic Psychology.   Forensic psychologists are involved in psychology and legal practice. They may look at criteria for determining legal insanity or work on questions regarding the validity of eyewitness testimony.

Exercise and Sport Psychology.   This specialty focuses on the application of psychological principles to exercise or athletic endeavors. Applications of psychological knowledge to influence the maintenance of exercise regimes, performance in competition, or rehabilitation from athletic injury are examples of work in this area.

Environmental Psychology.   Environmental psychology is concerned with the interactions people have with their physical settings. Areas of study include pollution effects, recycling efforts, and the study of stress generated by different physical settings.

Solved Problems

1.1   Upon moving into the dormitory, your new roommate asks you what your major will be. When you reply "psychology," your roommate's response is, "Gee, now I'll have to watch what I say all year long! You psychologists are always analyzing people's personality problems." Based upon the definition of psychology, explain why your roommate is wrong.

   The definition indicates that psychology studies all of behavior and cognitive processes—normal as well as abnormal, animal as well as human. Personality is included, but many other topics are investigated also. Your roommate's view of psychology is too limited.

1.2   Having been given the previous answer, your roommate says, "All of behavior? What for?" Explain the purposes of psychology.

   Psychology, although far from being complete, is trying to close the gaps in knowledge about behavior and cognitive processes in order to be able to understand, predict, modify, or improve actions or thoughts.

1.3   A psychologist presents the stimulus PS CH L GY to a subject, and the response given is "PSYCHOLOGY." Is this prediction or manipulation of behavior?

   The psychologist probably could predict the response. However, the fact that the psychologist creates the situation by presenting this particular stimulus makes this an example of behavioral manipulation. (The same psychologist might theorize that a person would tend to "complete" the word or sentence of a stutterer, in which case the psychologist would be predicting behavior.)

1.4   Some research studies involve human subjects; other studies use animals as subjects. Why?

It is generally quite easy to accept psychology as the study of human behavior and mental processes, but questions often arise about why psychologists study animals. There are several basic reasons, all of which are important: (1) Sometimes animals are studied simply because a psychologist is interested in animal behavior. Animals are an important part of the environment, and understanding their behaviors may be worthwhile for that reason alone. (2) Animals often are studied because it would be unethical or impossible to use humans in the research. For example, a psychologist can keep animal subjects in prolonged deprivation or stress situations, control their breeding, and maintain them for 24 hours a day for many months while holding the expenses for their housing and feeding to a reasonable level. (3) In many cases, the behaviors of animal subjects are similar to the behaviors of humans. Thus, psychologists are able to explore many problem areas with animals and predict, on the basis of the results obtained, what humans might do in comparable situations.

1.5   Describe a psychological study in which humans would not be suitable subjects and explain why animals would be used instead.

Consider a study investigating the effects of genetic patterns or hereditary influences on aging. While breeding rats for characteristics that make them "age" more quickly or slowly probably would be acceptable, conducting a similar study by pairing humans and having them make babies to be studied most certainly would be unethical. Moreover, a study with humans would be far too expensive and time-consuming, while the average two-year life span of a rat would make the study much more accessible and appropriate.

1.6   Is heredity important in influencing behavior?

Heredity certainly influences behavior. Characteristics such as skin color, height and weight tendencies, and hair and eye color, all of which are passed on from parents, may affect behavior. For example, a seven-foot-tall boy might well become an athlete, but it is far more likely that he will play basketball than be a jockey. More importantly, hereditary influences may produce brain damage, retardation, color blindness, or other characteristics that are likely to have significant effects on the behaviors in which a child may engage.

1.7   What is the relationship between hereditary and environmental influences on a person's behavior?

It is generally accepted that heredity and environment interact. This means that the behavior observed is the result of the combined effects of hereditary background, past and current environmental experience, and the interaction of inherited and learned characteristics. It is generally believed that the relative amount of each influence cannot be separated, for example, by percentage.

1.8   Psychology as a discipline appears to have considerable breadth. What considerations are common in describing the general topics covered by psychology?

Psychology is truly the study of all behavior and mental processes over the entire life span. Psychologists study human and animal behavior, normal and abnormal behaviors, conscious and unconscious influences on behavior, and behavior from conception to death. They are concerned with both the theory of behavior and the applications of the principles that are discovered.

1.9   Did psychology start suddenly when investigators decided to study behavior and mental processes?

The date usually given for the start of psychology as an independent discipline is 1879. (See Solved Problem 1.11.) Before that date, however, there was a rich and varied background to psychology. Many of the problems studied and the techniques used in psychology were taken from disciplines such as philosophy, the sciences, medicine, and education. In some cases, even nonscientific studies contributed to psychology's beginnings.

1.10 What were some of the background areas that affected the beginning of psychology?

Problems of learning, perception, and speech were concerns of philosophers that came to be studied as psychological topics. The experimental method was adopted from sciences such as biology and chemistry, as were areas of investigation such as the effects of nervous system functioning on behavior and thinking. Early clinical practice resulted from both educational or school concerns and from changes in medical practice. Even nonscientific or "quack" proposals generated investigations that tried to determine what really was happening.

1.11 The year 1879 usually is picked as the starting date for psychology. Why?

Many "psychological" investigations were conducted before 1879, but the people who did the research did not consider themselves psychologists. In 1879, Wilhelm Wundt established the first psychology laboratory in Leipzig, Germany, and called psychology an independent experimental science. He subsequently started a psychology journal and wrote a psychology textbook. Wundt and 1879 traditionally are chosen as the starting points for psychology because of his declaration of intent.

1.12 Why was Wundt's work important?

Three major factors made Wundt's work important. First, he got psychology started as an independent discipline. Second, his emphasis on experimental methodology gave psychology a strong scientific footing. Third, the system of Structuralism he espoused tested the method of introspection and thus provided a "target" for several other systems that followed.

1.13 How was Structuralism a "target"?

Wundt and the later Structuralists studied the introspective reports of normal adult humans. Later psychologists felt that the Structuralist position was too limited and argued that psychology should extend into new and different areas. For example, a Structuralist's subject would not look at a box and simply call it a box. Instead, the subject would have to describe a rectangular object having certain sensory properties. Later changes in psychological methodology allowed any kind of answer and then studied whatever the subject said or did.

1.14 Describe the systematic positions that developed after Structuralism.

Functionalism was the study of behavior as it was adjusted or adapted to the environment. Functionalists were concerned with the purpose of behavior, not the structure of the mind. Behaviorism studied behavior in a completely objective fashion. Behaviorists were interested only in muscular movements or glandular responses and denied the concept of mind. Gestalt psychology adopted a holistic viewpoint, emphasizing the interrelatedness of responses. Gestalt psychologists did not believe that a particular response could be isolated and then studied and understood. The phrase describing their position is "the whole is different from or greater than the sum of its parts." Psychoanalysis was developed by Freud as a method of therapy, not a systematic position. In time, however, a systematic position emerged, emphasizing the importance of early childhood experiences and unconscious motives in the development of a subject's personality.

1.15 How did these other systematic positions change the original psychology of the Structuralists?

The field of psychological investigation was broadened greatly. Because Structuralism depended on the introspective reports of normal adult humans, it could not cover developmental (child) psychology, learning principles, the study of abnormal behavior, or unconscious motives. Although all these systems subsequently lost favor, they provided psychology with a broad base on which to build.

1.16   What trend developed in psychology as the importance of systems diminished?

The general trend was (and continues to be) toward specialized areas of investigation. Smaller segments of behavior are studied, with little or no attempt to explain all of behavior by reference to only one system.

1.17   What are the current attempts to unify psychology?

Modern psychology features several different perspectives, each housing within it many specialized areas. These perspectives reflect both the beginnings of psychology and more modern theories or models. Psychologists often discuss the Psychodynamic outlook, based on Freudian principles and more recent clinical work, and the Behavioral perspective, which emphasizes the acquisition and alteration of observable responses. The Humanistic perspective stresses achievement or maximizing human potential, while the Biological and Evolutionary perspectives involve physiological and genetic explanations for behavior and thinking. The most recent perspectives are the Cognitive, stressing thinking and mental processes, and the Sociocultural, comparing ethnic or cultural groups.

1.18   Clinical and counseling psychology sound very much alike. How do they differ?

In many respects, clinical and counseling psychology are very much alike. Both are attempts to apply psychological principles to help people overcome problems, and these practitioners are thought of as health service providers. If differences exist, they are likely to involve the clientele rather than the techniques used. Clinical psychologists are more likely to treat more severe or abnormal problems, while counseling psychologists more often work with relatively normal problems. For example, a clinician might try to help a schizophrenic (see Chapter 13) regain socially acceptable behavior, while a counselor might help a person with occupational difficulties.

1.19   Realizing that one of her students is acting abnormally, a teacher contacts the student's parents and recommends that they obtain some help for the child. The parents are uncertain where to turn, wondering whether to call a psychologist or a psychiatrist. They call a local mental health agency and ask for help in understanding the difference between the two. What answer are they likely to be given?

Although the background of clinical psychology comes from medicine and psychiatry, there is a difference between the two. A *clinical psychologist* is generally university-trained and receives a Ph.D. (or, less frequently, a Psy.D.) degree. A *psychiatrist* is trained in a medical school and obtains an M.D. Both have specialized training in therapy and often use the same methods of diagnosis and treatment.

1.20   What percentage of U.S. psychologists are employed in clinical and counseling psychology?

Research indicates that nearly 60 percent of U.S. psychologists are clinicians or counselors. The remaining group is divided into segments of 10 percent or less for each of the remaining fields of psychology.

1.21   What makes applied psychology different from theoretical psychology?

The many fields of applied psychology are concerned with direct, practical applications of psychological principles. By contrast, a theoretical psychologist may simply want to test hypotheses and theories to judge whether they are tenable. The majority of psychologists today work in applied areas.

1.22 At their high school reunion, Luis asks his friend about her employment. She explains that she is conducting laboratory research, using monkeys, where she investigates the effects on behavior of stimulation of certain areas of the brain. Confused, Luis asks, "So what does that make you—an experimental psychologist? a biological psychologist? a neuropsychologist? a physiological psychologist? or what?" How might his friend respond?

The likely response is that any one of those labels or any combination of them might be correct. The primary concern here is that she is conducting scientific investigations that may provide information about brain functioning of either a theoretical *or* an applied nature. The label used is much less important than the work being done.

1.23 Give an example of an investigation that illustrates the kind of work done in cognitive psychology.

Because cognitive psychology is tied so closely to the use of computers, an excellent example is that of the *computer analogy* for memory. Psychologists propose that memory can be thought of as a three-stage process involving acquisition of the material, storage of what was learned, and then retrieval of that information at a later time. (Think of the name of your third-grade teacher; you acquired and stored that information a number of years ago and now retrieve it from memory.) Cognitive psychologists often use computers to try to mimic these memory processes, treating acquisition as the input, which is followed by storage and then the computer output. Programs that seem to parallel actual behavior are studied in an attempt to understand the cognitive processes involved.

1.24 What are the major concerns of a developmental psychologist?

A developmental psychologist studies behavioral changes over a time span. This may be a particular period such as early childhood, adolescence, or adulthood or the entire life of the individual. Developmental psychologists may pursue specialized interests such as cognitive development, social changes, physical growth, and identity formation.

1.25 The local parent–teacher organization believes that the educational effectiveness of the school system is inadequate. The organization would like to see the educational programs improved and decides to hire a full-time psychologist. What kind of psychologist is it likely to hire?

The answer to this problem probably depends on why the effectiveness seems inadequate. If the reason is that many students seem to have personal problems that affect their learning, the district will hire a school psychologist to get involved with testing, diagnosis, and counseling of the students. If the problems appear to lie in teaching or testing techniques, curriculum, technology, or facilities, the district will be better served by hiring an educational psychologist.

1.26 Ron, a college freshman, finds that the words he uses in conversation differ considerably when he is in the locker room, compared to when he is in the dining hall. What type of psychologist specializes in studying such differences?

The solution for this problem may take several forms, but the most likely answer is the social psychologist. Social psychology is the study of group influence on an individual's behavior. The group studied by a social psychologist may be a recreational group such as one found in a locker room after exercise, a more formal group such as might be found in the dining hall, or any number of other groups, such as those Ron might find himself in when in class, in church, or on a date. It is likely that Ron's behavior conforms to the standards of the group in which he finds himself.

1.27   Is social psychology an applied psychology?

There are particular types of social psychology that can be thought of as applied. For example, cross-cultural psychologists may study the effects of misinterpreting cultural gestures on the behavior of tourists. This certainly is the effect of one group's actions on the behavior of another group, but at the same time it has practical application to the success or failure of a trip.

1.28   What are some of the other applied psychologies that are popular?

Business-related psychologies are applied areas that have gained in importance in recent years. *Industrial/organizational (I/O) psychology* handles problems that develop in the work situation, including personnel evaluation, productivity, and management concerns. *Engineering psychology* focuses on improving the relationships between equipment and the person using that equipment, while *consumer psychology* looks at the motivation and buying habits of purchasers and investigates marketing strategies.

Other areas to which psychological principles have been applied are *exercise and sport psychology* and *environmental psychology*. Applied psychologists also work in hospital, prison, and governmental agency settings. Psychology is truly a young discipline and should continue to expand into new areas and diversify for a long time.

Key Terms

Abnormal behavior.   Behavior that produces distress or disability and is maladaptive, disruptive, or harmful for the person or for society.

Applied psychology.   Any branch of psychology that applies psychological principles to the solution of practical problems.

Behavior.   The observable or measurable response of a person or animal.

Behaviorism.   A system of psychology which studied observable stimuli and responses only and which denied the concept of mind.

Clinical psychology.   The branch of psychology concerned with the theory and practice of helping people with abnormal behavioral or mental disorders.

Cognitive psychology.   A branch of psychology which focuses on higher mental processes such as thinking, reasoning, and decision making.

Conscious.   An activity or condition of which an individual is aware and which the individual can recognize or describe.

Consumer psychology.   A branch of psychology concerned with market research or consumers' buying habits.

Counseling psychology.   A branch of psychology which employs techniques to help clients overcome "normal" problems.

Developmental psychology.   A branch of psychology which concentrates on changes in behavior over a time span, such as childhood or adolescence.

Educational psychology.   A branch of psychology which applies psychological principles to increase the effectiveness of the learning experience.

Engineering psychology.   A branch of psychology which concentrates on the relationships between people and machines.

Environment.   Any external factors or conditions which may influence an organism.

Environmental psychology. A branch of psychology which studies the interactions of organisms with their physical settings.

Exercise and sport psychology. A branch of psychology which applies psychological principles to exercise and athletic endeavors.

Experimental psychology. A theoretical branch of psychology that studies the basic or fundamental questions of behavior.

Forensic psychology. A branch of psychology which applies psychological principles to the legal profession.

Functionalism. A system of psychology which studied the purposes of behavior, focusing particularly on adaptations or adjustments to the environment.

Gestalt psychology. A system of psychology that adopted a holistic approach to the study of behavior.

Heredity. The genetic transmission of characteristics from parent to offspring.

Industrial/organizational psychology. A branch of psychology which applies psychological principles to the solution of work-related problems.

Introspection. A method of psychological investigation in which subjects report on their reactions to stimuli.

Psychiatry. A medical speciality dealing with the diagnosis and treatment of abnormal behaviors.

Psychoanalysis. A form of psychotherapy, started by Sigmund Freud, that stresses the importance of early childhood experiences and unconscious motives in the development of personality.

Psychoanalyst. A therapist trained at a special institute in the techniques developed by Freud.

Psychodynamic psychology. The outlook of psychology based on the work of Freud and emphasizing unconscious drives and the resolution of conflicts.

Psychology. The scientific study of behavior and cognitive processes.

School psychology. A branch of psychology which specializes in assessment of and counseling and guidance for students.

Sociocultural perspective. An approach to the study of psychology that uses comparisons of different ethnic or cultural groups.

Structuralism. A system of psychology which studied the adult, normal human mind by using the method of introspection.

System of psychology. A particular set of principles of psychology used to organize, interpret, and attempt to understand all of behavior.

Theory. A general principle, based on evidence or observation, suggested as an explanation for phenomena.

Unconscious. Refers to conditions of which the individual is unaware or barely aware yet which may influence behavior.

CHAPTER 2

Methodology and Statistics

Casual, undisciplined reports of behavior, such as gossip and rumors, occur frequently. Although these reports are descriptions of behavior, they are not acceptable to psychologists who study behavior. Psychologists require more reliable measures and accurate reports, and their methods for gathering information are established to meet those requirements. Once such information is gathered, psychologists often use statistics to present, analyze, and interpret numerical data. This chapter includes a discussion of the methods most often used by psychologists to measure and report on behavior and the statistical techniques that are commonly used.

2.1 THE EXPERIMENTAL METHOD

The most disciplined methodology used by psychologists is the *experimental method*. Using this method, an experimenter manipulates a variable to be studied, chooses the response to be measured, and controls extraneous influences that might inappropriately affect the results of an experiment. A *variable* is a characteristic of anything that can have two or more values.

EXAMPLE 2.1. An experimenter may wish to study the effects of room temperature on students' performance on an examination. Because both can take many different values, room temperature and the test scores obtained are variables.

The experimental method allows investigators to test cause-effect relationships. If changes in the variable that is manipulated produce differences in the response values obtained, a *causal* relationship can be assumed. Information gathered in this manner is called *research information*.

Properly conducted research usually satisfies several criteria. If these criteria are not met, the results obtained may be subject to question. However, when they are met, the psychologist is said to be studying a *meaningful problem*.

Objective. Research should be conducted so that the collection, analysis, and interpretation of behavioral information are done with maximum *objectivity*. This means that if possible, any conditions which might introduce bias or prejudice (*subjectivity*) must be avoided.

15

Repeatable.   Generally, a single research result that cannot be substantiated by a similar finding may be considered suspect and not widely accepted. To overcome this problem, a study should be written so that a skeptical or interested investigator has sufficient information to *repeat* or *replicate* the research and either confirm or disconfirm the reported results.

EXAMPLE 2.2.   If the researcher claims to have been in contact with ghosts and reports results that are impossible to replicate, the information is unlikely to gain credence in psychology. The procedures and results must be available *publicly* for questioning and replication to be understandable and accepted.

Empirical.   One characteristic that helps promote repeatability is for the study to be *empirical* in nature. An empirical study employs variables that are *measurable*, avoiding concepts that may be subject to many different interpretations and cannot be observed and recorded in an objective way. Experimenters often employ *operational definitions*, defining the variables used by the procedures used to produce or measure them.

Ethical.   Whether using humans or animals as subjects, psychologists are expected to justify the procedures they employ and conduct studies that will not lead to harm. Typically, a research proposal must be reviewed or evaluated before being started to assure that the study will meet ethical guidelines.

When the subjects are humans, they should provide *informed consent*, that is, be informed of and consent to the study's procedures, before starting. Researchers also should perform *debriefing* of the subjects after the study is completed, giving a complete explanation of what was done, and preserve the *confidentiality* of all subjects' results.

EXAMPLE 2.3.   While a researcher may be interested in the effects of maximum anxiety-producing stress on physical performance, knowing that such situations often occur in sport situations, it is unlikely that a review board would approve such a study in the laboratory. The potential for physical or mental harm would far outweigh the possible benefits of the results obtained. The researcher probably would have to be satisfied with studying naturally occurring instances of such behavior.

2.2   THE HYPOTHESIS

A *hypothesis* is a prediction of how one variable relates to another. As such, a hypothesis is a tentative premise or proposal suggested as an explanation for a phenomenon. This proposal must be stated so that it can be tested and either confirmed *or* disconfirmed.

Two forms of hypotheses—the null hypothesis and the directional hypothesis—often are used in psychological studies. The *null hypothesis* proposes that manipulations by the experimenter will *not* produce differences between the performances of the groups being studied. By contrast, a *directional hypothesis* states that the experimenter's manipulations *will* alter the outcome of the experiment.

EXAMPLE 2.4.   Using the situation suggested in Example 2.1, a null hypothesis would propose that changes in room temperature will have *no* effect on the test scores obtained by students, while a directional hypothesis might state that students tested in a room at normal temperature (72°F) will perform better than students tested in unusual temperatures (58 or 86°F).

No matter what kind of hypothesis is formulated, the psychologist will interpret the results and draft *tentative conclusions*. Although the conclusions reached are considered appropriate for the moment, the psychologist must realize that future research may reveal another conclusion that is more reasonable. In this sense, work in science is thought to be cumulative and ever-changing.

2.3 EXPERIMENTAL AND CONTROL GROUPS

Consider again the "temperature-exam" study. Assume that the experimenter sets out to confirm or disconfirm the null hypothesis "Changes in temperature have no effect on students' exam scores." To conduct the experiment it would be appropriate to administer the exam in at least three different conditions—once to a group that took the exam at "normal" room temperature (72°F), once to a group at the "high" (86°F) temperature, and once to the group at the "low" (58°F) temperature.

The students who took the exam at the "normal" temperature are called the *control group*. The purpose of a control group is to establish a basis for comparison. The students who took the exam at the "high" or the "low" temperature are members of *experimental groups*, experiencing what may be called the conditions of interest. The performance of the students in the experimental groups is compared with that of the students in the control group. Without the control group, the comparison of results would be inconclusive and the experimenter could neither confirm nor disconfirm the hypothesis.

EXAMPLE 2.5. Suppose the experimenter tested only two groups: the "high-temperature" and "low-temperature" groups. Suppose also that both groups scored equally well or equally poorly on the examination. This would *not* confirm the hypothesis. Only by examining the control group's performance can the experimenter justify a tentative conclusion, either confirming or disconfirming the hypothesis.

2.4 INDEPENDENT AND DEPENDENT VARIABLES

A condition manipulated by the experimenter is called the *independent variable*. The response caused or influenced by exposure to the independent variable and measured by the experimenter is called the *dependent variable*. Experiments in psychology attempt to confirm or disconfirm a hypothesis that proposes a relationship between an independent variable and a dependent variable.

EXAMPLE 2.6. In the "temperature-exam" study, the independent variable is the temperature of the room, which is manipulated by the experimenter. The dependent variable is the performance of the students on the exam.

It is important to remember that experimental and control groups differ only in the amount or level of the independent variable they experience. Furthermore, the responses of both groups are measured in terms of the same dependent variable.

By arbitrary agreement, psychologists plot the independent variable on the *abscissa* (*x*-axis) of a graph and the dependent variable on the *ordinate* (*y*-axis).

EXAMPLE 2.7. The "temperature-exam" study might be presented on a graph as in Fig. 2-1.

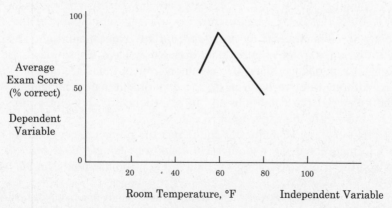

Fig. 2-1

2.5 EXTRANEOUS AND CONFOUNDING VARIABLES

Extraneous variables are irrelevant variables that may influence the results of an experiment. As much as possible, such variables should be eliminated or at least kept constant each time the experiment is conducted. Whenever possible, the experimenter should make certain that a subject's response is the result of the effect of the independent variable, not of some extraneous condition.

EXAMPLE 2.8. In the "temperature-exam" study, extraneous variables such as the noise level, illumination, or humidity of the room should be held constant each time a group takes the examination. In addition, care should be taken in selecting the students in each group; if all the "bright" students were assigned to one group, a confounding variable would exist. The experimenter would not be able to determine whether the scores obtained resulted from the manipulation of the independent variable, the differences in testing conditions, or the inappropriate assignment of students to groups.

2.6 SAMPLING

One way to avoid the influence of confounding variables is to use a careful *sample*, or selection of subjects for each group. Sampling is an attempt to select each group so that it is an equally accurate representation of the *population*, the entire group from which subjects may be chosen.

The most common form of sampling is *random sampling*, where each group selected from the population is chosen by "drawing numbers out of a hat" or by using a table of random numbers. Every potential subject has an equal chance of being chosen. The experimenter continues to choose subjects until a large enough sample has been chosen for all the groups. Occasionally, an experimenter may believe that certain subgroups or certain characteristics of subjects should be equally represented in all the groups chosen. In such cases, the experimenter may employ *stratified* or *matched* sampling techniques, assuring that each group has its fair share of subjects with the characteristics of concern.

EXAMPLE 2.9. The experimenter determining the groups for the "temperature-exam" study might use any of the sampling techniques mentioned above.

A *random sampling* technique would be used when all the members of the population were assigned numbers and groups were chosen by drawing numbers until all three groups were filled. Suppose, however, that the available population was composed of 80 percent first-year students and 20 percent upper-year students. The experimenter might want to assure that this percentage was reflected in the groups chosen and therefore would use a *stratified sample* or a *matched sample*, assigning similar percentages of subjects to each of the three groups.

Note: In some circumstances, a researcher cannot use any of these sampling techniques and must use whatever subjects are available. This is sometimes called *accidental sampling*. Confounding variables are more likely to affect the results in such situations.

2.7 EXPERIMENTER BIAS

Psychologists try to eliminate bias by using appropriate experimental and sampling techniques. They may, however, be unaware of unintentional biases they have. These biases are classified under the general heading of *experimenter bias*. Two common forms of bias are *demand characteristics* and *expectancy effects*. Although not recognizing it, the experimenter may anticipate certain responses from subjects and either set the conditions to "force" (demand) those responses or interpret the information received to satisfy the expectation.

Psychologists often employ techniques to counteract the possibilities of bias. In some studies the subjects are not informed about the hypothesized conditions (*single-blind control*), while in others both the subjects and the people collecting the data are kept uninformed (*double-blind control*).

EXAMPLE 2.10. The experimenter in the "temperature-exam" study inadvertently could indicate to the "high-temperature" or "low-temperature" subjects that they were not expected to do too well on the exam. Even a gesture or a casual remark to the subjects ("Do the best you can *under these conditions*") might introduce bias into the experiment.

2.8   OTHER PSYCHOLOGICAL METHODOLOGIES

Some psychological information cannot be obtained by using the experimental method. Psychologists use other techniques that are not as precise as that method but provide additional ways to gather and analyze research information.

Naturalistic Observation.   *Naturalistic observation* occurs when psychologists record the activities of everyday life in what is basically an unmanipulated environment. The psychologist does not control the circumstances in order to force or select a particular response from a subject. Observing the same kind of response in different settings may provide information for *cross-cultural research*.

EXAMPLE 2.11.   Interested in aggressive behaviors in schools, a psychologist might set up unobtrusive videotape cameras in the hallways of several school buildings. The naturally occurring activities thus recorded could then be analyzed to determine patterns of behavior and differences among settings.

Case Studies.   The primary purpose of most clinical or counseling psychologists is to help people overcome their personal problems. In the course of treating one person or a set of individuals, a psychologist will make a record of problems, insights, and techniques that were important in the treatment. Such reports are called *case studies* or *clinical case histories*. They often are studied by other psychologists because these studies may expose a factor that has general significance for the understanding of behavior.

EXAMPLE 2.12.   A psychologist who specializes in counseling couples considering divorce may combine the information gathered from a number of sessions into a case study report of the most likely causes of marital separation. Such a report would then provide others with problems to anticipate when confronting similar situations.

Tests and Surveys.   Psychologists often obtain information about behavior by asking subjects to respond to specially designed tests, surveys, interviews, and questionnaires. All of these techniques provide stimuli to which the subjects react. Psychologists study the responses to find out more about a particular subject's or group's behavior.

Tests, surveys, and questionnaires have been designed to investigate almost every aspect of behavior, including personality, intelligence, attitudes, and aptitudes. These techniques have two major advantages: they allow the rapid collection of information, and they give a psychologist the ability to compare the responses of one subject with those of thousands of others who have taken the same test. A disadvantage of these techniques is that there may be discrepancies between real-life behavior and test behavior, including purposely giving misleading responses.

EXAMPLE 2.13.   In Example 2.11, the psychologist interested in aggression in schools used naturalistic observation as a means of gathering information. Another method might be to administer tests oriented toward aggressive responses, analyze the results obtained, and try to determine whether particular patterns of response reveal any special indicators of aggressive responding for any groups of students in the school.

2.9   STATISTICS

Information gathered by psychologists often comes in numerical form. *Statistics* is the discipline that deals with the collection, analysis, interpretation, and presentation of numerical data.

Statistics has two major purposes in psychology: (1) to summarize or simplify the data that have been obtained and (2) to permit descriptions or inferences to be made from those data.

Descriptive Statistics. *Descriptive statistics* provide simplified or "shorthand" summaries of data. They are used to present the data collected in as concise a form as possible. Frequency distributions, measures of central tendency, and measures of variability are some of the descriptive statistics most frequently used.

Inferential Statistics. *Inferential statistics* provide a means for evaluating relationships that exist within the data obtained from a sample. Psychologists use inferential statistics when making predictions, often of the effect of a variable on responses.

Statistical Symbols. Regardless of the type of statistic being calculated, certain symbols have universal meaning in any formula. Some of the most common are included in the following list:

$$N = \text{number of scores}$$
$$X = \text{score (or scores)}$$
$$M \text{ or } \bar{X} = \text{mean (average score)}$$
$$d = \text{difference of a score from the mean}$$
$$\Sigma = \text{sum of}$$
$$D = \text{difference in rank}$$
$$r \text{ or } \rho = \text{correlation}$$
$$SD \text{ or } \sigma = \text{standard deviation}$$

EXAMPLE 2.14. These symbols can be used in combination. Thus, the formula

$$M = \frac{\Sigma X}{N}$$

would be read: "The mean is equal to the sum of the scores divided by the number of scores."

2.10 FREQUENCY DISTRIBUTIONS

To be able to comprehend items of raw data, it is often necessary to arrange the data in a *frequency distribution*. This is accomplished by dividing the measurement scale of the data into *class intervals*, which are portions of the scale determined by the investigator. Thus, each item of data will fall within one of the class intervals set up by the investigator.

Two forms of frequency distributions are used often. *Frequency polygons* are line graphs that present the data. A *histogram* is a bar graph that presents the distribution.

EXAMPLE 2.15. If a researcher collected data from the "temperature-exam score" study, the information obtained might be presented as it is in Figs. 2-2 and 2-3. (Both distributions reflect the same results, presenting the average test score and using the same temperatures as in the examples from the previous section.)

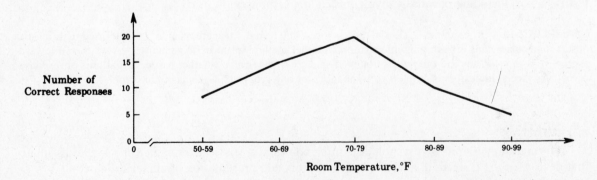

Fig. 2-2

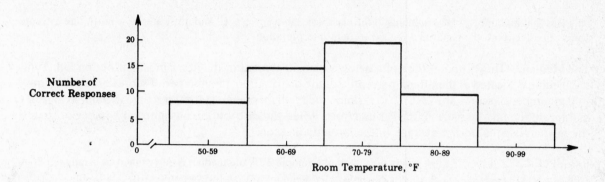

Fig. 2-3

Some frequency distributions have an equal number of scores (or other data) arranged in similar patterns on either side of the middle of the distribution. Such distributions are called *symmetrical distributions*. When scores "bunch up" at one end of the distribution, the distribution is said to be *skewed*.

2.11　MEASURES OF CENTRAL TENDENCY

A measure of *central tendency* is a statistical technique in which a single number is used to represent a group of numbers. Three different measures of central tendency are commonly used: the *mean*, the *median*, and the *mode*.

The Mean.　The *mean* is the average score for a distribution of scores. It is determined by summing all the scores in a distribution and dividing that figure by the number of scores. The formula for the mean is

$$M = \frac{\Sigma X}{N}$$

EXAMPLE 2.16.　Suppose on a 20-item quiz, seven students get the following scores:

$$14, 12, 7, 16, 12, 17, 13$$

To calculate the mean (M), you would divide the sum of the scores (X) by the number of scores (N) as follows:

$$M = \frac{\Sigma X}{N} = \frac{91}{7} = 13 \ ans.$$

It should be noted that the mean is sensitive to the effects of one extreme score. In such cases, one of the other measures of central tendency may be preferred.

EXAMPLE 2.17.　Suppose the same seven students take a 100-point exam and get the following scores:

$$92, 80, 90, 84, 84, 85, 87$$

In this case, the mean is 86. But suppose an eighth student starts to take the exam and then quits. This student's score is 6. If the eighth student's score is used in calculating the mean, the new average score is 76. This result indicates that all but one of the students in the class was "above average" and illustrates how much one extreme score can affect both the result and the subsequent interpretation.

The Median.   The *median* is the point below which 50 percent of the items in a distribution fall. Thus, the median is located at the fiftieth percentile of the distribution; the number of scores below it is equal to the number of scores above it. To determine the median, one must list the scores in numerical order and locate the middle score in the series. (*Note*: When the distribution has an even number of scores, the median is equal to the average of the two middle scores.)

EXAMPLE 2.18.   Using the test scores presented in Example 2.16, the median is determined by arranging those scores in order (7, 12, 12, 13, 14, 16, 17) and finding the middle score. In this case, the median is 13, matching the mean that was calculated before.

EXAMPLE 2.19.   Suppose an eighth student took the quiz and got a score of 9. The median now is calculated by averaging the two middle scores (12 and 13) and is reported as 12.5. (You also may want to calculate the mean for this eight-person distribution; it, too, is 12.5.)

The Mode.   The *mode* is the score that occurs with the greatest frequency in a distribution. The mode is the only one of the three measures of central tendency that may have more than one value.

EXAMPLE 2.20.   Examine again the distribution used in Examples 2.16, 2.18, and 2.19. The mode for all these distributions is 12.

EXAMPLE 2.21.   Suppose that when the eighth student takes the quiz, the score obtained is not 9, but 17. The distribution (7, 12, 12, 13, 14, 16, 17, 17) becomes a *bimodal distribution* with modes of 12 and 17. (You may want to verify that both the mean and the median for this new distribution equal 13.5.)

2.12   MEASURES OF VARIABILITY

Another characteristic of a distribution is its *variability*, or the dispersion of its scores. In other words, variability refers to whether the scores are clustered closely together or are spread out. Two measures of variability used commonly are the *range* and the *standard deviation*.

The Range.   The *range* is an easily calculated measure of variability. One simply subtracts the value of the lowest score from the value of the highest score. However, the range may give a misleading impression of a distribution in which all the scores but one are bunched closely together. If this single score's value is very different from the values of the other scores, the range may show great variability in the distribution when in fact there is very little variability.

EXAMPLE 2.22.   Using the test scores obtained in Example 2.21, the range is found to be 10 points. Note, however, that if the lowest score is ignored, the range is half as large (5 points) and perhaps gives a more representative indication of the variability of the distribution, or how bunched most of the scores really are. (The reader may want to go back to Example 2.17 for an even more extreme example where the range changes from 12 points to 86 points if the eighth student's score is used.)

The Standard Deviation.   The *standard deviation* is a more sensitive measure of variability than the range is because it takes into consideration every score rather than just the extreme scores. A basic formula for the standard deviation is as follows:

$$SD = \sqrt{\frac{\Sigma d^2}{N}}$$

EXAMPLE 2.23. Using the distribution of scores found in Example 2.16, calculation of the standard deviation would progress as follows:

Score	Difference from the Mean	d^2
17	$13 - 17 = -4$	16
16	$13 - 16 = -3$	9
14	$13 - 14 = -1$	1
13	$13 - 13 = 0$	0
12	$13 - 12 = 1$	1
12	$13 - 12 = 1$	1
7	$13 - 7 = 6$	36
$\Sigma X = 91$		
$N = 7$		
$M = 13$		

$$SD = \sqrt{\frac{\Sigma d^2}{N}} = \sqrt{\frac{64}{7}} = \sqrt{9.14} = 3.024 \; ans.$$

2.13 THE NORMAL PROBABILITY DISTRIBUTION

When many scores are collected and plotted on a graph, they often fall in a nearly symmetrical distribution called the *normal curve*. The normal curve is the graphical representation of the *normal probability distribution*, an idealized version of which is shown in Fig. 2-4.

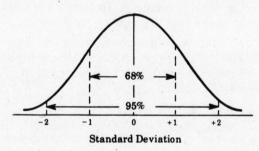

Standard Deviation

Fig. 2-4

The percentages shown are approximate but do indicate that about 68 percent of any set of scores (or other numerically valued responses) will fall somewhere between the mean-plus-one standard deviation and the mean-minus-one standard deviation. Furthermore, 95 percent will fall between plus-two and minus-two standard deviations from the mean.

Percentile Values. The normal curve (Fig. 2-4) can be redrawn to show what percentage of the scores falls between each indicator of deviation from the mean, as shown in Fig. 2-5.

It is then possible to calculate the *percentile* values for a given score. For example, the mean score represents the fiftieth percentile, a score one standard deviation above the mean is at the eighty-fourth percentile, and a score one standard deviation below the mean falls at the sixteenth percentile. (More detailed representations of percentile values can be found in statistics textbooks.)

One of the most common uses of the normal probability distribution is in interpreting the scores

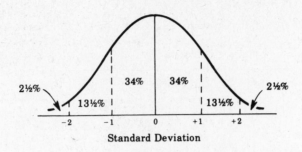

Standard Deviation

Fig. 2-5

obtained. If the mean and standard deviation of a distribution are known, a score obtained from any one subject can be compared to or located within the distribution.

EXAMPLE 2.24. If the test results from a scholastic achievement test distribute in a normal probability curve which has a mean of 500 and a standard deviation of 100, a score of 600 is in the eighty-fourth percentile. That is, the student's performance on the test was better than that of 84 percent of those who took the test. It is also possible to determine from the curve that 95 percent of the students who took the test had scores between 300 and 700.

2.14 CORRELATION

Correlation refers to the relationship between two variables. A correlation may be shown graphically by using what is called a *scattergram*, or *scatter diagram*. A relationship can be represented numerically by calculating the *coefficient of correlation*.

There are several ways to calculate a coefficient of correlation. Regardless of which one is used, the numerical values obtained will range from 0 (no correlation) to +1.00 or −1.00. If the correlation is *positive* (+0.01 to +1.00), the value of one variable increases as the value of the other variable increases. When the correlation obtained is *negative* (−0.01 to −1.00), the value of one variable increases as the value of the other variable decreases. The larger the absolute value of the correlation, regardless of sign, the better the predictions that can be made.

EXAMPLE 2.25. The scatter diagram such as the one in Fig. 2-6 can be used to plot the results obtained when measuring the time needed to run a mile as a function of the number of hours of training each person tested averages per week. A negative correlation would be illustrated by the scatter diagram in this figure.

The relationship indicates that the greater the number of hours of training, the shorter the time needed to run one mile. (The correlation coefficient obtained would be approximately −0.67.)

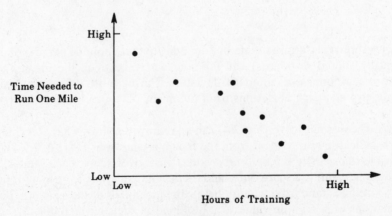

Fig. 2-6

Contingency and Regression. Correlation coefficients often are used for predictive purposes. However, a correlation does not automatically indicate a *contingency*, or causal relationship, between the two variables. Caution must be used in interpreting the meaning of an obtained correlation.

When there is ample evidence to support the acceptance of a contingent relationship, the use of a previously obtained correlation and the values of one variable to predict the values of a second variable is known as *regression*.

EXAMPLE 2.26. Public health officials have argued for years that a contingent relationship exists between smoking and increased health problems. Tobacco manufacturers have argued that no such contingency should be inferred, suggesting that additional investigation may reveal other causes for the increases in both variables. Insurance companies, accepting the health officials' arguments, have chosen to use the concept of regression to establish their rates, increasing policy costs for certain kinds of health care coverage for people who smoke.

2.15 INFERENTIAL STATISTICS

Once information is gathered, researchers often want to know what the likelihood is that the findings are the result of systematic, rather than chance, changes or manipulations. Predictions about the population are made from the data gathered from the samples used.

The results are described in terms of *significance*. Arbitrarily, psychologists usually define a *significant result* as one that could be expected to have occurred by chance fewer than 5 times out of 100. This often is written $p < .05$ (the probability of the result obtained being a chance occurrence is less than 5 times in 100).

Solved Problems

2.1 Why is the experimental method thought to be the most disciplined of the information-gathering techniques used by psychologists?

The experimental method allows psychologists to test cause-effect relationships. The investigator manipulates or measures a particular variable to be studied, selects the response that may be affected by such manipulations, and controls extraneous influences that could inappropriately affect the results obtained. None of the other data-gathering techniques assures that a causal relationship can be studied.

2.2 What characteristics of an experimental investigation assure that the researcher is studying a meaningful problem?

Generally, it is thought that a study must be objective, repeatable, and empirical to assure that the problem studied is meaningful. This means that the research is undertaken in an unbiased or unprejudiced fashion, is written in a manner that allows other to replicate it if desired, and employs variables that are measurable. Although other kinds of studies may be very interesting, they are unlikely to be widely accepted in psychology.

2.3 What are the essential ethical considerations that must be met in conducting psychological research?

Above all else, researchers must be certain to use procedures that will cause no mental or physical harm. This is true whether the subjects are humans or animals, and typically, the study must be evaluated and approved by a committee before being conducted.

Investigators who study human subjects have several considerations to fulfill. The subjects must be provided with enough information about the study before it begins to be able to give informed consent for participation. When the study is completed, the subjects should be debriefed, that is, given a complete explanation of what happened. In addition, the confidentiality of all subjects' responses must be preserved.

2.4   A common procedure for investigating a psychological problem is to develop a hypothesis and then test that hypothesis. What does this mean?

A hypothesis is a proposition or prediction of how one variable relates to another that is advanced as a possible explanation of a phenomenon. The hypothesis must be stated so that it can be either confirmed or disconfirmed.

2.5   What is the difference between a directional hypothesis and a null hypothesis?

A directional hypothesis proposes that if the conditions of an experiment are varied in a particular way, the outcome of the experiment also will vary in a particular way. The null hypothesis predicts that certain changes in the conditions of the experiment will *not* alter the outcome of the experiment. For example, a directional hypothesis might state that people who drink coffee will show faster reaction times than will people who do not drink coffee. The null hypothesis would propose that the reaction times of both groups will be the same. Both kinds of hypotheses can be tested by collecting information (in this case, the reaction times of the two groups—those who drank coffee and those who did not) and comparing the results.

2.6   What does it mean to say that psychologists often reach tentative conclusions?

Psychologists know that psychology is a "young" science and that many of the principles proposed so far may be superseded by future research findings. Psychology is thought to be cumulative and ever-changing. Conclusions therefore are viewed as temporary and are subject to revision if new information becomes available.

2.7   Explain why comparison is important in the conduct of an experiment.

Consider again the "coffee-drinking" experiment described in Solved Problem 2.5. If only those who drank coffee were tested for their reaction time, the experiment would not produce a meaningful result. To confirm or disconfirm a hypothesis—whether directional ("There will be a difference") or null ("There will be no difference")—at least two groups, including a control group, must be tested. The effects of drinking coffee can then be assessed by comparing the results from the two groups.

2.8   How many comparisons are necessary in an experiment?

The number of comparisons varies with the problem being studied. A psychologist should try to design an experiment so that all the necessary comparisons can be made. In the coffee experiment, two groups would be adequate, but the addition of a third group might improve the study considerably. It is possible that some subjects might *expect* their reaction times to be quicker simply because they drink coffee. To test for this possibility, the third group would drink decaffeinated coffee without knowing that it was decaffeinated. This third group's reaction times could be compared to those of the other two groups. Note that the use of decaffeinated coffee is similar to a *placebo treatment*, which often is used by psychologists and physicians. (A *placebo* is a chemically inert material that has the same appearance as an active drug. It allows psychologists to test the effects of a subject's expectations in an experiment.)

2.9   Consider the "coffee-drinking" experiment described in Solved Problem 2.8. Of the three groups, which are experimental and which is the control group?

Experimental groups usually receive "special" treatments manipulated by the experimenter. Control groups usually receive "normal" treatments; that is, they are not subject to all of or the same level of conditions manipulated by the experimenter. The two groups considered to be experimental groups in the "coffee-drinking" study are those drinking coffee, whether regular or decaffeinated. The other group, which drinks no coffee, is the control group and provides the standard of comparison. Note that the study described here is relatively simple. Many psychological investigations require far more elaborate arrangements to establish the experimental and control conditions.

2.10   Give an example of an extraneous variable that would have to be taken into account in conducting the "coffee-drinking" experiment described in the two previous problems.

One consideration the researcher would have to take into account would be the amount of fluid each subject ingested. If the coffee drinkers all have a cup of coffee, the control group should drink a comparable amount of fluid (for example, water) so that any effects produced, such as slight discomfort, will be likely to be the same for all the groups. Another method might be to ensure that none of the subjects drank excessive amounts of fluids before coming to the experiment. The experimenter tries to be certain the responses obtained are a result only of the independent variable rather than of an outside, inappropriate variable.

2.11   How does an experimenter, by reference to the responses of the experimental and control groups, reach a tentative conclusion?

The confirmation or disconfirmation of a hypothesis is made by comparing the results of the experimental group(s) with those of the control group. If a significant difference exists, the tentative conclusion is that the treatment conditions manipulated by the experimenter caused a difference in the performance of the experimental subjects compared to that of the control subjects.

2.12   In an experiment, what is an *independent variable* and what is a *dependent variable*?

A condition manipulated so that the effect can be investigated by the experimenter is called the independent variable. The response caused by the independent variable that is measured by the experimenter is called the dependent variable. In the "coffee-drinking" experiment, the condition manipulated was the beverage provided to the subjects. Thus, the independent variable was one of three conditions: coffee, decaffeinated coffee, or water. The dependent variable was the measured response: the reaction time of the subjects.

2.13   Suppose an experimenter ran the "coffee-drinking" study and found that all three groups had the same average reaction time. How would these results be shown on a graph?

The independent variable would be plotted on the abscissa (*x*-axis). The dependent variable would be plotted on the ordinate (*y*-axis). Figure 2-7 illustrates how the graph would look if the average reaction time for each group was 0.5 second.

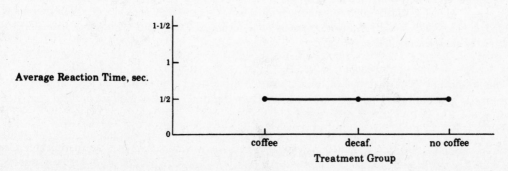

Fig. 2-7

2.14   How do experimenters avoid introducing bias when they pick the subjects for an experiment?

First, the experimenter must define the population from which the subjects will be drawn. (For example, the population could be the residents of a city who owned cell phones, all residents who had any kind of telephone service, or simply all the residents regardless of telephone service.) Once the population is defined, the experimenter either will use all its members as subjects or (more likely) will select a *sample* of the population. The purpose of sampling is to get a manageable number of subjects who are representative of the entire population.

2.15   If a psychologist was interested in investigating attitudes about a major social problem in different neighborhoods of a city, how might the sampling be done?

The psychologist must first establish the geographic boundaries of the neighborhoods. Once they are determined, *random sampling* would mean that every person within any one neighborhood would have an equal chance of being chosen as a representative of that neighborhood. The psychologist would "draw names out of a hat" until the necessary number was reached. If, for some reason, it appeared that it was significant whether the person being asked about the attitude was a homeowner as opposed to a renter, it might be necessary to establish the percentages of each category in each neighborhood and then select subjects accordingly. This would be a *stratified sample*.

2.16   In the study described in Solved Problem 2.15, what if the psychologist can get only volunteer subjects to participate?

When psychologists are unable to use sampling techniques such as those described here, yet still want to gather information, the last resort is to use an *accidental sample*, using only those people who are available and willing to take part. Less likely to be truly representative of the population, an accidental sample is used only when necessary.

2.17   Do sampling techniques eliminate all bias in the groups selected?

Sampling techniques *help* reduce bias, but it is unlikely that they ever completely eliminate it. The groups are selected to be as similar as possible before the study begins, but it is unlikely they will ever be perfectly alike.

2.18   What is experimenter bias? How can it be reduced or eliminated?

Unintentionally, experimenters may contribute bias to an investigation either in the design of the study or in the way they conduct it. For example, subjects may be able to tell, by the very design of the study, what kind of response is anticipated and make an effort to meet those expectations. In addition, even in a well-designed study, an experimenter may have some expectations about the subjects' performance and communicate those expectations by a gesture, tone of voice, or an offhand remark.

Bias can be reduced or eliminated by eliminating such expectations. In some studies, this is accomplished by preventing the subjects and those collecting the information from knowing the intent of the study, knowing which group is experimental or control, or being aware of other cues that might bias the responses. Such studies are said to employ *blind* techniques and typically require thorough debriefing after the study is completed.

2.19   The methodology and control of the experimental method are considered very important. Why, then, do psychologists accept information from relatively uncontrolled naturalistic observations?

In some cases, experiments are impossible. For example, it would be unethical to experimentally create conditions of severe nutritional deprivation for a young child. However, such conditions occasionally do exist. Psychologists can learn from these kinds of situations by employing careful, precise, and unbiased observation. Psychologists might be personally disgusted by the mistreatment of the child, but they would still study the situation to observe what effects these conditions had on the child's behavior.

2.20   How do case studies differ from naturalistic observations?

Case studies typically involve a record of the problems, insights, and techniques used in clinical or counseling treatment. Unlike naturalistic observations, the psychologist is an active participant in the process that produces this record. For both case studies and naturalistic observations, psychologists may want to confirm the ideas gathered, if possible, by using more systematic techniques.

2.21   Information about behavior that cannot be observed directly sometimes is gathered by using psychological tests and surveys. What are some of the advantages and disadvantages of tests and surveys?

Psychological tests and surveys allow for the rapid collection of large amounts of data and allow the investigator to compare the response of one subject to those of many others. Because most tests and surveys are standardized, they can be administered and interpreted easily and quickly. Disadvantages include the fact that respondents can falsify their answers and the fact that some tests or surveys may be invalid for the situation in which they are used.

2.22   In psychology, what roles do statistics play?

Statistics refers to the collection, analysis, interpretation, and presentation of numerical data. Statistics thus allow (1) simplification or summarizing of data through the use of descriptive statistics and (2) evaluation of the relationships within or between sets of data through the use of inferential statistics.

2.23   Would a psychologist be more likely to use descriptive or inferential statistics when making a prediction about a future behavior?

The psychologist might use both kinds of statistics. The descriptive statistics would provide the information about the values of scores that could be expected for the response being studied, while the inferential statistics would evaluate the probability of responding if similar situations occurred in the future.

2.24   As an officer of a charitable organization, Virginia is asked to create a visual record of donor levels that can be used in a forthcoming meeting. If Virginia plots a frequency polygon of the distribution, what might it look like? How would a histogram differ?

A frequency polygon such as Fig. 2-8, is often called a line graph. A histogram is a bar graph. Virginia's data would be plotted in a histogram, as shown in Fig. 2-9.

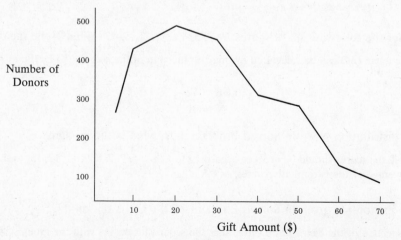

Fig. 2-8

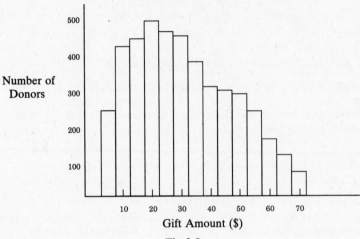

Fig 2-9

2.25 Is the information presented in Figs. 2-8 and 2-9 more likely to be called symmetrical or skewed? What types of skew can occur?

Virginia's data should be described as being skewed. Most of the donors make fairly small contributions, while fewer make large donations. If the distribution was symmetrical, the frequency of donations would occur in roughly equal numbers on both sides of the middle of the distribution.

When the data "bunch" toward the lower end of the scale, as in Virginia's donor records, the distribution is said to be positively skewed. If the scores were to "bunch" at the other end, the distribution would be negatively skewed.

2.26 What is a measure of central tendency? How does the mean represent a measure of central tendency? What other measures of central tendency are used commonly?

A measure of central tendency is a number that best represents a group of numbers. (This number is thought to be the best prediction of a score that might be made by any one of the people represented by the scores already collected.)

The *mean* gives the arithmetically calculated average score for the group. To calculate the mean, sum all the scores and divide that total by the number of scores. Other measures of central tendency include the *median*, which is the fiftieth percentile score (with an equal number of scores falling above and below it), and the *mode*, which is the score that occurs with the greatest frequency. (*Note*: There may be more than one mode in a distribution if two or more scores happen to occur with the equal greatest frequency.)

2.27 Consider the following set of scores: 7, 7, 5, 11, 9, 12, 8, 13. What is the mean?

The mean (M) can be calculated by dividing the sum of the scores (X) by the number of scores (N), as follows:

$$M = \frac{\Sigma X}{N} = \frac{72}{8} = 9 \; ans.$$

2.28 In the distribution given in Solved Problem 2.27, what is the median?

First, the scores should be ordered according to value: 5, 7, 7, 8, 9, 11, 12, 13. In this case, the median is the average of the two middle values, or 8.5.

2.29 In the distribution given in Solved Problem 2.27, what is the mode?

Inspection of the distribution shows that the score that occurs with the greatest frequency is 7; thus, 7 is the mode.

2.30 Suppose a score of 5 and a score of 13 were added to the distribution used in Solved Problem 2.27. What would the mean, median, and mode be for this new distribution?

The sum of the scores for the new distribution is 90. When divided by the number of scores (10), the mean of this distribution is the same as that found before, or 9.

The median differs from that of the previous distribution. It is the average of the two middle scores, or 10.

The new distribution has more than one score that occurs with the equal greatest frequency: 5, 7, and 13. Thus, this distribution has three modes, or is trimodal.

2.31 With the need to "downsize" his sales staff, an automobile dealer reviews the sales records of his employees. He finds that one person has sold as many as 44 cars in a month but also has had months when none were sold. Another employee's best month was 10 cars; in the worst month, 7 were sold.

The dealer's interest in these values illustrates what type of statistical consideration? What statistic can be calculated from the numbers provided in this problem? What values are obtained?

In this case, the employer is looking at variability, probably considering the consistency of sales performance. He can calculate the range, which equals the difference between the highest and lowest scores in a distribution. The range of performance for the first salesperson is 44 (44 − 0), while the range for the second person is 3 (10 − 7).

2.32 Consider the following distribution of scores: 4, 5, 6, 7, 8, 9, 10. What is the value of the standard deviation?

The formula for the standard deviation is as follows:

$$SD = \sqrt{\frac{\Sigma d^2}{N}}$$

N is simply the number of scores in the distribution, or 7. The other variable in the equation, d, must be calculated for each score (d is the difference between each score and the mean). The mean (M) is calculated as follows:

$$M = \frac{\Sigma X}{N} = \frac{49}{7} = 7$$

Thus, d and d^2 can be calculated for each score, and the squared differences can be summed to get Σd^2.

$X - M$	d	d^2
10 − 7	3	9
9 − 7	2	4
8 − 7	1	1
7 − 7	0	0
6 − 7	−1	1
5 − 7	−2	4
4 − 7	−3	9
		28

The values for N and d^2 can then be substituted in the formula for the standard deviation:

$$SD = \sqrt{\frac{28}{7}} = \sqrt{4} = 2 \quad ans.$$

2.33   Interested in determining how well the speed limits were being observed on a heavily-traveled street, the city police set up a radar checkpoint and measured the speed of hundreds of cars that passed by. When they plotted all the values obtained, they found that the curve obtained closely approximated a normal probability distribution. What was the shape of the curve?

The normal probability curve is a symmetrical distribution, with most cases falling near the middle of the distribution and the "tails" tapering off sharply at the very high or very low scores (or speeds, in this case).

2.34   Repeated investigations have shown that the normal probability curve has certain properties. Suppose the police (Solved Problem 2.33) found that the average speed of cars passing their checkpoint was 35 miles per hour and that the standard deviation had a value of 4. Sketch the curve they obtained, showing the appropriate percentages of the distribution.

The curve obtained would be similar to the one shown in Fig. 2-10.

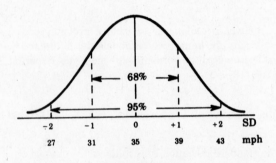

Fig. 2-10

This curve indicates that 68 percent of the cars passing the checkpoint were going between 31 and 39 miles per hour and approximately 95 percent were included in the range between 27 and 43 miles per hour. It also can be determined that $2\frac{1}{2}$ percent were going more than 43 miles per hour and another $2\frac{1}{2}$ percent were traveling at less than 27 miles per hour. (These two last groups are in the "tails" of the distribution.)

2.35   Another way to look at the normal probability curve is in terms of percentile values. Using the distribution given in Solved Problem 2.34, calculate the value (or speed) at the fiftieth percentile. Also, at what percentile would a speed of 39 miles per hour fall?

It is sometimes convenient to recast the normal probability curve in terms of percentage, as shown in Fig. 2-11.

Determination of percentile values can be done by adding percentage values from left to right; thus,

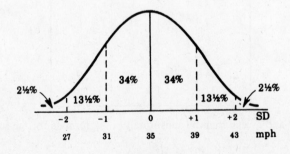

Fig. 2-11

the percentile value of $2\frac{1}{2}$ is reached at the -2 standard deviation indicator; the sixteenth percentile is at -1; the fiftieth percentile is at the mean; the eighty-fourth percentile at $+1$; and the percentile value of $97\frac{1}{2}$ is at the $+2$ standard deviation mark.

Solving the particular questions in this problem, the value at the fiftieth percentile is the mean value, or 35 miles per hour, and a speed of 39 miles per hour is located at the eighty-fourth percentile. (*Note*: Percentile values at other points on the curve have been determined and can be found by referring to a table of such values in a statistics handbook.)

2.36   Suppose you know you have a normal probability distribution with a standard deviation equal to 6 points and the value of the score at the eighty-fourth percentile equaling 90. What is the mean of the distribution?

Using the same kind of curve sketched in Solved Problem 2.35, you can determine that the score of 90 is one standard deviation above the mean. Therefore, subtracting the value of the standard deviation from that score will give you the mean of the distribution, which is 84.

2.37   Using the same values given in Solved Problem 2.36, what percentage of the group studied will fall between scores of 96 and 78?

The score of 96 is two standard deviation (SD) units above the mean, while 78 is one SD below the mean. Adding the percentages between these two points reveals that $81\frac{1}{2}$ percent of the group falls between these scores.

2.38   Intelligence tests often have a value of 100 for the mean and a value of 15 for the standard deviation. Scores above 130 or below 70 often are referred to as "exceptional." Based on the normal probability curve, does this label seem appropriate?

Scores above 130 or below 70 are more than two standard deviations from the mean and constitute the "tails" of the distribution. Thus, the label "exceptional" is probably appropriate.

2.39   In a campaign speech, a cynical politician reported that during the past term of his opponent, the average earnings per person in the city had gone up, as had the number of homeless people. He claimed that "homeless people just don't know how well off they are!"

What statistic was the politician using as the basis for his sarcastic remark? What caution should be heeded when using this statistic?

The politician based his remark on the calculation of a *correlation*. The statistic may have suggested a relationship between the two phenomena, but it is necessary to recognize that this may not be an indication of causality, or a contingency relationship. (For example, in this case, it could appear that as the "average person" in the city earns more money, more people become homeless. Such a conclusion makes little sense even though a correlation does exist.)

2.40   Interested in determining the effectiveness of a student workbook, a teacher asked her students how many hours they spent studying from the workbook and how much each student thought the workbook helped with preparation for the exam. The teacher then plotted the two graphs shown in Fig. 2-12. What are these graphs called, and what do they show?

The plots are called *scatter diagrams* or *scattergrams*. The scattergram relating hours of study to number of errors made on the exam shows a negative correlation; that is, the higher the value of one variable, the lower the value of the other. The scattergram relating the students' ratings of workbook helpfulness to the grade obtained shows a positive correlation, indicating that the higher the value of one variable, the higher the value of the other.

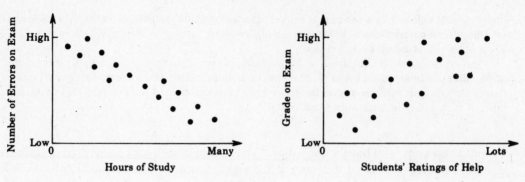

Fig. 2-12

2.41 The values of the correlations determined for the relationships shown in Solved Problem 2.40 are −0.68 and +0.32. Which correlation is the better predictor?

The negative correlation (−0.68) is a better predictor than the positive correlation (+0.32). Correlations may have any value from 0.00 to +1.00 or −1.00. The closer a correlation comes to an *absolute* value of 1.00 (either plus or minus), the more accurate the prediction that can be made from that correlation.

2.42 Suppose the teacher in Solved Problem 2.40 used the information obtained from her scatter diagrams and correlations to make a prediction about the performance of another class. By determining the number of hours of study each student reported, the teacher predicted the number of errors expected. Such a prediction, based on knowledge of one variable's value and a previous correlation, illustrates what statistical procedure? Is this a fairly common procedure?

Predictions of this nature illustrate the regression procedure, which is used fairly commonly. For example, admissions counselors correlate college entrance examination scores and the success of previous classes in college. These correlations allow the counselors to make predictions about the probable success of the members of each new class.

Key Terms

Abscissa. The *x*-axis, or horizontal axis, of a graph.

Central tendency. A number that best represents a group of numbers.

Class interval. Arbitrarily selected portions of a measurement scale; usually equal.

Clinical case history. Records or data from therapeutic situations; used to identify behaviors and suggest problems that need to be studied.

Contingency. The concept of causality or dependency; indicates that there is a meaningful relationship between two variables.

Control group. In a scientific experiment, the subjects whose responses are used as the basis for comparison; the experimenter compares the responses of the control group with the responses of experimental groups.

Correlation. The tendency of two or more variables to vary together (concomitantly); the numerical representation of the relationship between these two variables.

Debriefing.   At the end of an experiment with humans, informing the subjects about what has happened in a complete and accurate manner.

Dependent variable.   The measured response in an experiment.

Descriptive statistics.   Measures or techniques that allow a summary portrayal of collected data.

Directional hypothesis.   A prediction that a specific change in the conditions of an experiment will result in a particular change in the outcome of the experiment.

Double-blind control.   An experimental situation in which both the subjects *and* those who administer the experiment are unaware of how or when the variables are manipulated by the experimenter.

Empirical.   Refers to anything that is directly observable or measurable.

Experimental group.   In a scientific experiment, the subjects who respond to an independent variable that is "specially" manipulated by the experimenter; the responses of the experimental group can then be compared with the responses of the control group.

Experimental method.   A technique involving the controlled comparison of conditions to determine whether the variable investigated affects the results obtained.

Extraneous variable.   A condition that may affect the outcome of an experiment but is irrelevant to the purposes of the experiment.

Frequency distribution.   A graphic or tabular representation of the number of cases found in each class interval of a distribution.

Frequency polygon.   A line graph representing a frequency distribution.

Histogram.   A bar graph representing a frequency distribution.

Hypothesis.   A tentative explanation of a relationship or a proposition that a relationship exists; an experiment should be designed so that a hypothesis can be either confirmed or disconfirmed.

Independent variable.   A condition manipulated by the experimenter; the experimenter manipulates the independent variable to determine the effect of such manipulations on the dependent variable.

Inferential statistics.   Measures or techniques that allow the analysis or evaluation of relationships existing within a sample of data or between samples of data; can be used to make predictions.

Informed consent.   In experiments with humans, providing accurate and sufficient information about and obtaining consent to participate in the experiment.

Matched sampling.   A technique for selecting subjects in which the experimenter makes sure that each group in the experiment contains the same number of subjects who possess certain characteristics which might influence the outcome.

Mean (M or $\bar{X}$).   The average score in a distribution of scores; calculated by summing all the scores and dividing that sum by the number of scores.

Median.   The middle score in a distribution of scores; the number of scores above and below it are equal, and the score is at the fiftieth percentile.

Mode.   The score that occurs most frequently in a distribution; there may be more than one mode in a distribution.

Naturalistic observation.   The careful observation of events not manipulated by the observer.

Normal curve.   The graphic representation of the normal probability distribution.

Normal probability distribution.   An idealized distribution based on data collected from large samples; most scores are at or near the mean, with a few scores at the extremes; often used for making statistical inferences.

Null hypothesis.   A prediction that a specific change in the conditions of an experiment will not result in a change in the outcome.

Objectivity.   A condition that exists when judgments are free from bias or the influence of personal feeling.

Operational definition.   Defining a variable by the procedure used to produce or measure it.

Ordinate.   The *y*-axis, or vertical axis, of a graph.

Percentile.   The point below which a given percentage of the total number of scores in a distribution falls.

Placebo.   A chemically inert material that has the same appearance as an active drug; by analogy, the "placebo effect" occurs in any situation in which subjects believe they are experiencing a manipulation by the experimenter when in fact they are not.

Population.   The entire group from which samples may be chosen.

Random sampling.   A technique for selecting subjects in such a way that every potential subject in the population has an equal chance of being chosen.

Range.   A measure of variability calculated by determining the difference between the highest and lowest scores in a distribution.

Regression.   Use of the knowledge of a previously obtained correlation and the value of one variable to predict the value of another variable.

Sample.   A group selected from a population; an attempt should be made to make the sample as representative of the population as possible.

Scattergram.   The pictorial representation of a correlation.

Single-blind control.   An experimental situation in which the subjects are unaware of how or when the variables are manipulated by the experimenter.

Skew.   Occurs when the scores of a distribution occur with greater frequency at one end of a distribution.

Standard deviation (SD or σ).   A measure of variability based on the differences of each score from the mean.

Statistics.   The discipline that deals with the collection, analysis, interpretation, and presentation of numerical data.

Stratified sampling.   A technique for selecting subjects in such a way that significant subgroups within the population are reflected accurately in the composition of each group in the experiment.

Subjectivity.   A condition that exists when judgments are affected by bias, prejudice, or personal feeling.

Variability.   The extent to which scores are dispersed in a distribution.

Variable.   A characteristic of anything that can have two or more values.

CHAPTER 3

Biological Foundations

Physical structure plays an important role in determining the behavior of an individual. Understanding how physical structures influence behavior starts with the study of the individual components of the nervous system and how those components are arranged into systems and subsystems.

3.1 ELEMENTS OF A NEURON

A *neuron* is a single cell composed of three basic elements: the *cell body* (which contains the nucleus), *dendrites*, and an *axon*. There are billions of neurons in the human body. *Neuron fibers* are bunched together to form *nerves*, which carry signals throughout the body.

Cell Body.   The cell body (or soma) is the center of a neuron and assimilates and makes use of the nutrients that supply energy for neuronal activity. Unlike the cell body of most other cells, a neuron's cell body has two different kinds of branches or extensions: Many dendrites and the single axon extend from the cell body.

Dendrites.   The "receiving" portion of the neuron is formed by the many *dendrites*. They are usually short and thin and may number more than a thousand in a single cell.

The dendrites receive (or sense) signals in the form of neurotransmitters (see Section 3.2) emitted from other nerve cells. If enough excitatory messages are received, a neural signal is transmitted through the length of the cell as an impulse.

Axon.   Coming from the cell body, each neuron has only a single axon, although the axon may have branches with what are called *terminal buttons* at the end. The axon conducts the impulse away from the cell body to its end; the axon then passes the signal to the dendrites of the next neuron. Axons may vary in length from several microns to several feet, depending on the location of the cell.

While all of a neuron is covered by a cell membrane, many axons are covered with a fatty substance called *myelin*. Myelinated axons conduct a signal at a faster pace than do nonmyelinated axons.

EXAMPLE 3.1.   An easy way to picture a myelinated axon is to think of a string of somewhat irregular beads. The axon is the "string," while the "beads" are the myelin. The signal seems to skip from gap to gap between the beads and progresses faster than does a signal that flows smoothly through an unmyelinated axon.

3.2 TRANSMISSION OF A SIGNAL

Many factors are involved in signal transmission. Essentially, each signal travels the length of a cell and then crosses a gap to activate the next cell, where the process of transmission is repeated. Cells differ in their capacity to transmit and in the type of signal transmitted, but the basic process of all transmissions is the same.

Synapse. A signal first reaches a cell when a neurotransmitter (or transmitter substance) that is secreted by the axon of one cell crosses a gap between that axon and the dendrite of the next cell. This gap is called a *synapse*.

Synapses are one-way connections. Signals pass from axon to dendrite but do not travel in the opposite direction. In most cases, the signals are received by the dendrites of the next cell, although occasionally cell bodies or axons receive messages from across the synapse.

Neurotransmitters. At the end of each axon branch, there is a *terminal button* or knob that holds the *synaptic vesicles*. As a signal reaches the end of an axon, these vesicles discharge a chemical called a *neurotransmitter* (or *transmitter substance*), which is received by the next cell. Research has identified approximately 40 to 60 different substances that serve as neurotransmitters.

Neurotransmitters appear to interact chemically with the cell membrane of the next neuron and sometimes are described as "fitting into" receptors on the dendrite of the receiving cell. They tend to activate or constrain the firing of (transmission of a signal through) that next cell and are described, respectively, as *excitatory* or *inhibitory*. The sum of excitation and inhibition is called the *graded potential*. When the messages transmitted across the various synapses leading to the next cell surpass that cell's threshold for firing, it is activated and transmits a signal throughout its length.

EXAMPLE 3.2. Imagine a squirt gun full of ink pointed at a clean piece of white cotton cloth. When you pull the trigger of the squirt gun, the ink will cross the gap to the cloth and be absorbed. The synapse works in a similar fashion. When neurotransmitters are released from the axon, they cross the gap and are absorbed by the dendrites. Just as the ink cannot be released by the cloth and replaced in the squirt gun, the transmitter substances, once absorbed into the dendrite, cannot return to the axon.

Neurotransmitters are involved in all activities of the body, playing critical roles in behaviors as varied as memory, emotion, movement, learning, anxiety, and arousal. Among the neurotransmitters produced are *endorphins*, natural opiates that appear to regulate pain and pleasure. Endorphins are produced in the brain in response to stress or anxiety; they have been linked to "runner's high," the relief experienced by some athletes in extremely demanding physical conditions. Other neurotransmitters that have been studied extensively include *dopamine*, which is related to attention, movement, and learning, and *serotonin*, which is related to sleep, arousal, and mood.

EXAMPLE 3.3. Increased levels of endorphins lead to reduced pain. Interestingly, *opiates* (narcotic drugs such as heroin or morphine) mimic the effects of endorphins. Just as persons with a dependency on drugs experience anxiety and discomfort when prevented from having them, athletes often report similar discomfort when prevented from exercising.

Resting Potential. In a resting state, the cell membrane of a neuron maintains a certain level of permeability (penetrability) such that the inside of the cell is slightly negative in electrical charge compared to the outside. This relationship is called the *resting potential* of the neuron and exists because positive sodium ions (Na^+) are kept out of the cell by the membrane, while positive potassium ions (K^+) and negative chloride ions (Cl^-) can get in.

Action Potential. When the graded potential surpasses the neuron threshold, the signal passes through the length of the cell as an *action potential*. If an action potential begins, it always travels the entire length of the cell. There is no possibility that a signal can deteriorate and "die" within the length of a single cell. Thus, the firing of the cell is described by what is called the *all-or-none principle*.

The action potential travels much as a wave does. Each neuron fires at a fixed intensity; that is, the intensity is the same for every firing of the cell. The permeability of the axon membrane nearest the cell body shows a swift change and the electrical charges reverse so that the inside of the cell becomes positive and the outside becomes negative. This is called *depolarization*.

Although there is a rapid repolarization of the activated region, the signal does not fade. Rather, the adjoining section of the axon depolarizes. The depolarization-repolarization sequence repeats itself, conducting the impulse through the length of the axon.

EXAMPLE 3.4. Envision someone lighting a nonfilter cigarette. If the match is held too far from the end, the cigarette will not light. Once the heat is sufficient, however, the cigarette starts to burn. Now suppose this person places the cigarette in an ashtray and ignores it while it continues to burn. Eventually, the cigarette will burn completely.

A nerve signal operates in the same fashion. A neuron does not fire unless the stimulus strength is sufficient, but once it is started, it goes through the entire length of the fiber. (*Note*: The axon has an advantage that the cigarette does not have: When the axon has completed its task, it can repolarize and fire again. The tobacco turns to ash and cannot be reconstituted.)

Refractory Phase.   The *refractory phase* is the period of time required for the repolarization of a cell. Although this may be a very short period (less than 1/1000 of a second in some cases), no signal can pass through the cell during the first part of the phase, which is called the *absolute refractory period*. The remainder of the refractory period, which is called the *relative refractory period*, is the time during which the cell can be activated again, but only if the excitation is stronger than normal.

EXAMPLE 3.5. Perhaps you have experienced a "personal refractory period" comparable to that of a neuron. Suppose you have devoted an immense amount of time and energy to the preparation of a business plan for a potential customer. Perhaps you are truly "bushed" by the effort and feel you need a recovery period. If no new project demands your immediate attention, it may be possible to take a long rest before beginning the next undertaking. However, if another, potentially lucrative plan needs to be prepared quickly, your motivation may be so high that you will take a short rest break (absolute refractory period) and then start working again even though you are not yet fully rested (relative refractory period).

Signal Strength.   The action potential is always the same intensity for every firing of a neuron. The strength of a signal depends on factors other than the size of the action potential. Three variables appear to contribute to the identification of signal strength: the *frequency* with which any single neuron is being fired, the total *number* of neurons being fired by the signal, and the particular *route* of the neurons being fired. In general, a greater frequency of firing and a greater number being fired indicate greater intensity of the signal. Which neurons fire determines the type of stimulation that will be coded as a result of the signal.

3.3 ORGANIZATION OF THE NERVOUS SYSTEM

The billions of neurons that make up the nervous system of the human body can be categorized into two divisions: the *central nervous system* (*CNS*) and the *peripheral nervous system* (*PNS*). Each has subdivisions that function in specialized ways.

The Central Nervous System.   The central nervous system is composed of two major subdivisions: the brain and the spinal cord. These two parts are joined at the base of the brain so that there is constant passage of signals to and from the brain and body.

The CNS is encased in protective bone, with the skull surrounding the brain and the backbone (or spinal column) surrounding the spinal cord. Both parts receive sensory messages from the *afferent* (sensory) part of the peripheral nervous system, and both can send signals to the muscles and glands by connecting with the *efferent* (motor and autonomic) part of the PNS.

In general, the spinal cord serves two major functions: (1) carrying impulses back and forth from body to brain or brain to body and (2) controlling many reflexes. The brain controls many more sophisticated functions, including perception, memory, and voluntary movements as well as basic functions such as breathing and swallowing. (Brain signals even may modify actions that occur at the spinal cord level.)

Structure and Function of the Brain. The brain has three major anatomic regions or layers. The first layer forms the *hindbrain*, a well-protected central core that controls basic, rudimentary behaviors. The hindbrain of a human is very similar to that of other vertebrate animals. Above the hindbrain, the second layer, or *midbrain*, is the area through which all sensory and motor information going to and from the forebrain and the spinal cord must pass. The third layer is called the *forebrain*, which contains the cerebral cortex and the limbic system and controls higher mental processes.

EXAMPLE 3.6. Rather than thinking of a person standing, it is easier to envision the construction of the brain if one imagines a person "on hands and knees." The part of the brain pointing ahead is the forebrain, while the hindbrain is farthest toward the back, connecting with the spinal cord, which stretches toward the "tail."

Hindbrain. The hindbrain, or central core, includes the *medulla*, *pons*, and *cerebellum*; it has as its center the *reticular formation* (or reticular activating system). The behaviors controlled by the hindbrain include heartbeat and circulation, breathing, chewing, and salivating in the medulla; sleep and movement information in the pons; and movement and balance in the cerebellum. The reticular formation controls attention and arousal both for activity and when a person wants to sleep. The hindbrain is thought to be involved with basic survival and varies little among different species (see Fig. 3-1).

EXAMPLE 3.7. Damage to the cerebellum can cause *ataxia*, a condition of uncoordinated movement, loss of balance, and muscle tremors. Lack of control can be so bad that, for example, an ataxic person may reach for a cup of coffee only to knock it off the table and into a companion's lap.

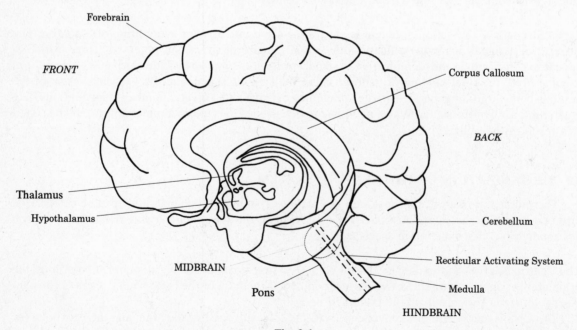

Fig. 3-1

Midbrain.   Located in front of (or above) the hindbrain, the midbrain is a small area with two major responsibilities. All sensory information that travels between the spinal cord and the forebrain must go through the midbrain. In addition, the midbrain has important centers that control body movement in response to auditory and visual information.

EXAMPLE 3.8.   The midbrain probably is more important in nonmammals than it is in mammals because it controls visual and auditory information. Much of that information in mammals is controlled by forebrain structures. Animals more dependent on auditory signals are likely to show increased development of the areas of the midbrain associated with auditory control, while those relying on visual information show more development of the visual areas of the midbrain.

Forebrain.   The third and most highly evolved layer of the brain, the forebrain, is composed of the *limbic system* and the two *cerebral hemispheres*. The outer layer of the cerebral hemispheres is called the cerebral *cortex*, an area that controls complex mental skills. If the cortex is peeled away, a highly connected group of structures called the *limbic system* is found inside.

The major components of the limbic system are the *thalamus*, the *hypothalamus*, the *hippocampus*, the *amygdala*, and the *septum*. The thalamus primarily serves to process and relay sensory information to specific parts of the forebrain. The hypothalamus functions in basic survival behaviors such as eating, drinking, sexual activity, aggression, and fear and also helps regulate the body's internal environment. It also regulates the activity of the *pituitary gland*, which in turn controls hormonal secretions from other glands. The hippocampus and the amygdala are involved in the formation of new memories, the retention of memory, and emotions. The septum also is involved with emotions in that it serves as an area determining experiences of pleasure.

EXAMPLE 3.9.   By accident, the researchers James Olds and Peter Milner found that electrical stimulation of the septum appeared to produce intense feelings of pleasure in rats. The rats would forsake food and other kinds of stimulation or reward to maintain the stimulation of the septum, even to the point of starving, and if given a chance to self-stimulate that area of the brain would work tirelessly to do so.

Careful study of the cerebral hemispheres has allowed the labeling of specific areas and the "mapping" of many of their functions. (Some of the most important functions are mapped in Solved Problem 3.19.) See Fig. 3-2.

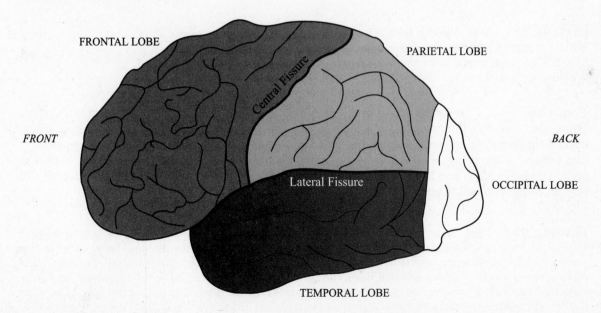

Fig. 3-2

EXAMPLE 3.10.   Because functions differ from one side of the brain to the other, the behaviors controlled by the two hemispheres sometimes are referred to as "left brain" and "right brain" activities. In general, there is a crossing over of control such that the left hemisphere controls activity of the right side of the body and vice versa. Thus, if a person has a stroke that affects the sensory or motor activities controlled by the left hemisphere of the brain, the responses of the right side of the body will be affected.

Central Fissure and Lateral Fissure.   While all of the cortical surface of the brain is convoluted (wrinkled), there are two especially deep convolutions. In each hemisphere, the central fissure runs from the top middle of the brain toward the center side; the lateral fissure runs from the lower front of the brain along the center side. (These structures are shown in Fig. 3-2.)

Cortical Lobes.   Each cerebral hemisphere is divided somewhat arbitrarily into four *cortical lobes.* The *frontal lobe* is in the area behind the forehead, found in front of the central fissure and the lateral fissure. The *parietal lobe* is at the top of the head and goes from the rear of the central fissure to the center back of the brain. The *occipital lobe* is the lower back portion of the brain. The *temporal lobe* is the area in front of the occipital lobe to the rear of the lateral fissure. (These structures are shown in Fig. 3-2.)

Localized Functions.   A number of functions have been identified for different areas of the cerebral hemispheres. The *motor area* is in the back portion of the frontal lobe, just in front of the central fissure. Just to the rear of the central fissure, at the front of the parietal lobe, is the *sensory area.* The initial analysis of visual stimuli occurs in the very back of the brain in the occipital lobe. Hearing, speech understanding, and speech production are located near the lateral fissure; for most people control of these appears to occur in the temporal lobe of the left hemisphere. Although much of the rest of the brain remains relatively unmapped, it is believed that association, memory, and other cognitive abilities are located there, especially in the frontal lobes.

Plasticity.   The brain appears to be able to adapt and change activity or function as a result of interchanges with the world. This is referred to as *plasticity*, a term that also is used more generally to describe adaptations to new circumstances, shown particularly by adults. It is likely that plasticity is the result of increased dendritic branching produced by practice, activity, and some medications.

EXAMPLE 3.11.   Several studies have shown that subjects asked to wear special glasses that invert the visual world are able to adjust within 2 to 4 days. The brain seems to "reprogram" itself and understand the new information. Interestingly, when the study is completed and the glasses are removed, the subjects have an additional adjustment period while returning to the "normal" environment.

Corpus Callosum.   The *corpus callosum* is a thick band of fibers connecting the cerebral hemispheres. These fibers serve as the pathway for signals to pass from one side of the brain to the other. These fibers sometimes are severed in patients with severe epilepsy, creating what has been called a "split-brain" individual. *Split-brain investigations* have shown that the two halves of the brain can operate independently and show differing functions. In general, such studies have shown that over 90 percent of the population is left-hemisphere-dominated.

EXAMPLE 3.12.   "Split-brain" research has shown that language skills usually depend on left hemisphere functioning. Suppose a subject has had the corpus callosum severed and is shown the word "matchbox" so that "match" is transmitted to the right hemisphere and "box" is transmitted to the left hemisphere. The subject will make a verbal report of seeing only the word "box." When asked what kind of box, the subject may guess "shoebox" or "hatbox," getting "matchbox" only by chance. However, if asked to use the left hand (controlled by the right hemisphere) to sort through objects on the table and identify the appropriate object, the subject is likely to be able to pick correctly, indicating that processing has occurred at a nonverbal level.

Methods for Observing or Evaluating Brain Activity.   Early investigations of brain activity in humans were limited primarily to two types: the study of the effects of brain damage and the use of recordings of the brain's electrical impulses. In the former type, changes in behavior after trauma to the brain were considered evidence of the control the damaged portion of the brain must have on the affected behavior. In the latter type, sensitive electrodes were attached to the outside of the head to produce an *electroencephalograph (EEG)*. Spontaneous changes in the pattern observed were correlated to corresponding mental states, such as dreaming. In addition, in limited situations, leads were implanted in the brain and used to deliver mild electric shocks. The effect on behaviors was attributed to the stimulation of the particular area of the brain.

Newer, more sophisticated methods have produced far more revealing looks at brain activity. *Computerized axial tomography (CAT scan)* uses x-rays to measure differences in tissue density from one area of the brain to others and is particularly helpful in revealing structural abnormalities. When radioactive glucose is injected into a person, *positron emission tomography (PET scan)* analyzes glucose metabolism in the brain, showing the differences in neural metabolic activity in the various regions of the brain at any given time. *Magnetic resonance imaging (MRI)* and *superconducting quantum interference devices (SQUID)* measure differences in the magnetic field throughout the brain, providing information about structure and neural activity. (*Note*: These techniques, for example, MRI, also are used to evaluate many other parts of the body.)

The Peripheral Nervous System.   The peripheral nervous system has two subdivisions: the *somatic system*, which is concerned with sensory and motor functions, and the *autonomic nervous system*, which controls the functions of many glands and smooth-muscle organs. The somatic system, especially sensory processes and perception, is treated thoroughly in Chapter 5.

The autonomic system is further divided into the *sympathetic system* and the *parasympathetic system*. Although there are some exceptions, these divisions usually work in an antagonistic, or opposite, manner.

Sympathetic System.   To either side of the thoracic and lumbar (middle) portions of the spinal cord, there are chains of nerve fibers and cell bodies linked to both the spinal cord and various visceral organs. These are the *sympathetic chains*. This system tends to act as a unit and is involved primarily in aroused or excited activity.

Parasympathetic System.   The fibers of the parasympathetic system connect with many of the same visceral organs as do those of the sympathetic system. These fibers originate in the cervical (top) and sacral (bottom) portions of the spinal cord. They tend to operate independently and are involved in the quiet, recuperative functions.

The autonomic system is so named because many of its functions are automatic and self-regulating, continuing whether or not conscious thought is involved.

EXAMPLE 3.13.   Antagonistic functioning within the autonomic nervous system can be illustrated by the inhibition of bladder release controlled by the sympathetic system and the stimulation of bladder release caused by the parasympathetic system. Another illustration is the sympathetic system's inhibition of digestion and the parasympathetic system's facilitation of digestive processes. In the latter case, athletes often are advised not to eat for several hours before a contest, because digestive processes will be shut down by the sympathetic system arousal associated with the athletic activity and the food will remain unprocessed in the digestive system.

3.4   THE GLANDULAR SYSTEMS

The human body contains two sets of glands that are important for body functions: the *exocrine glands* and the *endocrine glands*. In general, exocrine glands secrete fluids to outer surfaces of the body, while endocrine glands secrete *hormones*, distinctive chemicals which are similar to neurotransmitters and carry "messages" through the bloodstream to "target" organs or glands.

EXAMPLE 3.14.   Although exocrine glands often are thought to be less important to human functioning than the endocrine glands, it is hard to convince a very nervous individual who is perspiring copiously before an important ceremony of that fact. Certainly, the activity of exocrine glands is important in many day-to-day situations.

Hormones are essential to the proper functioning of the body, helping to control growth, nervous system activity, levels of energy, moods, and reactions to stress. The nervous system controls the activity of many endocrine glands, but some react directly to body conditions.

Pituitary Gland.   The *pituitary gland* has been designated as the body's "master gland." Connected to the hypothalamus, the pituitary gland secretes more different hormones than does any other endocrine gland. These hormones control numerous bodily processes, including activities such as reactions to stress, milk production in the mammary glands, the sequence of body growth, and the actions of other endocrine glands. The pituitary gland's connection with the brain provides an important reciprocal interaction between the nervous system and the endocrine system.

Other Endocrine Glands.   Several other endocrine glands provide good examples of the importance of this system in the overall functioning of the body. The *thyroid gland* secretes thyroxin, which regulates metabolism and influences psychological processes such as motivation and mood. The *adrenal glands* secrete adrenaline and noradrenaline, hormones that operate antagonistically to regulate mood, emotion, blood pressure and sugar level, and the distribution of blood between muscles and internal organs. More generally, these hormones are described as helping the organism prepare for emergencies and cope with stress. The *gonads*, or *sex glands*, secrete hormones concerned with sexual development, activity, and receptivity.

EXAMPLE 3.15.   Knowledge of hormonal control has allowed medical adjustments for physiological problems. Thus, the surgical necessity to remove the thyroid gland can be compensated for by appropriate doses of thyroxin (one of the gland's hormones) so that an appropriate activity level can be maintained.

Solved Problems

3.1   Sketch and label a simplified diagram of a neuron.

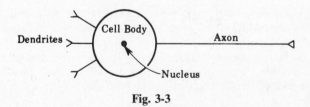

Fig. 3-3

3.2   Briefly describe the function of each of the parts of a neuron.

The dendrite is the "receiver part," picking up signals transmitted from other neurons or from external stimuli. The cell body, with its nucleus, has the specialized functions of absorbing and using nutrients to provide energy for the neuron's activities. The axon is the "transmitter part," carrying impulses from the neuron to other nerves or parts of the body.

3.3   How do axons and dendrites "hook up?" Sketch a simplified diagram to illustrate your answer.

There is a gap between the axon of one neuron and the dendrite of the next. This gap is called the synapse. (See Fig. 3.4.)

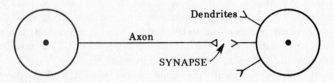

Fig. 3-4

The presence of the synaptic gap means there is no direct physical contact between the axon and the dendrite. The signal is carried across the synaptic gap by a neurotransmitter released by the axon.

3.4   If a neurotransmitter is released by the axon, will the next neuron (the one across the synapse) always fire?

Synapses may be excitatory or inhibitory; that is, the neurotransmitter crossing the gap may "encourage" or "discourage" the next nerve to fire. Only if the receiving neuron gets enough excitation and not too much inhibition will it fire.

3.5   Do signals ever go from the dendrite of one neuron to the axon of another?

No. The transmission of signals in the nervous system is a *one-way process*. The transmission of signals, whether they are excitatory or inhibitory, always goes from the axon to the next nerve. Usually, the neurotransmitter is received by the dendrite of the next cell, but cell bodies and axons also can receive messages across a synapse.

3.6   Are a neuron and a nerve the same thing?

Neurons are individual cells composed of dendrites, a cell body with a nucleus, and an axon. *Nerves* are bundles of neuron fibers which transmit signals over some distance in the body. The compilation of all nerves and neurons constitutes the nervous system.

3.7   What is myelin, and how does it affect the functioning of a nerve fiber?

Myelin is a fatty, beadlike sheath that surrounds the axons of certain nerve fibers. In general, signals travel faster and with less expenditure of energy in myelinated fibers than they do in unmyelinated fibers.

3.8   How does a signal pass through a neuron?

Whether a signal goes through a neuron is a function of several related properties. The input of both excitatory and inhibitory stimulation to the neuron is summated in the cell body. If the excitatory potential reaches a certain level (called the *graded potential*), the axon "fires," carrying the signal along its length. When a signal reaches the end of the axon (the axon terminal), it is transmitted to a dendrite or a body organ.

The actual "firing" of the neuron either occurs or it does not—there is no intermediate level. This is called the all-or-none principle. Before the axon fires, it is in a state called the *resting potential*. When it fires, an electrical charge called an *action potential* passes along its entire length.

3.9 What is the difference between a resting potential and an action potential? Can an action potential transmit different kinds of messages?

In a resting state, the cell membrane has a certain level of permeability which keeps out positively charged sodium ions (Na^+) while allowing in potassium ions (K^+) and negatively charged chloride ions (Cl^-). Thus, the inside of the cell is slightly negative compared to the outside.

When the axon is stimulated, the potential across the membrane is reduced. If this reduction in potential is great enough, a sudden change in membrane permeability occurs and the charges reverse—the outside is now slightly negative compared to the inside. This change affects the adjacent portion of the axon, and the process repeats itself along the entire length of the axon. This is the neural impulse, or action potential, which remains the same size throughout transmission.

A neuron always fires with exactly the same action potential. Thus, the signal (or "message") transmitted does not depend on the size of the action potential. Instead, the strength of the signal depends on the frequency with which a particular neuron is fired and the number of neurons firing at a particular moment. The type of message caused by the signal is determined by the pathway of the firing neurons.

3.10 The change in permeability of the membrane and the subsequent flow of ions is described by a particular term. What is this term, and what does it mean?

The term describing the change in membrane permeability and the flow of ions is *depolarization*. Depolarization occurs when the graded potential reaches or surpasses the cell threshold; there is a subsequent switch of negative potential from the inside to the outside.

3.11 Does an axon that has become depolarized stay that way as long as there is stimulation?

The transmission of an action potential is a brief burst (or firing) that is followed by a recovery period called the *refractory phase*. During the refractory phase, the cell is at first temporarily inactive and cannot transmit a signal. Later in the refractory phase, the cell can transmit a signal, but only if the graded potential is especially strong. Each transmission of a signal along an axon represents a depolarization; each refractory phase allows polarization to recur.

3.12 Are there different designations for the parts of the refractory phase? How long does the refractory phase last?

The two parts of the refractory phase are called the *absolute refractory period* (during which no signal can be transmitted) and the *relative refractory period* (during which only a strong graded potential will fire the cell). The entire refractory phase lasts only a few thousandths of a second.

3.13 The human body contains billions of neurons that make up the nervous system. What are the general designations for the different parts of the nervous system? What are the basic functions of each of these parts?

The nervous system is classified into two major divisions: the central nervous system (CNS) and the peripheral nervous system (PNS).

The CNS receives sensory messages via what is called the *afferent* nervous system. The CNS then processes or acts on these messages and on self-generated messages and initiates signals to be sent to all parts of the body via the nerves that constitute the *efferent* (or motor) system.

The PNS conducts information from various body organs to the CNS and takes messages from the CNS to the organs. The PNS has two subdivisions: the *autonomic nervous system* and the *somatic nervous system*. The former is concerned primarily with the control of internal body organ functions; the latter carries messages to and from the sense receptors, muscles, and the body surface.

3.14   What are the major parts of the central nervous system? How are they alike, and how do they differ?

   The central nervous system has two important components: the brain and the spinal cord. They are linked continuously so that the flow of messages remains unbroken from brain to body and from body to brain. Each component is well protected by a bony structure: the backbone for the spinal cord and the skull for the brain.

   The most important differences between the brain and the spinal cord are related to the complexity of function that can occur in each one. The spinal cord is capable of relaying many messages and carrying out simple stimulus-response sequences, such as reflexes. The brain can handle much more complex functions and can modify even the simple functions which occur at the spinal cord level.

3.15   Do specific areas of the brain control certain aspects of behavior?

   The brain appears to have developed into what are now described as three layers or sections. The hindbrain controls "survival" behaviors. All sensory information traveling between the spinal cord and the forebrain must go through the second layer, the midbrain. This layer also has centers that control movements in response to auditory and visual stimuli. The "upper" layer is called the forebrain. Consisting of the cerebral hemispheres and the limbic system, it is the area that controls advanced or sophisticated mental and cognitive processes.

3.16   What are the major components of the hindbrain? Name some examples of the "survival" behaviors controlled there.

   The major components in the hindbrain include the medulla, the pons, the cerebellum, and (in the center of the hindbrain) the reticular formation. Behaviors controlled in the hindbrain include heartbeat and circulation, sleep and waking, motor coordination, and attention and arousal.

3.17   The limbic system is thought to have many responsibilities in controlling behaviors. What are the major components of the limbic system, and what are some of the behaviors they control?

   Major parts of the limbic system include the thalamus, the hypothalamus, the hippocampus, the amygdala, and the septum. The thalamus relays sensory information to the forebrain. The hypothalamus influences basic survival behaviors and regulates the activity of the pituitary gland (the "master gland" that controls other glands). The hippocampus and amygdala affect the formation and retention of memories and emotions, while the septum also is involved with emotions.

3.18   It was mentioned in Solved Problem 3.15 that the forebrain is the location for higher mental processes. How well have these functions been "mapped"?

   The outer surface of the forebrain, the *cerebral cortex*, appears to control complex mental activity. Some of these activities, such as motor control, recognition of sensations, and speech control, have been mapped quite accurately. Other functions, not directly related to sensorimotor processes, are less well identified. These include functions such as association, memory, problem solving, and sophisticated differentiations. (See Fig. 3-5.)

3.19   Sketch a "map" of the areas and well-located functions of the cerebral cortex. (See Fig. 3-5.)

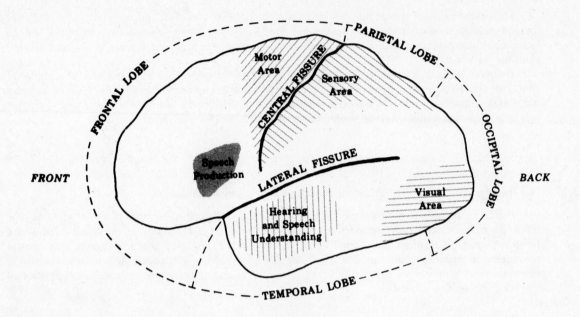

Fig. 3-5

3.20   Suppose an individual suffers some form of brain damage and loses a particular behavioral function. What term is used to describe the subsequent recovery of that function? How else is this term sometimes used by psychologists?

The term that describes the recovery of function is *plasticity*, meaning that the brain appears to be able to adapt or change function as a result of interchanges with the world. One part of the brain seems to be able to take over for another. *Plasticity* is used in a more general sense to describe adaptations to new circumstances, often shown particularly by adults.

3.21   The corpus callosum has a special function in the structure of the brain. What is this function, and what happens when it is terminated?

The corpus callosum is a broad band of fibers that connects the two cerebral hemispheres. It relays messages from one side of the brain to the other. When this function is terminated by a surgical cutting of the fibers, the two hemispheres operate independently. These "split-brain" situations have provided information for localization of function and have illustrated that most people are left-hemisphere-dominant.

3.22   Describe the techniques most often used for observing and evaluating the activity of the brain.

The earliest manner of observing or evaluating the activity of the brain was simply to determine the effects of brain damage on behavior. The behaviors of patients who experienced trauma or disease were analyzed, and attributions regarding the activities of brain areas were made.

Frequently used laboratory techniques include the electroencephalograph (EEG) to measure electrical activity, computerized axial tomography (CAT scans) using x-rays, positron emission tomography (PET scans) to record metabolic activity, and magnetic resonance imaging (MRI), and a superconducting quantum interference device (SQUID) to measure differences in magnetic fields throughout the brain.

3.23   If many areas of the brain seem to remain unmapped, how is it known that certain behaviors are controlled by them?

Research using organisms that have had damage to these areas has revealed which functions have been lost. In addition, occasional opportunities to stimulate these areas with an electrical probe have helped determine the functions present, and the use of the techniques described in Solved Problem 3.22 has helped correlate brain activity with certain mental functions.

3.24   Brain mapping indicates that sensory functions are located in the cerebral hemispheres. Does this mean that the somatic nervous system does not sense stimuli?

The somatic part of the peripheral nervous system *does* receive and transmit sensory signals, but the actual registration (or interpretation) of the signal is made in the CNS. This means that seeing, hearing, touching, and other sensations are completed only when the signals have reached the sensory areas of the brain. (A thorough treatment of these sensory processes is found in Chapter 5.)

3.25   Describe the autonomic nervous system. Why is it called autonomic? What basic controls does the autonomic nervous system exercise?

The autonomic nervous system is part of the peripheral nervous system. Subdivided into the sympathetic and parasympathetic systems, the autonomic system controls glands and smooth-muscle organs such as the heart, blood vessels, stomach, and intestines. The sympathetic part of the system has fibers located in *chains* which are found beside the spinal cord and are connected to the various visceral organs. The parasympathetic fibers originate in the cervical region (above those of the sympathetic system) and the sacral region (below the sympathetic system). The sympathetic and parasympathetic systems are called autonomic because they tend to operate in an involuntary (or self-regulating) fashion.

3.26   How do the functions of the sympathetic and parasympathetic systems differ?

Several aspects distinguish sympathetic from parasympathetic functioning. The sympathetic system tends to act as a unit and to prepare the body for activity. The parasympathetic system generally shows separate or particular functioning and operates when the body is in a relatively quiet state. Thus, the sympathetic system is oriented primarily toward energy expenditure and action, while the parasympathetic system tends to conserve energy and aid body recuperation.

3.27   Does this mean that the sympathetic and parasympathetic systems do not operate at the same time?

While many of the functions of these two systems appear to be *antagonistic* (for example, heart rate is speeded by the sympathetic system and slowed by the parasympathetic system), some functioning occurs when both systems are active at once or operate in sequence. Some of these interactions are understood. For example, the male sex act requires parasympathetic stimulation for erection and sympathetic stimulation for ejaculation. Many other interactions of the sympathetic and parasympathetic systems remain to be studied.

3.28   What system other than the nervous system carries messages to various parts of the body? How is this accomplished?

Endocrine glands secrete hormones, chemical communicators which circulate throughout the body in the bloodstream and affect "target" organs. This endocrine system helps control growth, sexual behavior, level of energy, reaction to stress, and even the functioning of the nervous system.

3.29   The pituitary gland has been called the *master gland* of the endocrine system. Why?

   The pituitary gland has been called the *master gland* because it controls the secretion of hormones in response to signals from the hypothalamus. It is important to note that much of the activity of the pituitary gland and other glands is monitored by the brain, and thus the hypothalamus is often called the *master of the master gland* because of the control it exerts on the pituitary gland. There is a complex interaction between the nervous system and the endocrine system.

3.30   What are other examples of endocrine glands, and what functions do they help control?

   The adrenal glands and the thyroid gland are two very important endocrine glands. The adrenals secrete adrenaline and noradrenaline, two hormones that operate antagonistically to regulate bodily functions affecting mood or emotion, blood pressure, and the circulation of blood. For example, adrenaline increases blood pressure while noradrenaline lowers blood pressure. Thyroxin, the hormone secreted by the thyroid gland, activates chemical reactions that help control the activity level of the body. Too little thyroxin is associated with lower metabolism, weight gain, and sluggishness, while too much thyroxin produces increased metabolism, high blood pressure, weight loss, and possible hyperactivity.

3.31   Why are psychologists interested in the biological foundations of behavior?

   Much biological or physiological information is gathered simply to increase knowledge about bodily functions. Often, however, practical applications of this information can help psychologists predict and control behavior. For instance, difficulties with appetite may result from malfunctioning of the hypothalamus, while damage to the occipital lobe of the brain may be associated with the development of blind spots in the visual field. Obviously, knowledge such as this may have practical applications in helping to alter such behaviors.

Key Terms

Action potential.   The signal which passes through a neuron.

All-or-none principle.   The finding that a signal, once started, always travels the length of a neuron at a fixed intensity.

Amygdala.   The part of the limbic system that controls the formation and retention of memories.

Autonomic nervous system (ANS).   The part of the peripheral nervous system that controls the function of many glands and smooth-muscle organs; divided into the sympathetic and parasympathetic systems.

Axon.   The single long fiber extending from the cell body of a neuron; carries the signal to the synapse.

Cell body.   Also called *soma*; the central part of a neuron from which the axon and dendrites extend.

Central nervous system (CNS).   Basically, the brain and spinal cord.

Cerebellum.   The part of the hindbrain that controls movement and balance.

Cerebrum.   The two cerebral hemispheres; control the more sophisticated mental processes; covered by the cortex.

Computerized axial tomography (CAT scan).   A machine that uses x-rays to measure tissue densities in the brain; helps reveal structural abnormalities.

Corpus callosum.   The broad band of fibers which connects the cerebral hemispheres.

Cortex.   The outer layer of the cerebral hemispheres; controls complex cognitive processes.

Cortical lobes.   The four arbitrarily designated divisions of the cortex.

Dendrite.   The branched fibers which serve as the receiving portion of a neuron.

Depolarization.   The process by which the electrical charge of a neuron reverses during the passage of an action potential.

Electroencephalograph (EEG).   A machine that uses electrodes on the outside of the head to record electrical activity in the brain.

Endocrine glands.   Glands which secrete hormones directly into the bloodstream.

Endorphin.   Substances produced in the brain in response to stress or anxiety; natural painkillers.

Exocrine glands.   Glands which secrete fluids onto the body's surface or into its cavities.

Forebrain.   Top layer of the brain; contains the cerebral hemispheres and the limbic system.

Frontal lobe.   The area of the cerebral hemispheres behind the forehead; located in front of the central fissure and the lateral fissure.

Graded potential.   The sum of excitation and inhibition at a synapse.

Hindbrain.   Also called the *lower brain*; controls basic survival needs.

Hippocampus.   The part of the limbic system that controls emotions and memory.

Hormones.   Distinctive chemicals, secreted by the endocrine glands, which carry information ("instructions") to certain areas of the body.

Hypothalamus.   The part of the limbic system that controls basic survival behaviors, regulates the internal environment, and controls the activity of the pituitary gland.

Limbic system.   Interrelated structures in the forebrain that are involved in the control of many cognitive functions.

Magnetic resonance imaging (MRI).   Measurement of differences in the magnetic field throughout the brain (or other areas of the body) to provide information about structure.

Medulla.   The part of the hindbrain that controls heartbeat, breathing, chewing, and salivating.

Midbrain.   The small area between the spinal cord and the forebrain that controls sensory messages and body movements.

Myelin.   A fatty substance which covers many axons, usually surrounding the axon in a beadlike arrangement.

Nerve.   A collection of neuron fibers.

Neuron.   The basic structural unit of the nervous system; composed of a cell body, an axon, and one or more dendrites.

Neurotransmitter.   Also called a *transmitter substance*; a chemical discharged from the axon's synaptic vesicles; may be either excitatory or inhibitory.

Occipital lobe.   The lower back portion of the cerebral hemispheres.

Parasympathetic system.   The part of the autonomic nervous system primarily involved with recuperative functions of the body.

Parietal lobe.   The area of the cerebral hemispheres at the top back of the brain, behind the central fissure.

Peripheral nervous system (PNS).   The nerves outside the central nervous system; has two subdivisions, the somatic and autonomic systems.

Pituitary gland.   An endocrine gland that controls the functions of many other glands; often called the *master gland*.

Plasticity.   The ability of the brain to adapt or change activity, often in response to changes in the environment or damage to the brain.

Pons.   The part of the hindbrain that controls movement and sleep.

Positron emission tomography (PET scan).   The use of radioactive glucose to measure neural metabolic activity in the brain.

Refractory phase.   The recovery period required by a neuron before another signal may be conducted.

Resting potential.   The nonactivated state of a neuron; the inside of the cell is slightly negative in potential compared to the outside.

Reticular formation.   Also called the *reticular activating system*; the center of the hindbrain which controls basic survival functions such as attention and arousal.

Septum.   The part of the limbic system that controls emotions, particularly pleasure.

Somatic system.   The part of the peripheral nervous system concerned with sensory and motor functions.

Split-brain investigations.   Research conducted when the corpus callosum has been severed; allows the two hemispheres of the brain to function independently.

Superconducting quantum interference device (SQUID).   A machine that uses magnetic field measurement to provide information about the structure of and neural activity in the brain.

Sympathetic system.   The part of the autonomic system that acts primarily when a person is aroused.

Synapse.   The gap between the axon of one cell and the dendrite of the next cell.

Synaptic vesicles.   Openings in the terminal buttons at the end of an axon from which neurotransmitters are discharged.

Temporal lobe.   The area of the cerebral hemispheres from in front of the occipital lobe to the rear of the lateral fissure.

CHAPTER 4

Developmental Psychology

Developmental psychology is the study of behavioral changes over a time span. A strong emphasis often is placed on physical development, but developmental psychologists also study social and cognitive development. The time span stretches from the moment of conception to the moment of death.

4.1 GENETICS

Genetics is the study of the biological transmission of characteristics from parents to offspring. In higher animals, this transmission takes place when the *germ cells* (sperm from the male and the egg, or ovum, from the female) unite during conception to form a *zygote*. The zygote is the single, original cell formed by the sperm and the egg. This cell then divides again and again to form a multicellular organism.

Chromosomes. In higher organisms, all cells except the germ cells contain one set of *chromosomes* inherited from each parent; for example, human body cells usually contain 46 chromosomes arranged in 23 pairs. Human germ cells contain only 23 single chromosomes. At conception, the egg and the sperm unite into a zygote, which then has the full complement of 46 chromosomes.

One particular pair of chromosomes determines the gender of the offspring. The gender-determining chromosomes are labeled X or Y. A female body cell is designated as XX; a male body cell is designated as XY. When the body forms germ cells, these chromosome pairs split. Thus, all female germs cells (eggs) carry the X designation, whereas half the male germ cells (sperm) carry the X chromosome and the other half carry the Y chromosome.

EXAMPLE 4.1. While it takes the germ cells from two parents to produce a conception, the gender of the child is determined at the moment of conception by the sperm cell that unites with the egg. If an "X sperm" arrives first, the child will be female. If a "Y sperm" arrives first, the child will be a male.

Genes. All chromosomes contain *genes*. Genes are found in a long molecule called *deoxyribonucleic acid (DNA)*, which combines with a protein structure to become organized into chromosomes.

Genes are the basic unit of hereditary transmission. They are paired, just as the chromosomes that hold them are paired. Genes hold "information" for the production of proteins; this information determines the way in which the organism will develop.

In rare cases, a spontaneous or sudden change occurs in the DNA, and as a result the cell does not replicate itself exactly. The resultant change is called a *mutation*. Mutations are permanent and frequently produce radical and harmful effects on human offspring.

Genetic Influences.   Once the zygote is formed, the presence or absence of various genes determines whether a particular characteristic will be observed in the offspring. In some cases, a characteristic of an offspring is determined by only one or two genes. In other cases, many genes work together to control some aspect of the offspring's development. Regardless, the total genetic pattern or script for any individual is called a *genome* and is created by the particular combination of chromosomes received from the biological parents.

EXAMPLE 4.2.   A single defective gene causes a disease called *phenylketonuria* (PKU) in which the body is unable to convert the protein phenylalanine into a usable form. If phenylalanine builds up to toxic levels, it attacks the cells of the central nervous system, causing mental retardation. (Research has indicated that more than 150 genes affect brain development. Therefore, that many or more *must* function correctly for a normal brain to develop.)

The characteristics determined by genes include skin color, eye color, hair color, height and weight tendencies, internal organ development, and the possibility of birth defects. Much debate continues about whether intellectual and personality characteristics can be inherited within the genome. Perhaps the most commonly accepted conclusion is that certain tendencies may be passed on from one generation to the next but specific behaviors learned by the parent cannot. Trying to separate the effects of hereditary and environmental factors in such studies has proved very difficult. (See the comments on twins below.)

Dominant and Recessive Genes.   Each pair of genes controls specific activities of development. The members of the pair are not always alike. If the paired genes are not alike, one of the pair (the *dominant gene*) will act as a controller while the other (the *recessive gene*) does not affect the process of development. Recessive characteristics appear in an offspring only when both members of the gene pair are recessive.

EXAMPLE 4.3.   Skin color may be either normal (which is dominant) or albino (which is recessive and is characterized by a lack of pigmentation). The offspring will be albino only if both parents transmit that trait in the germ cells that form the zygote. It is possible that both parents could have normal skin coloring and still produce an albino child, as Fig. 4-1 shows. Although both parents show normal skin coloring, on average one of four conceptions could be albino (aa).

		FATHER	
		N	a
MOTHER	N	NN	Na
	a	Na	aa

N = normal skin coloring (dominant)
a = albino skin coloring (recessive)

Fig. 4-1

Birth Defects.   Some birth defects, such as PKU (see Example 4.2), result from a defective gene. Other birth defects are a result of the disruption of the pregnancy by an environmental agent such as poor nutrition, drugs, or diseases such as AIDS and German measles. With advances in research, psychologists and other practitioners have been able to assist many couples with *genetic counseling*, presenting the probabilities for difficulties before or during pregnancy. The knowledge base has advanced so far that suggestions for *gene therapy* to correct those difficulties have arisen. In gene therapy, genes can be introduced into existing cells to prevent or cure a disorder.

EXAMPLE 4.4. A frequently observed example of an environmental agent affecting the development of an offspring is *fetal alcohol syndrome*. Children of mothers who consumed significant amounts of alcohol during pregnancy often show mental and growth retardation. In many cases, smoking or the use of physically addictive drugs produces similar effects.

Knowledge about genetic predispositions in itself may create psychological issues. Medical and psychological personnel must decide what information to present and how to present it and must anticipate the subsequent reactions.

EXAMPLE 4.5. *Huntington's disease* is an inherited neurodegenerative disorder that is determined by a single gene. A genetic test will reveal the presence or absence of this characteristic. If informed of the presence of this gene, the individual will know that the symptoms of erratic movement will begin after age 40 and will prove fatal within approximately 15 years. It also is known that there is a 50 percent chance of passing on this characteristic to the next generation. Having or not having this knowledge may have profound effects on the behaviors the individual will show.

Twins. Twins are of two types: *identical* and *fraternal*. Identical twins have the same hereditary pattern because they are the result of the same conception. In the process of cell division, the initial cell *cleavage* (division) may produce a complete separation and two offspring will develop. Each identical twin has the same genetic characteristics as the other.

Fraternal twins develop from separate conceptions. Their genetic characteristics are no more alike than are those of any other siblings. They are twins only because they develop and are born at about the same time.

The probability of fraternal twins (or any other siblings) having exactly the same genetic characteristics is exceedingly small. The chances of both parents repeating the same combination of chromosomes are about 1 in 70 trillion. The probability grows even slimmer if the transmission of exactly the same pattern of the many genes within the chromosomes is considered.

EXAMPLE 4.6. Although it is correlational research, many investigations have been conducted by using twins and other siblings or relatives to estimate the effects of heredity versus those of environment on certain behaviors. Of particular interest has been a series of studies using children who have been separated from each other and raised in differing environments (e.g., identical twins separated and adopted by different families in different geographic regions). Using *meta-analysis* (a summary analysis of many separate analyses from different studies), evaluations have shown that the greater the proportion of genetic characteristics shared by the children, the higher the correlation for showing similar behaviors whether the children live together or apart. It must be remembered, however, that even two unrelated children who have similar looks or personalities are more likely to be treated in the same way than are two siblings whose looks or personalities differ considerably. The effects of heredity and environment on behavior are very much interwoven.

Selective Breeding. Recognizing that hereditary characteristics sometimes seem to influence the offspring in a pronounced manner, it is reasonable to consider trying to mate parents in combinations that will produce favorable offspring. This procedure is called *selective breeding*; and it has been demonstrated for a number of different organisms, including pedigreed dogs, racehorses, and cattle. Humans have developed a number of social restrictions that keep them from applying these principles to breed "better" humans. However, a kind of selectivity is sometimes practiced by humans who breed only with members of a particular race, religion, or social class. The "science" of improving the human species through selective mating is called *eugenics*, but such activity is seldom taken seriously because few people can decide which characteristics should be encouraged or discouraged.

Behavioral Genetics. The study of the relative influences of heredity and environment on behavior is called *behavioral genetics*. Behavioral geneticists assume that differences in behaviors among individuals can be accounted for by the two major factors heredity (the *nature* side of the debate) and environment (the *nurture* side). The technical term that refers to the proportion of the difference or variation among subjects that can be attributed to heredity is *heritability*. When shared genetic factors and (as much as possible) shared environmental factors are evaluated, the remaining differences in behaviors can be attributed to unique or nonshared environmental factors.

4.2 EVOLUTION AND GENETICS

While *genetics* is the study of the transfer of hereditary characteristics from one generation to the next, *evolution* refers to the changes in a species that occur very gradually over very long time spans. Charles Darwin's *The Origin of Species*, published in 1859, was the first theoretical study of evolution. Darwin proposed that features of successive generations are modified through evolutionary processes. Darwin believed that qualities which allow an organism to adjust to the environment persist, while the qualities which do not help an organism adjust to the environment eventually drop out.

The major concepts of Darwin's theory are variability, adaptation, and selection. Changes in the genetic makeup of an organism that appear to enable the organism to adjust to the environment come under the heading *variability*.

The adjustments an organism makes are called *adaptation*. The essential aim of adaptation is survival of the species, although other, less dramatic functions also are served by adaptation.

Traits which seem to allow a species to adjust to the environment generally are passed on from one generation to the next. Traits that are not suitable generally do not recur in the species, most likely because the individuals possessing the traits cannot reproduce and therefore do not pass the trait to their offspring. This *selection* of characteristics has been summarized in the popular phrase "survival of the fittest." Although Darwin wrote about the *natural selection* of characteristics over long periods of time, *forced selection* through selective breeding is also possible. (See Section 4.1.)

Ethology. A related area of investigation is *ethology*, the study of the behavior of organisms in their natural habitats. The evolution of adaptive behavioral characteristics is often easier to illustrate for lower organisms than it is for humans. The patterns that have developed for different organisms frequently are *species-specific*; that is, the behavior pattern is common to all the members of that species and only that species.

Various labels have been used to identify different forms of species-specific behaviors. Perhaps the most common one is *instinct*, which is defined as the predisposition for complex patterns of behavior (or response patterns) that are completely controlled by hereditary factors.

Instincts may be *modified* by environmental factors. Thus, a bird's particular nesting behavior may depend on what materials are available in the environment, but the action itself is innate. Some behaviors are triggered by a *sign stimulus* or *releaser stimulus*.

EXAMPLE 4.7. Study of the male stickleback fish has shown that it will attack any fishlike model that has a red belly but will ignore an exact replica of another stickleback that does *not* have a red belly. The red marking, which is acquired by the male stickleback during the mating season, serves as the releaser stimulus for other male sticklebacks, often provoking an attack when they see it.

Similarly, instinctual behaviors may involve some learning, as occurs when *imprinting* is shown. Soon after being hatched, birds such as ducklings and chicks begin following moving objects in the environment. Most often this is the mother bird. However, when placed in special circumstances where the mother is not present, these baby birds still will express the instinct by learning to follow another moving object, such as the laboratory investigator.

Early explanations of *motivation* were based on instinct theory. As the complexity of human behavior was better understood, it became apparent that attributing behaviors to instinct was difficult, especially because agreement on what constituted primary instincts was impossible to reach. Some theories of personality and evolutionary psychology continue to emphasize the role of instinct in motivating behavior, but conceptions of motivation based on instinct have been supplanted by other, newer theories.

4.3 PHYSICAL DEVELOPMENT

Physical development, or *maturation*, may influence a human's behavior profoundly. Developmental psychologists therefore study both prenatal and postnatal development from the moment of conception, when (as seen above) the hereditary patterns are set, until death. A developmental psychologist may study only a part of the entire age span or a particular behavior within a time span.

Prenatal Development. For humans, *prenatal* development usually is divided into three periods. Although these designations are somewhat arbitrary, they are based on characteristics of typical patterns of physical development.

Germinal. During the first two weeks after conception, a period known as the *germinal stage*, the zygote begins the process of cell division, or *mitosis*. During this time, the bundle of cells is in the process of attaching to the mother by implanting itself in the wall of the uterus. That physical attachment occurs by the end of the second week and marks the beginning of the embryonic period. Only approximately half of all zygotes implant in the uterus, and approximately half of those zygotes fail to sustain the link and are miscarried soon after implantation.

Embryonic. During the next six weeks, the group of cells is called an *embryo*. The process of cell division and diversification continues during this period. By the completion of the *embryonic stage*, sufficient development has been completed that the basic physical features of the baby-to-be can be recognized.

Fetal. The label for the baby-to-be during the remaining 32 weeks of pregnancy (assuming a full-term pregnancy of 38 weeks) is *fetus*. By the end of this period, the fetus has grown to about 18 to 21 inches in length and to about seven pounds in weight. A fetus reaches the *age of viability*, the point at which it can survive if born prematurely, at approximately 28 weeks.

EXAMPLE 4.8. Medical technology is affecting the age of viability. Advances in the ability to sustain life in prematurely born children have made possible the survival of exceedingly small and frail babies. Just what limits will be reached has not been determined.

Postnatal Development. *Postnatal* development extends from the moment of birth to death. The labels often used to describe the sequence of development include infancy, childhood, adolescence, and adulthood. It must be noted, however, that psychologists are more inclined to look at development as a continuous process not divided into specific stages or periods. Regardless of the approach used, certain methods of study and general terminology usually are accepted.

Longitudinal and Cross-Sectional Investigations. Studies conducted over a fairly long period, using the same subjects throughout, are called *longitudinal studies*. The major advantages of such studies are that heredity is held constant throughout and the effects of early experiences on later development can be investigated. The disadvantages include the length of time involved, the possibility of a high dropout rate, and the concern that the problem being studied may lose its importance before the study is completed.

Cross-Sectional Studies can be conducted rapidly. Using subjects in different age groupings simultaneously, these studies typically are less expensive and have low dropout rates, but they lack the precision of experiential and hereditary control.

EXAMPLE 4.9. An investigator has identified two groups of children. By age 5, one of these groups has had extensive exposure to preschool activities, while the other has not. Trying to determine the effects of these experiences on subsequent cognitive and social development, the investigator begins a six-year longitudinal study of elementary school behaviors. In a parallel cross-sectional study, another psychologist selects children at ages

5, 7, 9, and 11 years who have or have not been to preschool before starting formal education and measures their social and cognitive skills. The assumption in this study is that the effects observed at any one age level will carry over to any other age level if the study is prolonged (as in a longitudinal study). Both studies may produce information of interest, although each has both advantages and disadvantages.

Deprivation and Enrichment.   When the level of stimulation or opportunity is significantly reduced, a *deprivation* condition exists. The usual result of prolonged deprivation is a level of accomplishment significantly below normal. *Enrichment* occurs when stimulation or opportunity is considerably above normal levels. In general, enrichment seems to produce beneficial results in terms of the development of physical, cognitive, and social skills.

Critical Periods.   Developmental psychologists extend concepts such as deprivation and enrichment when they study the *critical period*, a time of particular sensitivity, or *readiness*, to specific kinds of environmental stimulation. A critical period can be thought of as a time of opportunity: If the stimulation occurs, a behavioral development is likely to take place, while if the stimulation does not occur, the behavior will not develop.

EXAMPLE 4.10.   Research has shown that imprinting (the following response that was described earlier) will occur only if the baby chick is exposed to a moving stimulus the first day after hatching. If this experience is postponed, the critical period is passed, and imprinting does not occur. It is suggested that critical periods, although longer in duration, can be found for human behaviors as well. For reasons that are not well explained, it has become fairly evident that acquisition of language is far easier to accomplish if started before puberty than if started later.

Growth Trends.   Changes in physical development occur in predictable patterns. A newborn (or *neonate*) has all the neuron or muscle fibers he or she will ever have but has proportions that differ considerably from those which will be present in adulthood. Newborns exhibit many *reflexes* needed for basic physical survival.

EXAMPLE 4.11.   Two reflexes that show the adaptive survival pattern necessary for the newborn are *rooting* and *sucking*. If a newborn's cheek is stroked, the child turns toward (or roots for) the source of stimulation, for example, the nipple. Virtually any stimulation of the mouth will produce sucking behavior, as if a nipple were present. Many parents have learned that a knuckle will provide momentary satisfaction until milk can be provided.

All children develop in a top-to-bottom or head-to-toe fashion (sometimes called a *cephalo-caudal trend*) and in a center-to-outside (or *proximo-distal trend*). This latter pattern holds until adolescence, when the extremities grow rapidly to adult proportions. All physical development depends, at least in part, on factors such as nutrition or exercise, but in general, the sequence of the pattern is the same for all humans.

By the time a child has reached school age, the proportions are far closer to those of an adult. Height, weight, strength, coordination, and many other physical markers continue to change, although not all in the same manner. There are general standards that seem to apply to the growth and development of all humans, but any individual person's growth pattern may vary considerably from the norm. This variation in growth rate (and in social and cognitive development as well) is summarized by the term *individual differences*. Each person's development must be treated as a unique case.

EXAMPLE 4.12.   It is interesting to look at the differences in patterns of development for physical activities or physiological markers. Adolescence, for example, is marked by a seeming loss of coordination (the "awkward teenager") that probably results from the rapid growth of the extremities. Adolescence, or the very beginning of adulthood, is also the time when increases in height typically end. This is not true for weight, however, which often continues to increase at a slow but consistent rate throughout adulthood. Also likely for adults is a loss of muscle mass and strength associated with aging. Proper nutrition, exercise, and other variables may produce individual differences in the actual values noted.

Certain physical markers denote significant changes. *Puberty*, the point at which the sexual organs mature, is thought to signify the start of adolescence. In the majority of cases, puberty does occur in the early teens, although its onset may occur as early as age 8 or 9 or in the late teens. Early adulthood is thought to be the period of peak physical performance. *Menopause*, the cessation of menstrual periods, marks the end of fertility for women. There is no comparable event for men, who can remain fertile and father children into later adulthood. Older age often is marked by a reduction in hearing, vision, or other sensory capabilities; slower reaction times; and loss of strength. Some diseases, such as the progressive brain disorder *Alzheimer's disease*, are experienced primarily in older age.

4.4 COGNITIVE DEVELOPMENT

Psychologists have had great difficulty deciding what topics should or should not be included under the general heading "cognition." Broadly considered, cognition includes the total process of thinking, including language, perception, learning, memory, and problem solving or decision making. The development of these activities has been shown to start even before birth and is known to continue throughout one's life.

EXAMPLE 4.13. Researchers asked pregnant women to read a particular children's book aloud twice a day during the last six weeks of their pregnancies. In postnatal tests, the children were seen to recognize and prefer the sound of the story they had heard to the sound of other, comparable stories, indicating this by varying sucking patterns.

Perceptual Development. One aspect of cognitive development is *perception*, the integration, interpretation, and understanding of sensory stimuli. Evidence indicates that even very young children have the capacity to receive signals and react in more than a reflexive fashion. Using measures such as heart rate, sucking behavior, and facial imitation responses, psychologists have been able to identify and document the progression of perceptual development in neonates. As with physical development, improved perceptual skills are expected throughout the formative years. (Perception and sensation are considered in more depth in Chapter 5.)

Language Acquisition. All children seem to have the potential to learn any language and, for some time after birth, generate all the sounds necessary to do so. The sequence of language development is basically the same for all languages, with environmental variables determining which language will be learned. Comprehension of language usually precedes language production. A typical pattern of language production includes cooing, followed by babbling, then one-word utterances, short "telegraphic speech" patterns, longer phrases, longer sentences, and finally, by about age 4, speech patterning that is very similar to that of adults. Many psychologists view language acquisition as the primary basis for thinking and memory.

Piaget's Theory of Cognitive Development. One of the most influential approaches to understanding cognitive development was proposed by Jean Piaget (1896–1980), a Swiss psychologist. Although the stages of development described below have been questioned, challenged, and in some cases refuted, Piaget's theory has been extremely important in prompting explorations into cognitive development.

Two concepts are crucial to all the stages in Piaget's theory: *Assimilation* refers to a child's ability to incorporate incoming material into already existing *schema* (conceptions of the world), and *accommodation* describes modification of the existing schema to include new information.

EXAMPLE 4.14. Because he thinks that all fluids can be ingested, Jeffrey's word for all fluids is "milk." When given the chance to drink lemonade for the first time, Jeffrey enjoys it and asks for more "milk." Lemonade is assimilated into Jeffrey's already existing schema concerning fluids. However, left alone for a moment in the garage one day, Jeffrey finds an open can of motor oil. When he tries to drink from it, he quickly finds that some fluids do not fit his schema of "milk" and perhaps develops new schema for nondrinkable fluids. New information forces such an accommodation.

Sensorimotor Stage. According to Piaget, the *sensorimotor stage* lasts from birth until about age 2. During this period, children are egocentric and fail to distinguish between themselves and outer reality. They have little ability to use language or symbolic representations and therefore are unable to exhibit *object permanence*, the awareness that people or objects continue to exist when they are not in sight.

EXAMPLE 4.15. Object permanence is truly an "out-of-sight, out-of-mind" situation. If a series of clouds blows in front of the sun so that the view is blocked, the sun no longer exists in the cognition of a child in the sensorimotor stage of development.

Preoperational Stage. During the *preoperational stage*, which lasts from about age 2 until age 7, a child shows considerable progress in the ability to represent things by using language, drawings, numerical systems, and symbolic play. Conceptualization and prelogical reasoning develop, although the child's viewpoint of the world continues to be primarily self-centered.

Concrete Operational Stage. From ages 7 until 11, during the *concrete operational stage*, a child's thoughts are characterized by logic, the understanding of relationships, and the development of coordinated series of ideas. The child's thoughts are tied to concrete or observable things, however, and abstract thought remains at a rudimentary level. This is particularly evident in testing a principle such as *conservation*, the knowledge that quantity is unrelated to the arrangement or appearance of objects; for example, if able to observe them, a child at this stage understands that seven pennies are seven whether they are spread across a table or grouped closely together.

Formal Operational Stage. From age 11 years until adulthood, during the *formal operational stage*, a child's thoughts progress to incorporate formal rules of logic. Abstract concepts become understandable, and the child can generalize from one situation to another. The child shows interest in the future and can use theories and hypotheses to propose what may happen.

EXAMPLE 4.16. Suppose a child is asked to describe the concept of heating the house. A child in the sensorimotor stage would only react with "Hot!" or "Cold!" A child in the preoperational stage might respond by saying, "My daddy can change it with the dial." A child in the concrete operational stage might understand the relationship of the thermostat and the temperature level, but this understanding would be based on the concrete operation of actually turning the thermostat's dial. At the formal operational level, the child could hypothesize relationships involving different kinds of thermostats or heating devices without necessarily having such objects available.

Piaget's theories stress the *sequence* of events in cognitive development. The ages are suggested as average or typical but not necessarily binding. This emphasis on sequence tends to underplay the *amount* of cognitive development, which usually is studied under the heading of intelligence. (See Chapter 11.)

Information-Processing Approach to Cognitive Development. An alternative explanation for the behaviors described as occurring in stages by Piaget is that of the *information-processing approach*. From this perspective, cognitive development is an active process of continuous increases in language and verbal fluency, numerical skills, knowledge and memory, ability to solve problems, and proficiency in applying these skills in various circumstances. Similar to Piaget's theories, information-processing approaches envision changing conceptualizations of the world as a child becomes increasingly sophisticated in cognitive skills. However, information-processing approaches do not propose stages or establish cutoff points for the behaviors being observed, emphasizing instead the changes in efficiency and understanding with which information is processed.

EXAMPLE 4.17. Younger children often do not understand that they do not understand; given a problem to solve, they may be unaware of their errors. It is only after he or she has had the opportunity to develop the necessary cognitive skills that a child will be able to say, "I don't understand what's going on here." An information-processing approach emphasizes the increases in skill learning, experiences, and abilities that allow the development of cognitive strategies *and* the understanding of when such strategies are missing.

Cultural Influences on Cognitive Development.   Differences in attitudes toward cognitive development are recognized as affecting the patterns exhibited by children. Language skills, the importance of working hard in school, and career goals are emphasized more or less, depending on cultural background. Children moving from one location to another often confront the differences in cultural expectations, finding their cognitive patterns inappropriate for the group into which they move.

4.5   SOCIAL DEVELOPMENT

Along with physical and cognitive development, social development has been studied over the entire life span. A child's social development is marked particularly by *integration*, the connection to society through relationships and responsibilities, and *differentiation*, the formation of a separate social identity.

Attachment.   The initial phase of social development typically consists of *attachment*, a positive, close emotional bond with a particular individual. That individual often is the primary caregiver for the infant, and the relationship that develops between the child and the caregiver appears to be a function of the interactions they experience. Indeed, the child's reaction to the caregiver is as important in the establishment of the relationship as are the caregiver's responses to the child.

During the first year of life, the child's link to the caregiver strengthens to the point where "separation anxiety" may be displayed when the caregiver leaves the child. This does not mean that the child will suffer from such separations; research evidence indicated no significant developmental handicaps for children who were placed in high-quality day care while their parents worked, and in some cases there were many positive effects.

Peer Influence.   By age 2, children become more self-reliant and likely to interact with peers. As a child grows older, play becomes less egocentric and more interactive. Play serves to foster an understanding of others' behaviors, development of physical and social control, and the capacity to respond appropriately. The child learns *role taking*, the ability to predict another person's point of view. In general, as children grow older, their values are more and more determined by what is acceptable to peers (*peer-group influence*) and less influenced by the values of older persons.

Gender Roles.   What is considered "typical" or "acceptable" behavior for males and females seems to change with each succeeding generation. Some types of behaviors are labeled "feminine" or "masculine," but the *gender roles*—the values, traits, and social motives thought to be appropriate for males and females—vary considerably with cultural and environmental conditions. Much of the development of gender roles appears to be a function of others in the child's environment.

EXAMPLE 4.18.   Consider how men's hairstyles change. Both the "acceptable" length of hair and the amount of facial hair have varied tremendously in recent years, depending on society's whim. By contrast, the stereotype of "men are the warriors" has persisted largely unchallenged for a long time. This is noted in an activity such as play, where girls have "dolls" and boys have "action figures."

Moral Development.   *Morality* is based on learning what is considered right and wrong and how to act on the differences. Obviously a function of the society in which the child lives, this area has been studied extensively in social development.

A popular three-stage approach to understanding moral judgment is found in the work of Lawrence Kohlberg, who extended ideas originated by Piaget. In the first, or *preconventional*, stage, the child behaves appropriately because of fear of punishment or the chance to receive a reward but does not recognize any higher principle. Other people's expectations of what is good or what conforms are the basis for behaviors in the second, *conventional* stage. Kohlberg called the third stage *postconventional*, with appropriate behaviors determined by universal, abstract moral principles rather than by conformity or by rewards and punishments.

EXAMPLE 4.19.   A very young child might say it was wrong to steal from a store because one might get caught and be punished, an illustration of preconventional thinking. In the conventional stage, the child might feel that stealing was acceptable because "everybody" does it; if the child did believe that stealing was wrong, it would be because "good" people do not do things like that. In the third stage, postconventional thinking, the child would come to the conclusion that stealing was wrong because it was contrary to the principles of honesty and fairness.

One criticism of Kohlberg's work is that it was based almost exclusively on work with male subjects. Carol Gilligan has suggested that a morality of *caring* or *compassion* is an orientation that is more likely among females and deserves greater consideration. Research has not supported such differences between males and females, but the emphasis on compassion has increased in recent years.

Erikson's States of Psychosocial Development.   Although much work in developmental psychology has focused on children, the periods of adolescence and adulthood have received increasing attention. Perhaps the best known of the theories regarding development through the life span is the work on *identity formation* done by Erik Erikson. Erikson's eight-stage theory of psychosocial development spans the life cycle and highlights a particular developmental crisis at each stage. The eight stages, with the associated age range and crisis condition, are as follows:

Stage	Age Range, Years	Crisis Condition
1. Trust versus mistrust	0–1	Relationship with caregiver and satisfaction of basic needs versus lack of care and deprivation
2. Autonomy versus shame and doubt	1–3	Support and permission for learning versus lack of support and overprotection
3. Initiative versus guilt	4–5	Encouragement of exploration and independent behavior versus lack of encouragement
4. Industry versus inferiority	6–11	Training for and mastery of social and school skills versus poor training and lack of support
5. Identity versus role confusion	12–20	Establishing unique social roles (e.g., political, work, religious) versus confusion of identity or purpose
6. Intimacy versus isolation	20–40	Warm, interactive relationships versus loneliness
7. Generativity versus self-absorption	40–65	Purpose, productivity and sense of contribution versus lack of success and regression
8. Integrity versus despair	Over 65	Fulfillment and acceptance of life versus disgust and dissatisfaction

Dying and Death. The most widely accepted proposal associated with dying and death is found in the work of Elisabeth Kubler-Ross, who proposed a series of stages that precede death. Subsequent research has indicated that all of the behaviors she reported are likely to occur, but not necessarily all of them for everyone, and not necessarily in the order she presented.

Kubler-Ross described the first stage of dying as *denial*, an unwillingness to accept the diagnosis of a terminal disease or the idea that one might die. Next comes *anger*, which may be directed at those "allowing this to happen," such as healthy people, the physicians treating the person, and God. *Bargaining*, the third stage, includes attempts to create "agreements" that may extend one's life, while the fourth stage, *depression*, is accompanied by the realization that life really is ending. The final stage is *acceptance* of impending death.

Solved Problems

4.1 How much of the human life span do developmental psychologists study?

As a group, developmental psychologists are concerned with the *entire* life span, including both prenatal and postnatal development. An individual psychologist may be concerned with only a part of the life span or single behavior within the life span. The study of developmental psychology begins with the moment of conception and extends until death.

4.2 How does the transmission of hereditary characteristics take place in higher animals?

The biological transmission of hereditary characteristics from parents to offspring, which is studied as the topic of *genetics*, takes place when germ cells (sperm from the male and an egg from the female) unite during conception to form a *zygote*. The zygote is a single cell formed from the union of the sperm and the egg. Physiological hereditary characteristics are set at the moment the zygote is formed.

4.3 What are some similarities and differences between chromosomes and genes?

Chromosomes are structures that contain genes. Chromosomes are found in the nucleus of each cell. Genes are the actual units of hereditary transmission. In humans, all cells except the germ cells contain 46 chromosomes arranged in 23 pairs. The number of genes contained within these chromosomes has not been determined but is known to be very large. Genes are found in deoxyribonucleic acid (DNA), which combines with a protein structure to form chromosomes. The germ cells (egg and sperm) carry only one member of the pair of chromosomes for each of the 23 pairs. When they unite, the resultant zygote has the 23 pairs.

4.4 How is the gender of a human offspring determined?

One of the pairs of chromosomes determines the child's gender. Designated as X and Y, the gender-determining chromosomes link at the moment of conception to form either an XX pattern for a female or an XY pattern for a male. Because only males carry both X and Y possibilities, it is the sperm cell that determines the gender of the child—an X or Y sperm unites with an X egg, creating either the XX or the XY pattern.

4.5 Is the transmission process invariant?

The actual transmission must involve male and female germ cells. However, on rare occasions, spontaneous changes may occur in the DNA. These changes alter some aspect of the transmission code contained in the genes and produce what is called a *mutation*. A mutation occurs with a sudden, permanent, and often radical effect. Generally, mutations in humans produce mostly harmful effects, although mutations in plants and some animals are considered favorable and are manipulated to breed better strains for commercial use.

4.6   Once the zygote is formed, what characteristics of the offspring are determined?

The particular combination of chromosomes received from the two parents creates the genome, the total genetic pattern or script. Many characteristics are set at the moment of conception, including gender; skin color; eye color; height and weight tendencies; the development of the nervous system, organs, and glands; and in some cases physiological characteristics which will eventually appear as birth defects. Many psychologists also believe that personality tendencies can be passed from parent to child, but specific behaviors learned by the parent cannot.

4.7   Some hereditary characteristics are described as dominant, and others as recessive. What does this mean? What determines whether the characteristics are evident in the offspring?

Each chromosome contains pairs of genes. The paired genes in one chromosome may or may not be alike. In general, if the pair members are not alike, one of the pair (the dominant gene) will determine the trait that appears, while the other trait (from the recessive gene) does not appear. Recessive characteristics appear only when the recessive genes from both parents are joined in the zygote.

For example, eye color is determined in this way: Suppose both parents are brown-eyed but carry the blue, recessive gene. (Both parents are Bb, where B = brown and b = blue.) The children of such a couple should follow the pattern shown in Fig. 4-2.

```
                          FATHER
                         B     b
                      ┌──────────────
                   B  │  BB    Bb
          MOTHER      │
                   b  │  Bb    bb
```

Fig. 4-2

On average, three of every four children would be brown-eyed, while the fourth would have blue eyes. However, three of four could pass on the recessive characteristic to successive generations. Only one child in four, the BB, would not carry the recessive gene.

4.8   Are human birth defects always the result of genetic transmission?

Birth defects may be the result of hereditarily determined characteristics *or* an environmental condition that affects the prenatal development of the child. For example, Down syndrome (called *mongolism* in the past because of the shape of the eyes in these children) is caused by a chromosomal defect. Instead of inheriting the normal complement of 46 chromosomes, the child has 47 chromosomes, with the extra chromosome in the twenty-first pair. The result is mental retardation and certain physical characteristics, including stubby fingers, small ears, and eyelids with an unusual configuration.

The effects of some drugs (such as thalidomide) and diseases (such as German measles) also may produce birth defects. Although chromosomally correct at conception, the child is born with a defect because of environmental influences on development during the pregnancy.

4.9   Suppose a couple wants advice about possible genetic problems. What kind of counseling is available?

Biologists, medical doctors, and psychologists working together have developed techniques for identifying potential genetic effects. Before a couple conceives a child, their chromosomes can be analyzed to determine whether their germ cells might carry abnormal characteristics. During pregnancy, fetal cells in the amniotic fluid of the woman can be tested for the presence or absence of abnormal chromosomes.

Using such knowledge, genetic counseling allows the couple to weigh the probabilities of genetic influences on the structure and/or behavior of a child they might have. Such pre- or postconception counseling can relieve much anxiety and allow planning for eventualities the couple will experience.

4.10   Is it possible for two individuals to have exactly the same hereditary characteristics?

Two or more individuals may have exactly the same hereditary characteristics. Identical twins, for example, result when a single zygote divides and, in the process, the resultant cells separate. Each separate cell continues to develop and becomes an individual. These individuals have identical hereditary characteristics.

The possibility that two different conceptions will result in exactly the same hereditary characteristics is exceedingly small. The chances of such an occurrence are less than 1 in 70 trillion because of the vast number of combinations of chromosomes each parent may provide in the germ cell.

4.11   Explain the difference between identical and fraternal twins. Is it possible for identical and nonidentical siblings to be born at the same time?

When a single zygote splits completely and develops as two separate individuals, identical twins are produced. Because they come from a single conception, they carry the same hereditary pattern. Fraternal twins are the result of two separate conceptions occurring at about the same time. They are independent individuals from the moment of conception and may or may not be of the same gender.

Identical and nonidentical siblings may be born at the same time. For example, one highly publicized set of quintuplets consisted of three identical girls, one fraternal girl, and one fraternal boy.

4.12   What have "twin studies" shown about the likelihood of shared personality or behavioral characteristics in children who share some or all of the same hereditary characteristics?

In general, it has been found that higher proportions of shared genetic characteristics are associated with higher correlations of personality or behavioral characteristics whether the children live together or apart. Determining whether this is a function of hereditary influence or environmental variables has proven very difficult; most psychologists believe that the effects of "nature" and "nurture" are interwoven.

4.13   What use do humans make of the knowledge that the characteristics of adult organisms are important in determining the characteristics of their offspring?

Selective breeding of nonhuman organisms has been a common procedure for many years. The results of such breeding often yield obvious benefits, such as cows that produce more milk, thoroughbred horses that run faster, and chickens that lay more eggs.

Humans usually do not practice selective breeding. Although the science of eugenics has been proposed as the way of "improving" the human species, social standards, ethical questions, and the lack of certainty about what characteristics ought to be encouraged through selective breeding have combined to discourage such practices. Note, however, that many humans *are* somewhat selective in choosing mates, with religious, racial, or social class preferences serving as examples of considerations that affect choices.

4.14   How do the study of evolution and the study of genetics differ? Why are psychologists interested in evolution?

Genetics is the study of the transfer of characteristics from one generation to the next. Evolution looks at the gradual changes in species that occur over very long periods and may involve many generations.

Understanding evolution helps psychologists comprehend the heritage of human behavior. Humans have developed unique patterns of behavior in the same way they have developed unique configurations of physiological characteristics. These patterns of behavior are species-specific and are comparable to the behavior patterns found in other organisms.

4.15 Who is given credit for initiating the study of evolution? What primary considerations were set forth in his theory?

Charles Darwin, an English naturalist, published *The Origin of Species* in 1859. This work was the initial statement of his theory of evolution. Darwin's primary considerations were *variability*, in which changes in the genetic makeup of an organism lead to adaptation to the environment; *adaptation*, or the ability to adjust and survive within the environment; and *selection*, the tendency for adaptive characteristics to persist and for other characteristics to disappear.

4.16 Darwin's theory has been summarized in a single, well-known phrase. What is this phrase, and what does it imply?

The phrase often used to summarize Darwin's viewpoint is "survival of the fittest." The implication is that the characteristics that best help an organism adjust to the environment are those which persevere through natural selection and appear in succeeding generations. While the most fit characteristics continue to develop, the less fit tend to disappear.

4.17 How do ethologists conduct their research? What kinds of behaviors receive their attention?

Ethologists study the behaviors of organisms in their natural habitat. Thus, ethologists employ naturalistic observation when conducting research. The behavior patterns most likely to be studied are those which are species-specific, that is, common to all the members of that species and only that species.

4.18 If a behavior pattern is called an instinct, why may it be possible for that behavior to be modified by conditions in the environment or to involve learning?

An instinct is a species-specific predisposition for a complex behavior pattern that is completely controlled by hereditary factors. However, instincts are susceptible to environmental influences and may require learning to show they have occurred. An excellent example of instinct that illustrates both influences is *imprinting*. Newly hatched ducklings or chicks will follow a moving object in the environment. Although this object is usually the mother, if the baby birds are placed in an environment where the parents are absent and another moving object (for example, the researcher) is present, they learn to follow the human. Imprinting is illustrated by the following responses the birds show after being exposed to the moving stimulus. Thus, both learning and the conditions of the environment influence the expression of an instinct in all members of the species.

4.19 What is the difference between "maturation" as used in developmental psychology and "being mature" as it is used popularly? Is maturation the only concern of developmental psychology?

In developmental psychology, "maturation" refers specifically to physical growth, whereas "being mature" is a colloquial phrase used to describe a person (usually a child or adolescent) who acts more like an older individual than like his or her age mates. "Being mature" is not dependent on physical growth.

Developmental psychology includes the study of maturation processes but is more encompassing. Studying characteristics throughout the entire life span—including physical development, cognitive development, and social development—may be part of developmental psychology.

4.20 How much of the human life span is studied by developmental psychologists?

As a group, developmental psychologists are concerned with the *entire* life span, including both prenatal and postnatal development. An individual psychologist may be interested in only a part of the life span or a single behavior within the life span. The study of developmental psychology begins at the moment of conception and continues until death.

4.21   What are the periods of prenatal development? How do they differ from one another?

Three identifiable periods of prenatal development exist. The *germinal* period covers the first two weeks after conception. During this period, there is initial cell division but there is no physical attachment between the fertilized ovum and the mother.

At the beginning of the third week, attachment occurs. From then until the end of the sixth week, very rapid growth continues during what is called the *embryonic* period. At the end of this period, the cell development of the embryo has progressed to a point where the basic physical features of the future child are identifiable.

The time from the end of the embryonic period until birth (usually about the thirty-eighth week if the pregnancy is full-term) is called the *fetal* period. During this time, physical growth continues at a very rapid pace, although not as rapidly as in the previous periods.

4.22   What is the age of viability? How has technology affected this age?

The age of viability is the point during pregnancy at which a baby can survive if it is born prematurely. Medical technology has provided ways to sustain life for babies born in exceedingly frail states, making the age of viability much earlier in pregnancy.

4.23   Professor Graskool is interested in studying the changes in social behaviors that occur during the elementary school years. Describe the differences between longitudinal studies and cross-sectional studies performed for this purpose.

If Professor Graskool conducted a longitudinal study, she would use the same children throughout the study. Assuming she started with first-grade children, she would measure social behaviors at that age and then again, for the same children, during the next five years of school. The study would take nearly six years to complete but would reveal the patterns of change in a consistent group of subjects. However, many of the children might move during the five-year period, resulting in a high dropout rate.

A cross-sectional study could be conducted in a matter of weeks. Professor Graskool might test the social behaviors of all the children in an elementary school, and then compare the results obtained from the children in one grade to those of the children in the other grades. She would have to assume that the overall characteristics of each class did not differ significantly from those of the children in the other classes. Cross-sectional studies are relatively inexpensive and have a low dropout rate.

Professor Graskool would have to weigh the advantages and disadvantages of each of these techniques before deciding which to use in conducting her study.

4.24   The directors of a community preschool program wish to help parents, teachers, and other adult leaders recognize those situations which encourage and those which hinder child development. To this end, they hire a developmental psychologist to speak to them. The psychologist titles the presentation "Deprivation and Enrichment." What would be the basic points of the talk?

The psychologist points out that deprivation means "doing without" and that research studies have shown that depriving children of opportunities to develop usually results in an incomplete or reduced level of accomplishment. The psychologist indicates that all children should be supported so that motor, cognitive, and social skills will develop. For example, the psychologist may suggest that the parents not use "baby talk" when speaking to their children. ("Baby talk" deprives children of the chance to hear and learn from models of standard language.)

The talk continues with the suggestion that something more than minimal support may be very beneficial for children. The psychologist refers to this as enrichment of the environment and informs the audience about the vast potentials children have that may be developed if opportunities exist. The caution is given that heredity may place some limits on the characteristics that will develop, but the benefits of enrichment are stressed. The psychologist may suggest, for example, that storytelling and conversational activities be provided to give children opportunities to develop their verbal skills.

4.25 It often is suggested that children should begin learning a second language before they reach the age of puberty. How might developmental psychologists describe this suggestion?

Although the time period involved may represent a rather lengthy example, this suggestion proposes that there is a *critical period* in which children have particular sensitivity to second-language learning. Given the right kinds of stimulation, children may grasp concepts and language learning in a seemingly easy manner.

4.26 What are some typical physical characteristics of infants? How do these characteristics change over a period of time?

While a newborn has all the neuron and muscle fibers he or she will ever have, the responses available are rather limited and the infant relies on reflexes for many of the necessary survival responses. In addition, the infant's proportions differ considerably from those of older children or adults, with the head and the center of the body developing earlier than do the other parts. The head-to-toe developmental pattern is called the *cephalo-caudal trend*, while the development of the center before the outside is referred to as the *proximo-distal trend*. There may be considerable variation in development in one child compared with another—individual differences—but the overall pattern is usually very similar for all children.

4.27 Using the concept of "hot," provide an illustration of both assimilation and accommodation in a child's behavior.

Imagine the toddler Samantha waking from her nap while her mother is ironing. Samantha comes into the room and starts to reach for the iron. Mother stops her and says "Oh, don't do that, Sammi—that iron is *hot!*" Samantha adds this knowledge to her existing concepts of hot, which include the oven, a candle flame, and a fire in the fireplace, all of which she has explored and learned about. This is assimilation of new material into a concept that already exists.

That evening Samantha tries tacos for the first time. The sauce is very spicy and "burns" in her mouth. When she indicates this to her parents by making a series of panting noises, they tell her that tacos can be "*hot!*" Incorporating this version of "hot" into her concepts requires accommodation, because a modification of what the word means is necessary.

4.28 Describe the sequence of cognitive development proposed by the Swiss psychologist Jean Piaget.

Very careful and extensive study of cognitive processes led Piaget to propose the following sequence of cognitive development:

Sensorimotor period (birth to 2 years): Child learns the difference between the self and other objects, the influence of action on the environment, and the concept of object permanence.

Preoperational period (2 to 7 years): Child learns the use of language, more sophisticated classification of objects, the use of numbers, and the principle of conservation.

Concrete operational period (7 to 11 years): Child becomes capable of logical thought and continues to develop ideas of relationships but uses abstract terms only in relation to concrete (observable) objects.

Formal operational period (11 years and up): Child can think in abstract terms, can create and reason by using hypotheses, and shows concern for the future and for ideological problems.

4.29 Create illustrations of Piaget's concepts of object permanence, conservation, and concrete operations versus formal operations.

Object permanence means that the child understands that something continues to exist even when it cannot be directly observed. For example, if a toy is hidden under a blanket, a child with object permanence will try to pull the blanket to reveal and retrieve the toy.

Conservation refers to a child's ability to recognize that properties such as number, mass, and weight do not change simply because the materials are rearranged. For example, the amount of fluid remains the same when poured from a short, squat glass into a tall, thin glass.

Concrete operations mean that cognitive processes are tied intimately to actual objects, whereas *formal operations* can be wholly abstract. For example, a child's decisions regarding weight relationships require the actual presence of weights in the concrete operational period but not in the formal operational period.

4.30 How does the information-processing approach to cognitive development differ from the approach proposed by Piaget?

While both the information-processing approach and Piaget suggest that conceptualizations of the world change as cognitions develop, information processing proposes that these changes are continuous and does not establish cutoff points or particular periods in the manner of the Piaget approach. Skills learning and understanding of strategies for learning are important aspects of the information-processing approach.

4.31 A noticeable difference between elementary school preparation for children in the United States and that for children in European and Asian countries is the concern for second-language learning. Give a cultural influence explanation of this difference.

Cultural expectations produce differences in attitudes toward cognitive development. An obvious example is of second-language learning for elementary school children, which is almost totally ignored in the United States but is emphasized in many European and Asian countries. Simply stated, this reflects the cultural patterns of the various countries, perhaps, for example, revealing a greater "globality" for European and Asian countries than for the United States.

4.32 Distinguish between integration and differentiation as social development concepts. Then give an example of how these two concepts may overlap.

A child's social development involves both integration and differentiation. *Integration* refers to the child's connection to society through relationships and responsibilities, while *differentiation* is thought of as the formation of a separate or unique social identity. These concepts certainly overlap in situations where a child feels that his or her identity is defined by or depends on the friends with whom he or she plays.

4.33 What is considered the first phase of social development? How important are the parents in this phase?

Most developmental psychologists emphasize *attachment*—the establishing of a close, emotional bond with a particular individual—as the first phase of social development. Research has shown that while links with the parents certainly can produce many positive effects, separation from parents can be mitigated by high-quality day care, which also may have many positive effects.

4.34 Parents often are amazed at the values their children express. What would research on peer-group influence indicate about the development of values?

What the parents often do not realize is that peer-group influence becomes more important as a child grows older. While a parent serves as a role model for younger children, continued interaction with age mates assumes greater importance in determining an older child's values. This results in the adoption of values that may differ significantly from those held by the parents.

4.35   Are "traditional" gender roles an outgrowth of a child's social development?

They seem to be. Many individuals claim to be able to describe inherently "masculine" and "feminine" characteristics, but gender roles appear to be changeable and to be affected by the customs of society. What is accepted as "traditional" by one generation often is changed by the next. Interestingly, the influence of peers and parents in the development of gender roles seems to be comparable to their influences on other behaviors.

4.36   Does Kohlberg's explanation of moral development follow a sequence? How has this explanation been criticized?

Like explanations of many other behaviors, Lawrence Kohlberg's proposals regarding moral development follow a particular stage sequence. In the first, or *preconventional*, stage, the child acts correctly because of fear of punishment or the possibility of reward but does not understand the underlying principles. In the second, or *conventional*, stage, the child recognizes "duty" and maintains order because that is what is expected. Kohlberg's third, or *postconventional*, stage represents standards that involve conscience and principles.

Kohlberg's proposals have been criticized as not including sufficient consideration of caring or compassion. Such criticism arose because of Kohlberg's seemingly exclusive concern with the behavior of males, but research has shown that the criticism applies to both male and female concerns; that is, both females and males are more caring and compassionate than Kohlberg allowed for in creating his proposals. Recent proposals concerning morality have emphasized compassionate behavior to a much greater degree than did the original three-stage explanation.

4.37   Leonard, an adolescent, has taken on the role of "class clown," pulling practical jokes, tormenting people, and acting absurdly in an attempt to get attention. If Erikson were analyzing these behaviors, what interpretation might he give?

Erikson's eight-stage theory of psychosocial development emphasizes a series of crises the individual must face and resolve. In Leonard's situation, the crisis is between identity and role confusion. Apparently unable to resolve the identity crisis, Leonard has become confused and has adopted a "negative" identity. Ultimate psychosocial development, according to Erikson, depends on how well a person resolves the conflicts found at the eight specified stages.

4.38   Faced with probable terminal lung cancer, Shawn begins to make promises to anyone who will listen: "I'll quit smoking right now. I'll never touch another cigarette again. I'll begin an exercise program to restore my lungs. I'll teach all my children and their kids the right way to take care of themselves." In terms of Kubler-Ross's theories of dying and death, what stage is Shawn exhibiting in making such promises?

Shawn would appear to be in the *bargaining* stage, attempting to make agreements that might extend his life. In the sequence suggested by Kubler-Ross, this is the third stage. It is likely to have been preceded by *denial* and *anger* and to be followed by *depression* and finally *acceptance* of impending death.

Key Terms

Accommodation.   Modification of existing schema to include new information.

Age of viability.   The point at which a fetus can survive if born prematurely.

Assimilation.   A child's ability to incorporate new information into already existing schema.

Attachment.   The relationship of a child to parents and other significant individuals; usually develops during the first six months of postnatal development.

Behavioral genetics.   The study of the relative influences of heredity and environment on behavior.

Cephalo-caudal trend.   The tendency for the head to develop before and more quickly than the lower portions of the body.

Chromosomes.   Structures in each cell that contain genes; the units of hereditary transmission.

Concrete operational stage.   According to Piaget, the third stage of cognitive development; from approximately age 7 to age 11.

Critical period.   A stage during which the organism is able to learn a new behavior; this state is limited in time—it has both a beginning and an end.

Cross-sectional study.   An investigation that makes use of subjects in different age groups to determine how age, the independent variable, affects behavior.

Deprivation.   Doing without; in developmental psychology, a significant reduction of stimulation or opportunity.

Developmental psychology.   The study of behavioral changes over a time span.

Dominant gene.   In a pair of genes, the one which controls the hereditary characteristic that appears.

Embryonic stage.   The second period in prenatal development; from approximately the third week after conception until the end of the sixth week.

Enrichment.   In developmental psychology, stimulation or opportunity considerably above normal levels.

Ethology.   The study of organisms in their natural habitats.

Evolution.   Changes in a species that occur very gradually over lengthy periods.

Fetal stage.   The third period in prenatal development, from approximately the seventh week until delivery; in a full-term pregnancy (of 38 weeks), the last 32 weeks.

Formal operational stage.   According to Piaget, the fourth (and final) stage of cognitive development; from approximately age 11 to cognitive adulthood.

Gender roles.   The values, traits, or social motives thought to be appropriate for males and females.

Genes.   Units of hereditary transmission; found in the molecule called deoxyribonucleic acid (DNA).

Genetics.   The study of the biological transmission of characteristics from parents to offspring.

Genome.   The genetic pattern for any individual.

Germ cells.   The sperm from a male and the egg (ovum) from a female that unite to form a zygote.

Germinal stage.   The first period in prenatal development; from conception until approximately the end of the second week.

Heritability.   The proportion of the difference or variation among subjects that can be attributed to heredity.

Instincts.   Predispositions for complex behaviors that are completely controlled by hereditary factors.

Longitudinal study.   An investigation conducted over a fairly long period, using the same subjects throughout; the study may be used to determine how age, the independent variable, affects behavior.

Maturation.   In developmental psychology, the physical development of the body.

Mitosis.   The process of cell division involving differentiation and halving of the chromosomes.

Mutation.   A spontaneous or sudden change in DNA.

Peer-group influence.   The attachment to and the effects of interactions with age mates; increasingly important as a child grows older.

Postnatal.   After birth; the period from delivery to death.

Prenatal.   Before birth; the period from conception to delivery.

Preoperational stage.   According to Piaget, the second stage of cognitive development; from approximately age 2 to age 7.

Proximo-distal trend.   The tendency for the central portions of the body to develop before and more quickly than the peripheral parts.

Puberty.   The physiological changes associated with adolescence; marked by the development of the capacity to reproduce and the appearance of secondary sex characteristics.

Readiness.   The state in which an organism is ready and able to learn a new behavior; once readiness is reached, the organism always will have the ability to learn the new behavior.

Recessive gene.   In a pair of genes, the one which does not control the hereditary characteristic shown unless only the recessive gene is found in that pair.

Sensorimotor stage.   According to Piaget, the first stage of cognitive development; from birth to about age 2.

Zygote.   The single, original cell formed when the sperm and the egg unite.

CHAPTER 5

Sensation and Perception

Sensation is the process by which stimuli are detected, identified, and gauged. Sensation merely reveals or conveys information, while *perception* is the *interpretation* of the information received. It is important to recognize that humans have more sensory processes than usually are attributed to them. Many descriptions of human sensory processes detail a "basic five" senses, but probably it is more appropriate to identify a "basic seven" and then realize that each of them appears to have subcategories. The five most often mentioned senses receive signals from outside (vision, audition, smell, taste, and cutaneous or skin), while the other two (equilibrium and kinesthesis) sense internal states.

5.1 BASIC SENSORY PROCESSES

The study of basic sensory processes often is called *psychophysics*, the measurement of the functioning of the senses that looks at the physical nature of stimuli and the responses that are provoked. No matter which sensation is being described, a certain sequence of events appears to be necessary for the sense to operate. First, a stimulus appropriate to that sense must be present in sufficient strength to initiate reception. The signal is picked up by a *receptor* (a nerve ending that is specialized for this task) and transmitted through the sensory (or somatic) peripheral nervous system to the brain. The signal activates a part of the brain that records the signal as a sensation. Not until the signal reaches the brain does sensation occur.

Most sensory receptors are located in relatively well-protected portions of the body. (All but some skin receptors are at some distance from the surface of the body and are therefore difficult to damage.) Each sensory process is limited in its range of reception. A human's sensory capabilities are generally quite good, although they sometimes are surpassed by other organisms' abilities. Stimuli occurring outside an organism's range of reception are not recorded by the organism.

EXAMPLE 5.1. Receptors for hearing are not located in the outer (or visible) ear but well within the skull, guarded by the outer ear, skin, bone, and other tissue. Normal human hearing is quite good, but special "dog whistles" illustrate that dogs can hear sounds that are inaudible to humans.

Thresholds. Stimulation must be of sufficient strength for reception to occur. This necessary level of strength is called a *threshold*. A distinction is made between thresholds for revealing the presence or absence of a stimulus and those for detecting a change in the value of a stimulus.

Absolute Threshold.   If correct detection of the presence or absence of a stimulus occurs 50 percent of the time, the stimulus is said to be at the *absolute threshold*. (This percentage has been determined arbitrarily.)

EXAMPLE 5.2.   Figure 5-1 shows how the value for an absolute threshold is determined.

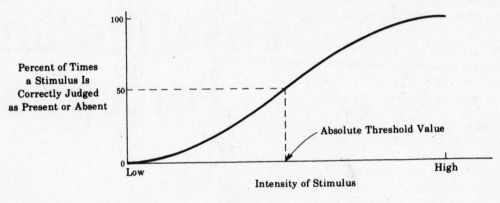

Fig. 5-1

Difference Threshold.   The minimum change in a stimulus value that can be detected as a change represents the *difference threshold*, often called the *just noticeable difference (j.n.d.)*. The relationship between the value of the original stimulus and the amount of change needed to be noticed is described as *Weber's law*, which states that a j.n.d. is a constant proportion of the intensity of the original stimulus.

EXAMPLE 5.3.   If it takes a 1-inch increase in the 20-inch diameter of a circle to be noticed, Weber's law would predict that a 2-inch change is needed when the original diameter of a circle is 40 inches. "Larger" changes are needed if the original stimulus is "larger"; thus, a small change in noise will be noticed in a quiet environment, while a much greater change will be needed to be recognized in a noisy room.

Sensory Adaptation.   On occasion, stimulation is of prolonged duration or at an unusual level compared to normal circumstances. In most of these cases, humans appear to be able to make adjustments and adopt a pattern of behavior that allows them to cope with the new level of stimulation. This process of coping is called *sensory adaptation*, a decrease in sensitivity or an adjustment in sensory capacity in reaction to the stimulation.

EXAMPLE 5.4.   Sensory adaptation may be illustrated by a newly married person wearing a wedding band. At first the ring seems very noticeable and perhaps somewhat awkward. The person may twist, pull, or "fool around" with the ring. With some experience, however, the individual usually adjusts to the "new" stimulation and no longer is aware of the ring, although the actual sensory stimulation remains the same.

Transduction.   When the stimulus (mechanical, chemical, radiant, etc.) is picked up by a receptor, its energy is changed into an action potential that then begins the sequence of events leading to the brain's registration of the sensation. This change from energy to action potential is called the *transduction* of the signal. Of course, the incoming energy level must be at least at the absolute threshold value before transduction can occur.

5.2 SIGNAL DETECTION THEORY

Early theories of sensory reception implied that each stimulus must have some minimum, unchanging value for its absolute threshold and some constant amount or ratio of change for its difference threshold. Later work (*signal detection theory*) has shown that those concepts are relatively naive. Absolute threshold values and difference thresholds may vary, depending on a number of conditions.

Motivation.   Research has suggested that certain payoffs or costs can affect a person's judgments regarding the presence or absence of a stimulus or a change in stimulus level. Evidence indicates that threshold values differ depending on motivation, with greater or lesser sensitivity resulting.

Analysis of such situations often is presented in terms of the outcomes possible. If the stimulus is present (or has changed), the person can either note this (a "hit") or not recognize it (a "miss"). If the stimulus is not present (or has not changed), the person can either recognize this (a "correct reject") or say that stimulation has occurred when it has not (a "false alarm"). In every case, the consequences of the response must be weighed against the possible alternatives.

EXAMPLE 5.5.   Signal detection theory arose in part from concerns during World War II. Sailors on watch had to decide whether enemy submarines were nearby and then respond accordingly. If a submarine was nearby and a sailor noted this by activating the alarm for "battle stations," this represented a *hit*. If there was no submarine nearby and the sailor sounded no alarm, a *correct reject* occurred. However, the sailor's errors could take two forms. If no submarine was present but the sailor saw an iceberg or a whale and mistakenly believed a submarine was present, sounding the call to battle stations represented a *false alarm*. The potentially more serious form of error happened when there was a submarine present and the sailor did not note this. Making no response placed the ship in jeopardy and constituted a *miss*. Obviously, in such circumstances, the relative payoffs and costs favored sounding the alarm whenever the possibility existed that an enemy submarine was in the area.

Extraneous Stimuli.   Example 5.5 introduced a second important consideration in signal detection theory. The possibility that a whale or an iceberg is misidentified as a submarine represents the influence of extraneous stimuli on the stimulus recognition process. Such irrelevant stimuli often are classified as *noise*. Excesses of noise may raise threshold values by making it more difficult to detect the appropriate stimulus.

Probability of Stimulus.   Past experience frequently provides information regarding the likelihood that a stimulus will occur again in the future. With a great likelihood, a person can be expected to detect the stimulus, whereas a very small likelihood means the person will devote his or her energies to other stimuli and miss this particular one. A threshold therefore varies with the probability of stimulus occurrence. Understanding stimulus probability in signal detection is affected by early experience, the importance of which is seen in situations where a restricted environment has existed. Organisms raised in restricted circumstances are less likely to recognize the possible stimulus occurrence than are those raised in normal situations.

Some organisms appear to be "hardwired" to respond to certain stimulus occurrences; this is a hereditary or evolutionary influence. Detection of a stimulus is more or less likely depending on how the organism is suited to that class of stimuli.

EXAMPLE 5.6.   Evidence for "hardwiring" to detect certain patterns of stimulation is seen in the ability of frogs to feed on insects. The frogs appear to have built-in "bug detectors" that provide excellent sensitivity to what is their source of food.

5.3   TYPES OF SENSORY PROCESSES

Vision.   The most thoroughly researched sensory process is vision, probably because the visual apparatus is relatively accessible and because early philosophers believed vision to be the "dominant" sense.

The chain of visual reception follows the basic sensory sequence described in Section 5.1. Light energies (the visible range of wavelengths in the electromagnetic spectrum) enter the eye by passing through the cornea, the pupil (the hole in the center of the iris), and the lens. They are picked up by the visual receptors located at the back of the eye, in the retina. There they pass through three layers of neuronal tissue, are transduced into action potentials, and are transmitted via the *occipital nerve* to the visual region of the brain, where they are registered and interpreted as sights. The image is brought to the retina in an upside-down position but is transformed to an upright position by the brain. Many neurons in the visual cortex, called *feature detectors*, are specialized and are activated only by stimuli of a specific shape or pattern.

The Retina. The *retina* is the light-sensitive surface at the back of the eyeball. It contains two kinds of receptors, called cones and rods, which serve different purposes.

Cones are receptors that function primarily in daylight or highly illuminated visual circumstances. They are concentrated toward the center of the eye, particularly in the *fovea*, an area directly across from the lens where maximum visual acuity occurs. Cones provide the receptors for color vision and sharp details.

Rods are receptors that function in dim light. More numerous than cones, they are found throughout the retina, except in the center of the fovea. Rods are largely insensitive to color and fine detail.

EXAMPLE 5.7. When looking at a dim star, it sometimes is easier to focus by tilting the head a little to the side. This is the case because cones do not operate well in dim light conditions and the stimulus must be brought into focus on rod receptors, which are located more in the periphery of the retina.

Dark adaptation is an increased sensitivity to light that occurs after one has been in a place of relative dimness for some period. Dark adaptation results from changes in the chemical composition of the rods and cones during that period.

EXAMPLE 5.8. A common example of dark adaptation occurs when one goes to the movies on a sunny afternoon. Stepping into the theater from the bright sunlight requires a period of adjustment before one can see the aisles and seats. Some psychologists also suggest that there is a comparable, although quicker, process of light adaptation when one comes from a darkened area into bright light. Squinting or closing the eyes for several moments is required for light adaptation.

The *blind spot* is a place in each retina that contains no receptors. The blind spot is an opening in the retina where the optic nerve exits to the brain. In general, because of the dual operation of the eyes and past visual learning experiences, the blind spot in the visual field of either eye is not readily apparent. (See Solved Problem 5.15 for a demonstration of the blind spot.)

Color vision is a function of the cones. Research has shown that not all cones receive all colors. A popular explanation of the differences among cones is the *trichromatic theory* of color vision, which states that some cones are most sensitive to reds, some to greens, and a third group to blues. According to the trichromatic theory, the color received is a result of how many of each of these receptors are activated by a stimulus. A second theory, that of *opponent-process channels*, extends the trichromatic theory by suggesting that the activity of the cones or color receptors takes place in ways that pair red with green and blue with yellow (the color resulting from the combination of red and green). These pairs of color receptors are thought to be sensitive to stimuli in ways that suggest they are in competition or opposition for dominance. Activation of specific cones produces the activity of the channels that determines the color perceived. For example, when red is detected at a particular spot on the retina, it is thought to be physiologically impossible to detect the opposite—green—at that same point. Some variations of the opponent-process theories include a black-white channel as well.

Properties of Light. The *color* (or *hue*) of the stimulus, the *intensity* of the light source, and the *saturation* of the stimulus are all properties of light stimuli.

Color, or *hue*, is determined by the *wavelength* of light. Humans are able to see colors ranging from reds (the longest visible wavelengths) to blues (the shortest) and any wavelengths between. This range of color vision has been named the *visible spectrum*. Stimulation by only a narrow band of these wavelengths produces a *pure spectral color*.

Intensity is the amount of physical energy produced by a light source. The viewer's reaction to this intensity is usually labeled the *brightness* of the light.

Saturation is determined by the variety of wavelengths in a light source. A pure spectral color is said to be completely saturated. When a color is composed of light of many wavelengths, the saturation is decreased; that is, the color becomes "washed out."

Visual Dysfunctions.   Several fairly common visual dysfunctions exist. Obviously, the most severe is total blindness, which often results from traumatic damage to nerve tissue. Nearsightedness, farsightedness, and astigmatism are dysfunctions in which the rays that are received are not focused properly on the retina. Correction by the use of glasses or contact lenses or by laser surgery is often possible.

Color blindness and color deficiency occur when particular cones are missing or malfunctioning. The most common color deficiency is an inability to recognize reds and greens. Much less common are inaccuracies in receiving blues or yellows, and total color blindness, where virtually no color reception exists. In general, color deficiencies and color blindness are not correctable.

EXAMPLE 5.9.   Individuals with red-green color deficiency must rely on position and brightness cues to determine whether a traffic signal is red or green. Universal standards have been adopted so that red is always above green in the signal. (Placing the green above the red, as a highway system in Canada once did, created confusion and hazard for drivers with color deficiency or color blindness.)

Hearing.   *Hearing* (or *audition*) is an organism's ability to receive mechanical energy in the form of sound waves. The sound waves are generated when a source is made to vibrate, resulting in compression and expansion of adjacent molecules. The repeated compression and expansion are carried by some medium to the hearing receptors. Most frequently, the transmission medium is air molecules, although sound can pass through other gases, liquids, and solids.

The reception and registration of sound waves follow the basic sensory sequence described in Section 5.1. The specific parts of the body involved in (normal) hearing are as follows: The *outer ear* (or *pinna*) "traps" the sound waves and funnels them to the eardrum. The *middle ear* contains three small bones or *ossicles*, the *malleus*, *incus*, and *stapes* (also frequently called the *hammer*, *anvil*, and *stirrup*), which transfer the vibrations from the eardrum to a second membrane, called the *oval window*. The *inner ear* contains the *cochlea*, a snaillike structure filled with fluid and hairlike receptors (*hair cells*) that transduce the mechanical energy into an action potential. From the cochlea, the signals are transmitted through the *auditory nerve* to the *auditory cortex* of the brain, where the actual registration of the sound takes place.

Properties of Sound Waves.   The distinguishing characteristics of a sound wave are its *frequency*, *amplitude*, and *complexity*. Frequency, the number of sound waves per second, determines the *pitch* a listener hears. The greater the number of waves per second, the higher the pitch. Amplitude represents the amount of energy in each wave as measured by the height of the wave. Amplitude determines the intensity of the sound reported as decibels, that is, how loud the sound will be. Complexity refers to the number of different sound waves that occur simultaneously. Complexity determines the *timbre* of the sound, the type of quality the sound has.

EXAMPLE 5.10.   It is easy to think of the three properties of a sound if one considers how music "sounds different" if produced by different instruments. Although a tune may be exactly the same, it does not sound the same if produced by a trumpet versus a guitar. The pitch may be the same, but the intensity and the timbre are likely to be perceived as being quite different.

Auditory Localization.   In many instances, the receiver is interested not only in how the stimulus sounds but from where the stimulus is coming. Identifying the direction of the sound source is called *auditory localization*. Basically, localization depends on the discrepancy between the time one ear receives the sound and the time the other ear receives it. When the sound source is exactly equidistant from both ears, the receiver may have to rely on another sensory process (for example, vision) or turn the head slightly to create a time differential in order to determine direction.

EXAMPLE 5.11.   To demonstrate the difficulty in determining the location of auditory stimuli that arrive at both ears simultaneously, do the following. Sit with your eyes closed and have someone sound a noise source directly in front or directly in back of you. Try to point to the location of the source. You may find that you are unable to determine where the source is located unless you either open your eyes or turn your head slightly.

Auditory Dysfunctions.   The most severe auditory dysfunction is total deafness. Other hearing losses are mild dysfunctions throughout the hearing range or partial dysfunctions in which only a segment of the range cannot be heard. Damage to the conductive mechanisms (*conduction deafness*) or to the nerves involved (*nerve deafness*) may be the cause of such losses.

EXAMPLE 5.12.   Exposure to very loud noise (120 decibels or above) can produce permanent damage to the hair cells in the cochlea and resultant loss of hearing. Loud sounds between 70 and 120 decibels also can produce damage if there is continual exposure. This latter finding is of particular importance in today's society because of technological changes that have made it possible to listen to music at such levels. Rock musicians and, in some instances, people who have worn headset listening devices for extended periods have shown loss of auditory capacity.

The Chemical Senses—Smell and Taste.   *Smell* (olfaction) and *taste* (gustation) are sensory processes that receive stimulus energy in the form of chemical substances. As with the other senses, the signals are transduced into action potentials which are relayed to specialized areas of the brain to be recorded as odors or tastes.

Smell.   The receptors for smell are hair cells in the membranes of each nasal passage (olfactory epithelium). Human receptors are quite sensitive to certain odors but relatively insensitive to changes in the concentration of an odor.

EXAMPLE 5.13.   Animals are known to produce chemicals called *pheromones* that convey messages through the scent they produce. For example, female ring-tailed lemurs "mark" branches with secretions that signal sexual availability to males in the group. Whether humans produce similar scents is a matter of debate.

Taste.   Taste receptors are specialized cells with hairlike endings grouped together in *taste buds*. Found in the tongue, the taste receptors have been classified as sensitive to sweet, sour, salty, and bitter, with each type most sensitive to only one of these stimuli.

Flavor.   The combination of taste and smell results in *flavor*. This probably results from the fact that the two types of receptors are sensitive to very similar chemical stimuli.

EXAMPLE 5.14.   An experiment demonstrates how important odor reception is to the perception of flavor. If a subject is blindfolded and has the nasal passages completely blocked, different foods, such as an onion, a potato, and an apple, that are chopped into similar-sized bites cannot be differentiated. However, once the nasal passages are unblocked, the subject can make rapid distinctions among the foods. (This is an easy demonstration to try for yourself.)

Dysfunctions.   Unless some kind of nervous tissue damage occurs, dysfunctions of the chemical senses are likely to be mild. Most occur, for example, when a person has a bad attack of hay fever or "burns" the tongue. Permanent difficulties such as *anosmia*, the inability to smell normally, may result from head injury or long-term asthma.

The Skin Senses.　　The skin (or *cutaneous*) senses provide sensory experiences from receptors in and under the skin. Four varieties have been identified: *warm*, *cold*, *pressure*, and *pain*. These receptors are *not* distributed evenly throughout the body. Certain areas, such as the face and hands, have many more receptors than do other areas, such as the back.

The stimuli received may be provided by either mechanical or radiant energy, although the latter does not create pressure stimuli. There also is evidence that modification of the signals received, particularly those of pain, can occur. The *gate-control theory of pain* suggests there are receptors that can send signals that make an individual more or less sensitive to pain experience. Two variations have been identified. One shows that when another set of neural receptors is activated, the experience of pain is lessened. The other indicates that psychological factors can initiate signals from the brain that "close" the gate to pain from the injured area.

EXAMPLE 5.15.　　Young children are prone to run into things. If a child slams into the dining room table and hits a shoulder, the parent is likely to say "Let me rub that for you; it will feel better." The parent's rubbing demonstrates the first of the two gate-control proposals: rubbing the skin around the injured area will relieve the pain by activating other neurons and competing with the pain message.

The Kinesthetic Senses.　　*Kinesthetic* receptors are located in muscles, joints, tendons, and the skin. They provide information about changes in the activity and position of the body (*kinesthesis*). This in turn aids in coordination.

Which receptors are activated depends on the direction and angle of movement. The signals from the kinesthetic receptors are registered and interpreted in the brain, just as occurs with the other senses. Dysfunctions occur when nervous system damage prevents signals from the receptors from being registered in the brain.

Balance.　　*Balance* (the *vestibular* sense) has receptors in the inner ear, next to the hearing apparatus. These receptors consist of three *semicircular canals* and the *vestibular sacs*.

The semicircular canals and vestibular sacs contain hair cells that respond to changes in body orientation. Fluid in the semicircular canals moves with body rotation and generates displacement of the receptors. The hair cells of the vestibular sacs respond to the body's position or angle, such as when it is at rest.

Dysfunctions of balance may lead to vertigo or nystagmus (involuntary oscillation of the eyeballs). These dysfunctions frequently can be overcome by relying on other sensory processes.

EXAMPLE 5.16.　　A trip to a "fun house" can show how maintaining a vertical or upright position may be difficult. When visual cues make the relationship between floor and walls appear to be different from what it really is, a person may have to rely on kinesthetic, touch, or vestibular cues. It is easy to demonstrate the complex interactions of these sensory processes by trying to stand on one foot, first with the eyes open and the head in an upright position and then with the eyes closed and the head tilted forward.

5.4　PERCEPTION: EXTERNAL CUES

Perception is the process by which a person *interprets* sensory stimuli. For the most part, perception appears to be a function of experience. Research evidence indicates that a subject whose perceptual experience is restricted or eliminated will be unable to develop normal perceptual reactions. Even assuming normal development, only a small portion of the information received will be processed and interpreted. All organisms must choose from among the many sources of stimulation, a process known as *selective attention*.

EXAMPLE 5.17. A popular example of selective attention has come to be known as the *cocktail party phenomenon*. Imagine attending a party where several conversations are going on at once. You are talking with several people when someone in another conversational group mentions your name. It is likely that your attention will shift to the other group's conversation, at least momentarily, because of attention to something relating to you.

Two types of factors influence perception. In this section, *external* (stimulus) *cues* are investigated, while *internal* (personal) cues are considered later. External cues develop from the properties of a stimulus or a group of stimuli. Interest in the effects of external stimuli on attention and perceptual development arose during the early years of Gestalt psychology. The Gestaltists realized that stimuli provided the start for more than just sensation. They stated that perception was more than just an additive function of sensations, a theory now often expressed as "the whole is greater than the sum of its parts."

EXAMPLE 5.18. Consider the following: "fisihtsekamesnes, er'uoyaprahsrekniht!" Rearranged, these letters read: "if this makes sense, you're a sharp thinker!" However, you have to have the correct arrangement and spacing of the letters to appreciate the meaning. In other words, the whole is *more* than its parts. In and of themselves, the stimulus components do not always allow someone to understand or interpret the stimulus environment.

Figure-Ground Relationship. The relationship between the main or featured stimulus and any surrounding stimuli is called the *figure-ground relationship*. This relationship determines how distinct the main stimulus (the figure) is within the total context (the ground). In general, the greater the *intensity* of a stimulus is, the more likely it is that a subject will attend to it. In addition, a stimulus that differs noticeably from the ground surrounding it (by virtue of quality or quantity) is more likely to be noticed. This is the principle of *contrast*.

EXAMPLE 5.19. Much perceptual research is done with vision, but a figure-ground relationship also can be illustrated by listening to music. The melody represents the figure, and the harmony provides the ground. If one or both of these elements is varied, the figure-ground relationship may change.

Figure-ground relationships are called *unstable* if the figure sometimes can be perceived as the ground and the ground can be perceived as the figure. Figures also may be described as *ambiguous* if they can be "correctly" interpreted in more than one way. (See Solved Problems 5.36 and 5.37.)

Other Gestalt Principles. The placement or arrangement of stimuli can affect how one attends to and understands them. In general, stimuli that are categorized as being alike, perhaps because of appearance or common behaviors, will be grouped together because of *similarity*. Stimuli that are close together physically will tend to be grouped together, a principle referred to as *proximity*. *Good continuation* or *continuity* refers to the uninterrupted "flow" of a stimulus. A subject is likely to perceive a stimulus situation as a combination of regular or continuous stimuli rather than a combination of irregular or discontinuous stimuli.

EXAMPLE 5.20. In Fig. 5-2, drawing *a* usually is perceived as the combination of a straight line and an "accordion" line (drawing *b*) rather than as the combination of two "sawtooth" lines (drawing *c*).

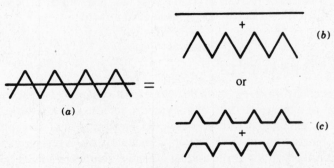

Fig. 5-2

Closure is defined most easily as filling in gaps in information. A subject receives "incomplete" information, but enough so that it is possible to "finish" the stimulus. (A person's ability to show closure depends on previous knowledge of what "fits" the situation.)

EXAMPLE 5.21. Television game shows often make use of the principle of closure. Incomplete phrases, pictures, or musical themes are presented to a contestant, who must quickly complete the cue in order to win a prize. Advertising often employs the same principle, letting the viewer mentally complete a phrase related to the product.

Some psychologists believe that the overriding Gestalt principle is that of *simplicity*. Given a choice of interpretations of a stimulus situation, people are likely to choose the less complex option.

Perceptual Constancies.   The stimulus a person receives from an object may change as the position or condition of the object changes. (For example, as you move away from a dinner plate on a table, the image on your retinas will become less like a circle and more like an oval.) Despite such stimulus changes, a person perceives that the object has not changed. (The plate still is perceived as a circular object.)

This phenomenon is called *perceptual constancy*. Research has shown that people perceive size, shape, brightness, and color constancies.

EXAMPLE 5.22.   Imagine throwing a model plane so that it moves away from you, loops, and returns toward you. The retinal image you receive is of an object that first grows smaller and then seems to increase in size. However, you perceive that the actual size of the plane remains constant throughout the flight. This is an example of size constancy.

Monocular Depth Cues.   In visual perception, some of the most important stimulus properties provide *depth cues*. If these cues can be perceived accurately using one eye alone, they are called *monocular depth cues*. Examples of monocular cues are *interposition*, *perspective*, *texture gradient*, and *shadow*.

Interposition occurs when one object appears to "block out" part of another object in the visual field. Interposition provides information about the size, distance, and location of the various stimulus objects.

Perspective and texture gradient often operate together to provide information about three-dimensionality. *Perspective* is the apparent "drawing together" of parallel lines as they recede into the distance. *Texture gradient* is the change in the distinctiveness of the surface texture of a stimulus from noticeable or coarse when close to smooth or fine when at a distance. Both allow understanding of the visual field.

Shadow also offers cues that aid in the perception of three dimensions. The distance, height, and shape of an object may become more intelligible when shadow cues are present.

Binocular Depth Cues.   When the perceptual cue depends on the operation of both eyes, these cues are called *binocular depth cues*. The fact that the visual images on the retinas of the two eyes at a given moment are never exactly the same is called *retinal disparity*. The brain is able to "blend" the two images so that one sees just one image, which carries information about depth and dimensionality. As objects draw closer to a person, the muscular movement involved in focusing the image on the retinas is called *convergence*. Interpretation of that movement provides information about depth and other visual properties.

EXAMPLE 5.23.   Stereoscopic viewers rely on retinal disparity to provide the impression of three dimensions. A pair of two-dimensional pictures is viewed through special lenses. Each picture sends a slightly different image to each retina. The brain then combines those images into what appears to be a three-dimensional view.

5.5   PERCEPTION: INTERNAL CUES

Internal cues that affect perception appear to be a function of a subject's cognitive processes. Perceptual interpretations may be influenced by factors such as expectations, motivation, and past learning. Processing proceeds in two manners that often occur simultaneously: top-down processing and bottom-up processing.

Top-Down Processing.   Previous learning, situational context, expectations of the moment, and other cognitive factors all play a role in *top-down processing*, influences on perceptions that are based on "filling in" missing or confusing stimuli to interpret the stimulus situation. Selection of the stimuli to which one attends and organization of the incoming signals into a meaningful pattern are seen as a function of the previous experience of the individual and the current motivational and expectation conditions.

An example of such influence has been called *set*, the temporary tendency (or expectation) to respond in a certain fashion. This tendency may change as the subject is confronted with different instructions or rewards.

EXAMPLE 5.24.   Read the following sentence: "If Frieda follows Fred frantically, Fred flees fleetingly!" How many *f*'s do you count in that sentence? If you counted eight, your set was accurate. If you counted only seven, you probably were caught by the first-letter set and missed the *f* in the word "if."

Bottom-Up Processing.   Top-down processing is very important to perceptual processes, but cannot happen without *bottom-up processing*, the recognition and processing of information about the individual components of stimuli. For example, if you were unable to recognize or understand what a letter *f* is, the question asked in Example 5.24 would be meaningless.

Bottom-up processing allows processing of the basic characteristics of incoming stimuli, while top-down processing illustrates the influence of experience on the interpretations made. Both types of processing occur simultaneously and in most cases enable a person to make responses appropriate to the situation.

5.6   UNUSUAL PERCEPTUAL EXPERIENCES

Illusions.   Sometimes stimuli can be interpreted incorrectly. Some stimuli exist in a configuration that almost always leads to incorrect perception. When this occurs, the perception is described as an *illusion*.

EXAMPLE 5.25.   The famous Mueller-Lyer illusion (see Fig. 5-3) shows how stimulus cues may lead to

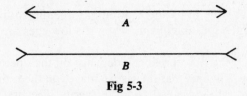

Fig 5-3

perceptual misunderstanding. Lines *A* and *B* are exactly the same length, but *A* appears shorter than *B*.

(*Note*: Illusions often are confused in everyday speech with *hallucinations*, which are perceptions of "stimuli" that actually do not exist.)

Extremes of Sensory Load.   *Sensory deprivation* (very little stimulation) and *sensory overload* (a great amount of stimulation) may exceed a person's "normal" capabilities for sensory adaptation. When this happens, unusual patterns of responding (such as hallucinations) may result. A person may be unable to continue to interpret the stimulus environment correctly if extreme deprivation or extreme overload is maintained for a prolonged period.

Subliminal Perception.   Years ago, attempts were made to create advertisements that would be presented at stimulus values just below the conscious threshold. The idea was that a person would receive the advertising message without being aware of the stimulation. Such perception without awareness is called *subliminal perception.*

In general, subliminal campaigns have been abandoned. Thresholds vary for individuals, making stimulus values difficult to determine. In addition, research has shown that no significant changes could be produced in carefully controlled experimental situations designed to create subliminal effects. The same studies did show, however, that the expectations subjects brought to the studies did have an influence on their behaviors, often making the subjects believe that subliminal effects had been produced even when response values indicated that this had not occurred.

Extrasensory Perception.   *Extrasensory perception (ESP)* is said to have occurred when a correct interpretation or manipulation of the environment has taken place without any information being provided by regular sensory processes. Several varieties of ESP have been studied, including telepathy, precognition, clairvoyance, and psychokinesis.

Telepathy is the transfer of thought from one person to another without the aid of the usual sensory channels. *Precognition* refers to the ability to anticipate future events. *Clairvoyance* is the ability to disclose information that could not have been received through regular sensations. *Psychokinesis* is the capacity to make objects move by using only thought processes.

Solved Problems

5.1   Describe the difference between sensation and perception and give an example of each.

> Sensation is simply a part of overall perceptual processes. Using the nervous system (see Chapter 3), energies of various kinds are detected, distinguished as to kind, and interpreted for strength and difference from other stimuli. Thus, the sensory processes only "report" information, whereas perception then makes inferences from or interprets the information.

> Imagine riding in a boat on a wide river. Far in the distance you can see a bridge spanning the river. If you raise your hand and hold it in front of your eyes, you will be able to block out any visual image of the bridge completely. However, at this point you still realize the bridge is much bigger than your hand and must be at least as long as the river is wide.

> The "tiny" image of the bridge represents sensation, the actual stimulation being received by the receptors and transmitted to the brain. The interpretation of these signals, in which you realize that they represent a large structure, is perception.

5.2   What kind of energies are detected as sensations?

> The human body receives and translates energies which are detected as sights, sounds, tastes, odors, various touch sensations, information about balance, and information about body position.

5.3   The usual list of human sensations includes five sensory processes, but Solved Problem 5.2 implies that there are more. What are they?

> The designation of five basic senses is too limited, based on receiving signals from outside the body. There are at least seven sensory processes that correspond to the descriptions in Solved Problem 5.2. They are vision, hearing, taste, smell, skin or cutaneous senses, balance, and kinesthesis.

Each of these sensory processes appears to have a number of separate receptors that receive particular types of energy.

5.4   Are sensations recognized when a receptor is activated? Is the process of sensation the same or different for each type of sensation?

Activation of a specialized nerve ending (or receptor) begins the sensory process, but that signal must be transduced into an action potential, transmitted through the sensory peripheral nervous system to the central nervous system, and "recorded" in the brain before the recognition of a sensation takes place.

This sequence—stimulus, receptor, sensory peripheral nerve, and central nervous system—is essentially the same for all sensory processes. Differences exist in the types of stimuli that activate the receptors, which parts of the sensory peripheral nervous system are called into play, and which specialized areas of the cortex are activated.

5.5   How good are the human senses?

All human sensory processes have a limited range. However, human senses are thought to be quite good, even though comparable sensory processes in other organisms may on occasion be more sensitive or have a greater range.

5.6   What is a threshold?

If the stimulus strength is sufficient to be detected, it has reached or passed the *threshold* for detection. The concept of threshold has two subdivisions: (1) *Absolute threshold* indicates the level at which the presence or absence of a stimulus can be detected correctly 50 percent of the time, and (2) *difference threshold* indicates the smallest change in a stimulus value that can be detected correctly as a change 50 percent of the time. (The difference threshold of a stimulus is also referred to as the *just noticeable difference*, or *j.n.d.*)

5.7   Describe Weber's law. If a sound of 30 decibels requires a 2-decibel change for the change to be noticed, how big must the change be to be noticed if the base stimulus is 45 decibels?

Weber's law says that a just noticeable difference is a constant proportion of the intensity of the original stimulus. Thus, if the base stimulus is at 45 decibels, a 3-decibel change will have to occur in order to be noticed ($2/30 = X/45$ yields $90/30 = X$, or $3 = X$).

5.8   What is sensory adaptation?

Sensory adaptation occurs when sensory sensitivity changes or adjusts to the amount and type of prolonged incoming stimuli. For example, a worker who has been employed for years in a candy-making factory may no longer notice the very sweet smell of the workplace except perhaps for a brief moment upon arriving each day. The consistency and amount of stimulation appear to lead to a decrease in sensitivity or an adjustment in sensory capacity in reaction to the stimulation.

5.9   What factors may influence threshold values?

Absolute and difference threshold values may vary, depending on a number of factors. Three that have been studied extensively and form the basis for *signal detection theory* are motivation, the probability of the stimulus, and extraneous stimuli (noise). Motivation is concerned primarily with the payoffs and costs associated with recognizing that the stimulus is present or has changed. Probability of the stimulus evaluates whether its occurrence is a "sure thing" or fairly unlikely. Extraneous stimuli, or noise, looks at how many distracting or irrelevant stimuli may interfere with stimulus identification.

5.10 Imagine driving on a rainy day when the temperature is dropping. The pavement is wet, and you realize the moisture may freeze on the surface of the road. In threshold terms, you are looking for a just noticeable difference. Using signal detection theory possible outcomes, explain what decisions you might make and what they would be called.

Four possible outcomes can occur. They are based on whether there actually is ice on the road and whether you accurately recognize what the conditions are. If ice is there and you note the change, your decision is called a *hit*. If no ice is there and you correctly realize the road is still wet but not icy, your decision is called a *correct reject*. If the road is only wet but you believe there is ice present (and probably act accordingly), your decision is called a *false alarm*. Finally, if there is ice present but you do not recognize that it is there, your decision is called a *miss*.

5.11 Barnyard chickens are known to seek shelter when a short-necked bird (such as a hawk) flies over, hurrying to safety even if they see only the shadow of such a bird. What seems to explain this extreme sensitivity to short-necked bird stimuli?

There is evidence that certain organisms are "hardwired" to be particularly sensitive to certain kinds of stimuli. This is attributed to hereditary or evolutionary development and often is associated with survival.

5.12 The process of seeing often is described as being very similar to the process by which a camera takes a picture. Try to describe vision by relating it to how a camera works.

Basically, a camera is a container with an opening (the lens) on one side and film on the opposite side. The eye has a somewhat comparable structure. The pupil of the eye serves as the opening, which can adjust to the amount of light being received. Directly behind the pupil is the lens, which focuses the stimuli being received on the retina. The retina is similar to the film, located at the back of the eyeball and receiving the stimuli. Carrying the analogy a step further, the visual area of the brain serves as the processor, "developing" the signals transmitted from the retina and completing the visual process. (*Note*: The image projected on the retina is upside-down, but after it is received, the brain converts the signal to an upright position.)

5.13 Besides their shape, how do cones and rods differ?

There are two kinds of visual receptors: cones and rods. Both show adaptation to light and darkness, but cones operate primarily in daylight conditions and rods function in dim or dark situations. Cones provide color vision; rods provide vision only for light and dark (achromatic vision).

5.14 The distribution of cones and rods is not uniform throughout the retina. How are they distributed, and what effect does this have on vision?

Cones tend to be located toward the center of the retina; rods generally are located more in the periphery. The greatest concentration of cones occurs in a central area called the *fovea*, which is the point of maximum visual acuity. Thus, vision under bright illumination is best if the signal is focused toward the center of the retina. Vision in dim light is generally better if the stimulus is directed toward the periphery of the retina.

5.15 Describe how to locate the blind spot. Why does it exist?

Using the X and O below, close one eye and focus on the center of the stimulus on the opposite side. Slowly move the page toward you. At some point, you will no longer be able to see the mark on which you are *not* focusing.

X   O

The blind spot exists because there are no receptors at the point in the retina where the optic nerve leaves the eye. The blind spot usually is not noticed because of the dual operation of the eyes and the ability of the brain to "fill in the gaps." (This is a form of *closure*. See Solved Problem 5.40.)

5.16 Do all cones in the retina receive all colors? What causes color deficiency or color blindness?

Research evidence indicates that not all cones receive all colors. The most widely accepted theory is called the *trichromatic theory* of color vision. It states that some cones respond best to red light, others to green, and still others to blue. The colors a person sees depend on how many of each of these types of cones are activated.

Color deficiency or color blindness results from missing or malfunctioning cones. Most commonly, reds and greens are not received correctly. The inability to distinguish blues and yellows is much more rare, as is the inability to distinguish any color (total color blindness).

5.17 How does evidence from color deficiency appear to support the opponent-process channels concept?

The concept of opponent-process channels extends the trichromatic theory of color vision by suggesting that the activity of the three types of cones works together in ways that set red against green, blue against yellow (a combination of red and green), and, for some theorists, white against black. Deficiencies appear to match these channels, in that failure to distinguish red is almost always accompanied by inability to see green, with the same pattern found for blues and yellows.

5.18 What are the three basic properties of light?

One basic property of light is *color* (or, more properly, *hue*). It is determined by the wavelength of the light. The range of wavelengths seen by humans is called the visible spectrum; the longest visible wavelengths appear as red, and the shortest appear as blue. A second basic property of light is *intensity* (or brightness). Intensity describes the amount of physical energy produced by the light source, while brightness refers to the viewer's response to intensity. In general, more intense lights appear brighter. The third basic property of light, *saturation*, is determined by the number of light-wave components mixed with a pure spectral color; the more components mixed in, the less the light's saturation.

5.19 What dysfunctions other than those involving color can affect visual processes?

Other visual dysfunctions include farsightedness, nearsightedness, and astigmatism. All create situations where the incoming rays do not focus properly on the retina because the cornea and lens do not bend the rays correctly. All usually are correctable by means of glasses or contact lenses, which are shaped to compensate for the improper focus, or in some cases by laser surgery, which changes the eye structure.

Another visual dysfunction is total blindness. In this case there is no vision at all, a condition that usually is not correctable.

5.20 Sound stimuli reach us as waves. Describe these sound waves and the basic properties of sound.

Sound waves are a form of mechanical energy. When a source is made to vibrate, the resultant compressions and expansions of molecules are conducted much as in a chain reaction through some medium (usually air) until they reach the receptors. A basic property of sound waves is *frequency*, the number of waves per second, which determines the sound's *pitch*. Another property is *amplitude*, the height of the wave, which determines the *intensity* of the sound or how loud it seems. A third property of sound waves is *complexity*, the number of different sound waves occurring simultaneously. Complexity determines the *timbre*, or type of quality, the sound has.

5.21   While shopping in a department store, your friend calls to you from an adjoining aisle. Describe the chain of reception of the sound of your friend's voice.

The chain involves the outer ear, the middle ear, the inner ear, and the brain. The outer ear (what ordinarily is called the "ear") traps the sound waves and funnels them into the auditory canal, where they strike the eardrum. The eardrum vibrates, relaying the signal into the middle ear, which consists of three small bones called the ossicles (malleus, incus, and stapes). These bones transmit the vibrations to a second membrane, called the oval window, which is found at the start of the cochlea, a coiled tube filled with fluid and hair cells, the actual sound receptors. The hair cells are found between two membranes (basilar and tectorial), which expand or contract according to the signal being received. This causes deflection of the hair cells, which sends signals through the auditory nerve to the brain, where they are registered in the auditory cortex. At that point, you have "heard" your friend's voice.

5.22   One of the functions of the outer ears is to trap incoming sound waves. What other function do the outer ears, working in conjunction, serve?

Auditory localization, the ability to determine from where a sound has come, occurs because humans have two ears which are some distance apart. In general, a sound which comes from any direction except directly in front or in back arrives at one ear slightly before arriving at the other. Although the time differential is small, it is sufficient to allow location of the source. To locate sound sources directly in front or in back of the head, a person may have to use visual cues or turn the head to create a time differential.

5.23   Distinguish between the two general causes for partial or complete deafness. What kinds of compensations can be made for loss of hearing?

Some hearing losses are caused by damage to or deterioration of the conductive mechanisms and are called conductive deafness. Damage to the nervous system produces nerve deafness. Compensation for hearing loss may be accomplished with the use of hearing aids, by learning speech (lip) reading techniques, or by learning sign language using one's hands.

5.24   Which senses are called the "chemical senses"? Explain why they have this name and identify where their receptors are located.

Smell (olfaction) and taste (gustation) are called the chemical senses because stimuli come in the form of chemical substances that make contact with their receptors. The receptors for smell are millions of hair cells in the olfactory epithelium, a membrane in the nasal passages. Taste receptors are specialized cells with hairlike endings grouped in taste buds in the tongue. As with other senses, these receptors are well protected and show variety in their receptivity to certain kinds of stimulation. For example, taste receptors are identified by how sensitive they are to sweet, sour, salty, or bitter stimuli.

5.25   A severe head cold can make food "taste" bland and unappealing. Why?

Generally, the word "taste" is used in too broad a sense. The reason a person with a severe head cold may find food unappetizing is that the person's smell receptors are disrupted by the head cold. It is more appropriate to say that the *flavor* of the food has been affected because flavor is a result of the interaction of taste and smell.

5.26   The skin (cutaneous) senses are of various types. What are these types, and how are they distributed?

Receptors for the skin senses appear to be sensitive to pressure, pain, warmth, and cold. The distribution of receptors is uneven, with only certain parts of the body having heavy concentrations of them. For example, the face and fingertips have numerous receptors, while the back has relatively few. It is interesting to note that the proportion of cortical tissue associated with the different skin areas of the body is comparable to the concentrations of receptors in those skin areas.

5.27   Athletes sometimes appear to "play through the pain." Using the gate-control theory, explain how this may occur.

The gate-control theory of pain suggests that signals can be sent that make an individual less sensitive to the pain experience. Two proposals explain this effect. The first says that activation of another (perhaps competing) set of neural receptors will block the signals from the pain receptors. The athlete might squeeze or rub the area surrounding the painful part of the body to create this effect. The second proposal suggests that psychological factors can initiate signals from the brain that close the gate to pain. The athlete creates a "I can't feel that now" reaction that shuts the gate to the pain signals.

5.28   Give an example of a kinesthetic sensation.

If a person stands on one foot, holds the other foot behind, and wiggles the toes, he or she will realize that the toes are wiggling because of kinesthetic reception. The toes cannot be seen, heard, tasted, smelled, or touched in such a position, yet the activity is recognized. Kinesthetic senses, which tell people about the activity of the muscles, joints, and tendons, are as much a basic sensory process as are the five senses mentioned above.

5.29   Explain why balance is considered a basic sensory process yet balancing oneself may depend on more than one sensory process.

Balance (vestibular reception) is considered a basic sensory process because there are specific receptors particularly concerned with this type of stimulation. These receptors are the three semicircular canals (located in the inner ear, very near the cochlea) and the vestibular sacs (located between the canals and the cochlea).

Balancing often is a function of more than one sensory process. Just as flavor is the combination of taste and smell, balancing may depend on vision, kinesthesis, and touch sensations as well as on strictly vestibular sensations.

5.30   After some kinds of movements, such as spinning, why does a person sometimes feel dizzy?

Assuming the person's nervous system is normal, dizziness may result when movement of the fluid in one or more of the semicircular canals does not terminate immediately when the body stops moving. In other words, the fluid continues to "slosh around" after the body has stopped moving, and signals sent from the affected hair cells are interpreted as dizziness.

5.31   A famous writer was hurt badly when struck by a minivan. The driver of the minivan admitted that he had been distracted by his dog. What term describes the situation experienced by the driver?

Taking his eyes off the road and trying to deal with the dog are best explained by referring to *selective attention*. All organisms must choose from the many sources of stimulation occurring at any given time. In this case, the driver's selectivity created a problem that led to the accident.

5.32   How is past experience important to perception?

Previous experience is very important to perception. Research studies have indicated that subjects must have experience with the environment to be able to perceive stimuli within it. Furthermore, a subject must be able to interact with these stimuli to develop perceptual skills. For example, one study compared the behavior of pairs of cats that were exposed to exactly the same environment. One cat in each pair was permitted to be active, while the other was allowed only to view the situation passively. The active cats were able to develop fairly sophisticated perceptual skills, whereas the passive cats could not.

5.33 The characteristics of a stimulus often are called external cues. Distinguish these cues from internal cues and explain why external cues may be very important in determining perception.

External cues are the properties of the stimulus environment. Internal cues are self-generated stimuli (usually in the form of thoughts) that may be the result of previous learning, motivation, or a particular set. External cues play an important role in determining whether or to what a subject will pay attention. Moreover, the particular qualities of an external cue affect the way in which a subject understands and interprets a stimulus.

5.34 Early in the development of psychology, one group of researchers showed particular concern with questions of perception and investigated them extensively. Who were they, what was the general statement describing their position, and how could that statement be worded in terms of sensation and perception?

The Gestalt psychologists were among the first to study perception. The statement that summarized their position was "the whole is greater than the sum of its parts." Reworded, that statement might read: "While each separate stimulus might be received and recognized as a sensation, the totality of stimuli and the interaction among stimuli form a perception, which is more than just the sum of the sensations received."

5.35 On the back cover of many popular magazines there are cigarette advertisements. Suppose you are now looking at such an ad. Describe the location of the cigarette pack and name the perceptual principle that was used to determine its position.

The cigarette pack probably is located off center and at an angle to the other features of the advertisement. The principle used in its placement is the figure-ground relationship, where the figure (or main feature) is made to "stand out" from the background by its position, angle, or other contrasting characteristics.

5.36 Distinguish between stable and unstable figure-ground relationships.

Many figure-ground relationships, such as the cigarette pack on the background, are stable. Others, however, are unstable—one cannot be certain which part of the stimulus is the figure and which is the ground. Figure 5-4 is an example of an unstable figure-ground relationship because it can be perceived as either a dark X on a light background or a light X on a dark background.

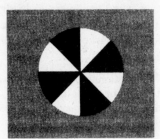

Fig. 5-4

5.37 What is an ambiguous figure? Give an example.

An ambiguous figure is one that can be interpreted in more than one way. Drawing (a) in Fig. 5-5 can be perceived as representing either drawing (b) or drawing (c). Place your hand over (c) and compare (a) and (*b*). Then place your hand over (*b*) and compare (*a*) and (*c*). Furthermore, it is impossible to tell whether the X in drawing (*a*) is on the front or back of the box.

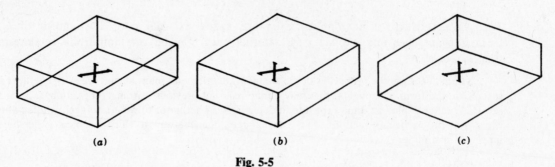

(*a*)   (*b*)   (*c*)

Fig. 5-5

5.38   Watching birds at a bird feeder, Karl is asked how many he has seen. He replies, "There have been about half a dozen sparrows, maybe four or five cardinals, a couple of blue jays, and one grackle." Explain how Karl's answer represents the Gestalt principle of similarity.

Asked how many birds he has seen, Karl does not give a simple count, such as "There have been about a dozen." Rather, he identifies and counts the birds seen by the similarity in breed that each has, grouping according to those similarities.

5.39   What are the Gestalt principles of proximity and good continuation? What typical effects do these principles have on perception?

Proximity states that stimuli that are close together physically will be grouped together and perceived as belonging together. Good continuation states that there is an uninterrupted "flow" of a stimulus. A person is likely to perceive a complex stimulus as a combination of continuous stimuli rather than a combination of discontinuous stimuli.

5.40   People who talk with a stutterer often feel the need to complete a word or sentence that the stutterer is having trouble completing. What perceptual principle does this tendency illustrate?

The principle described is closure, the tendency to complete an otherwise incomplete stimulus. Note, however, that the response "filled in" by the listener may be wrong, especially if the previous knowledge of what fits the situation differs between the speaker and the listener.

5.41   In Solved Problem 5.1, you were asked to imagine a bridge that you could see at some distance down the river. Although you were able to block out the image of the bridge with your hand, you still perceived that the bridge was large enough to span the river. What perceptual principle is operating in this situation?

The ability to interpret the "small" stimulus as a full-size bridge is characteristic of *size constancy*, the ability to recognize the consistent size of an object despite the varying stimulus presentations one receives. Size constancy is one of several perceptual constancies, which include shape, brightness, and color constancies.

5.42   Distinguish between monocular and binocular depth cues, giving examples of each. Related to this distinction, why does the demonstration of the blind spot (Solved Problem 5.15) require that one eye be closed or covered?

Monocular depth cues are properties of a stimulus that permit a viewer to perceive depth even if only one eye is used. *Interposition*, which occurs when one object partially blocks the vision of another;

perspective, the apparent "drawing together" of parallel lines as they recede into the distance; *texture gradient*, the coarseness or smoothness of the image seen; and *shadow* are all monocular depth cues. Binocular depth cues require that both eyes be involved in the visual process. *Retinal disparity*, the "blending" of the two images obtained by the eyes, and *convergence*, the muscular movement involved in focusing images on both eyes, are examples of binocular depth cues.

The blind spot illustrated in Solved Problem 5.15 is not experienced with binocular vision because the "information" missing at one eye's blind spot is probably *sensed* by the other eye (retinal disparity) and the brain is able to blend and complete the stimulus image.

5.43 A classroom demonstration (which you may want to do as you read this) involves the following sequence:

> The teacher says to the class, "Please respond aloud to the requests I make. Ready?"
> "How do you spell the word 'soap'?"
> **S ... O ... A ... P**
> "What do you do at a green light?"

If your initial reaction was to think or say "Stop" (which is what many students will do when responding out loud), what perceptual principle was illustrated?

Because the correct response (of course) is to say "Go," those who respond by saying "Stop" are illustrating the temporary tendency to respond in a certain, in this case incorrect, fashion. This is evidence of *set*, a momentary expectation established by the context of the situation.

5.44 Distinguish between bottom-up processing and top-down processing. Why is it thought that both types of processing must operate simultaneously for an individual to be able to have accurate perceptions of the environment?

Bottom-up processing refers to the recognition and processing of information found in individual components of a stimulus situation. *Top-down processing* describes the selection and interpretation process applied to the stimulus situation, usually a function of both previous experience and the current motivation and expectation conditions that exist. Evidence indicates that both types of processing occur simultaneously, with each being dependent in some ways on the other. For instance, the italic *f* used in Example 5.24 is very much like Old English script for the letter *s*. Obviously, the context of seeing the word "paffage" in a sentence "The passage was open" would influence the bottom-up processing of the *f*, and the reader would be likely to interpret the word and sentence correctly.

5.45 Suppose a person looking at Fig. 5-6 says that the vertical line is longer than the horizontal line. (The lines are actually the same length.) Is this an example of an illusion or a hallucination? What is the difference between an illusion and a hallucination?

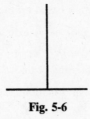

Fig. 5-6

The arrangement of the two lines creates an *illusion*, which is a misperception of a stimulus situation that really exists. A hallucination is a perception of something that does *not* exist, such as seeing an object or hearing a voice that is not really there.

5.46   What is subliminal perception?

Subliminal perception refers to situations in which a person supposedly responds to stimuli that are just below threshold (limen) value. In general, research has shown that subliminal techniques for modifying behavior (for example, sleeping with a tape recorder beside the bed playing information that will be on tomorrow's exam) have not been successful. However, the same studies have shown that the expectations people bring to such situations have an effect on the behavior they show.

5.47   Solved Problem 5.6 presented the concept of sensory adaptation to overload or deprivation of stimulation. What happens to perception if such conditions are maintained at an extreme level for a prolonged period?

Apparently, prolonged periods of extreme deprivation or overload may exceed a person's usual capacity for sensory adaptation. This sometimes results in unusual patterns of responding, such as hallucinations and other attempts to perceive an environment that is more "normal."

5.48   Why do psychologists tend to discount extrasensory perception (ESP) as a part of psychological study?

The difficulty with ESP seems to result from the unreliability of the phenomena. They cannot be produced with consistency or regularity and are very difficult to study scientifically. Many ESP reports are made after the fact and may be subject to misinterpretation because of the time lag between the event and the report. It is difficult to confirm or disconfirm most ESP research.

5.49   What types of ESP have been reported? What are the differences among them?

Four different types of ESP have been reported: *telepathy*, the transfer of thought from one person to another without external stimuli; *precognition*, the ability to predict the future correctly; *clairvoyance*, the ability to report events not detectable by normal sensory processes; and *psychokinesis*, the ability to move objects without exerting physical force on them.

Key Terms

Absolute threshold.   The lowest level of a stimulus at which its presence or absence can be detected correctly 50 percent of the time.

Auditory localization.   Identifying the direction from which a sound was produced; often a function of the slight discrepancy between the times at which the signal reaches the ears.

Binocular depth cues.   Cues to depth perception based on the simultaneous functioning of two eyes.

Blind spot.   The area in the retina where the optic nerve exits to the brain; no vision is possible here because there are no receptors.

Bottom-up processing.   Recognition and processing of information about individual components of stimuli.

Clairvoyance.   The disclosure of knowledge or information that could not have been received through regular sensory channels.

Closure.   In perception, filling in or completing an "incomplete" stimulus or piece of information.

Cochlea.   The structure within the inner ear that transduces the mechanical energy of sound waves into signals for hearing.

Color.   The hue of a visual stimulus; determined by the wavelength of the light.

Cones.   The visual receptors which function primarily in lighted conditions; they are located toward the center of the retina and provide color vision.

Difference threshold.   The minimum change in stimulus value that can be identified correctly as a change 50 percent of the time; also known as the *just noticeable difference* (*j.n.d.*).

Extrasensory perception (ESP).   Correct interpretation or manipulation of the environment in the absence of regular sensory processes.

Feature detectors.   Specialized neurons in the visual cortex activated only by stimuli of a specific shape or pattern.

Figure-ground relationship.   The distinctiveness from or interconnection of the principal stimulus (figure) with surrounding stimuli (ground).

Flavor.   A combination of taste and smell; the term most appropriately used in discussing food.

Fovea.   The area in the center of the retina containing only cones; the point of maximum visual acuity.

Gate-control theory of pain.   A proposal that there are receptors that can send signals which make an individual more or less sensitive to pain.

Hallucination.   A perception of "stimuli" that actually do not exist.

Illusion.   Stimuli that exist in a configuration that creates a misinterpretation or incorrect perception.

Interposition.   A monocular depth cue in which one object appears closer to the viewer because it partly blocks the view of another object.

Kinesthesis.   The sensations concerned with perception of body position and body movement.

Monocular depth cues.   Cues to depth perception that are dependent on only one eye; perspective and interposition are examples.

Noise.   In detection theory, the term used to describe extraneous stimuli.

Opponent-process theory.   An explanation of color vision that proposes activity of retinal receptors in competing or opposing pairs (e.g., if red is activated at a point in the retina, green cannot be activated at the same point).

Ossicles.   The three bones of the middle ear (malleus, incus, stapes) that transfer vibrations from the eardrum to the oval window of the cochlea.

Perception.   Basically, the interpretation or understanding of sensory receptions.

Perceptual constancy.   Understanding or interpreting that a stimulus has not changed even though the sensation from that stimulus varies.

Perspective.   A monocular depth cue in which perception of distance is based on previous knowledge of size-distance and shape-slant relationships.

Precognition.   The correct prediction of events that have not yet occurred.

Psychokinesis.   The capacity to make objects move by using only thought processes.

Psychophysics.   The measurement of the functioning of the senses.

Receptor.   A specialized nerve ending that is sensitive to a particular type of stimulus.

Retina.   The part of the eye containing the receptors for vision; located at the back of the eyeball.

Retinal disparity.   The fact that visual images on the retinas of the two eyes are never exactly the same at any moment.

Rods.   The visual receptors which function primarily in dim or dark conditions; they are located toward the periphery of the retina and operate only in a black-and-white dimension.

Selective attention.   The process by which organisms choose from among many sources of stimulation.

Semicircular canals.   Three tubes in the inner ear; they are filled with fluid and are sensitive to changes in body and head orientation.

Sensation.   The process which detects, judges, and identifies stimuli.

Sensory adaptation.   The process of adjustment to unusual levels of stimulation.

Sensory deprivation.   Extreme restriction of the sensory environment.

Sensory overload.   An excessive amount of stimulation.

Set.   The temporary tendency or expectation to respond in a certain manner.

Signal detection theory.   A theory that stresses the effects of motivation, stimulus probability, and extraneous stimuli on the decision regarding the presence or absence of a given stimulus or a change in stimulus value.

Subliminal perception.   The supposed reception and understanding of stimulation presented at a level slightly below the threshold value.

Taste buds.   Receptors for taste; located in the pits of the tongue.

Telepathy.   The transfer of thought from one person to another without the use of regular sensory channels.

Texture gradient.   The change in the appearance of texture based on distance from the viewer; a monocular depth cue.

Threshold.   The level of stimulation necessary for reception to occur.

Top-down processing.   Interpretation of sensations based on previous experience or other cognitive factors.

Transduction.   The change of stimulus energy into an action potential.

Trichromatic theory.   A popular explanation of color vision based on the idea that there are three types of cones that are sensitive, respectively, to red, green, and blue.

Vestibular sense.   Balance; the function of the three semicircular canals and the vestibular sacs.

Visible spectrum.   The range of wavelengths of light received by humans.

Weber's law.   The relationship which states that a just noticeable difference is a constant proportion of the intensity of the original stimulus.

CHAPTER 6

Consciousness

Consciousness is the term for the internal mental experiences of which a person is aware. These experiences may include sensations, thoughts, feelings, and an awareness of the self, others, and the world around a person. There may be an interaction between these mental experiences and the physiological processes of the body, but the definition of consciousness is limited to the internal characteristics that make up a person's mental experiences. Note, however, that not all conscious experience falls in the same realm; psychologists are interested in "altered states of consciousness" and "expanded consciousness" as well as the experiences described above.

6.1 CHARACTERISTICS OF CONSCIOUSNESS

Many types of consciousness may be experienced by an individual. A few examples are thoughts and ideas, feelings, attention, memories, control of one's behavior, and dreams. It appears that consciousness is a function of brain activity and that each individual may have several consciousnesses.

Levels of Consciousness.   Starting with proposals advanced by Sigmund Freud, differing levels of consciousness have been accepted by many psychologists. Most commonly, in addition to consciousness, both preconscious and unconscious (or subconscious) levels have been thought to be important for behavior.

A *preconscious* level consists of information that could reach conscious consideration easily but is not continuously in awareness. Included in this level are automatic behaviors such as driving a car and throwing a ball.

EXAMPLE 6.1.   It is very unlikely that as you read this sentence you are thinking about your relatives. Yet as soon as the topic is raised, it is possible for you to call forth the names of brothers, sisters, uncles, aunts, parents, or other relatives with little or no difficulty. Such information is at a preconscious level—not always in awareness but readily available.

The *unconscious* (or *subconscious*) level is thought to be much less readily accessible. Information stored at the unconscious level often cannot be recalled or, if it is, requires considerable effort to access.

EXAMPLE 6.2.   Freud suggested that information at the unconscious level may be there because it is upsetting and has been purposely forgotten or repressed (see Chapter 12 for a more thorough explanation of repression). Recovering such information may require therapy or another special effort.

Differentiation of Consciousness. By using techniques such as *electroencephalography* (*EEG*), *magnetic resonance imaging* (*MRI*), *computerized axial tomography* (*CAT*) *scans*, and *positron emission tomography* (*PET*) *scans*, psychologists and neuroscientists have been able to monitor and record activity in certain parts of the brain. The type of activity observed may vary as the subject's state of consciousness changes, but different states of consciousness do not necessarily show markedly different types of brain activity.

EXAMPLE 6.3. Consider your recollection of waking events as opposed to your recollection of dreams. The activity of the brain is very similar in both states of consciousness, yet dreams often include illogical, dramatic, or vivid mental experiences that differ very much from mental experiences in a waking state. You may dream of flying by flapping your arms, but such a mental experience would not fit into your usual waking consciousness.

Psychologists distinguish conscious processes in terms of control. Some tasks require *controlled processing*, in which full concentration is necessary for the task to be completed. Other tasks are completed without full awareness, requiring little concentration and operating with what has been called *automatic processing*. Many tasks advance from controlled to automatic processing as familiarity with a task increases.

EXAMPLE 6.4. Think about learning to use the keyboard of a computer. Initial attempts require great concentration to learn the location of the letters, numbers, and command keys. As one develops familiarity with the task, however, the "typing" becomes automatic and soon allows other mental processes, such as creating the paragraph being typed, to occur simultaneously.

There are other indications that an individual has more than one level or state of consciousness. Split-brain studies (see Section 3.3) have revealed that the left and right hemispheres of the brain may have different conscious processes. Studies also have shown that some individuals demonstrate abnormal personality patterns, appearing to have multiple personalities, with unique conscious processes accompanying each personality.

EXAMPLE 6.5. Famous depictions of cases of multiple personalities appear in the movies *The Three Faces of Eve* and *Sybil*. Based on actual clinical cases, these movies showed the totally separate and quite dissimilar personality patterns of certain female clients.

Limitations of Consciousness. Limitations of consciousness can be documented in at least three ways. First, if brain processes are disrupted or destroyed, conscious process may be upset or eliminated. Consciousness is a function of the brain and therefore depends on the appropriate operation of the brain.

A second limitation is found even when all brain functioning is normal. Similar to the effect of attention on perception (see Section 5.4), consciousness is limited to the person's capacity to receive and process information. In general, a person can concentrate on only one thought at a time, although switching from one thought to another often is accomplished very rapidly.

Third, environmental conditions may alter conscious processes. Interruptions, conditions of sensory deprivation or overload, fatigue, and ecstasy are examples of interferences that may place limitations on a person's consciousness.

Finally, behaviors such as meditation (see Section 6.2) and drugs such as LSD (see Section 6.3) seem to affect the limitations of consciousness, producing a so-called expansion of consciousness. Conditions considered to be outside the normal range of consciousness are referred to as *altered states of consciousness*. However, even these states seem to have limits.

6.2 ALTERED STATES OF CONSCIOUSNESS: INTERNAL INFLUENCES

Consciousness may be influenced by both internal states and external stimuli. Internal influences on consciousness may be the result of purposeful or nonpurposeful behavior on the part of an individual. Frequently, the decision to act or think in a certain manner is a function of the social restrictions a person has learned from past experience in a particular society, but many altered states of consciousness, such as sleep, seem not to be affected by social controls.

Sleep. Some of the most widely studied conscious processes are those which occur during sleep. Extensive research has shown that several variables are significant in the study of sleeping and associated dreaming.

Circadian Rhythms. Humans appear to have a biological clock that operates in a regular, rhythmic fashion. This "clock" develops as a child becomes accustomed to particular environmental circumstances, resulting in daily rhythms (*circadian rhythms*) of behavior such as hunger, body temperature, hormonal flow, and sleeping. These rhythms usually match the 24-hour day, although research has shown that a person placed in an environment where time cues are completely eliminated may establish a rhythm on a shorter or longer cycle. A person whose sleep patterns are upset may require a period of adjustment (often several days) before a new, workable sleep pattern is established.

EXAMPLE 6.6. College students frequently find that rhythmic patterns control perceived hunger. If a student is accustomed to eating a midday meal at noon, a new term's schedule that requires attending a class at that time may be difficult to cope with at first. It is likely to take several days before "hunger pangs" seem to be delayed until the class is over.

Sleep Rhythms. Sleep not only occurs at rhythmic times during the 24-hour day but also shows rhythmic patterns within the sleeping period. Research done mostly with subjects willing to sleep in laboratory situations has identified four different *stages of sleep*, or depths of sleep, by recording changes in EEG frequencies and magnitudes. A person is likely to move through this four-stage cycle several times during a night's sleep.

In general, stage 1 sleep is preceded by *alpha* brain waves (a rhythm of approximately 10 cycles per second), which are then replaced by slower, more irregular *theta* waves. The period just before sleep actually begins often is referred to as a *hypnagogic state*. Stage 2 includes continued theta activity, together with occasional *spindles* (bursts of 14-cycle-per-second activity), while in stage 3, *delta* waves (2 cycles per second) are added. Finally, stage 4 shows almost exclusive delta wave activity. This series of stages is marked by a slowing of brain wave activity and accompanied by reduced responsiveness to outside stimuli. It usually lasts about 90 minutes.

REM Sleep. At the end of each 90-minute sleep cycle, a period of heightened brain activity, increased cerebral blood flow, and *rapid eye movement (REM)* occurs. Waking someone during this period produces the report of a dream more than 80 percent of the time. (Waking someone during non-REM sleep produces reports of dreams less than 15 percent of the time.) *Rapid-eye movement (REM) sleep* gets longer with each successive sleep cycle, often lasting 30 to 60 minutes by the end of a night's sleep.

REM sleep sometimes is called *paradoxical sleep* because the subject's heart rate, respiration rate, and EEG patterns closely resemble those observed when the subject is awake. Interestingly, however, activity of the cranial and spinal motor neurons is inhibited during this period, leading to loss of muscle tone and a considerably diminished chance of movement.

EXAMPLE 6.7. Studies have shown that some patients suffering from severe depression have disturbing dreams during REM sleep and awaken only to be more depressed. One form of therapy incorporates interrupting REM sleep (to prevent such dreams) or teaching these patients to interrupt a dream and create a more pleasant ending for the dream "script." The symptoms of depression often improve when therapies such as these are used.

Dreams.   Dreams appear to be a part of almost everyone's behavior, although some people are much more capable of recalling dreams than are others. Some research has suggested that dreams serve a recuperative function. If REM sleep is not allowed to occur for several sleeping periods in a row, irritability, anxiety, and even hallucinations may result. Given the opportunity to sleep without interruption, people deprived of REM sleep show a "rebound effect," incorporating more than the usual amount of REM sleep into the sleep pattern. Interestingly, sleepwalking and sleep talking usually do not occur during REM sleep and do not seem to be coordinated with dreams that are remembered upon awakening.

Several explanations for why people dream have been proposed. Probably the best known is that of Sigmund Freud, who suggested that dreams represent unconscious wish fulfillment. Freud also thought that dreams often might threaten conscious awareness and distinguished between the *manifest content* of the dream (the actual "script" of the dream) and the *latent content*, or symbolic meaning, of the dream. Dream analysis was thought to be an important source of information for psychotherapy. Other explanations of dreaming are likely to focus less on threat than on the need to dream as a means of dealing with daily concerns or "cleaning house" mentally. Little agreement has been reached regarding the functions of dreaming.

Restorative Function of Sleep.   Evidence has accumulated to support the belief that sleep serves a restorative function. Sleep deprivation can produce intense fatigue, perceptual distortion, diminished cerebral functioning, and disruption of bodily processes. It is known, for example, that the pituitary gland releases growth hormone only during slow-wave sleep stages. This may be why children appear to need more sleep than adults do.

Sleep Disorders.   Not all people experience smooth patterns of sleeping. Disturbances take several forms, including insomnia, sleep apnea, narcolepsy, and somnambulism (sleepwalking). *Insomnia*, the inability to fall asleep, is the most common sleep disorder. It may occur at the start of the sleeping period or may be experienced as waking during the night and being unable to fall asleep again. *Sleep apnea* is marked by complete stoppage of breathing for a few seconds to more than a minute. Associated with obesity and alcohol use in adults, sleep apnea also is thought to be a possible cause of sudden infant death syndrome (SIDS) in children. Sudden, uncontrollable attacks of sleep during the normal waking period mark *narcolepsy*. A narcoleptic usually sleeps for about 15 to 20 minutes with each incident. Narcolepsy can be dangerous if, for example, the sleeping urge occurs while one is operating machinery. *Somnambulism* (or *sleepwalking*) typically occurs during non-REM sleep. Most incidents of sleepwalking occur in children, who typically outgrow the behavior as they grow older, although some adults experience sleepwalking. Most sleepwalkers do not remember the incident upon awakening.

EXAMPLE 6.8.   The disorder of sleepwalking has taken on legal considerations. Several cases of spousal abuse or murder have been attributed to sleepwalking behavior. Juries have had to decide if the behavior truly was sleepwalking and if the person had no memory of the actions.

Meditation.   *Meditation* techniques are used to try to "focus" conscious processes in a manner unlike that used in everyday circumstances. Two types of meditation are employed frequently: concentrative meditation and opening-up meditation.

Concentrative Meditation.   *Concentrative meditation* limits conscious attention to a specific object or sound in an attempt to narrow attention to that direction only and block out other stimuli from the environment. The result of concentrative meditation is supposed to be a state of emptiness or void accompanied by increased clarity of thought.

Opening-Up Meditation.   *Opening-up meditation* is an attempt to develop continuous attention to everything that is happening. This technique is supposed to produce a broad understanding of the total environment.

EXAMPLE 6.9.   One form of opening-up meditation occurs when the individual performs typical daily activities in a slightly different manner. This change in routine is supposed to allow the person to become more aware of the totality of experience and to develop a new focus or attention within that environment.

Both techniques produce changed states of consciousness for some users. Many meditators claim profound benefits from meditation, including increased understanding of the self and the relationship of the self to the environment. Sometimes meditation is accompanied by changes in physiological processes such as those found in biofeedback. Meditation even has been used as therapy for drug abuse.

Biofeedback.   *Biofeedback* is a technique in which a person can observe measurements of bodily processes that are otherwise unobservable. The individual is then able to find ways to regulate processes, such as heart rate and blood pressure, that usually are thought to be involuntary physiological responses. Frequently this is accomplished by using a monitoring device that indicates the status of the otherwise "hidden" variable. As the person learns to control the bodily process, this is reflected by a change in the signal. The feedback provides information that helps the person focus conscious processes in order to manipulate the bodily activity.

EXAMPLE 6.10.   Evidence indicates that migraine headaches may result from excessive blood flow in the brain area. To overcome this process, biofeedback techniques have been used to teach a person to adjust blood flow so that more blood goes to other parts of the body, such as the hands or feet, thus decreasing the headache symptoms. The monitoring device helps the person learn conscious control of blood flow increases to areas other than the head.

6.3   ALTERED STATES OF CONSCIOUSNESS: EXTERNAL INFLUENCES

External stimuli may influence an individual's consciousness in many ways. The use of drugs, accidental or intentional damage to brain tissue, and hypnosis all fall within the category of external influences.

Psychoactive Drugs.   *Psychoactive drugs* are drugs that affect the central nervous system, causing subjective changes in perception, emotion, and other conscious processes. These agents include depressant drugs, narcotic drugs, stimulants, hallucinogens, and many more. The primary reason for using psychoactive drugs appears to be social influence from peers. Other reasons for use may involve a physical problem such as insomnia, or a psychological need such as relief from anxiety. The study of the psychological effect of drugs is called *psychopharmacology*.

Psychologists make several distinctions regarding behaviors associated with drugs. First, they distinguish between *drug use*, where no impairment or actions harmful to others seem to occur, and *drug abuse*, where users' daily actions or health may be significantly impaired and harmful actions toward others may result.

EXAMPLE 6.11.   A casual alcoholic drink with friends at an evening party constitutes drug use but is unlikely to result in drug abuse. Repeated binge drinking that impairs health, jeopardizes others (for example, driving while intoxicated), or impairs normal functioning on the job would be classified as drug abuse. Interestingly, some forms of abuse may not be readily recognized: Many people abuse the intake of caffeine, drinking coffee or soft drinks to the extent that failure to have the beverages causes various forms of impairment.

Psychologists also distinguish between *physiological drug dependence* and *psychological drug dependence*. Physiological drug dependence occurs when the use of a drug causes a change in the body's chemical balance and only continued use can maintain that changed status. Psychological drug dependence is the continued belief that the drug is needed even if the physical demand has been eliminated. The use of many drugs leads to both physical *and* psychological dependence.

EXAMPLE 6.12.   Many people recognize the dependencies associated with drugs when they try to quit smoking. The physiological need for nicotine (one of the active components associated with smoking) persists for several weeks after one stops smoking. Even when the physiological need has dissipated completely and is no longer a concern, many people find that the psychological draw of smoking is difficult to overcome, thinking of smoking as a stress reliever or a social necessity.

As the body becomes accustomed to the use of a drug, it often develops a *drug tolerance*, meaning that the effect produced by the drug can be achieved only if a greater amount is used. Stopping the use of drugs often leads to *withdrawal effects*, which are unpleasant side effects produced by the body's compensatory or tolerance mechanisms.

Depressants.   Also known as "downers," central nervous system (CNS) depressants slow the operation of the CNS. In therapeutic use, they often are prescribed to relieve anxiety or combat insomnia.

Alcohol.   Alcohol, a depressant, is one of the most widely used psychoactive drugs. When taken in sufficient quantities (which vary from one individual to the next), alcohol can depress certain aspects of CNS functioning, causing conscious reactions that differ noticeably from those produced in a nonalcoholic state. The mental "high" produced by alcohol ingestion is accompanied by lowered inhibitions and impairment of motor coordination. Extreme excessive use can cause death.

EXAMPLE 6.13.   The flirtatiousness of a person at a cocktail party may be the result of the depression of certain brain activity by alcohol. Continued drinking may lead to continued changes in brain activity, with the result that the "life of the party" may become hostile, lose motor coordination, and even pass out.

Barbiturates.   Another category of depressant drugs is barbiturates. These drugs frequently are prescribed by physicians to induce sleep (counteracting insomnia, for example) or relieve stress. Nembutal and Seconal are common barbiturates.

Narcotic Drugs.   *Narcotic drugs* are agents that relieve anxiety, produce relaxation, or reduce pain. Abuse of the two most common narcotic drugs, *heroin* and *morphine*, has become widespread. Initial misuse of narcotics commonly occurs for social reasons, but repeated dosages lead to a physiological dependence that continues to increase. This dependence has two aspects, the need for larger doses to prevent withdrawal symptoms (which can be quite severe) and the need for larger doses to produce the euphoric effect. Often, satisfaction of these needs leads to illegal activities to procure the narcotic.

Stimulants.   Drugs that elevate heart rate, blood pressure, and muscle tension are referred to as *stimulants*. Included in this category are drugs such as caffeine, nicotine, amphetamines, and cocaine.

Caffeine is present in many commonly used products, including coffee, tea, soft drinks, and chocolate. Many people develop a physiological dependence on caffeine, often without recognizing that this is the case.

EXAMPLE 6.14.   Evidence for caffeine dependence is found in the "weekend headache." Many people become accustomed to early-morning ingestion of coffee, tea, or soft drinks but vary this routine on the weekend. Failure to have the early-morning beverage produces headaches and in some cases may produce depression as well.

Nicotine, which is present in tobacco products, activates neurons in much the same manner as does *cocaine*, although the effects of cocaine are thought to be more pronounced. Both, however, are highly addictive.

Cocaine creates feelings of euphoria, confidence, and physical and mental alertness. The fastest-acting version of cocaine is "crack," which is smoked and therefore enters the bloodstream, affecting the brain, within seconds. In extreme cases, prolonged use of cocaine or "crack" can lead to psychotic behavior, including hallucinations, delusions, and extreme emotional disturbance.

Amphetamines, such as Benzedrine or Dexedrine, are popularly known as "speed." The use of amphetamines in relatively small amounts usually produces increased alertness, a sense of energy, and positive emotional feelings. When used excessively or for a prolonged periods, amphetamines can produce feelings of persecution, negative emotions, and even convulsions or death.

Hallucinogenic Drugs. Many psychologists classify *marijuana* as a *hallucinogenic drug*. Smoking marijuana or eating it after it has been cooked may produce a psychoactive drug effect. Often the marijuana "high" is a state of elation in which the user claims an enrichment of sensory experiences.

Research into the effects of marijuana has shown that the effects produced may be a function not only of the amount and characteristics of the marijuana used but also of the expectations of the user. Motivation, past experience, and many other variables may create potential effects greater or lesser than those expected from the properties of the marijuana itself. Some studies have suggested a *reverse tolerance effect* in which less drug is needed to produce the same "high." This seems attributable to expectations and familiarity with the techniques for using the drug.

EXAMPLE 6.15. Expectations sometimes produce remarkable effects. People have been known to get "drunk" when drinking cola or "high" when smoking oregano. The social setting, a person's beliefs, and many additional factors contribute to such behavior.

Other hallucinogenic drugs, such as *LSD*, *PCP*, and *mescaline*, are available legally only in controlled circumstances such as medical research. These drugs typically produce strong hallucinations, with extreme distortion of "normal world" experiences. One characteristic of these drugs is that the effect produced by their use cannot be predicted reliably. It is even difficult to predict whether the mental experiences that result will be considered favorable or unfavorable. In addition, with LSD particularly, users report "flashbacks" long after the initial use of the drug.

Hypnosis. Dramatic demonstrations of external control of consciousness often are provided by *hypnosis*. Not all people are equally susceptible to hypnosis. Five to 10 percent of the population cannot be hypnotized at all, while a similar percentage can reach deep hypnotic trances. However, the effects of hypnosis tend to be similar for most people between these extremes.

A hypnotized individual accepts the hypnotist's directions, showing little or no emotional feeling (unless prompted to do so) and increased suggestibility. The hypnotist usually can restrict or direct the subject's attention. Furthermore, a hypnotized subject may experience a distorted perception of reality or show pronounced relaxation or alertness, depending on the hypnotist's instructions. People who achieve a very deep hypnotic state often report a feeling of a mystical experience, but some psychologists believe that reports of hypnotic states are "faked behaviors" that represent the subjects' desire to please or satisfy the hypnotist.

EXAMPLE 6.16. One use of hypnosis that has had much media attention is that of trying to increase or enhance memory by using the technique. Victims of crimes have been hypnotized in attempts to generate memories that will reveal something about the crime and lead to capturing the criminal. While some dramatic cases appear to support this use of hypnosis, such as remembering the license plate number of a vehicle used in a crime, the general finding is that success in using the technique in this manner is not well substantiated.

Brain Damage.   Consciousness may be affected by certain types of brain damage, including both accidental damage and some intentional surgical techniques.

EXAMPLE 6.17.   The case of Phineas Gage is renowned in psychology as one of the first documented examples of the effects of the destruction of brain tissue on conscious processes. Struck in a work accident by a piece of pipe that entered his eye socket and exited through the front top portion of the skull, Gage lived but lost brain tissue in the region of the frontal lobe. Very noticeable changes in his behavior were noted, especially in his emotional reactions to certain events. The loss of brain tissue apparently changed his way of responding, while all other variables remained basically the same.

The most obvious example of a surgical effect on consciousness is the split-brain procedure, which separates the functioning of the two cerebral hemispheres by dividing the corpus callosum (see Section 3.3). The separated hemispheres show individualized consciousnesses and in some cases respond differently to the same stimulus.

It is not possible to predict all the effects that may be produced by damage to the brain, whether accidental or intentional. Changes in emotional reactions, memory skills, or perceptual understandings have been demonstrated by testing patients before and after surgery. However, mapping of the brain is not complete enough for consistently accurate predictions to be made.

Solved Problems

6.1   A person may say, "My consciousness is personal." Is such a statement true, and if it is, how can psychologists investigate consciousness?

Consciousness includes mental experiences—such as thoughts, dreams, and perceptions—of which only the individual may be aware. Thus, these experiences are personal. However, psychologists can study consciousness by soliciting verbal reports of these processes or inferring from observable behaviors what kinds of conscious processes are going on.

6.2   In addition to the mental experiences of which a person is aware—consciousness—psychologists distinguish two other levels of mental activity. What are these levels, and how do they differ?

Psychologists identify preconscious and unconscious (or subconscious) levels of mental activity. The preconscious level refers to thoughts, ideas, and memories that are not currently active but can be called to conscious awareness with relative ease. Remembering multiplication values such as $7 \times 6 = 42$ represents the preconscious level of mental activity. The unconscious level, also sometimes called the subconscious level, refers to thoughts, ideas, and memories that are *not* readily available to conscious awareness. Sigmund Freud suggested that these thoughts were repressed, that is, purposely forgotten because of potential threat or upset that could occur if they were remembered.

6.3   Think about tying a shoelace. Does this represent controlled processing or automatic processing? Why?

For most people who have considerable experience, tying a shoelace represents automatic processing. Other conscious tasks can be accomplished (for example, a conversation) while the shoelace is being tied. For a young child, however, who is only beginning to learn how to tie the shoelace, controlled processing is required. Full concentration is necessary for the child to be able to complete the task.

6.4   Do there seem to be limitations on the kinds and intensity of consciousness a person can experience?

Three types of evidence point to limitations of consciousness. First, disruption or damage to the brain may limit consciousness. A person's consciousness thus seems to depend on the functioning of the brain. Second, even when the brain is functioning properly, a person's capacity to receive and process information is limited by learning and other previous experiences. Third, conditions in the stimulus environment, such as sensory overload or deprivation and disruptions, limit consciousness.

6.5   What kinds of disruption might affect a person's conscious processes?

Interference by an outside stimulus may disrupt conscious processes. (A person may accuse another of "interrupting my train of thought" when this happens.) Other environmental or personal conditions also may disrupt consciousness. These conditions include things such as sensory deprivation, fatigue, and ecstasy.

6.6   A major influence creating internal control of consciousness seems to be social learning. What kinds of effects might be expected from social learning?

Most simply stated, social learning may lead to the facilitation or inhibition of conscious processes. That is, learning may "encourage" or "discourage" certain kinds of mental experiences in a person's consciousness. For example, if a well-trained botanist and a well-trained geologist hiked through a forest together, it would be very likely that each would have a distinctly different consciousness of the experience.

6.7   Do conscious processes go on even when a person is asleep? Are there different consciousnesses which exist within one person?

Consciousness appears to be an active brain process. When the brain is functioning normally, conscious processes may occur. Because the brain functions during sleep, dreams are included in the category of conscious processes. Someone who is unconscious (perhaps in a coma) does not appear to have comparable brain functioning.

Several consciousnesses appear to exist in one person. Not only is there a sleeping consciousness and a waking consciousness, but split-brain research, for example, indicates a left-hemisphere consciousness that is separate from the right-hemisphere consciousness. Furthermore, research in abnormal personality patterns has revealed rare cases of multiple personalities, that is, individuals with more than one distinctive set of personality characteristics accompanied by independent sets of conscious processes.

6.8   Explain how "jet lag"—the fatigue and disorientation experienced by air travelers who have flown a great distance—may be the result of circadian rhythm.

Circadian rhythm is the term used to label the "biological clock" each individual develops. Eventually, as a child grows older, a pattern is established for activities such as sleeping and bodily functions such as temperature regulation. This pattern "fits" observable time cues such as darkness and daylight.

A traveler who has crossed several time zones in a short period (as in a transoceanic jet flight) will experience tiredness at the "wrong times." The circadian rhythms the traveler established in one time zone will not match the time cues of another time zone. For example, the traveler may feel wide awake at midnight and exhausted at noon. It may take several days for the traveler's circadian rhythms to adjust to the new time zone.

6.9   Sleep often is described as occurring in stages. How are these stages identified?

The stages of sleep are identified by differences in EEG patterns, the measure of brain waves. Four levels have been agreed upon, based in general on the reduction in frequency and the increase in magnitude of the brain waves.

In addition, sleeping stages have been divided into periods accompanied by rapid eye movement (REM) and those where no rapid eye movement is observed (non-REM).

Both the depth of sleep, identified as the four stages, and the REM periods appear to be cyclical in nature. The sleeping cycles repeat themselves at roughly 80- to 90-minute intervals throughout a typical eight-hour night's sleep.

6.10 Is REM activity marked by particular EEG patterns? Other than eye-movement activity, what difference exists between REM and non-REM sleep?

REM sleep occurs almost exclusively after the four-stage sleep cycle has been completed such that it can be considered as preceding or as the first part of stage 1 sleep. There is both heightened brain activity and increased cerebral blood flow during REM sleep. REM sleep differs from non-REM sleep in that most dreaming appears to occur during REM sleep. Research reports show that waking from REM sleep yields an account of a dream about 80 percent of the time, while the percentage is about 15 percent when non-REM sleep is interrupted.

6.11 Explain why REM sleep sometimes is called paradoxical sleep.

The term *paradoxical sleep* is used to describe REM sleep because during REM sleep several bodily functions—such as EEG, heart rate, and breathing—operate in patterns very similar to those found in a waking state. Dreaming, the conscious activity of sleep, appears to occur most frequently in REM sleep. Other bodily functions, such as responses to external stimuli and muscle tone, are similar in REM sleep to those present during deep sleep.

6.12 Dreams have been a subject of great interest for the general population. Now that psychologists have subjected dreams to careful study, what are some of the basic understandings that have developed?

A very basic principle is that almost everyone seems to dream. A second finding is that dreaming is good for a person. Repeated interruption of REM sleep for several days has been shown to cause irritability, anxiety, and even hallucinations in some cases. People deprived of REM sleep show a "rebound effect" when given the opportunity to sleep in uninterrupted patterns, incorporating more than the usual amount of REM sleep into the nightly pattern. Also, if REM sleep is accepted as evidence of dreaming, the differences which appear to exist among individuals lie in the ability to *recall* dreams rather than in the ability to experience them.

6.13 Distinguish between the manifest content and the latent content of a dream.

Sigmund Freud proposed that dreams may represent unconscious wish fulfillment. While the manifest content of the dream—the actual content of what is dreamed—may seem strange, confusing, or innocuous, Freud believed there could be symbolic meaning to the ideas expressed in the dream. He called these ideas the latent content of the dream and believed that being able to expose the "real" meaning of the dream could be helpful in psychotherapy.

6.14 Are sleepwalking and sleep talking functions of dreams?

Research evidence supports the idea that both sleepwalking and sleep talking usually do not occur during REM-sleep dreaming periods but during stage 2, 3, or 4 sleep. Dreams recalled the following morning usually have little or no connection with the sleepwalking or sleep talking periods.

6.15 Tomas finds that he wakes during the night and then cannot get back to sleep. What sleep disorder is Tomas experiencing? What other common sleep disorders have been studied by psychologists?

Tomas's inability to get back to sleep is a form of insomnia. The most common sleep disorder, insomnia also occurs frequently when a person is unable to get to sleep at the start of the sleep period.

Other common sleep disorders that have been studied include sleep apnea, the complete stoppage of breathing during sleep for a few seconds to more than a minute; narcolepsy, which is marked by sudden, uncontrollable attacks of sleep during the normal waking period; and somnambulism, or sleepwalking.

6.16   Describe the basic types of meditation.

Meditation techniques fall into two main categories: concentrative meditation and opening-up meditation. Concentrative meditation establishes a single point of focus, such as a *mantra* (a personal chant given to the learner by the meditation instructor), and restricts attention to that focus. Opening-up meditation is an attempt to pay complete attention to the total stimulus environment. It is supposed to produce complete perception of the world at that moment, while concentrative meditation produces as its aftereffect a "clearness of thought" about the world.

6.17   What is biofeedback, and why might it be used?

Biofeedback is the term popularly used to describe situations in which an individual, through observation, is able to gain control over physiological processes that are not ordinarily under voluntary control. In general, the procedure used is to create a signal that allows the individual to monitor functions that are otherwise difficult or impossible to observe.

As the person becomes accustomed to the situation, research evidence indicates that the ability to concentrate on the feedback allows the development of control over the physiological functions. Thus, heart rate, blood flow, blood pressure, respiration rate, and EEG rhythm have been manipulated successfully by learning to concentrate conscious processes in an appropriate manner.

6.18   Is meditation the same as biofeedback?

Not necessarily. Meditation may be a way in which a person can enhance the biofeedback process. However, other kinds of training, such as progressive relaxation and hypnosis, may prove effective in establishing the control associated with biofeedback.

6.19   What are some of the reasons people use psychoactive drugs?

More than any other factor, peer influence encourages or discourages the use of psychoactive drugs. Social pressure often leads to initial use, and with some drugs (such as heroin) physiological dependence eventually may result.

Other important reasons for the use of psychoactive drugs include situational circumstances, for example, the use of a stimulant to stay awake while studying for exams or smoking as a means for maintaining weight.

6.20   Are drug abuse and drug dependence the same thing?

Drug abuse is *any* misuse of a drug but does not necessarily indicate physiological or psychological dependence. For example, a person who is *not* an alcoholic may drink beer at a party to the point of passing out. This certainly is abuse of the drug (alcohol) but is not necessarily an indication of drug dependence.

6.21   What is the difference between physiological and psychological drug dependence? Is it possible to have both at the same time?

A change in the body's chemical balance is associated with physiological drug dependence. Only continued use of the drug will maintain the changed status, while discontinuation will lead to withdrawal symptoms. Psychological dependence is the belief that one *must* have the drug. Psychological dependence can exist even when physiological dependence has been terminated. It is possible, however, to have simultaneous physiological and psychological dependence, for example, when one continues smoking both for the effects of the nicotine and for "relaxing."

6.22   Does the use of alcohol lead to an altered state of consciousness? What is the general effect of alcohol on an individual?

Alcohol is classified as a psychoactive drug, that is, a drug which affects the central nervous system, creating subjective or psychological effects. Using alcohol may lead to conditions or actions outside the normal range of behavior: an altered state of consciousness. Alcohol is a depressant and may, if taken in sufficient quantities, depress central nervous system functioning to significantly alter conscious reactions to stimuli. (*Note*: The commonly accepted notion that alcohol stimulates an individual is incorrect. The effect produced is a *depression* of inhibitory mechanisms, thus making the individual appear to be stimulated.)

6.23   Narcotic drugs have valuable medical uses, yet they have become a serious social problem. Why?

Repeated use of narcotic drugs such as morphine and its derivative heroin causes a person to develop a physiological dependence. This dependence creates an ever-increasing tolerance to the drug, with larger and larger doses needed to produce euphoria and prevent withdrawal symptoms. While often started for social motives, the use of narcotic drugs becomes necessary to satisfy physiological needs. Nonmedical use of narcotic drugs thus can result in illegal sales and use, with those dependent on the drug committing crimes to obtain money to buy it.

6.24   Why is caution suggested whenever the use of stimulant drugs is proposed?

Stimulant drugs, whether legal or illegal, are likely to lead to physiological and/or psychological dependence. The resultant difficulties often are hard to overcome, and range from an inability to quit smoking to a complete loss of lifestyle associated with the use of "crack" cocaine.

6.25   In a typical marijuana "high," what kinds of reactions can be expected? Can marijuana's effect on consciousness be predicted accurately?

The reported effects of marijuana most often include an enhancement of sensations accompanied by some kind of elation or euphoria. It is difficult to make accurate predictions about the effects of marijuana for several reasons. First, there are many types of marijuana, and because it is illegal, "dosages" are not controlled accurately. Furthermore, the potential effect of the drug depends not only on the quantity and quality of the drug but also on the expectations of the user. Perception, emotions, sense of time, motor performance, and other behaviors may be altered radically because of the user's expectations rather than by the pure drug effect.

6.26   Why does a drug get classified as a hallucinogenic drug? How consistent are the effects of such drugs?

Certain drugs are labeled hallucinogenic because their use produces extreme distortions of "normal world" experiences. LSD, PCP, and mescaline are examples of hallucinogenic drugs. Such drugs do not seem to have consistent effects; as with marijuana, expectations play a large role in the effect produced. Moreover, the effects achieved may produce "good trip" or "bad trip" results at any given time.

6.27   A popular misconception is that hypnosis puts the subject in a "deep sleep." What evidence contradicts this belief?

The EEG measurements of a hypnotized subject are comparable to those of a waking subject rather than those of a sleeping subject. Furthermore, although most subjects in hypnotic states are very relaxed, it is possible to create hyperalert hypnosis, in which the subject shows increased tension and recognition of stimuli.

6.28   What, then, are the characteristics of a hypnotic state?

Several attributes seem to mark the hypnotic state. In general, a hypnotized subject shows heightened suggestibility, develops selective attention (especially to the hypnotist's voice), and is more likely to distort reality than is a person under normal conditions. In addition, the subject does all this because of direction from the hypnotist rather than as self-initiated behavior. It is possible for some subjects to reach very deep hypnotic states in which they experience mystical feelings.

6.29   If confronted with the task of trying to hypnotize someone, what kind of person would you select?

Not everyone is equally susceptible to hypnosis. Interestingly, your selection probably should be made on the basis of willingness to participate and the capacity the individual shows for imaginative experience. Additionally, it appears important that the subject trust the hypnotist. Perhaps 5 to 10 percent of the population cannot be hypnotized at all, while about the same percentage can achieve deep hypnotic states. The rest of the population falls somewhere between these two extremes.

6.30   Imagine a brain surgeon who is about to operate on a patient. The patient asks, "Will this operation affect the way I think?" What is the surgeon's answer?

The answer has to be based on the type of surgery being performed. As was mentioned previously, an operation to sever the corpus callosum will create "split-brain" consciousness, preventing the transfer of conscious processes from one cerebral hemisphere to the other, although both sides can learn the same things if exposed to the same stimuli. However, information about the function of many of the brain's areas is so limited that it will be difficult to respond to the patient's question with a definitive yes or no unless one of the well-mapped areas of the brain is involved. Furthermore, plasticity of brain functioning means that one area may be able to assume the function of another, given appropriate training.

Key Terms

Biofeedback.   The use of a monitoring device to reveal the status of physiological processes not otherwise easily observed.

Circadian rhythms.   Cyclical patterns of change in physiological function, such as hunger, sleep, and body temperature.

Concentrative meditation.   Meditation that limits attention to one specific object or sound.

Consciousness.   The internal mental experiences of which a person is aware.

Electroencephalography (EEG).   A technique used to measure the electrical activity of the brain.

Hallucinogenic drugs.   Drugs which have as a major characteristic the production of hallucinations.

Hypnosis.   A technique or group of techniques for inducing an altered state of consciousness that is characterized by increased suggestibility, relaxation or alertness, and possible distortion of reality.

Insomnia.   Inability to fall asleep; the most common sleep disorder.

Latent content.   In the interpretation of dreams, the symbolic meaning of a dream.

Manifest content.   In the interpretation of dreams, the actual content ("script") of the dream.

Meditation.   Technique used to focus or concentrate conscious processes.

Narcolepsy.   Sudden, uncontrollable attacks of sleep during normal waking activity.

Narcotic drugs.   Drugs that can be used for anxiety relief or relaxation or as painkillers, such as heroin and morphine.

Opening-up meditation.   An attempt to produce continuous attention to all aspects of the stimulus environment.

Preconscious.   Information that could reach conscious consideration easily but is not currently in awareness.

Psychoactive drugs.   Drugs that can cause subjective or psychological effects in a person.

Psychopharmacology.   The study of the psychological effects of drugs.

Rapid-eye movement (REM) sleep.   Also called *paradoxical sleep*; the movement of the eyes during sleep provides the name; often the period in which dreams occur.

Sleep apnea.   A sleep disorder marked by complete stoppage of breathing for short periods.

Somnambulism (sleepwalking).   A sleep disorder most likely to occur in children; marked by walking that is not remembered when the person awakes.

Stimulants.   Also known as *uppers*; drugs that elevate heart rate, blood pressure, and muscle tension.

Unconscious.   The cognitive state in which information is not readily available.

Withdrawal effects.   Unpleasant side effects that accompany the cessation of drug use.

CHAPTER 7

Learning

The next three chapters deal with the acquisition of new responses, storage of the new information, and the ability to retrieve and use that information at a later time. This sequence thus represents learning, memory, problem solving, cognition, and many additional topics. This chapter starts with various ways in which new information is acquired.

Learning is defined as a relatively permanent change in behavior that occurs as a result of experience. This definition implies that there is *acquisition* of the response and *storage* (or *retention*) of the response once it becomes part of an organism's behavior. (This chapter looks at several different forms of response acquisition. The retention and *retrieval* of the learned responses—*memory*—are considered in Chapter 8.)

At least three considerations play a role in this definition of learning. First, the definition does not diminish the importance of physical maturation; indeed, physical development may be a necessary condition for response acquisition to occur. However, physical development alone is not sufficient; for learning to take place, an organism must have experience.

EXAMPLE 7.1. Infants are not developed enough to be able to speak a language. Only when they are older can they begin to learn to speak. However, in the absence of the right kinds of experience—including appropriate models, practice, and reinforcement—even a much older child or adolescent will not be able to speak a particular language.

Additionally, it must be recognized that learning and performance are not necessarily the same. An organism's observable behavior (*performance*) does not always reveal what that organism has learned. This second consideration often has been labeled *latent learning*, indicating that the response has been acquired but the conditions are not appropriate for showing it.

EXAMPLE 7.2. A young child who is lost in a large crowd at the county fair may cry but be unwilling to talk. A callous observer may react by saying, "The kid doesn't even know his name." Actually, the child may have committed to memory his name, address, and telephone number. However, the child may have been taught not to speak to strangers, and this learning keeps him from responding to questions he knows how to answer.

Finally, the debate regarding the influences of internal and external factors on the acquisition of new materials has produced a great deal of controversy. Many psychologists have come to accept both *cognitive* (internal) and *behaviorist* (external) approaches to learning, recognizing that a combination of the two may yield the best understanding of what occurs during the learning process.

7.1 CLASSICAL CONDITIONING

Classical conditioning is a process in which an organism learns to respond in a particular way to a stimulus that previously did not produce that response. This stimulus, which was once "neutral," becomes response-producing because it is paired (or associated) with another stimulus that does produce the response. A behaviorist explanation of why classical conditioning takes place emphasizes *contiguity*, the "external" arrangement of the occurrence in a relatively close time frame of the two stimuli. By contrast, a cognitive explanation stresses the "internal" perceived *contingency* that one stimulus (that which is originally neutral) comes to predict the onset of the other, response-producing stimulus.

Classical conditioning also has been called *respondent conditioning* or *Pavlovian conditioning*. The term "respondent" implies that the learned response is elicited involuntarily from the subject rather than being produced in a voluntary (or operant) manner. Calling classical conditioning Pavlovian conditioning gives credit to the Russian physiologist Ivan Pavlov (1849–1936), the first person to investigate classical conditioning extensively. Pavlov devoted over 30 years to the study of this type of learning.

The Classical Conditioning Paradigm. A stimulus that is originally neutral and comes to be response-producing is called a *conditioned stimulus* (abbreviated *CS*). A stimulus that produces the response on the first trial and every trial afterward is called an *unconditioned stimulus* (abbreviated *US* or *US*).

The response elicited by a US is called an *unconditioned response* (*UR* or *UR*). Eventually, the same type of response will occur at the presentation of the CS; this response is called the *conditioned response* (*CR*). A diagram representing the classical conditioning paradigm or design appears in Fig. 7-1.

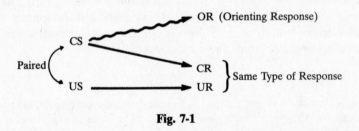

Fig. 7-1

The *orienting response* (*OR*) indicated in Fig. 7-1 often occurs for the first few trials. The subject responds by determining where the stimulus comes from or what stimuli are being presented.

EXAMPLE 7.3. In his original investigations, Pavlov used dogs as subjects. He found that presentation of meat powder (US) would cause the dogs to salivate (UR). Pavlov then paired the ringing of a bell (CS) with the presentation of the meat powder. The pairing soon led the dogs to salivate at the sound of the bell (CR). The OR in this situation occurred in the first few trials when the dogs turned their heads in an attempt to determine the origin of the bell sound.

The timing of the presentation of the two stimuli has been studied extensively. The paired CS and US may occur exactly together, or there may be a time interval between them. The time between the onset of the CS and the onset of the US is called the *interstimulus interval* (*ISI*). *Contiguity* describes the timing of the relationship between the CS and the US, while *contingency* refers to the perceived cognitive connection that develops. Example 7.4 illustrates the ISI arrangements researchers have studied.

EXAMPLE 7.4. The Pavlovian experiment described in Example 7.3 may be conducted with several different ISI arrangements for the bell (CS) and the meat powder (US):

> *Simultaneous conditioning.* The bell and the meat powder are presented at exactly the same time.
> *Delayed conditioning.* The bell comes on first and stays on until the meat powder is presented.
> *Trace conditioning.* The bell comes on and goes off before the meat powder is presented.
> *Backward conditioning.* The meat powder is presented before the bell is rung.
> *Temporal conditioning.* The bell is never rung. The CS in this situation is a constant time period, such as five minutes. The meat powder is presented every five minutes.

In general, conditioned responses are more likely to develop in ISI situations where the CS precedes the US. Usually the timing is quite brief (a matter of seconds or fractions of a second) for most successful conditioning, although some examples "stretch" the ISI to much longer periods.

EXAMPLE 7.5. Research on *learned taste aversions* has shown that classical conditioning can take place when the ISI is as long as several hours. Ingestion of a food, especially if it is an unusual one for the subject, that is followed by illness (such as nausea) some time later will lead to a learned aversion to the food.

Extinction and Spontaneous Recovery. *Extinction* in classical conditioning is the procedure of presenting the CS alone (without the US) for repeated trials. The word "extinction" also is used to refer to the result of such a procedure, in which the CR returns to its original (preconditioning) level.

EXAMPLE 7.6. In Pavlov's experiment (see Example 7.3), extinction was produced by repeatedly sounding the bell without presenting the meat powder. Eventually, the dogs stopped salivating at the sound of the bell. That is, the CR (salivating) returned to its original, preconditioning level.

Resistance to extinction is one measure of the strength of a CR. In general, it is felt that the greater the resistance to extinction, the greater the strength of the established CR. Assuming the US can be treated as a *reinforcer* (an event which strengthens or maintains the response), resistance to extinction can be increased by using *partial reinforcement* while establishing the CR. In this interpretation, partial reinforcement occurs when the CS is paired with the US on some but not all of the trials. A partial reinforcement situation is described in terms of a percentage; for example, if the CS is paired with the US on half the trials, the subject experiences 50 percent reinforcement.

Research has shown that a CR acquired under partial reinforcement conditions takes longer to learn but, once acquired, is more resistant to extinction than is a response established under continuous (100 percent) reinforcement. This is called the *partial reinforcement effect* (*PRE*).

EXAMPLE 7.7. Suppose two dogs were trained to make the salivation response to the sound of a bell. One dog was trained in a continuous reinforcement situation, while the other heard the bell on every trial but was presented with meat powder on only some of the trials. The CR of the latter dog would take longer to acquire but eventually would be more resistant to extinction than would the CR of the first dog.

If, after a period of rest after extinction, the CS is presented (alone, with no US present), the CR sometimes will reappear. This is called *spontaneous recovery* of the response. The strength of the CR will not be as great as it was originally, but partial recovery of the CR will occur.

EXAMPLE 7.8. Suppose the CR of one of Pavlov's dogs was extinguished and the dog was kept out of the experimental setting for several days. If the dog was then placed again in the experimental setting, it would salivate (CR) at the sound of the bell (CS). Evidence of salivation under these circumstances would indicate spontaneous recovery of the dog's CR.

Generalization and Discrimination. In a classical conditioning paradigm, *stimulus generalization* is demonstrated when a CR is made not only to the original CS but also to other stimuli that are similar to that CS. Stimulus generalization that is based on the physical properties of the stimulus is called *primary stimulus generalization.*

Humans, who have a command of language and other symbols, are able to show an additional form of stimulus generalization called *secondary stimulus generalization.* A human's CR may be given not only to the original CS but also to other stimuli that are judged to be similar because they have the same meaning as the original CS.

EXAMPLE 7.9. One of Pavlov's dogs might salivate in response to both a bell and a similar-sounding chime. Humans may show comparable primary stimulus generalization by responding to a variety of automobile horns, all of which may sound similar.

However, humans also have the capacity to make the same response to stimuli that do not have similar physical properties but have equivalent meaning. Thus, humans may respond in the same way to stimuli such as the following:

Raise = rays. When spoken, the same sounds yield primary stimulus generalization.
Lift = raise. Secondary stimulus generalization based on word meaning.
Lift = elevator. Secondary stimulus generalization if one is familiar with British use of the words.

A subject who gives the CR to a particular CS but does not respond to similar stimuli shows *discrimination* (or *differentiation*). Generalization and discrimination can be thought to represent a *continuum*; responding only to the original CS and not to any similar stimuli represents complete discrimination at one end of the continuum, while giving the CR indiscriminately to all stimuli represents complete generalization at the other end. Many instances fall somewhere between these two poles, with difficulty distinguishing differences among stimuli with very similar characteristics, but ease of distinguishing those which are quite different.

EXAMPLE 7.10. Pavlov's dogs would have shown complete stimulus generalization if they had salivated in response to any noise. If they had responded to the original bell but not to other similar sounds, they would have shown complete discrimination. Pavlov showed that when dogs were forced to make choices (that is, differentiate) between two stimuli that were very similar, they sometimes showed confusion and distress. Pavlov called this phenomenon *experimental neurosis.*

Higher-Order Conditioning. When the strength of the CR is near its maximum value, the CS that elicits the CR may take the role of a US. A new pairing is established in which a new CS is paired with the well-established CS. Repeated presentation leads to the elicitation of the same type of CR by presentation of the new CS alone. This is called *higher-order conditioning.*

It should be noted that each new-CS/old-CS pairing is both a conditioning trial for the new-CS/CR attachment and an extinction trial for the old-CS/CR link. A weakly established original CR may extinguish before the new bond can be formed.

Special Applications of Classical Conditioning. The principles of classical conditioning can provide interesting perspectives on other psychological principles. Two of these perspectives are the development of secondary (conditioned) reinforcers and the topic of phobias.

Secondary Reinforcement. When a previously neutral stimulus (a CS) is paired with a reinforcer (US) and the CS takes on reinforcing properties, a *secondary (conditioned) reinforcer* is said to have been established. Frequently, secondary reinforcers are verbal stimuli that become meaningful as reinforcers only after pairings of this sort. This principle applies in establishing conditioned aversive stimuli.

EXAMPLE 7.11. Two-year-old Bailey tries to eat a bug. Her grandmother stops her and, while doing so, says, "Oh don't eat that ... it's pooky!" Bailey sees "Grammy" make an unpleasant face and unpleasant sounds and throw the bug away. Several additional pairings of "pooky" with similar unpleasant reactions are all it takes for Bailey to understand that "pooky" means something is bad. This is a conditioned aversive stimulus.

Phobias.   Phobias are intense, compelling fears that are thought to be established in the same manner as other classically conditioned responses. A previously neutral stimulus (CS) is paired with a fear-producing stimulus (US), and the CS takes on fear-producing attributes. Similar to establishing secondary reinforcers, this is an illustration of secondary or conditioned emotion.

EXAMPLE 7.12.   Imagine stepping into an elevator that plunged 20 floors before the emergency brake saved you from crashing at the bottom of the shaft. It is probably easy to understand that your next confrontation with an elevator might be highly fear-producing. The previously neutral stimulus (the elevator) takes on fear-producing qualities from the single (CS-US) pairing.

7.2   OPERANT CONDITIONING

Operant conditioning is a learning process that involves changing the probability of a response by manipulating the consequences of that response. The underlying principle on which operant conditioning investigations were undertaken was the *law of effect* proposed by E. L. Thorndike (1874–1949), which stated that responses followed by satisfaction are more likely to be repeated, while responses followed by unpleasant or annoying circumstances are less likely to be repeated. It is important to note that Thorndike believed that the law of effect was "automatic"; that is, the organism did not have to understand the link between the response and the result for the effect to occur.

Operant conditioning is sometimes called *instrumental conditioning* or *Skinnerian conditioning*. The term *instrumental* is used because the response is thought to be helpful or essential in achieving the desired goal. The label "Skinnerian" gives credit to the work of B. F. Skinner (1904–1990), a leading investigator of the principles of operant conditioning.

Characteristics of Operant Conditioning.   Operant conditioning is concerned with the acquisition and retention of operant responses as well as the elimination of undesired responses. The *operant response* is a voluntary response made by an organism. Voluntary does not mean necessarily that the organism has complete choice in the matter or that the action is purposive but rather that the response involves voluntary muscle actions and some degree of mediated responding. Operant responses may be learned in sequence (a *chain* of behavior), with the end result being the attainment of a desired goal.

Reinforcement.   Typically, the goal achieved is referred to as a *reinforcement*. A reinforcer is any event that maintains or increases the probability of the response that led to that event.

Psychologists distinguish between positive and negative reinforcement. *Positive reinforcement* means that the presence of a particular stimulus strengthens or maintains a response. *Negative reinforcement* means that the removal or absence of a particular stimulus (usually an aversive stimulus) strengthens or maintains the response. An *aversive stimulus* is one the organism finds noxious or unpleasant.

EXAMPLE 7.13.   "Going outside" provides illustrations of both positive and negative reinforcers, depending on the circumstances. If the children in an elementary school are told that good behavior will be rewarded with an "extra" recess period during which they can go to the playground, going outside is a positive reinforcer. But if they find that when they are outside, the sunlight is very strong and they feel exceptionally hot, getting into the shade represents a negative reinforcer; the children get away from the unpleasant or aversive "hot sun" and find relief in the shade.

Using a Response as a Reinforcer.   When a less probable or less desired response is encouraged by the promise of the opportunity to perform a more desired response, the more desired response serves as a reinforcer. Sometimes called the *Premack principle* after David Premack, who first studied this arrangement, the hierarchy of preference is recognized as being a very personal thing.

EXAMPLE 7.14. The Premack principle also has been called *Grandma's rule*. A child may be informed that an "if-then" contingency exists: Only when a particular low-probability response (such as shoveling snow from the driveway) has been completed will a higher-probability response (such as going sledding) be allowed. Sledding thus serves as a reinforcement for snow shoveling *if* the child enjoys playing in the snow. If the personal hierarchy does not put sledding at a higher level of preference, the contingency for getting the driveway shoveled will not work.

Contingency.   Generally, operant conditioning occurs in situations where the actual delivery of the reinforcer depends on the appropriate responses being made. This is called the *contingency* of the reinforcement on the response. Interestingly, a behaviorist understanding of the relationship stresses only the link between the response and the result, while a cognitive approach emphasizes the understanding of that link. Regardless of the interpretation, there is evidence to show that *delay of reinforcement*, when some time elapses between the completion of a response and the delivery of a reinforcer, is likely to reduce acquisition efficiency.

Occasionally, misinterpretations of a circumstance occur when a reinforcer happens to follow a response by chance (a *noncontingent* reinforcer). Organisms sometimes appear to create a perceived link between the response that preceded the reinforcer and the outcome of reinforcement, a result that may lead to *superstitious behavior*. The organism continues to make the response as if it would produce the reinforcer when, in fact, no contingency exists.

EXAMPLE 7.15.   Although the possibility of parking closer exists, Irene continues to park her car in a fairly remote parking lot she has identified as her "lucky lot." During her first term in college, when going to take a final exam, Irene was forced to park in this lot because of unusual snowy weather conditions that had closed several other lots. She did very well on that exam. While no contingency truly exists between the lot and her academic success, Irene still trusts in the luck of the lot and superstitiously repeats her parking behavior for all examinations.

Acquisition.   The acquisition of an operant response occurs as the organism learns the contingency between the response and the reinforcement. Unlike classical conditioning, where the response is elicited from the subject by a US, most operant situations allow the subject to "find" or emit the correct response over a series of trials. The key relationship in operant conditioning is not between a CS and a US but between a response and a reinforcement.

The most common measure of whether an operant response has been conditioned is to use a *cumulative record* of that response. A cumulative record simply indicates the number of satisfactory responses made in a given time period.

A type of apparatus used frequently in operant conditioning research is called an *operant conditioning chamber* (more popularly known as a *Skinner box*). Figure 7-2 illustrates the basic form of a Skinner box.

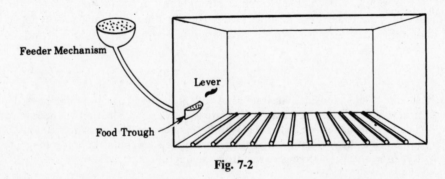

Fig. 7-2

EXAMPLE 7.16.   An untrained and hungry laboratory rat placed in a Skinner box eventually may learn to press the lever, which will activate the feeder mechanism and deliver food pellets into the trough. This represents a positive reinforcement situation. If the grid floor were electrified so that a mild electric shock could be used as an aversive stimulus, the rat could learn to press the lever to turn off the shock. That situation would illustrate negative reinforcement.

To encourage the acquisition of the operant response, the process of *shaping*—the reinforcing of closer and closer approximations to the desired response—sometimes is used. It may be necessary in some cases to encourage the first response so that it can be reinforced and begin the process of shaping.

EXAMPLE 7.17.   When an untrained rat is placed in a Skinner box, it often is possible to speed the acquisition of the lever-pressing response by using a shaping procedure. With a remote control apparatus, the experimenter can reinforce the rat's approaches to the lever, any indications of interest in the lever, placing a paw on the lever, and finally pressing the lever—a sequence of responses that leads to the appropriate response.

With humans, exactly the same kind of pattern may develop. Language learning frequently involves shaping, for instance, when a child's first approximations of words are reinforced, as are the better and better attempts produced later. At first, a child may say that the flower is "pweee," followed by "pwit-tee" and finally by "pretty."

When aversive stimuli are involved, acquisition is categorized in several different ways. If the response being made terminates an already present aversive stimulus, this is classified as an *escape response*. An *avoidance response* means that an organism responds in a way that keeps an aversive stimulus from being delivered. *Punishment* occurs when a response leads to or is followed by an aversive stimulus.

Punishment can be classified as *positive punishment*, where the response leads to the administration of an unpleasant stimulus, or *negative punishment*, where the response leads to the removal of a pleasant stimulus. Both are aversive for the recipient.

It also must be recognized that punishment situations usually involve a contingency relationship; that is, the aversive stimulus occurs because the response was made. However, occasionally, an aversive stimulus may occur contiguously with some response even though no contingency exists. In such cases, a superstitious relationship may develop.

EXAMPLE 7.18.   Behavior as simple as running may illustrate escape, avoidance, or punishment. If the aversive stimulus of a thunderstorm is present, one may run to get inside and away from the storm. If one fears heart trouble, one may run to achieve physical fitness, hoping to avoid later physical difficulties. Children who misbehave during gym class may have to "run laps" as punishment for their actions.

Extinction and the Partial Reinforcement Effect.   Extinction in operant conditioning is accomplished by terminating the delivery of reinforcement after the response. The result of this procedure should be a decrease in the rate of responding until it reaches the preconditioning level.

EXAMPLE 7.19.   Suppose a rat has been conditioned to make the lever-pressing response in order to receive food pellets. Extinction is accomplished simply by turning off the feeder mechanism so that additional responses will *not* lead to the delivery of food pellets. Although the rat may continue to respond for some time, the expected change in the response rate should be observed eventually. A cumulative record of extinction might be illustrated as in Fig. 7-3.

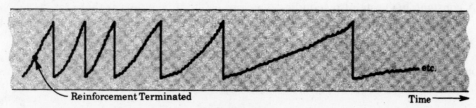

Fig. 7-3

Generally, the effect of partial reinforcement in operant conditioning is the same as it is in classical conditioning; that is, acquisition of the response under partial reinforcement conditions leads to greater resistance to extinction than does continuous reinforcement. Certain special effects of the PRE in operant conditioning have been studied extensively.

Schedules of Reinforcement.   The effects of partial reinforcement have been investigated by arranging the contingency conditions according to several principles. These arrangements have been called *schedules of reinforcement.*

Four variables appear most important in determining basic schedules of reinforcement. They are (1) *fixed schedules*, where the schedule never changes, (2) *variable schedules*, where the schedule may change, although usually around an average value, (3) *ratio schedules*, which are based on the number of responses made, and (4) *interval schedules*, which are based on time.

Combining these variables produces the four basic schedule formats, as follows:

Fixed ratio (FR): The reinforcement is contingent on the subject making a certain number of responses (or *n* responses). This number remains constant throughout the procedure.

Fixed interval (FI): The reinforcement is contingent on a correct response being made at the end of a specified time interval. This time interval never varies.

Variable ratio (VR): The reinforcement is contingent on the subject's responding. However, the number of responses varies from trial to trial, usually in a random pattern. (There may be an average number of responses required, but this will not be readily apparent to the subject.)

Variable interval (VI): The reinforcement is contingent on the subject giving a correct response at the end of a period of time, but the time period changes, usually in a random fashion. (There may be an average amount of time, but it will not be readily apparent to the subject.)

EXAMPLE 7.20.   The rat in the Skinner box might demonstrate each of the basic schedules as follows:

FR. The rat must make 10 lever presses before a food pellet will be delivered to the trough. The speed or pattern of responding does not matter as long as the 10 responses are made.

FI. The rat must make one correct response at the end of a 30-second interval. Responding is not required at any other time during the interval, and the interval never changes.

VR. The rat is reinforced after 3, 13, 7, 10, 7, 15, 17, 10, and 5 responses. While this pattern averages 10 required responses per reinforcement, sometimes fewer are needed, while at other times many more must be made before the reinforcement will be given.

VI. The rat is reinforced when a correct response is made at the end of 15-, 27-, 45-, 30-, 33-, 10-, 30-, and 50-second intervals. Although the average time is 30 seconds, the interval may be either shorter or much longer.

Each of the basic schedules of reinforcement usually produces a particular or distinctive pattern of responding, as follows:

FR. Bursts of responses closely matching the required number of responses are followed by brief pauses just after the reinforcement is delivered.

FI. There is no or very slow responding during the early part of the interval that then gives way to a high rate of responding just as the interval nears completion.

VR. A constant, high rate of responding develops as the subject learns that more responses mean more reinforcements; however, the subject cannot determine how many responses must be made for each reinforcement.

VI. A slow, steady rate of responding occurs. The rate of responding is not important, but a correct response must be made at the end of each time period. The subject "protects" against missing the end of an interval by continuing to deliver steady performance.

The cumulative record of responses for each of the four basic formats would tend to look like the results shown in Figure 7-4. (*Note*: Each "hash mark" denotes the delivery of a reinforcement.)

Combinations or variations of the basic schedules lead to more complex or advanced schedules of reinforcement. A *multiple schedule* requires the subject to satisfy two or more independent schedules that are presented successively, each in the presence of a cue (or identifying) stimulus. A *compound schedule* reinforces a single response according to the requirements of two or more schedules

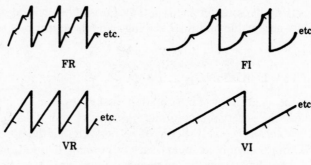

Fig. 7-4

operating simultaneously. A *concurrent schedule* reinforces the subject when two or more responses are made to satisfy the requirements of two or more schedules at the same time.

EXAMPLE 7.21.   Using profanity may be considered appropriate by some people when talking with a peer group, thought to be less appropriate when talking with parents, and judged totally inappropriate when talking with a religious leader. The different conversational partners serve as the cue stimuli for what is essentially a multiple schedule of reinforcement.

Generalization and Discrimination.   In some operant conditioning situations, *discriminative stimuli* (cues) indicate to the subject when responding is appropriate or inappropriate. These are not considered conditioned stimuli because they do not elicit specific responses, but they do serve as signals for the general class of operant responses.

Just as in classical conditioning, stimulus generalization is shown when the subject responds not only to the original (discriminative) stimulus but to other, similar stimuli. The class of discriminative stimuli cues the operant response in several similar situations.

Discrimination or differentiation occurs when the organism distinguishes between the original discriminative stimulus and other similar stimuli, making the operant response in the presence of the original stimulus but not to other similar stimuli.

EXAMPLE 7.22.   Children often become very sensitive to discriminative cues that indicate when parents are approachable and when they are not. The children may recognize facial expressions, certain postures, and particular gestures that indicate that this is a good time to tease a parent and to expect to be reinforced for doing so. (*Note*: The operant class of responses used for teasing may vary considerably. These responses are emitted by, not elicited from, the children.) However, slight changes in any or all of the indicators will signal that the parent is "busy" with something else and does not want to be disturbed. Using the cues illustrates discrimination in an operant responding situation.

In operant situations, psychologists sometimes refer to *response generalization* as having occurred. They do this because there is not a specific response that is required to perform most operant tasks but rather a "family" of responses. If the subject learns to perform a task using one particular response but then finds that response blocked, the subject may substitute another response that works equally well, thus illustrating response generalization.

EXAMPLE 7.23.   Usually one pushes the drawer of a desk shut by using a hand. If, however, the drawer has been opened to get several things from inside it and the hands are now full, response generalization is illustrated when a knee is used to push the drawer shut. The operant class of responses is "shutting the drawer," although the means for accomplishing this task vary.

There are many possible applications of operant conditioning in family life, education, business, animal training, and many other circumstances. Many computer programs require operant responses from the user, as do *behavior modification* techniques used in therapeutic settings. In behavior modification, the emphasis is not on understanding the causes of behavioral symptoms but on creating responses that are socially acceptable and thus helping patients return to a relatively "normal" life.

7.3   COGNITIVE SOCIAL LEARNING

Cognitive learning is the acquisition of information or skills by using mental (cognitive) processes. Very often, this occurs after the observation of others' behaviors; thus, many psychologists refer to this learning style as *cognitive social learning*. It should be recognized that the observation may be of actual behavior or may occur through a symbolic means such as reading. In addition, there is not necessarily any observable response from the learner during the acquisition period, as acquisition may result from watching, listening, reading, or other relatively passive means rather than from the action of stimuli, as in classical conditioning or from the effects of reinforcement as in operant situations.

Although there is some evidence that cognitive learning occurs in other species (within the skill ranges available and appropriate to those species' patterns), most research has been conducted with humans. In general, what seems to be learned is abstract representation (a *schema*) of the behavior being observed, although there are occasional examples of *pure imitation* involving exact modeling of another's behavior.

EXAMPLE 7.24.   In some cases, pure imitation occurs without understanding; that is, the response is copied, but the meaning of the response is not recognized by the imitator. This can produce humorous results, as occurs when children sing Christmas carols without learning the correct words (or the meaning of those words), singing about "Round John Virgin" or "Hark the hairless angels sing." Although good attempts at imitative modeling, these responses obviously are done without understanding.

Observational Learning.   The schemas formed through watching, listening to, and reading about others are used to guide one's own behavior. Most of these schemas are a combination of patterns observed in several different situations, leading to a personal style of behavior that differs from any of the observed models.

This typically is referred to as *observational learning*; other labels for such cognitive activity include *modeling*, *learning by imitation*, and *social learning*. A number of considerations influence the results.

Reinforcement and Vicarious Learning.   Two considerations about reinforcement seem relevant to the understanding of cognitive learning. First, external reinforcement appears to facilitate cognitive learning, but the response gets into the behavior pattern because it has been observed, not because it has been reinforced. Second, many activities provoke a sense of *intrinsic* (or internal) reinforcement, inner reactions associated with performing the response. While the emphasis here is on learning through observation, reinforcement can be seen to influence the behaviors.

Vicarious learning occurs when an observer is able to note not only the response being made but also the consequences of that response for the person performing it. The schema (or expectation) that develops includes both the pattern of responding and the knowledge of what the consequence of making that response might be.

Vicarious reinforcement seems to be quite helpful in many situations for learning a new, previously untrained response. However, vicarious reinforcement alone is unlikely to maintain that response because the learner will come to expect actual reinforcement.

EXAMPLE 7.25.   You may have experienced vicarious learning if you have observed someone suffer a very painful burn. For instance, suppose you watched your older sister lean against an electric range just after one of the surface units was turned off. You saw the nasty burn she received and the pain and distress she experienced. You did not have to lean on the hot burner and also get burned to know that it could hurt you. This is a case of vicarious *suppression* of a response; situations involving positive reinforcement for the person being observed may lead to vicarious *facilitation* of a response.

Symbolic Learning.   Much cognitive learning depends on verbal representation of a behavior rather than observation of an actual behavior. More than any other characteristic, this ability distinguishes humans from other species and makes a human's range of behavior exceptionally broad. *Symbolic learning* considerably reduces the time and effort necessary for learning many behaviors.

EXAMPLE 7.26.   Suppose you discovered a timesaving shortcut from your home to a local theater. You could use a verbal description to represent this path to a neighbor. In effect, that neighbor will model your behavior, but no direct, physical observation of the shortcut is necessary. The neighbor relies instead on a sequence of verbal guides such as "Left on McKenzie until you reach Riverside, then right to Bittersweet."

Model Status.   Research has shown that observers are selective in their choice of models. This selectivity is based on the *status* of the potential model, including characteristics such as the position the model holds, the role the model adopts, the power or influence the model has, and the ability of the model to communicate. Even "strangers" can act as models if they are accorded status in the mass media. Observers have not met the model personally but still confer high status on the person. This is an individualistic activity; each observer may choose differently, depending on the qualities he or she judges to be most important.

EXAMPLE 7.27.   Television has made it possible for most people to observe the behaviors of people with special abilities. Thus, schemas may develop that are based on qualities that receive attention through media confirmation of status. For example, recent years have been marked by increase in tattoo and body piercing behaviors copied from entertainment and sports figures accorded status by the media.

Benefits of Observational Learning.   For the safety of the learner or others, some responses are best learned through observational learning. In some cases, forcing a response is impossible, and learning by shaping an operant response may place the learner, teacher, or others in unreasonable jeopardy.

EXAMPLE 7.28.   Learning to shoot a pistol or rifle could be accomplished by using classical conditioning or operant conditioning techniques. However, such techniques might turn out to be very dangerous. In classical conditioning, for example, a learner's orienting responses might result in the unintentional firing of the weapon. In operant conditioning, the trial-and-error shaping of an appropriate response might be time-consuming and unsafe. By contrast, the correct, safe use of a weapon can be observed and modeled with relative safety and speed.

Solved Problems

7.1   The processes of a computer often are described as input-storage-output. How do psychologists view the same sequence in learning, and what terms do they use?

Psychologists essentially adopt exactly the same sequence to explain learning. The terminology is slightly different in that "input" becomes *acquisition*, "storage" stays the same, and "output" becomes *retrieval*. Acquisition refers to the relatively permanent change in behavior that is stored, while storage and retrieval combine to represent *memory*.

7.2   Do a child's physical growth and development assure that learning will take place? Will a child who has learned a particular response always be able to perform it?

Simply maturing (growing physically) is not enough to guarantee that learning will take place. Physical development in many cases may be a necessary condition for learning, but it is not sufficient. Learning results from experience and may or may not come to pass, depending on whether the experience occurs. There is a difference between learning and performance. A child may learn a response yet be unable to perform it. (Conditions of the moment may prevent the child from revealing what she or he has learned.) This sometimes is referred to as *latent learning*, indicating that the response has been learned but currently is not being shown.

7.3   Are all learning processes the same?

Some characteristics of all learning processes are the same. For example, experience is always necessary if learning is to take place, and all learning produces relatively permanent changes in behavior. However, the actual acquisition of learned responses may result from several different types of learning processes. Psychologists study these processes—such as classical conditioning, operant conditioning, and cognitive learning—in an attempt to understand the various types of acquisition situations.

7.4   The acquisition of a response in classical conditioning often is described as involuntary. Why? What counterproposal has been advanced to suggest something different?

The classical conditioning situation involves the pairing of an originally neutral stimulus with a response-producing stimulus. Both stimuli are presented to the subject, and a "forcing" of the response occurs. In effect, the subject does not have a choice of what response will be made, or the stimulus to which the response will be attached. This explanation stresses the *contiguity* of the two stimuli, an external arrangement not under the control of the subject.

Another interpretation of classical conditioning emphasizes the perceived *contingency* of one stimulus (that which is originally neutral) coming to predict the onset of the other, response-producing stimulus. This approach is a cognitive explanation. Many psychologists believe that both the "automatic" behaviorist approach and the cognitive approach have merit in explaining the classical conditioning process.

7.5   Classical conditioning also has been called *respondent conditioning* and *Pavlovian conditioning*. How did it get these labels?

The word "respondent" implies the involuntary nature of the subject's response in classical conditioning. This is in contrast to a subject operating in a voluntary manner on the environment, which is characteristic of operant conditioning.

Classical conditioning also is called *Pavlovian conditioning* in honor of Ivan Pavlov, a Russian physiologist who first explored many of its principles. His studies concerned the salivary responses of dogs.

7.6   Playing in the backyard one day, 3-year-old Kyle is on a swing when a rabbit suddenly appears out of the bushes and startles her. She slips off the swing, falls against the sandbox, and hurts her arm. Kyle cries from the pain. Later, after calming down and having a bandage put on her arm, Kyle returns to the backyard; while she is standing in the grass, another rabbit hops into view. Kyle begins to cry. Identify the US, UR, CS, and CR in this situation.

The US is the pain. It is response-producing and in this case generates the UR of crying. The CS is the appearance of the rabbit. Presumably, the rabbit's appearance was originally a neutral stimulus; however, it came to be paired with the pain and later produced the CR: crying at the sight of the rabbit.

7.7   In Solved Problem 7.6, both the UR and the CR are crying. Does this mean the UR and the CR are always the same?

No. The UR and the CR are the same *type* of response, although they may differ quantitatively or qualitatively. For example, Kyle's crying in response to the pain might be classified as sobbing, while the later crying (at the sight of the rabbit) might be called whimpering, and the quantity of tears may differ.

7.8   In a classroom demonstration, Professor Puffit is going to illustrate classical conditioning. He asks for a student volunteer to come to the front of the room and seats the student facing the class. Puffit asks the student to "look straight ahead" and then takes an empty syringe in one hand and points it at the student's eye. Puffit reaches to the desk beside the student and rings a small bell, intending to puff air from the syringe into the student's eye immediately afterward to generate an eye blink response. However, the student looks to the side to see where the noise came from, and the air puff is delivered to the student's ear! Explain what Puffit is trying to accomplish and what has happened to prevent it.

Puffit is trying to pair the noise of the bell (a neutral stimulus) with the air puff (a response-producing stimulus) to illustrate how classical conditioning occurs. Unfortunately for Puffit, the student shows a strong orienting response to the noise of the bell and turns to try to identify the source of the noise. At least for this first trial, Puffit's design is unsuccessful. It is likely that an additional reminder to look straight ahead and a growing familiarity with the sound of the bell will lead to a diminishing OR. With more trials, Puffit should be able to condition an eye blink to the sound of the bell.

7.9   Using Professor Puffit's proposed plan, describe the various interstimulus interval arrangements that could be created.

If Puffit used a *delayed* conditioning paradigm, he first would ring the bell and continue to ring it until he puffed the air. In a *trace* conditioning arrangement, he would ring the bell and stop, and then puff the air. *Simultaneous* conditioning would require Puffit to ring the bell and puff the air at exactly the same time, while *backward* conditioning would mean puffing the air before ringing the bell. (If Puffit established *temporal* conditioning, he would puff the air at a repetitive pace, such as every 30 seconds. The time would become the CS.)

7.10   Refer to Solved Problem 7.6 again. Suppose Kyle's parents recognized her distress when she saw a rabbit. What should they do to extinguish this distress?

Extinction of a classically conditioned response involves repeated presentations of the CS alone. The result of such a procedure is that CR strength returns to its original (preconditioning) level. In Kyle's case, repeated presentations of a rabbit without any accompanying pain should lead to the cessation of crying in the presence of rabbits.

To facilitate this, Kyle's parents might want to institute a *counterconditioning* procedure. This probably would mean pairing something positive (such as hugs or candy) with the sight of a rabbit. This should create a new classically conditioned CR to replace the old one.

7.11   Observing the speed with which Kyle's crying response is extinguished is one way of measuring the strength of a CR. Explain.

In general, it is assumed that CR strength is revealed by the amount of time or the number of trials necessary to extinguish the response. Very short extinction represents a weak CR, while longer extinction means the CR was stronger.

7.12   Kyle and her parents spend a week's vacation in Washington, D.C. When they return home, Kyle goes into the backyard to play, only to come back into the house a few minutes later, sniffling a little. Questioning reveals that she has once again seen the rabbit. What principle explains Kyle's response?

Kyle has shown spontaneous recovery of the CR (crying). Presentation of the CS (rabbit) after extinction and a period of rest may elicit the CR once again. Kyle's response is typical of those observed in spontaneous recovery because the strength of the response is not as great as the original CR. (Kyle is only sniffling, not crying uncontrollably.)

7.13   After World War II, many residents of countries that were bombed expressed great hatred for and fear of the sound of low-flying planes. When questioned why they so disliked the sound, many people said, "You never knew whether a bombing attack would be a bad one . . . or even if the planes intended to bomb." Explain how these responses illustrate the effect of partial reinforcement.

The sound of the low-flying planes often was associated with damage, destruction, and death, but not always. Bombs could fall harmlessly in fields, lakes, or remote regions, or they could be "duds." Furthermore, the planes might have been on reconnaissance missions or have might not been enemy planes. The uncertainty of the result produced a partial reinforcement effect, making the fear response *very* resistant to extinction. Even years later, comparable aircraft sounds would generate fear and hatred even though no bombs were falling.

7.14   Solved Problem 7.13 also illustrates another important principle. Why do the people report experiencing feelings of fear and hatred when they hear planes that are in no way associated with war?

The principle that explains the "carryover" is that of stimulus generalization. The sound of planes, which came to be associated with bombing, became response-producing (fear, hatred). Subsequent sounds from planes, even though not exactly the same as those experienced during the war, are enough like the original sounds to provoke the same kinds of responses. The people are responding not only to the original stimulus but to other similar stimuli.

7.15   Distinguish between (1) responding in the same manner to the sound of a bell and the sound of a buzzer and (2) responding in the same manner to the words "bell" and "gong."

If the same response is made to the sound of a bell and the sound of a buzzer, primary stimulus generalization has been shown. The responses are made to the similarity of the *physical* properties of the stimuli.

If the same response is made to the words "bell" and "gong," secondary stimulus generalization has been demonstrated. The subject responds in a like manner because of the similar *meaning* of the two stimuli, even though their physical properties differ.

7.16   Suppose you receive invitations to two different parties that are to be held the same evening. You immediately accept the invitation to the party where you expect good food, drinks, and companionship. You send regrets to the host of the other party. (In the past, this person's parties have been boring, full of business talk and have had poor food and drink.) Your decision illustrates what psychological principle?

When you first were invited to each host's party, the stimuli were essentially neutral. However, one has been paired with pleasure (positive reinforcement), while the other has been associated with boredom (an aversive stimulus). Thus, you have developed a distinction between these two similar stimuli. This illustrates discrimination (differentiation).

7.17   Why is it hard to illustrate the concept of a generalization continuum by using the notes of a musical scale?

The idea of a generalization continuum proposes that as the stimulus changes more from the value of the original CS, the strength of the response will be weaker. The problem with a musical scale is that more than one dimension comes into play when trying to test this. If the original CS is "middle C," for example, moving a few notes in either direction might illustrate diminished responding quite nicely. However, moving farther away would complete the scale and bring the tone back to "C" above "middle C" or "C" below "middle C," both of which might be judged to be very similar to the original CS and lead to strong responding.

7.18 Pavlov's dogs often started salivating as soon as the experimenter walked into the room, even when the experimenter was there for a purpose other than conducting the research studies. Explain how this response pattern might have developed.

This may be an illustration of higher-order conditioning. The appearance of the experimenter preceded the onset of the bell, which in turn preceded the presentation of meat powder. Even if the experimenter was not visible when the bell was rung and the food was presented, it is possible that the dogs associated the experimenter's presence (a new CS) with the likelihood that the bell (the old CS) would be rung. The bell had such a strong association with the food that it served as a US when paired with the experimenter's presence.

7.19 Any language contains words that are used as conditioned reinforcers. Explain what would be necessary to make the phrases "bad girl" and "bad boy" pleasant, *positive* reinforcers.

At first, words are neutral (to a very young child, for example). Words acquire meaning only by being paired with other stimuli. To make the phrases "bad girl" and "bad boy" positive reinforcers, it would be necessary to pair those phrases with rewarding or pleasant circumstances. Repeated association of the phrase (CS) with the reward (US) should produce conditioned reinforcement, and "bad" would be "good." (*Note*: The phrases given here are in English. They could have been arranged as "dab yob" and "dab lirg" and, if paired appropriately, could then take on reinforcing properties.)

7.20 Fran shows an intense, compelling fear of spiders. If a spider is present, her anxiety increases markedly and her performance deteriorates rapidly. Explain how this fear could be the result of classical conditioning.

A spider (CS) probably was paired with a strong fear-producing stimulus (US) one or more times in Fran's past. Fran's fear (a phobia) resulted when the association between the two stimuli became well established.

7.21 Consider where you are sitting as you read this problem and imagine you are hungry. Briefly describe the sequence of operant responses you might make to reach a goal that would satisfy your motive.

Depending on where you are reading at this moment, the sequence of operant responses might be as follows: (1) stand, (2) walk to the kitchen, (3) take a package of microwave popcorn from the shelf, (4) put the package in the microwave and activate the machine, (5) remove the package when the timer goes off, (6) open the package and pour the popcorn in a bowl, (7) return to where you were studying and eat the popcorn. The actual eating of the popcorn is called a *consummatory response*, while the preceding responses are operant responses that lead toward the desired goal.

7.22 Operant conditioning also has been called *instrumental conditioning* and *Skinnerian conditioning*. Why?

The term *instrumental* implies that the response is helpful or essential in achieving the goal. Operant or instrumental responding is in contrast to *respondent* conditioning, in which the organism's response is a reaction to stimulation from the environment.

Operant conditioning is called *Skinnerian conditioning* because of the influence of B. F. Skinner, an American psychologist who developed theories and techniques that greatly expanded knowledge of operant conditioning.

7.23 Why is operant conditioning described as a contingency situation?

Operant responses are voluntary responses that lead to a goal or reinforcement. Unless the response is made, the reinforcement will not be attained. Thus, the reinforcement is dependent on, or contingent on, performance of the response. (*Note*: Psychologists who take a behaviorist approach emphasize only the link between the response and the reinforcer, while cognitive psychologists emphasize the understanding of that link.)

7.24   Contingency implies that the operant response becomes conditioned because it is followed by the reinforcement. What principle was proposed as a general explanation for such situations?

The *law of effect* proposed that when a response led to either a satisfying state of affairs or the removal of an annoyance, that response would become conditioned. Responses followed by an aversive stimulus—something unpleasant or noxious—would become less likely to be repeated. This principle was set forth by E. L. Thorndike very early in the development of the psychology of learning and has been well supported ever since.

7.25   Donna has been attempting to lose weight. She has made a written record of everything she eats and has calculated the number of calories consumed each day. While it took a while to adjust her patterns, decreased caloric intake, combined with increased exercise, has produced a loss of weight and led several friends to make very pleasant comments about Donna's "new shape." What principles of operant conditioning can be used to describe this situation?

The change in eating behavior toward better approximations of a desirable diet represents shaping. The associated weight loss is a negative reinforcer (removal of an aversive stimulus), while the compliments from her friends are positive reinforcers. Recording the caloric intake (the change in eating is the operant response pattern) represents a cumulative record of responding.

7.26   Aversive stimuli play a role in both negative reinforcement and punishment situations. What distinguishes these two situations?

Negative reinforcement occurs when a response leads to the *removal* or termination of an aversive stimulus; that is, something unpleasant or noxious is taken away because an operant response was made. By contrast, punishment occurs in situations in which the performance of a response leads to the *delivery* of an aversive stimulus. (It is important to understand that punishment is *not* negative reinforcement.)

7.27   Many parents use "time out" as a way to change their children's behaviors. In terms of punishment, how is this procedure classified?

The "time out" procedure is thought to be *negative punishment* in that a pleasant stimulus such as playing or watching television is taken away, thus creating an unpleasant circumstance for the child. This is used rather than *positive punishment*, where the response leads to the administration of an aversive stimulus such as spanking.

7.28   Michael, who travels major highways quite frequently, sets the cruise control on his car because he knows the state police patrol the roads looking for speeders. Often, as he approaches someone who has been stopped, he sees the other driver gesturing and explaining, obviously trying to keep from being arrested. What principles associated with aversive stimuli explain the behaviors described here?

By using his cruise control, Michael is illustrating avoidance behavior. He is making a response that he knows will keep him from being arrested, which could be unpleasant and expensive (aversive). The other drivers are showing escape and avoidance behaviors. They are attempting to make responses that will remove an already present aversive stimulus (the state patrol) and prevent the subsequent fine.

7.29   What principle is illustrated when a parent tells a child, "As soon as you have cleared the table, you may go out and play"?

In this case, one response is being used to reinforce another. A low-probability response (clearing the table) will be performed so that a high-probability response (playing) may follow. This is called the *Premack principle*.

7.30   Teachers frequently are accused of failing to show concern for their students because they assign and collect papers, but do not return them to the students for a long time. Students claim that this practice reduces learning efficiency. A psychological principle seems to explain why this accusation probably is correct. Name the principle and explain how it fits the situation.

The principle is *delay of reinforcement*, which states that if there is a long period between response and reinforcement, especially if that period is unfilled, learning efficiency will diminish considerably. In this instance, the *feedback* from the teacher would serve as reinforcement (or punishment), and the long delay reduces performance.

7.31   Robert believes that his wedding day was "the luckiest day" of his life. Because of this, when he stops to fill his car's gas tank, he buys a lottery ticket using the date of his wedding, his birthday, and his wife's birthday. He is convinced this will lead to a big payoff. Robert's behavior illustrates what principle of psychology?

Robert is showing superstitious behavior. Although there really is no contingency between the dates and "good luck," the fact that reinforcers happened on those dates (their births and their wedding) has created the appearance of a contingency. (It is difficult to predict what Robert will do when the couple have children.)

7.32   Young children often learn to operate on their environment (that is, their parents) by crying. This seems particularly true at times when children do not want to go to bed, even though they are very tired and need sleep. What parental response is necessary to eliminate this type of crying?

The parents should *not* respond. By reacting, the parents will reinforce the crying. By not reacting, the parents establish an extinction procedure, that if carried through will lead to the elimination of the crying. Consistency is necessary, however, because an occasional reaction to the crying will serve as partial reinforcement and make the response very resistant to extinction. Similarly, punishment may suppress the response but not eliminate its recurrence at a later date.

7.33   In Solved Problem 7.32, the partial reinforcement effect is described in the same fashion as it is in classical conditioning. Is the effect of the PRE the same in both classical and operant conditioning?

The effect of the PRE is the same in both classical and operant conditioning situations: partial reinforcement results in greater resistance to extinction than does continuous reinforcement.

7.34   Briefly explain the variables that are considered most basic in establishing schedules of reinforcement.

The variables that seem most important in the determination of schedules of reinforcement are whether the schedule is fixed or variable and whether the schedule is based on a ratio of responses to reinforcement or on an interval of time. Fixed schedules do not change, with the same number of responses required or the same amount of time used throughout. Variable schedules may change, although frequently an average number of responses or amount of time is used. Ratio schedules are based on the number of responses, while interval schedules are based on a time period.

7.35   A student seeking to make extra money finds a job painting shutters for a construction firm. The student is told that the work can be done at whatever time fits best into the school schedule and that the wages paid will be $50 each time 12 shutters are completed. Analyze this situation in terms of schedules of reinforcement.

The important consideration is the payoff. Fifty dollars is given after 12 shutters have been completed, a fixed ratio circumstance in which a certain consistent amount of responding is rewarded with a monetary reinforcer.

7.36   Telephone solicitation has become a popular means for selling things. What is the likely schedule of reinforcement for someone working in this way?

It is likely that a telephone solicitor is paid on a variable ratio schedule of reinforcement. As more responses (calls) are made, the chances of getting a payoff are increased. However, there is no guarantee that after a certain number of responses are made a payoff will occur. The inconsistent schedule based on responses made (rather than time working) means this is a VR schedule of reinforcement.

7.37   A student attending a class where the instructor gives unannounced ("pop") quizzes probably should study according to one of the basic schedules of reinforcement. Which one?

Unannounced quizzes may occur at any time. Therefore, the student needs to be ready for one at any class meeting and should study a little bit every day in anticipation of an exam. This is a variable interval schedule of reinforcement, where the payoff comes after a certain amount of time but the time periods are not always the same.

7.38   In many classes students are assigned a term paper. While the paper may be completed and turned in any time during the course, it *must* be finished by a certain date. Responding to complete such an assignment illustrates which basic schedule of reinforcement?

This is a fixed interval schedule of reinforcement. The work must be completed within a certain period but not at any specific time within that period. (*Note*: Psychologists often refer to FI schedules of reinforcement as illustrating the "term paper effect." No matter what length of time is allowed, many students complete their work with desperate "all-nighters" the day before the paper is due. The burst of responding at the end of the interval is comparable to that produced by a lever-pressing rat.)

7.39   An interlocking schedule (an example of a compound schedule of reinforcement) may demand that the number of responses increase as the length of time since the previous reinforcement increases. Why might such a schedule create a major problem for children learning to read?

The required number of responses for reinforcement may become exceedingly large very quickly. If first-grade children do not produce the appropriate responses to begin with, the ever-increasing demands of the second and third grades will mean those children will fall further and further behind the children who are able to keep up.

7.40   When Lacinda first got her cellular phone, she would turn it on and immediately start dialing a number. She learned that when she turns on that phone, unlike her home telephone, there is a brief delay before she gets a dial tone. She has learned to wait for the dial tone before beginning to dial a number. What principle is illustrated by Lacinda's behavior?

Waiting to hear the dial tone illustrates differentiation in an operant situation. The response made (dialing) is an operant response that leads to a goal (making a call). By waiting until the discriminative cue (dial tone) is present, Lacinda has differentiated between an appropriate time to respond and an inappropriate time.

7.41   Harold's job requires him to do a lot of "schmoozing." Most of the customers he meets are interested in automobiles, sports, and food. Harold has developed a standard set of questions he uses in almost all these situations regardless of the person he is with. Explain Harold's behavior in terms of discriminative stimuli.

Harold is making a series of operant responses that should lead to his goal of making his customers feel good. However, his response pattern indicates stimulus generalization in that he makes the same set of responses to many similar stimuli ("If it's a customer, stick to these questions. If it isn't a customer, maybe we can talk about something else.").

7.42   Distinguish between stimulus generalization and response generalization. Give an example of response generalization.

Stimulus generalization involves giving one response to several similar stimuli. Response generalization involves giving several similar (or equivalent) responses to one stimulus. Greetings illustrate response generalization. If someone approaches and says "Hello," you may respond by saying "Hello," "Hi," "How's it going?" "Hey," or even "Howdy." All these responses fit into the category of a return greeting.

7.43   In both classical conditioning and operant conditioning there is an important relationship between the desired response and reinforcement. In cognitive learning, is reinforcement considered important? What is the major emphasis of cognitive learning?

Reinforcement is important in cognitive learning, but not for the same reasons it is important in classical or operant conditioning. Reinforcement neither forces a response (as in classical conditioning) nor serves as a necessary condition (as in operant conditioning). Instead, reinforcement in cognitive learning appears to *facilitate* a subject's response. The major emphasis in cognitive learning is that the subject observes a response and then incorporates the actual response pattern or a schema based on that pattern into subsequent behavior.

7.44   What are some of the other names given to cognitive learning, and what do they imply?

Cognitive learning also has been called *cognitive social learning*, *observational learning*, *modeling*, *vicarious learning*, and *learning by imitation*. The implication of all these labels is that the learner develops responses by observing the responding of others either directly or symbolically. Watching, listening, reading, and other observational techniques are involved in the cognitive learning process.

7.45   A research study investigated subjects who were shown a videotape of aggressive behavior that ordinarily is disapproved. However, the aggressive behavior shown on the tapes went unpunished. The subjects who saw those tapes were as likely to imitate the aggressive behaviors as were subjects shown a videotape which depicted the same behaviors being rewarded. What term describes this situation, and what explanation seems to fit these circumstances?

The subjects are experiencing vicarious reinforcement. They are seeing the positive results of normally disapproved responses. In the latter videotape, the responses yield direct positive reinforcement, while in the first situation, the absence of anticipated punishment apparently indicates permissiveness and reduces the fears that might otherwise accompany such behaviors. This fear reduction seems to serve as negative reinforcement, with the removal of the aversive stimulus (fear) strengthening the likelihood of copying the observed behaviors.

7.46   Suppose instead that the videotaped aggressive responses in Solved Problem 7.46 were punished. What would be the expected effect on the subjects who observed such tapes?

Vicarious observation may influence behavior in both facilitatory and inhibitory manners. Thus, the punishment noted here would be likely to reduce the potential modeling of responses. Research studies have shown that observed responses that are consistently punished produce almost no imitation.

7.47   Lower organisms appear to demonstrate some cognitive learning, but humans seem to have a much greater capacity for such activity. Why is this? What limitations might exist for humans?

Humans have an immense capacity for language learning. This means that humans can make verbal representations of behavior that can be retained for long periods. In addition, language gives humans the ability to pass on information to others who did not observe the original activity. With the most advanced language or communication skills, humans have the greatest opportunity for verbal or symbolic modeling. Modeling through language probably is limited only by the language development of a person.

7.48   "He acts *just* like his father!" is probably only a partially accurate statement. Why?

Unless the son's behavior has been restricted tremendously, it is exceedingly unlikely that his environment has been exactly comparable to that of his father. Moreover, even if many of the son's behaviors are modeled after those of the father, research has shown that the son may be unable to imitate all of his father's responses. The son's responding is more apt to be based on a combination of several models' attributes. Careful observation of the son's behaviors probably would reveal characteristics in imitation of his mother, other relatives, significant peers, and even media models from advertising, television shows, sports, and other sources.

7.49   Suppose that a person is confronted with the behavior of two highly valued models (for example, a teacher and a member of the clergy) and that their behaviors differ somewhat. What kind of situation is this? What kind of behavior might be expected from the observer?

This is a conflict situation (see Section 10.4). The observer may make a comparison and possibly a choice between the two somewhat different responses. Resolution of a conflict of this nature may depend on the strength of status of each model. If one is more important to the observer than the other, responding is likely to favor the more highly valued model's style. If the models are equivalent, the observer may adopt a combination of attitudes that reflects selected aspects of each model's actions.

7.50   Why is observational learning considered the "best" kind of learning for certain behaviors, such as swimming and driving an automobile?

Compared to other forms of learning, observational learning is the most efficient and the least dangerous. For those two behaviors, there are no readily available stimuli to force the correct responses, thus ruling out classical conditioning. Furthermore, shaping closer and closer approximations to a desired response may be part of learning either behavior, but the initial model seems necessary to avoid what might be tragic errors. In both cases, providing an opportunity for the observation of correct responses helps ensure a relatively high level of safety for the learner.

Key Terms

Acquisition.   The process by which an organism makes a response part of its behavioral repertoire.

Aversive stimulus.   Any stimulus an organism judges to be noxious or unpleasant.

Avoidance response.   Any response an organism makes to keep from experiencing an anticipated aversive stimulus.

Backward conditioning.   In classical conditioning, a trial in which the onset of the US occurs before the onset of the CS.

Behavior modification.   Also called *behavior therapy*; the use of operant conditioning procedures to help create socially acceptable behaviors.

Classical conditioning.   The acquisition procedure in which a previously neutral stimulus is paired with a response-producing stimulus until the neutral stimulus elicits the same type of response; also called *respondent conditioning* and *Pavlovian conditioning*.

Cognitive learning.   The acquisition of information or skills by using mental (cognitive) processes.

Compound schedules.   Partial reinforcement schedules in which a response is reinforced according to the requirements of two or more schedules that operate at the same time.

Conditioned reinforcer.   See *secondary reinforcer*.

Conditioned response (CR).   In classical conditioning, a response elicited by the CS; usually similar to the UR.

Conditioned stimulus (CS).   In classical conditioning, a stimulus that was originally neutral and comes to be response-producing.

Contiguity.   The occurrence of two or more events in close temporal proximity.

Contingency.   A perceived cognitive connection between two events, usually that one depends on the other; in operant conditioning, a situation in which a reinforcement is not delivered unless certain responses are made.

Cumulative record.   The tally or record of appropriate or satisfactory operant responses made in a given time period.

Delay of reinforcement.   A period of time between the response and the reinforcement in a contingency situation.

Delayed conditioning.   In classical conditioning, a trial in which the onset of the CS precedes a US, with the CS staying on at least until the US has occurred.

Differentiation.   Responding to the original stimulus but not to other, similar stimuli.

Discrimination.   See *differentiation*.

Discriminative stimulus.   A cue stimulus that indicates when it is appropriate or inappropriate to make an operant response.

Escape response.   Any response made by an organism to get away from or terminate an already present aversive stimulus.

Extinction.   In classical conditioning, both the procedure of presenting the CS alone repeatedly and the result of this procedure, which returns the CR to its original (preconditioning) level; in operant conditioning, the termination of reinforcement after the response, followed by a decrease in the rate of response until it reaches the preconditioning level.

Feedback.   An organism's knowledge of the results of its response.

Fixed schedules.   Partial reinforcement schedules that remain unchanged.

Higher-order conditioning.   A conditioning procedure in which a new CS is paired with a well-established CS from a previous instance of classical conditioning; the new CS comes to elicit the same type of CR.

Interstimulus interval.   The time between the onset of a CS and the onset of the US.

Interval schedules.   Partial reinforcement schedules in which reinforcement is delivered after a response that has been made at the end of a given time period.

Law of effect.   Thorndike's proposal that a response followed by the presence of a satisfying stimulus or the termination of an annoying stimulus will become conditioned.

Learning.   A relatively permanent change in behavior as a result of experience.

Negative reinforcement.   A type of event in which the removal or absence of a stimulus strengthens or maintains a response.

Noncontingent reinforcement.   Reinforcement that follows a response but is not dependent on that response.

Operant conditioning.   A learning process that involves changing the probability of a response by manipulating the consequences of that response; also called *instrumental conditioning* and *Skinnerian conditioning*.

Operant conditioning chamber.   An apparatus for the experimental testing of operant conditioning; several varieties exist.

Operant response.   A response that leads toward a goal.

Orienting response (OR).   In classical conditioning, any of a number of adjustment responses made when the CS first occurs.

Partial reinforcement.   In classical conditioning, when the CS is presented on every trial but the US occurs on only some of the trials; in operant conditioning, when the appropriate response is followed by reinforcement on only some of the trials (see *schedules of reinforcement*).

Partial reinforcement effect (PRE).   The finding that responses conditioned under partial reinforcement are more resistant to extinction than are those conditioned under continuous reinforcement.

Performance.   The responses an organism actually shows; may or may not reveal what the organism has learned.

Positive reinforcement.   A type of event in which the presence of a stimulus condition strengthens or maintains a response.

Primary stimulus generalization.   Stimulus generalization based on the physical properties of the stimulus.

Punishment.   A type of event in which the delivery of an aversive stimulus is contingent on a certain response.

Ratio schedules.   Partial reinforcement schedules in which the reinforcement is delivered on the basis of number of responses made.

Reinforcement.   Any event that maintains or increases the probability of the response that led to that event.

Response generalization.   Responding to the original stimulus not only with the original response but with other similar responses.

Schedules of reinforcement.   Ways of arranging partial reinforcement in operant conditioning situations.

Schema.   An abstract representation of behavior being observed or otherwise acquired.

Secondary reinforcer.   Also called a *conditioned reinforcer*; when a previously neutral stimulus is paired with a reinforcer and comes to take on reinforcing properties.

Secondary stimulus generalization.   Stimulus generalization based on the subject's knowledge of language or another type of symbol.

Shaping.   Reinforcing closer and closer approximations of a desired behavior.

Simultaneous conditioning.   A classical conditioning procedure when the ISI equals zero; that is, the CS and the US occur at the same time.

Stimulus generalization.   Making a response not only to the original stimulus but also to other similar stimuli.

Superstitious behavior.   When an organism performs as if the particular response caused reinforcement but in fact there is no contingency.

Symbolic learning.   Cognitive learning which depends on verbal representation of a behavior rather than actual observation of that behavior.

Temporal conditioning.   A classical conditioning procedure in which the US occurs at regular intervals; these regular intervals are treated as the CS.

Trace conditioning.   A classical conditioning procedure in which the onset and cessation of the CS occur before the US is presented.

Unconditioned response (UR).   In classical conditioning, the response elicited by the US.

Unconditioned stimulus (US).   In classical conditioning, the stimulus that is response-producing on the first trial and every other trial.

Variable schedules.   Partial reinforcement schedules that can change, usually around an average value.

Vicarious learning.   When an observer notes not only the response being made but also the consequences of making that response.

CHAPTER 8

Retention and Forgetting

The learning process is divided easily into two subcategories: the *acquisition* of new materials and the *memory* of those materials as measured by retention. This chapter focuses on the second aspect: the retention of or failure to retain learned materials.

8.1 DEFINITIONS

Several terms are used in discussing retention. *Retention* is thought of as the storage of learning over a period of time called the *retention interval*. Memory includes both retention (storage) and *retrieval*, which involves getting the response out of storage. If for some reason the subject is unable to produce the response at the end of the retention interval, *forgetting*—the loss of retention or the inability to retrieve—has occurred.

Retention often is evaluated by using an *information-processing approach*. Psychologists interested in trying to represent learning functions in terms of computer programming have analyzed the learning process as an *input-processing-output* sequence. By knowing the stimuli to which the subject is exposed and the response the subject later makes, they hope to program computers to simulate the learning process and thus better understand acquisition, retention, and retrieval.

EXAMPLE 8.1. Computers have reached a capacity that allows them to match or exceed human capabilities at many tasks. For example, a properly programmed computer will never lose (but may tie) a game of tic-tac-toe and now is able to match or surpass even the world champion of chess, a game that requires both retention and creativity at an extremely sophisticated level.

8.2 TYPES OF STORAGE

The most widely accepted explanations of storage propose three levels or categories: sensory storage, short-term storage, and long-term storage. When measured by the retrieval of information, these levels also are referred to as sensory memory, short-term memory, and long-term memory.

Sensory Storage. The basic concept of *sensory storage* is that information is held in an unprocessed form before being "read out," categorized, or interpreted. This kind of storage is thought to last for a very brief period, although the length of the retention interval may vary from hundredths of a second to several seconds, depending on the sensory process involved.

Two forms of sensory storage have been studied most extensively: *echoic* storage of auditory signals and *iconic* storage of visual signals. Research has shown that materials either are processed from sensory storage into short-term or long-term storage or are lost or discarded.

EXAMPLE 8.2. Ingenious investigations of sensory storage have made use of very brief (fractions of a second) exposures to auditory or visual signals. Subjects are given a very short exposure (perhaps one-tenth of a second) to a fairly complex stimulus item. This is followed by a very brief delay interval, and then a marker (such as an arrow for visual signals) indicates what part of the stimulus item is to be recalled. The subject is *not* seeing the stimulus item at this time. Instead, the subject "sees" a visual trace of that image. Research of this type has shown that the visual trace persists for less than two seconds.

Short-Term Storage.   *Short-term storage* is thought to extend from 1 to 30 seconds after exposure to a stimulus item. Initial processing of the material, in which information is taken from sensory storage, takes place during this period. Short-term storage is viewed as a temporary or interim period. It is one step past unprocessed sensory storage, but if further processing does not take place, the material is lost or discarded.

Short-term storage sometimes is called *working memory*, implying that conscious activity is being devoted to the information being dealt with. Studies of short-term storage have indicated that the amount of material that can be held in this active state at any one time is quite limited, usually thought to be seven plus or minus two units of information. The size of the units of information appears to vary, depending on how much effort must be used to process the information and whether separate items can be grouped together (a process called *chunking*) so that one item contains multiple pieces of information.

EXAMPLE 8.3. A task seemingly as simple as remembering a string of digits can be altered to be easier or harder. Consider the single digits 2-7-5-8-7-3-5-2-1-9-7-5. If all you are asked to do is to remember them in the order they are presented, research indicates that you should remember at least the first five digits ($7 - 2$ units of information), usually will remember seven, and may remember nine ($7 + 2$ units of information). It is easy to expand the total number of digits remembered by chunking them into two-digit numbers, that is, as 27 (twenty-seven), 58, 73, 52, 19, and 75. Now there are only six units of information to be remembered, less than what is typically thought to be the capacity of short-term storage but already containing more total information than it would if the digits were treated individually. By contrast, processing can be made much harder if you are asked to do something with the numbers, such as add them as you practice them; 2 plus 7 is 9, plus 5 is 14, plus 8 is 22, etc. Much of the short-term capacity is devoted to activity other than learning the numbers.

It should be noted that some psychologists consider working memory to be a special part of long-term memory that moves currently activated information to and from short-term storage. The idea here is that *parallel processing* may occur, so that disparate elements of information may be active simultaneously, and that working memory differs from short-term memory but incorporates it.

Long-Term Storage.   *Long-term storage* occurs when materials in sensory storage or short-term storage are processed, rehearsed, encoded, or otherwise treated for retention over a period of more than 30 seconds (and maybe for 30 years). Long-term storage is thought to have unlimited capacity, and as long as initial acquisition has taken place and the subject retains the ability to make the appropriate response, items in long-term storage may have unlimited retention intervals.

How items become part of long-term storage is a matter of debate. Psychologists often suggest that a process of *consolidation*, the forming of a fixed or stable memory, must occur and that this process involves activity of the central nervous system. Recent studies have focused on the activation of a protein in nerve cells that causes growth of dendrites and therefore strengthening of the connections at the synapse.

EXAMPLE 8.4. You probably can recall an event from your childhood. Perhaps you remember a happy moment such as receiving a special present from your parents, or you may remember a sad incident such as the death of a pet. All such memories are retrieved from long-term storage.

Psychologists have developed several different ways of interpreting or categorizing the components of long-term storage. For instance, a distinction is made between *semantic memory* and *episodic memory*, with the former referring to storage based on the meaning of words and the latter identifying autobiographical memory of a particular event that happened to you. Differences also are seen between *declarative memory* and *procedural memory*. Declarative knowledge refers to remembered facts (a "knowing that" kind of understanding), while procedural knowledge includes skills and abilities (grasping "knowing how to"). In addition, some psychologists distinguish between *explicit memory* and *implicit memory*, depending on whether a conscious attempt to produce the information in memory is being made. Explicit memory seems to involve effort, while implicit memory is produced relatively effortlessly.

EXAMPLE 8.5. Riding a bicycle can produce examples of many of the types of long-term storage described above. Talking about biking with someone else involves semantic memory ("The frame I have is made of space-age materials!") or episodic memory ("That day I was pushing hard to get to the top of a very steep hill, when I crashed."). Declarative memory is illustrated by knowing facts about bicycles ("Many bikes today have at least 18 gears."), while procedural knowledge is shown when one actually rides a bicycle (the skill or motor performance). Recognizing landmarks that identify when to make turns and unconsciously doing so while talking about another topic with a riding partner illustrates implicit memory. Actually naming the roads that made up the route that was ridden that day, a conscious effort to recall each one, is evidence of explicit memory.

The mental structures developed and stored in long-term storage are called schema (see also Section 4.4). Consisting of already encoded knowledge and beliefs, schema serve to filter new experiences, creating context and meaning for each one.

8.3   MEASURES OF RETENTION

Psychologists have devised a number of different ways to evaluate retention. Each is an attempt to retrieve and measure information held in storage.

Recognition. In *recognition* measures of retention, the subject is presented with the correct answer, usually as one of a number of available answers. The subject then responds by selecting the answer that is thought to be correct. Objective scoring of such tests is possible because a result, such as the number of correct answers, can be determined without the possibility of scorer bias.

EXAMPLE 8.6. Matching or multiple choice questions are usually recognition tests of retention. Suppose you are asked the following question:
Name the city represented by a baseball team named the Red Sox.

1. Boston
2. Kansas City
3. Chicago
4. Cincinnati

You should select the first answer, recognizing that it is the correct answer, and eliminate the others.

Recall. In *recall* measures of retention, a minimum cue statement or question is presented and the subject is required to supply additional information. Correct or incorrect answers are not presented before the subject responds.

EXAMPLE 8.7. Essay questions and "completion" questions often are recall tests of retention. For example, suppose you are asked, "What are the names of the major league baseball teams in Kansas City, Cincinnati, and Chicago?" No selection of names is furnished; you are expected to generate the answers without any additional prompting. (The answers would be the Kansas City Royals, the Cincinnati Reds, and the White Sox *and* Cubs in Chicago.)

Relearning. In some situations, subjects may have to *relearn* materials they have learned before. The amount of time or the number of trials required for *relearning* then may be compared to the amount of time or number of trials required for original learning. Measurement of retention can be computed in terms of the *savings score* shown in relearning:

Savings score = original learning (OL) − relearning (RL)/ original learning (OL)

By multiplying this value by 100, one arrives at a percentage to report as retention.

EXAMPLE 8.8. On Wednesday it takes Fred 20 minutes to memorize a vocabulary list for one perfect recitation. On Friday, when he is tested for retention, Fred relearns the list perfectly in five minutes. Thus, his savings score (retention) is calculated as 75 percent:

$$Savings\ score = OL - RL/\ OL \times 100$$
$$= 20 - 5/20 \times 100$$
$$= 15/20 \times 100$$
$$= 75\%$$

Comparison of Retention Measures. It is important to understand that an estimate of retention may vary, depending on the measure of retention that has been used. Because of differences in presentation and scoring, recognition tests should never give a zero value for retention, while recall measures may. Relearning, however, may show a negative score if the time or trials necessary for relearning exceed what was required for original learning.

EXAMPLE 8.9. A subject might be taught the names of all the major league baseball teams. Having accomplished this, the subject might then learn the names of all the teams in the National Football League. Later, when retention for baseball team names is tested, a recognition test using matching might yield a score of 65 percent, recall might be 40 percent, yet relearning might be −5 percent. The last result could occur because of the subject's confusion produced by the fact that many cities have one or more teams in both leagues and/or from nicknames appearing in both leagues but for different cities (New York has the baseball Mets and Yankees and the football Giants and Jets, but San Francisco has the baseball Giants, for example).

Note: A seldom used measurement of retention (at least in psychological investigations) is called *qualitative measurement*. Qualitative measurement involves a more subjective judgment than do any of the previously mentioned techniques, often requiring literary, artistic, or musical ability. As a result, memory sometimes is not as important as skill and the evaluator's judgment, and conclusions regarding retention may be difficult to make.

EXAMPLE 8.10. A famous study of the ability to reproduce a drawing started with an original drawing like the one shown in Fig. 8-1.

Fig. 8-1

Fig. 8-2

The first subject had a brief exposure to this drawing and, from memory, attempted to duplicate it. The second subject saw the first subject's drawing and, again from memory, attempted to duplicate it. By the time the tenth subject made an attempt, the drawing looked something like the one in Fig. 8-2. Each subject's recollection of the previous subject's drawing contained some distortion, with the cumulative effect of the distortions resulting in a considerably changed figure.

The Learning Curve.   Psychologists have attempted to illustrate the progress of acquisition and storage with pictorial or graphical representations of performance plotted as a function of time or trials. These representations are called *learning curves*. (Remember, however, that performance is not always an accurate indicator of what has been learned.)

EXAMPLE 8.11.   Students in elementary school learn "keyboarding," or the ability to "type" using the letters and numbers on the keyboard of a computer. The performance measure used might be the number of words correctly typed in two minutes. This can be plotted against the amount of time spent practicing. Different students may show quite different patterns of performance, as illustrated in Fig. 8-3. Each of the lines represents a "learning curve," although student D does not seem to be learning very much.

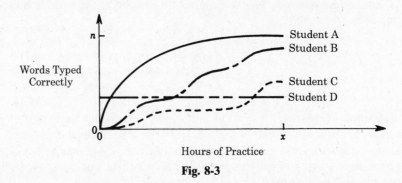

Fig. 8-3

Plateau.   Occasionally, during the course of the trials, the learning curve will "flatten out," and no apparent progress will be made. After this period, performance once again improves. This period of no improvement, preceded and followed by periods of improvement in performance, is called a *plateau* in the learning curve.

Asymptote.   When a subject achieves maximum or nearly maximum performance, the learning curve levels off. This final leveling of the curve is called an *asymptote*. (*Note*: The asymptote may be less than the maximum possible on the task but is maximal or nearly maximal for the subject being tested.)

The Curve of Forgetting.   Early in the history of psychology, Hermann Ebbinghaus devoted much of his career to studies of the acquisition and retention processes in verbal learning. One conclusion he reached has remained relatively unchallenged for over 100 years: The general pattern for loss of retention is that the greatest loss occurs soon after acquisition, with the rate of loss diminishing after that. This is represented by what has come to be called the *curve of forgetting*, as shown in Fig. 8-4.

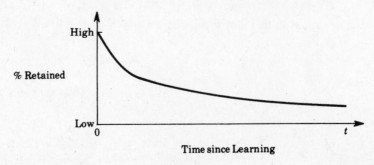

Fig. 8-4

While the general form of the curve seems to hold for many cases, the exact level and shape may vary somewhat, depending on individual variables such as motivation, the materials learned, fatigue, and the amount of rehearsal. This is illustrated dramatically by what has come to be known as the *von Restorff effect* (or sometimes the *isolation effect*). When an especially distinctive stimulus is inserted into any part of a list, it almost always is retained at a very high level. The remainder of the items in the list will show a fairly typical position in the curve of retention: the first and last learned will be remembered better than those in the middle of the list. This is called the *serial position effect*. Both phenomena are illustrated in Fig. 8-5.

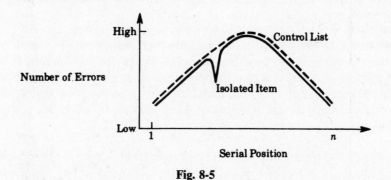

Fig. 8-5

EXAMPLE 8.12. Suppose a group of subjects is asked to memorize the items in the following list: "horse, cow, giraffe, Oklahoma, mouse, dog, monkey, pig, cat, lamb, bird, snake, rat, bear." The von Restorff effect would be shown if the subjects tended to learn and remember the one distinctive item—"Oklahoma"—better than they learned and retained most of the rest of the list. The subjects also would be likely to remember the first ("horse, cow") and last items ("rat, bear") quite well, illustrating the serial position effect.

8.4 THEORIES OF FORGETTING

Several theories of forgetting have gained prominence in the psychological literature. Theories based on retrieval difficulties, loss of memory trace, lack of motivation, and interference have been proposed and supported in part by research results.

Forgetting as a Failure to Retrieve.   One theory suggests that forgetting is the result of a person's failure to retrieve materials that are already stored. The theory suggests that acquisition has taken place but that poor organization in storage, poor prompting, inappropriate motivation, or another variable keeps the person from achieving the performance that would reveal the stored materials. Changes in the cue, suggestions for new ways to organize the material, and other alterations in attempting retrieval have shown that the subject's performance can improve considerably.

EXAMPLE 8.13. A young child who is asked to "replicate the design you saw" may appear to have no recollection of the stimulus. However, if the request is changed to "draw me a copy of the picture you just saw," the child does much better. In this case, the change of cue makes the task much more comprehensible.

Forgetting as Fading of the Memory Trace.   Another theory of forgetting proposes that loss of retention occurs because of disuse of learned materials. Failure to call upon the memory trace means that the trace will somehow "fade" and the memory eventually will be lost. To counteract this "fading," a subject must practice. Evidence for this theory comes from research studies in which the typical "curve of forgetting" (see Section 8.3) appears even though there is no indication that anything except the passage of time has contributed to the loss of retention.

EXAMPLE 8.14. Highway restaurants sometimes entertain their waiting customers by putting puzzles on the tables. One of these puzzles involves a triangular-shaped arrangement of golf tees in which all the holes in the block of wood holding the tees except one are filled. The task is to "jump" one tee over another, always removing the tee that has been jumped, until only one tee remains. Customers find this challenging and somewhat difficult but often discover a pattern that allows them to succeed and repeatedly practice this successful solution.

Returning to such a restaurant and being confronted once again with such a puzzle, many customers reach for it confidently, only to find that they cannot remember the solution they previously found. Statements such as "I knew how to do this; now just a moment" are fairly common. Because it is doubtful that other puzzles of this nature have been encountered during the interim period, it would appear that the trace of the previous solution has faded through disuse. However, it can be very difficult to determine whether other contributing factors also might have been operating.

Forgetting as Distortion of the Memory Trace. Another theory suggests that forgetting occurs because of distortions of the memory trace. This theory proposes that some materials incorporated into memory are only partially accurate and that inappropriate descriptive labels are attached to them. In such cases, the altered meanings of the stored materials make accurate recollection impossible. Again, some research evidence supports this conclusion; when inaccurate labels are provided for learned materials, distorted memories may result.

Motivated Forgetting. The psychoanalytic theory of *repression* suggests that some forgetting comes to pass because a person wishes to forget something. Originally proposed by Sigmund Freud, this view suggests that forgetting is one means by which an individual can "protect" his or her personality. (The term for such protections is *ego defense mechanisms*; see Chapter 12 for a more thorough discussion.)

Freud believed that readily accessible memories were found in the *preconscious*. Memories that might arouse great anxiety were pushed "deeper" into memory, into the *unconscious*, where they could not be called forth easily. Repression was likely to put memories in the unconscious, but Freud believed that such memories continued to influence behavior in the form of *unconscious motives*. While experimental evidence to support the notion of repression has not been produced, repression has been used in case histories to account for forgetting.

EXAMPLE 8.15. One clinical case history illustrates how repression occurs and how it affects behavior. Hilda, a young girl, misbehaved badly one day and ran away from her parents. In the process, she fell into a rushing stream and ruined her good clothes. Although she was hurt and in need of attention and comfort, her parents punished her. The memory of that day became very anxiety-producing for Hilda. She eventually managed to repress her conscious memories of those events, but unconscious aftereffects persisted. The key stimulus appeared to be rushing water; as Hilda grew older, she found comparable stimuli (such as a running shower) very anxiety-producing. Fortunately, she was able to uncover this repressed memory and ultimately overcome her fears.

Forgetting as a Result of Interference. One of the best documented theories of forgetting proposes that loss of retention results from interference from other materials. This has been studied with what are known as *proactive interference* (PI) and *retroactive interference* (RI) experimental designs. In each case, the question investigated is what effect one learning task will have on the retention of other learning.

Proactive Interference. The experimental design for testing *proactive interference* is as follows:

	Step 1	Step 2		Step 3
Experimental group	Learn A	Learn B	REST	Test B
Control group	Put in time	Learn B	REST	Test B

When the material of task B is tested, if the control group does better than the experimental group, it may be concluded (assuming no experimental flaws exist) that PI has taken place; that is, the task A materials interfered with the later retention of task B materials.

Retroactive Interference. *Retroactive interference* is studied by using the following experimental design:

	Step 1	Step 2		Step 3
Experimental group	Learn 1	Learn 2	Rest	Test 1
Control group	Learn 1	Put in time	Rest	Test 1

Again, if the control group's performance is significantly better in step 3, task 2 learning has interfered with the retention of task 1. (*Note*: Most research on both PI and RI has studied interfering or inhibiting effects in an attempt to determine the reasons for the loss of retention. If one learning made retention of the other appear easier, however, the word "facilitation" would be used.)

EXAMPLE 8.16. Learning names to go with faces eventually may lead to either PI or RI when similar-looking people are involved. Recalling a first-learned name when a second would be appropriate is an instance of PI. If a second-learned name is called forth when the first is appropriate, RI is shown. This is a difficulty people in "public" jobs such as teaching and selling often encounter.

8.5   WAYS TO IMPROVE MEMORY

Educators and psychologists have devoted much time and effort to determine the factors that help or hinder the acquisition and storage of new materials. Some of the most important findings are reported in this section.

Rehearsal. Among all influences on the acquisition and storage of materials, *rehearsal*—the repetition of the materials being learned—is perhaps the most important. Rehearsal allows for the consolidation of information into long-term storage.

It is important to note, however, that the type of rehearsal carried out affects the formation of memories. If mere repetition is used, the information may stay only in short-term storage and not be consolidated into long-term storage. Repetition sometimes is referred to as *maintenance rehearsal* or *shallow processing*. To assure a greater likelihood that the information will be held in long-term storage, *elaborative rehearsal* or *deep processing* involving additional processing should be used. Several considerations affect elaborative rehearsal.

EXAMPLE 8.17. Something as simple as remembering a telephone number illustrates the differences between maintenance rehearsal and elaborative rehearsal. If you need the number for just a moment, such as when you are calling a movie theater to check the times of a show, you may repeat the number several times while dialing but then make no effort to hold that number in storage once the call has been completed. By contrast, if the person you have asked to accompany you to that movie gives you a telephone number to remember, you will try to find some means of being certain you will recall it at a later time. For example, you might look for some obvious link to the number given (268-4272) by thinking, "Two plus 6 is 8; 268 plus 4 is 272." The mathematical manipulations represent elaborative rehearsal.

Organization. Organization may be imposed either by the material itself or by the learner. More organization, if it is sensible and does not contradict other factors in the materials, usually leads to improved acquisition and retrieval. This appears to be especially true if the learner takes an active part in developing the organization of the materials. An obvious example of this is that sentences are remembered more easily than are groups of random words, especially if the learner creates the sentences.

Imagery. Information that lends itself to creating images, or "mental pictures," is generally more likely to be acquired and retained than is abstract information. Interestingly, research has indicated that the more bizarre the image is, the more likely it is that the thought will be retained.

Other Mnemonics. Other memory-enhancing techniques, called *mnemonics* (from the Greek word *mneme*, meaning "memory"), include a number of ways to improve retention. Among them are the *method of loci*, where information is cataloged as if in particular places; the *keyword technique*, which involves linking the information to be retained with specific prompts; and *rhyming*, where information is "forced" into a sound-alike format.

EXAMPLE 8.18. Caught without anything on which to write a grocery list, you might mentally walk through your apartment and "picture" the items you need to remember in various locales. For example, the loaf of bread could be on top of the television set, the orange juice pouring into a plant, an egg smashed on the floor, and strips of bacon hanging from the shades. Thus, you will remember the things you need for tomorrow's breakfast!

Overlearning. Suppose a criterion of performance (such as one perfect recitation of a poem) is used to represent learning. (Once the subject has recited the poem perfectly from memory, learning has been achieved.) Any practice that occurs *after* this criterion has been reached is called *overlearning*. Overlearning usually is reported as a percentage of the time or the number of trials needed for original learning.

EXAMPLE 8.19. Suppose a subject took 16 trials to learn a list of nonsense syllables (consonant-vowel-consonant sequences such as YOF, which do not make a word). If the subject then continues to practice the correct order of this list for eight more trials, 50 percent overlearning will have occurred.

Research has shown that the law of diminishing returns seems to operate for overlearning. While 50 percent overlearning usually results in a significant improvement in a subject's acquisition and retention of material, 100 percent overlearning helps some more, but not tremendously. Overlearning beyond 100 percent (such as 24 overlearning trials in Example 8.19, which would equal 150 percent) seems to result in little additional improvement. (*Note*: Overlearning helps increase the acquisition and retention of responses, but one must be careful to determine that the responses being practiced are the desired ones.)

EXAMPLE 8.20. A popular phrase said to many children learning all kinds of tasks is "Practice makes perfect." In reality, this phrase should be "Practice makes permanent," for if the wrong response is being practiced to the point of overlearning, it is likely to be well ingrained in the behavior repertoire but far from "perfect."

Transfer of Training. *Transfer of training* (also called *transfer of learning*) occurs when the learning of one set of materials influences the later learning of another set. Some psychologists claim this is the most important learning principle that can be applied in educational situations.

The experimental design used to test transfer of training is as follows:

	Step 1	Step 2
Experimental group	Learn task A	Learn task B
Control group	Put in time	Learn task B

Both groups are alike as possible before the experiment begins. (See Chapter 2 for a discussion of experimental methodology.) To avoid possible biases because of warm-up or fatigue effects, the control group is kept busy doing an unrelated task during step 1, while the experimental group is learning task A.

The test of transfer comes in step 2. If the experimental group learns and retains task B more easily than does the control group (that is, in less time, with fewer trials, or with fewer errors), *positive transfer* has occurred. *Positive transfer* means that the learning of one task has facilitated the learning of the second task. If the experimental group has more difficulty than the control group has learning and retaining task B, *negative transfer* has occurred. (Learning task A has hindered the learning of task B.) If both groups learn Task B equally well, *no transfer* (or *neutral transfer*) has occurred.

EXAMPLE 8.21. Learning to play the piano probably would lead to positive transfer when one started to play the organ or the harpsichord. However, learning to play the piano might hinder learning to play the drums. (Negative transfer might occur because the manual skills developed in piano playing are very different from those required for drumming.) Finally, learning to play the piano probably would have no transfer effects for learning to speak Spanish.

A special case of transfer is called *learning to learn*. A person may learn general principles rather than specific items of information and then use those general principles in a later situation. In such cases, the subject has learned how to learn, retaining an approach to learning rather than particular materials.

EXAMPLE 8.22. A thief might show learning to learn in a series of break-ins. Having learned the general principles of how to force a lock, the thief may apply those principles to each new lock confronted, determining the specific technique that works for each.

Other Practice Variables. Several other variables influence the acquisition and retention of materials. Included among these are *knowledge of results* (*KR*), or *feedback*, the information about the effect of a response. In general, immediate KR is more beneficial than delayed KR, because the subject often treats KR as if it were reinforcement (see Section 7.2 regarding delay of reinforcement).

Another important consideration is *distribution of practice*. In general, the distribution of practice so that blocks of acquisition trials are interspersed with rest periods seems to improve acquisition and retention. When acquisition trials are massed together, performance suffers.

EXAMPLE 8.23. A practical application of distribution of practice occurs in study situations. Acquisition and retention of new materials seem to proceed more easily if studying is divided into study sessions and breaks. (Of course, this assumes that the study sessions are not too short and the breaks are not too long.)

Practice also tends to be more effective if it is done in an *active* rather than a *passive* manner. Educators have translated this result into a "recitation-reading" comparison, showing that active discussion of new materials is likely to promote acquisition and retention of those materials, while a more passive, reading-only approach is less likely to do so.

One aspect of an active approach to learning involves the concept of *warm-up*. It appears that for some tasks, an initial period of adjustment and introduction is necessary before acquisition can take place. A learning curve revealing warm-up effects might be illustrated as in Fig. 8-6.

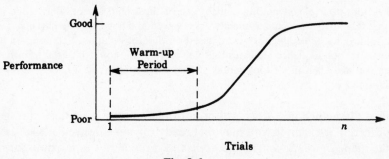

Fig. 8-6

One more variable that has been found to be important for acquisition and retention is called the *whole-part* distinction. Efforts to acquire and retain new materials may be attempts to acquire all of the materials to be learned at one time (the whole method) or only segments of the materials at one time (the part method). In the part method, the subject may divide the materials into several units, studying each separately and trying to bring them all together only after each has been learned individually. The subject also may incorporate an "add-on" technique in which one unit is learned, a second is added to it, and then each succeeding unit until all the materials are learned. This is called the *progressive-part* method.

Research indicates that the choice of whole, part, or progressive-part methods may best be made by analyzing the materials to be learned. Certain tasks seem to lend themselves more to one type of procedure than to another.

EXAMPLE 8.24.   Diving provides a good example of how method selection may depend on the task to be learned and retained. A simple forward dive from a standing position usually is taught by using the whole method. A running approach may be practiced as a separate skill and then connected with the dive. More sophisticated dives, such as a somersault with a full twist, may best be practiced by using the progressive-part method.

8.6   SPECIAL ISSUES IN RETENTION

Retention is not without its unusual aspects. Several are presented in this section to give a sense of the many considerations psychologists must evaluate when working with memory concerns.

Amnesia.   Several types of reduced memory functioning of several sorts have been grouped under the general heading *amnesia*. Evidence that amnesia results when there is an inability to acquire and then consolidate memories into long-term storage comes from studies of *retrograde amnesia*, where there is an inability to retrieve memory of events that occurred *before* the trauma that caused the memory loss. *Anterograde amnesia* refers to an inability to form memories for events that occur *after* the precipitating trauma. *Infantile amnesia* describes the common finding that memories for the first few years of life are typically nonexistent. In all cases of amnesia, the difficulty of consolidating a memory into long-term storage seems to be the crucial consideration.

EXAMPLE 8.25.   Some psychologists believe that in some instances, amnesia may be a good thing. Consider, for example, a person who suffers head trauma in a serious automobile accident. The inability to recall the pain and distress associated with that event may be thought to be a positive result of retrograde amnesia.

Context.   *Context* can influence acquisition and retention in two basic ways. First, the meaning of the material to be learned may be inferred from the use of that material in a particular setting. Second, associations that promote acquisition and retention may result when material is presented in a particular setting. (This phenomenon sometimes is referred to as *state-dependent or mood-dependent memory*.)

EXAMPLE 8.26.   Both principles related to context can be illustrated by considering the meaning of the word "abvoc." If you find that abvocs are cute; some abvocs cry, wet, and have moving parts; and children love abvocs, you may be able to develop a meaning for abvoc based on that information. Suppose you are in a happy mood while learning about abvocs. Evidence indicates that you will be able to retrieve the information about abvocs at a later time when you are again in a happy mood. If, however, your mood differs, you may have more trouble retrieving that information.

Tip-of-the-Tongue Phenomenon.   Retrieval of information from long-term storage sometimes is not readily accomplished. For example, you may feel ready to give a desired answer only to find that you cannot—thus the name *tip-of-the-tongue phenomenon*. Frequently, approximations of the answer are attempted. Similar sounds, the same number of syllables, or the same initial letter may be used in attempts to determine the correct response. Such a memory is not random and retrieval attempts may include synonyms as well.

EXAMPLE 8.27. Someone asks for the name of the British island grouping in the Atlantic Ocean. For some reason, you cannot recall that response immediately, but you say, "Let's see. Is it Burnworth?, Mermaid?, NO, wait. It's like the onion. It's Bermuda!" Your responses include the initial letter, similar sounds, and a related meaning, all evidences of the tip-of-the-tongue phenomenon.

Eyewitness Testimony. A special case of memory occurs in legal proceedings. The reports of witnesses to a crime provide information used in many legal settings. Research evidence has shown that these reports often are inaccurate and moreover are subject to manipulation by the kinds of questions asked.

Some witnesses make substantial errors when asked to report the occurrences they observed because they are eager to "help" and manufacture reports that seem appropriate for the situation. These responses may be a mixture of fact and fiction, but the witnesses are likely to believe the reports are true even when they contain combinations of truth and errors.

The specific wording of the questions asked of witnesses also has been shown to influence the responses given. This seems especially true for children, whose reports of memories seem vulnerable to others' influences.

EXAMPLE 8.28. Laboratory evidence for the inaccuracy of eyewitness testimony includes a series of studies where all the subjects were exposed to the same stimuli but the questions were phrased in varying manners. For example, when asked how fast cars were going when they "smashed" into each other, subjects estimated a speed almost 10 miles per hour faster than the speed estimated by subjects who were asked the speed when the cars "contacted" each other.

Solved Problems

8.1 A college teacher wanted to demonstrate the relationship of retention to forgetting. To do that, the teacher instructed her students to listen to a series of numbers and pay very close attention. When the list was completed, the teacher asked one student to name the numbers in the series he "had forgotten." The student immediately responded by saying, "Forty-three, fifty-eight ..." until he realized he did not know what numbers he had forgotten. What point does this incident illustrate?

The student's responses showed that one cannot tell what one has forgotten, only what one has remembered. Thus, psychologists never measure forgetting directly; they measure retention and assume that what was not retained has been forgotten.

8.2 Is memory different from retention?

Retention is the storage of learned material over a period of time called the *retention interval*. Memory is a more inclusive term, implying that the materials have passed through an acquisition phase, have been stored, and are available for retrieval.

8.3 What is the information-processing approach to the study of retention?

The information-processing approach is an attempt to draw analogies between human mental processes and the processes of computers. The learning of material is seen as an input-processing-output sequence, with acquisition occurring at the input stage, storage occurring during the processing stage, and retrieval (the measurement of retention) as output. Psychologists who attempt to imitate human functions by using computers hope that by analyzing the computer's sequence they will develop a greater understanding of what goes on during human learning.

8.4   Suppose you are sitting in a totally darkened room. Someone else in the room waves a small flashlight in a figure-eight pattern. What do you see, and why?

What you are likely to "see" is a tracery of light rather than a single moving point of light. Although the entire figure eight probably is not recorded at one time (unless the person is moving the light at a very rapid pace), at least part of the figure seems to be present. (You may "see" this even though you realize there is only one moving point of light.) The explanation of this phenomenon is that you are holding a sensory storage of the moving stimulus and thus see the visual path along which it is moving.

8.5   What evidence exists that not all sensory memories operate in the same way?

Most research in sensory memory has looked at *iconic* (visual) and *echoic* (auditory) memories. While both types seem to hold information in a totally unprocessed form, auditory sensory memory appears to last longer than does visual sensory memory.

8.6   Your daughter is getting married. At the reception you stand in line and meet many of her husband's relatives and friends for the first time. A short while later an acquaintance of yours comes over, points to one of those people, and asks who she is. You find you are unable to recall the woman's name, even though you heard it only a few minutes ago. Why?

The explanation is that you have held the name in short-term storage but have not processed it for longer retention. Short-term storage usually is defined as a 1- to 30-second period during which the stimulus item may be used. After that period, however, the item is rapidly discarded or blocked. The information appears to be processed from sensory memory to short-term storage but goes no further.

8.7   How much information can be held in short-term storage?

There are two ways to answer this question. First, evidence indicates that the typical person can hold "seven plus or minus two units of information" in short-term storage. Additionally, however, there is evidence that shows that the size of those units can vary, thus producing differing total amounts of information being processed. One of the most common ways to increase the size of each unit is to employ *chunking*, or grouping separate items together to form larger, cohesive units.

8.8   A study by three psychologists showed that many people were able to recall names and events from their high school days as much as 30 or 40 years later. Their accuracy, as checked against documentation from yearbooks, was quite high. What storage process is involved here? What limitations exist?

The ability to recall items over such a long period indicates long-term storage of the materials. This is the third stage of processing, following sensory storage and short-term storage, and may be almost limitless, depending on the type of information retained. Thus, names and events may be recalled with great accuracy, while learned motor movements may not.

8.9   On your eleventh birthday you and your family took a ferry ride across the Rhine River in Germany. Many years later you can still "picture" the day and remember the food you ate to celebrate the trip. What type of long-term storage is this? How does it contrast with other forms of long-term storage?

Several labels apply to this kind of long-term storage. First, it is an *episodic memory*, an autobiographical memory of an event in which you participated. Episodic memories often are contrasted with *semantic memories*, long-term storage based on the meaning of words, which are generally descriptive without being so specific. It also is appropriate to describe this memory as *declarative*, remembering facts, as opposed to *procedural*, remembering how to do something, and it is likely that this memory is *explicit*, being intentionally recalled, rather than *implicit*, in which case no conscious effort is involved.

8.10   Can you create an example of a procedural, implicit memory?

An excellent example of a procedural, implicit memory is tying one's shoe. The memory is of how to do a particular task, but having been learned very well, the task requires almost no conscious effort to fulfill.

8.11   What general term is used to describe the establishing of long-term storage? What likely explanation is there for this process?

The forming of a fixed or stable memory in long-term storage is referred to as *consolidation*. Consolidation appears to involve the activity of the central nervous system. Recent research has emphasized the activity of proteins in the nucleus of nerve cells that cause the growth of dendrites and, seemingly, the strengthening of connections at the synapses.

8.12   Create recognition, recall, and relearning measures of long-term storage about a play by Shakespeare.

A recognition question about a Shakespearean play might be:

Which of the following plays by Shakespeare features a "balcony scene"?

1. *Twelfth Night*
2. *Much Ado about Nothing*
3. *Hamlet*
4. *Romeo and Juliet*

A recall question would be:

Name the play by Shakespeare that contains the famous balcony scene.

A relearning measure could be:

You played the balcony scene from Shakespeare's *Romeo and Juliet* in a high school drama club production. Learn those lines again for this summer camp production. How long does that take compared to the original learning?

8.13   Suppose it took you 10 days to learn your lines for the balcony scene when you were in the high school drama club. Now, at summer camp, you find that it takes only four days for you to be ready. What is the savings score you obtain for relearning?

The savings score measure of relearning compares the amount of time or the number of trials required for original learning (OL) with the same measure for relearning (RL), creating a percentage called *savings*. In this case, the solution would be as follows:

$$OL - RL/OL \times 100 = \text{savings score}$$
$$10 - 4/10 \times 100 = \text{savings score}$$
$$6/10 \times 100 = \text{savings score}$$
$$60\% = \text{savings score}$$

8.14   Suppose an instructor gives a class the chance to choose the method of retention measurement that will be used on the final exam. If the students want to start the exam with the biggest possible advantage, which measurement of retention should they choose?

The class should choose a recognition test. As long as they are not penalized for guessing, the students can anticipate receiving some credit for correct answers chosen by chance. For example, with four-choice multiple-choice questions, students might get 25 percent correct just by guessing. A recall test may produce a zero percent retention score, while a relearning measure (which probably would not be used in a classroom setting) can produce a "minus savings" when relearning takes longer than the original learning. (*Note*: Some instructors realize these differences and adjust the grading scale so that no actual advantage exists for any single measure.)

8.15. A famous study of learning to interpret Morse code showed that subjects first learned to understand each separate letter, held that level for a while, and then somewhat suddenly seemed to be able to receive whole words. Ultimately, the subjects became quite skilled at interpreting the code. Sketch the learning curve that represents the performance described, labeling the significant components of the curve.

The learning curve is illustrated in Fig. 8-7. Two noticeable components are the *plateau*, which represents the pause before the total words are grasped, and the *asymptote*, the maximum performance possible.

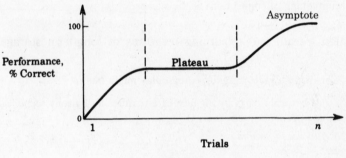

Fig. 8-7

8.16 Another famous study in psychology has come to be known as the "sleep-waking study." The subjects were trained for a task and then measured for retention at various intervals afterward. In half the cases the subjects went about their normal daily activities after training (waking condition), while the other half rested or slept after training (sleeping condition). Activity, as opposed to sleep, appeared to interfere more with retention. Sketch the "curves of forgetting," with the appropriate labels, for these two groups.

See Fig. 8-8. Both groups show the "typical curve of forgetting," with the most rapid loss of retention occurring soon after learning. In addition, the loss of the waking group was greater than that of the sleeping group.

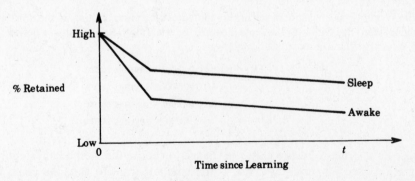

Fig. 8-8

8.17 A grandfather and granddaughter are talking about elementary school. The grandfather is asked, "Well, what was it like when you were in grade school?" He responds, "You know, I don't remember too much of that anymore except that it was fun and my third-grade teacher's name was Mrs. Wakenhut. Was she ever nice!" When asked if he can remember any of his other teachers, the grandfather finds that he cannot. His recall of Mrs. Wakenhut's name seems to illustrate which principle of retention?

It can be assumed that the grandfather learned the names of all his elementary school teachers quite well. His recall of Mrs. Wakenhut but none of the others may illustrate the von Restorff effect, in which one distinct response is remembered in the right place and in the midst of many others that are not recalled.

8.18 If you are interviewing for a job and know that the interviewer will be talking to potential candidates all day long, which time slot should you request for the interview? Why?

Assuming you do not intend to do something outrageous to make the interviewer remember you (the von Restorff effect), you probably should ask for one of the first or one of the last time slots. The reason for doing this is that items (people) at the start of a list (the *primacy effect*) and items at the end of a list (the *recency effect*) usually are remembered better than are those in the middle of a list. This is called the serial position effect.

8.19 A popular notion is that people never forget anything that has happened to them; that is, everything is "stored away" somewhere in memory. What theory of retention seems to support this idea? Is there evidence to support the theory?

The theory of memory that supports this notion is based on the concept of failure to retrieve. The theory suggests that the memories are indeed present but that lack of organization, proper cues, or some other variable keeps a person from producing the memory. Research studies have shown that when stimulus cues are altered to generate new attempts at retrieval, many additional responses can be provoked. Also, electrical and chemical stimulation of certain areas of the brain sometimes generates memories that otherwise seem to be lost.

8.20 Arriving early for his piano lesson, Charlie is surprised to find his teacher practicing scales and other basic exercises. When he asks why the teacher is practicing such "simple stuff," the answer he gets is, "Why, if I didn't, I might forget how to play them!" The teacher's answer shows a belief in which theory of forgetting?

The teacher seems to think that memory depends on use, while forgetting will occur with disuse. This theory proposes that memory is held as a trace which may fade if it is not renewed periodically. (*Note*: Such a theory would help explain the "curve of forgetting" obtained for the sleeping group in Solved Problem 8.16.)

8.21 Look at the three drawings in Fig. 8-9. The subjects in one group were told that drawing (*a*) resembled a tree. The subjects in a second group were told that drawing (*a*) resembled a light bulb. Later, in an attempt to reproduce drawing (*a*) from memory, the first group of subjects tended to make drawings like drawing (*b*), while the second group's drawings tended to look like drawing (*c*). What theory of forgetting explains these results?

(*a*)

(*b*)

(*c*)

Fig. 8-9

The theory is that forgetting may occur because changes or distortions may develop with the passage of time. In this experiment, the potential distortions are provided by the experimenter. The *meaning* first attributed to a stimulus is likely to determine (at least in part) how it will be recalled later.

8.22   When she was fired from her sales position, Susan reacted by saying, "I just can't understand it. Why, I remember how well I did with that customer from Portland, and then there was that other one from Yorktown. My goodness, I shouldn't have been fired." Suppose you knew that Susan had had great difficulty with a customer from Anderson and had lost an important customer from Cammack. What theory of memory and forgetting might then be used to explain her response?

Susan's responses seem selective; she remembers the favorable circumstances and forgets the unpleasant ones. Such forgetting is called *motivated forgetting* and is attributed to *repression*, a psychoanalytic concept that proposes that some memories are deliberately forgotten to help protect one's self-image. This concept was stressed by Sigmund Freud and many of his followers as a possible explanation of what they called *unconscious motives*.

8.23   Experimental investigations in verbal learning revealed that if subjects learned various responses from one conceptual category (such as the names of vegetables) and were asked to recall them after a short-term storage period, performance declined with succeeding trials. Additionally, if after several such trials the response materials were changed in regard to conceptual category, the recall percentage improved. The improvement was related to how much difference appeared to exist between the original materials and the new items. Fig. 8-10 presents these results. In the first three trials, subjects memorized lists of vegetables. In the fourth trial, they memorized either another list of vegetables or the names of fruits or sports.

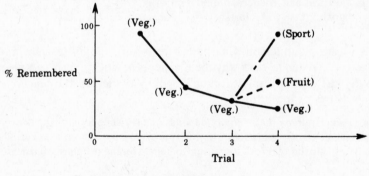

Fig. 8-10

What theory seems to explain the decline in performance on the second and third trials? How does this principle help account for the results on the fourth trial?

The decline in performance can be attributed to proactive interference (PI), in which learning earlier materials interferes with the retention of material learned later. The apparent release from PI on the fourth trial is greater for the sports words than for the fruit words because there is less conceptual overlap between vegetables and sports than there is between vegetables and fruits.

8.24   Lucky enough to receive an overseas travel grant, Professor Pritchard first spent three months studying in France. He then moved to Barcelona, Spain, for three more months. As he prepared to leave Europe, Pritchard returned briefly to Paris, where he found that he used Spanish phrases instead of French phrases. How does the interference theory of forgetting help account for his trouble?

Pritchard's difficulties illustrate *retroactive interference* (RI), in which new learning (Spanish) interferes with the retention of previously learned materials (French). Both RI and PI studies support the concept that forgetting may occur because of the inhibiting or interfering effects of materials other than those being tested.

8.25   Return to Solved Problem 8.16 and look at the "curves of forgetting" for the sleeping and waking groups. The "decay theory" helps explain the shape of the curves. But how does interference theory seem to account for the difference in the performance levels of the two groups?

Retroactive interference (RI) appears to be important in this study. The sleep group has little or no opportunity to be exposed to materials that may interfere with later retention; this group learns and then goes to sleep. The waking group, by contrast, may experience many interfering or inhibiting situations after learning. (It is assumed that both groups had equal opportunity for PI effects before the study started, and so RI seems to account for the differences found.)

8.26   Suppose, for a hiking trip; your friend calls to remind you that you must remember to pack bug spray, lotion, petroleum jelly, and bandages. You will not be able to resume packing for a little while. What kind of rehearsal should you use so that you will remember these supplies when you get back to packing?

Rehearsal, the repetition of materials to be learned, can take different forms. Maintenance rehearsal would mean that you simply kept repeating the items over and over until you began to pack again. This would be relatively inefficient and likely to be disrupted. Elaborative rehearsal, or deep processing, would involve finding one or more ways to "do something" with the list that would enhance the chances of remembering what was included. In this case, you might want to envision a "worst-case scenario" and picture yourself sitting in a blazing sun, surrounded by bugs, trying to repair blister damage on your feet. You would put lotion on for the sun, apply bug spray for the insects, and petroleum jelly on the blisters before covering them with bandages.

8.27   Identify the "memory tricks" used in the answer to the Solved Problem 8.26.

Memory is improved if the materials are *organized*. Simply creating sentences about the items to be remembered represents a basic level of organization. In addition, picturing the worst-case scenario involves creating *imagery*, another memory aid that improves retention. Other mnemonic devices that could have been employed include the method of loci, the keyword technique, and rhyming.

8.28   Sometimes peers seem to deride a fellow student by saying, "You goof, you really wasted your time and *overlearned* that stuff!" Why would psychologists say the peers are wrong?

Overlearning refers to practice beyond a level of competence. For example, if it took two hours to get ready for a quiz, an additional one hour of study would represent 50 percent overlearning. Evidence indicates that overlearning helps assure retention of the materials being learned and is beneficial. In this case, the student being teased probably can be expected to do well on the quiz.

8.29   Psychologists and educators spend many hours and dollars trying to design school curricula so that each step in the learning program leads logically to the next. Why?

The obvious answer is that programs are designed in this fashion to try to maximize the students' learning experiences. The principle involved is positive transfer of training. If curricula are designed carefully, it can be expected that many of the students' learning experiences will make succeeding learning easier to accomplish. In a sense, the learning process is a series of "steps" students take in the proper sequence for learning and retention to be most efficient.

8.30   Suppose that when you study, you follow a set routine of study techniques regardless of the material to be learned. What learning principle would your study habits represent?

Learning general principles that then are applied in a number of different situations is called *learning to learn*. In this situation, your general principles of how to study are applicable to many different types of subjects.

8.31   In recent years flight students have used computer-controlled flight simulators for practice. In the simulator, the "pilot" manipulates controls while observing a "flight," learning the skills needed when actually flying a plane. Such simulators have been found to be helpful both for maintaining skills already learned and for learning new skills. This type of machine operates according to which learning principle?

Each "flight" is judged by the machine for success or failure of the manipulations made, providing the "pilot" with knowledge of results (KR) or feedback. This immediate feedback is particularly helpful if the pilot is trying to modify existing techniques because it provides KR without placing the person in the threatening or dangerous environment that actual flight might.

8.32   People who are studying or working often take "coffee breaks." What principle of learning are they putting to use when they take such breaks?

The principle is distribution of practice. In general, distributing practice into practice sequences and rest sequences seems to facilitate learning and retention. Thus, coffee breaks probably facilitate study or work performance compared to working straight through.

8.33   Guides describing how to study, counselors' suggestions, and practical experience all tend to favor certain attitudes toward acquiring the materials used in a school course. One attitude in particular emphasizes the *active approach* toward learning. What does this mean? What are some examples of this approach?

The active approach means that the learner actively takes part in the learning process. Research evidence indicates that being active in an attempt to learn is usually more beneficial than remaining passive. Examples of active studying include underlining and making notes while reading rather than just reading and trying to answer questions about the material rather than just reviewing it. The wise student incorporates an active approach and many of the other principles mentioned in this chapter, such as distributing practice rather than "cramming" and seeking knowledge of results while learning.

8.34   Two students have to memorize a poem that each will have to recite in front of the class. One practices each stanza separately, memorizing one at a time and not trying to recite the entire poem until all the stanzas have been learned. The second learns the first stanza, then repeats the first while learning the second, and continues adding each successive stanza in this manner until the entire poem has been learned. Distinguish between the two methods of learning.

The first student is using the part method of learning, while the second is using the progressive-part method. While both are part methods and differ from trying to learn the whole poem at once, they differ in the amount of practice given to each stanza. The first student devotes enough time to each stanza to learn it. The second student not only learns each stanza but because of the progressive-part technique experiences overlearning for the earlier stanzas.

8.35   Jordan was riding her bicycle but not wearing a protective helmet. She crashed and struck her head against the curb, sustaining a severe concussion. After several days in the hospital, Jordan was released, but when asked by her friends to describe her accident, she found that she could not recall anything about it. What principle describes Jordan's inability to recall?

Jordan is exhibiting retrograde amnesia. She is unable to remember events that occurred before the trauma that produced the memory loss. Although it is likely that she eventually will recall some of the events preceding the accident, it is unlikely that she ever will recall the accident itself; the memory probably never was consolidated into long-term storage.

8.36 Contrast infantile amnesia with anterograde or retrograde amnesia. What are the similarities and differences?

Infantile, anterograde, and retrograde amnesias are all marked by some form of memory loss. The major difference among them is that infantile amnesia is not caused by a trauma or accident, while the other two typically are. It is more likely that infantile amnesia is simply the result of the immaturity of the nervous system in a very young child.

8.37 Consider the following experimental design: Two groups of rats are to learn to solve a maze. One group does this in a sober condition, while the other does so after having been given alcohol ("drunk" rats). For testing later retention of the maze pattern, both groups are divided, with half of each group remaining sober and the other half "getting drunk." Based on your understanding of state-dependent learning, predict which groups will show best retention of the responses (sober-sober, sober-drunk, drunk-sober, drunk-drunk).

If you picked the first and fourth groups, you predicted correctly. Rats that were tested in the same state in which they had learned the maze responses showed the best retention of those responses, illustrating the importance of state-dependent learning for subsequent retention.

8.38 A contestant is given some cues and asked to recall the name of a famous actress from early film history. The contestant responds, "Fairbanks." The host tells the contestant this is wrong and actually is the name of a famous actor. Before the host can give the correct response, the contestant blurts out, "Fairborn, Fairburn, Burnbank, Fairheart," and finally responds correctly with "Bernhardt." The sequence of these responses illustrates what pattern of retention?

The contestant's responses seem to illustrate the tip-of-the-tongue phenomenon. Searching through the stored memories, the contestant selects names which approximate the category (acting), the correct number of syllables (two), and similar sounds (such as "burn" and "heart"), before determining the correct answer. It is unlikely the contestant would have chosen a name such as "Jones" because it has none of the appropriate characteristics.

8.39 In the courtroom, attorneys often very carefully plan the phrasing of questions they will ask eyewitnesses. Why?

Research evidence has indicated that eyewitness testimony can be subject to influence, especially by the question being asked. For example, asking "Did you see him _____ the defendant?" probably will produce differing attitudes if one of the words "strike," "hit," or "slug" is inserted in the blank. Regardless of the response given to that question, the phrasing is likely to affect the subsequent responses.

Key Terms

Amnesia.   Reduced memory functioning.

Anterograde amnesia.   An inability to form memories for events that occur after a precipitating trauma.

Asymptote.   The point at which a learning curve levels near maximum performance.

Chunking.   Grouping separate items to enable easier retention of the collective materials.

Consolidation.   The forming of a fixed or stable memory because of activity of the central nervous system.

Curve of forgetting.   The graph plotting the percentage of learned materials retained as a function of time since learning; generally shows that most loss of retention occurs soon after acquisition.

Declarative memory.   Storage of facts.

Echoic storage.   Storage of information as sounds.

Episodic memory.   Autobiographical storage of an event, based on personal experience.

Explicit memory.   An effortful attempt to create storage of information.

Forgetting.   The loss of retention or the inability to retrieve a stored memory.

Iconic storage.   Storage of information as visual signals.

Implicit memory.   Storage of information involving little or no intention or effort.

Infantile amnesia.   The common finding that memories for the first several years of life are typically nonexistent.

Information-processing approach.   Using the computer analogy (input-storage-output) to evaluate memory.

Knowledge of results (KR).   Also called *feedback*; information about the effect of a response.

Learning curves.   A graphical representation of the acquisition and storage of information as a function of time or trials.

Long-term storage.   Retention of a response for more than 30 seconds; materials from sensory or short-term storage are processed or encoded for this type of storage.

Memory.   The storage and later measured retention of a response that was previously acquired.

Mnemonics.   Memory-enhancing techniques that may improve retention.

Overlearning.   Any practice that occurs after the criterion for retention has been achieved.

Parallel processing.   Occurs when more than one component of memory (storage) is activated and processed simultaneously.

Plateau.   During the acquisition of information, a period of little or no progress preceded and followed by increases in storage.

Proactive interference (PI).   Also called *proactive inhibition*; the effect of previous learning on the retention of later learning.

Procedural memory.   Storage of skills and abilities; knowing "how to."

Qualitative measurement.   A measure of retention involving subjective judgment.

Recall.   A measure of retention in which a subject is given only a minimal cue and must produce the requested materials.

Recognition.   A measure of retention in which the correct answer is presented to the subject, who must select it from among several alternatives.

Relearning.   A measure of retention in which the time or trials necessary for the second learning of a task are compared to the time or trials necessary for original learning; see also *savings score*.

Repression.   Motivated forgetting; one of the defense mechanisms proposed by Freud.

Retention.   The storage of learning over a period of time.

Retention interval.   The period between acquisition of a response and retrieval of that response from storage.

Retrieval.   The process of bringing materials from storage.

Retroactive interference (RI).   Also called *retroactive inhibition*; the effect of later learning on the retention of previous learning.

Retrograde amnesia.   The inability to retrieve memories of events that occurred before the trauma that caused memory loss.

Savings score.   A percentage that expresses the difference between the time or number of trials required for original learning and the time or number of trials required for relearning.

Semantic memory.   Storage based on the meaning of words.

Sensory storage.   The very brief retention of a signal in its unprocessed sensory form.

Serial position effect.   The finding that the first and last items of a list are remembered better than are items in the middle of the list.

Short-term storage.   Also called *working memory*; retention of a stimulus for a 1- to 30-second period; during this period, some initial processing takes place.

State-dependent memory.   Also called *mood-dependent memory*; occurs when retrieval of information is dependent on recreating the setting or emotional state that existed when the material was first acquired.

Tip-of-the-tongue phenomenon (TOT).   Occurs when retrieval (usually verbal) from long-term storage seems almost possible but cannot quite be accomplished.

Transfer of training.   Also called *transfer of learning*; occurs when the learning of one set of materials influences the later acquisition of another set.

Unconscious motives.   Information that is held in memory and continues to influence responding but is not recognized at a conscious level.

Von Restorff effect.   Also called the *isolation effect*; occurs when an exceedingly distinctive stimulus within a list is remembered very well compared to the surrounding items.

CHAPTER 9

Cognitive Processes

Once psychologists gained some knowledge about the processes of acquisition and retention in learning (see Chapters 7 and 8), a number of them turned to consideration of the uses of learning. Ultimately, these studies have focused on the "things that go on in the head," the mental content and activity called *cognitive processes*. This chapter concentrates on four major aspects of cognitive processes: conceptual thinking, problem solving, decision making, and the development and use of language.

9.1 CONCEPTUAL THINKING

The contents of memory, as described in Chapter 8, provide the bases on which conceptual thinking is formed. *Thinking* is symbolic mediation, or the use of symbols to span the time interval between presentation of a stimulus and the responses made to it. Thinking is an internal, personal process that often is attributed to the activity of the mind. The mental manipulation of the *representation* of information, thinking cannot be observed directly but must be assumed from observable behaviors.

EXAMPLE 9.1. One college instructor is known to demonstrate the individuality and "hiddenness" of thinking by asking the class to "think of the dirtiest word you can!" The instructor then points out that unless one of the students calls out a word, there is no way for any member of the class to know what choice another student made. However, one of the students could speak, write, or gesture in a way that would indicate his or her thought. The other students could interpret this as representative of that student's thinking.

Symbols. A *symbol* is any stimulus that has become a commonly accepted representation of an object, event, action, or idea. A symbol may take any form or meaning as long as there is general agreement that it stands for another particular thing.

Concepts. *Concepts* are symbols that summarize or generalize attributes typical of several objects, events, actions, or ideas that are dissimilar in other important aspects. Concepts distinguish between members and nonmembers of the conceptual category on the basis of specified characteristics and thus create basic categories of knowledge or meaning. They simplify, summarize, and give structure or predictability to what otherwise might be an overly complex and uncontrollable world.

Concepts often are thought to fall into *hierarchies* or levels of understanding. These levels are classified as *superordinate* (the highest level), *basic* (an intermediate level), and *subordinate* (the lowest level). Typical speech employs mostly basic-level concepts.

154

EXAMPLE 9.2. When a person asks a companion to "please hand me a beer," a basic-level concept is being used. Such a request is much more likely to be made than is a request for "a chilled alcoholic beverage brewed from barley and hops and encased in an aluminum can" or for a "drink." The first (subordinate) is far more specific than is needed for ordinary conversation, while the second (superordinate) is far too vague to convey the intended message.

Concepts are stored in memory by their *defining features* and, thus, may be *well defined* or *fuzzy*. A well-defined concept has precise features, ones that allow for little ambiguity. Fuzzy concepts are less clear and usually are explained by giving examples.

EXAMPLE 9.3. Concepts in the sciences or mathematics are likely to be well defined. Although its size may differ from one example to the next, a "circle" otherwise always has exactly the same properties. By contrast, the concept of "bird" is far less exact. Some birds fly, others do not, some have songs, and others are silent—the defining features are much less clear.

Concepts are classified as *simple* when they represent a single stimulus property. (For example, all things are round or they are not round.) Concepts are *complex* when more than one stimulus property is considered simultaneously.

Complex concepts take several forms. *Conjunctive concepts* are defined by the simultaneous presence of two or more properties. *Disjunctive concepts* may be based on two or more properties, but any one property or a combination of properties is adequate to satisfy the concept. *Relational concepts* establish a relationship between two properties.

EXAMPLE 9.4. The various types of complex concepts can be illustrated by considering beverages. The word "highball" represents a conjunctive concept because to satisfy (or fit into) the concept, a drink must have at least two properties: the presence of alcohol and that of another fluid (such as water or soda). The word "beverage" is a disjunctive concept because any one of a number of drinks (such as water, beer, and milk) or a combination of drinks (such as coffee with milk) satisfies the concept. Any comparison, such as the statement "Milkshakes are thicker than sodas," expresses a relational concept.

Ambiguous or "fuzzy" concepts often are described by citing a *prototype*, a typical or highly representative example of the concept. Prototypes produce high agreement among persons asked to designate which examples fit the category and which do not, most likely because a prototype contains more features associated with the concept than do other examples. Some psychologists modify the definition of a prototype and treat it as an abstract or idealized concept made up of the "best" characteristics of the category. Individual examples of the category are then called *exemplars*.

EXAMPLE 9.5. By far the most likely prototype responses to the question "What is a pet?" are "dog" and "cat." It is much less likely that the responses will include "fish" or "snake," even though both of those animals are kept as pets by some people. Consider what the properties are that make a dog or a cat the more appropriate response, and you will list the features associated with the concept. Note that you may have to do this by citing exemplars such as "Labrador retriever," "boxer," and "poodle" but probably will be much less likely to cite "corgi" (which has no tail) or "basenji" (which has no bark).

9.2 PROBLEM SOLVING

A major consideration in cognitive psychology has been *problem solving*. Problem solving occurs when an individual or group establishes a goal and seeks ways to reach that goal. Careful research on problem-solving processes has disclosed a fairly common sequence of events leading to the attainment of that goal.

The Problem-Solving Sequence.   The steps in problem solving seem to be as follows:

Recognize that there is a problem.   Not being able to understand that there is a problem stops the process at this point.

Define the problem accurately.   This seems to involve representing the problem correctly and recognizing concepts that are pertinent to the problem. If the key concepts are not available, the problem may not be solved.

Produce hypotheses about the problem's solution.   Based on the concepts selected in the previous step, guesses about how to resolve the problem are developed.

Test the hypotheses.   Each hypothesis should be confirmed or disconfirmed. While several hypotheses may solve the problem, it often is possible to select a single best solution. If all are disconfirmed, checking and repeating the previous steps to create different hypotheses is necessary to attain the goal.

EXAMPLE 9.6.   The sequence of events leading to a goal is easily demonstrated if your boss asks you to travel to "Athens" to evaluate a building. You realize that you must find an appropriate mode of transportation to get to Athens. However, if you interpret the request to mean Athens, Greece when the intent is to send you to Athens, Ohio, the problem is not defined correctly and no solution you generate is going to work. If you do understand that the city is in Ohio, you then can generate possible solutions (hypotheses) involving various ways to get there—take a car and drive, fly to the nearest airport and rent a car to drive to the city, take a train, take a bus—and then test each to determine which might be the most efficient and cost-effective, selecting the one that seems to fit best with attaining the goal.

While Example 9.6 is fairly straightforward, it should be recognized that the same sequence may apply to a problem as intricate and subtle as a personality difficulty or an emotional disturbance. An individual first must recognize that there is a problem and define it correctly, then determine the key concepts necessary for solving the problem, and finally complete the problem-solving sequence as described above.

Problem-Solving Strategies.   If successful problem solving requires resolving the sequence presented above, a crucial aspect is producing the possible solutions. This solution-process production generally falls into one of two categories: *algorithms* or *heuristics*.

An *algorithm* is a procedure or set of actions that guarantees a solution to the problem. Many computers are programmed with algorithmic procedures which assure that once the information is entered correctly, a solution (if one is possible) will be found. Although this process is relatively inefficient, the speed of computers sometimes makes this approach reasonable.

EXAMPLE 9.7.   Many psychologists like to use anagrams to illustrate algorithmic solutions. For example, if one is presented with the letters "TEHAR," the algorithmic way to find an English word composed of those letters is to try every possible arrangement, such as "TERAH," "TERHA," "TEARH," "TEAHR," "TEHRA," "TEHAR" (these exhaust the possibilities starting with *TE*) and continue until all possible combinations have been evaluated to determine whether any one forms a word in English. For a five-letter word, 120 combinations of letters are possible. If every anagram had to be solved in this manner, the problem solver might say, "Have a *HEART!*"

Because algorithms require so much energy expenditure, problem solving often is done using *heuristics*, "rules of thumb" or shortcut strategies that reduce the complexity of the problem and focus on the most likely solutions. Heuristics cannot guarantee a solution but typically are far more efficient than an algorithm when they produce a successful resolution to the problem.

Some heuristics are specific to a particular kind of problem, but others are general and may be applied to many situations. These include *means-end analysis*, which compares a current position with the desired end and then tries to find ways (the means) to get from the position to the end, and *backward search*, which begins at the end point of the problem and works backward.

EXAMPLE 9.8.   When given a pencil maze to solve, some people employ a backward search heuristic, beginning the track by starting at the goal and following the successful path back to the starting point. Although some wrong paths can be entered (a solution is not guaranteed), the use of backward search increases the probability that a correct solution will be found rapidly.

Psychologists also have noted general categories referred to as the *availability heuristic* and the *representativeness heuristic*. In the former, solutions are based on how easily an event can be recalled from memory, with those more easily recalled being overestimated in regard to how frequently they may occur. In the latter, judgment is based on how much a person or event "fits" a particular category, with those "fitting" better being attributed a greater than deserved likelihood of fulfilling an expectation.

EXAMPLE 9.9.   People often solve problems using the representativeness heuristic by judging an individual in regard to how closely that person matches the characteristics of a given group. For example, the decision to hire a teenage potential employee as a Web page creator and moderator may be based on "surface characteristics" because the employer believes that teenagers with tattoos and body piercings are less reliable than are those who do not have such adornments. It is possible that this way of thinking came from an availability heuristic in that the employer may remember better some instances of teenagers with tattoos and body piercings being "in trouble" than instances involving "clean-cut" teenagers.

Creativity.   An additional consideration for problem solving is *creativity*, the structuring of ideas or responses in original or novel yet productive ways. Psychologists recognize differences in goal-seeking strategies when they distinguish between *convergent thinking* and *divergent thinking*. Convergent thinking occurs when a problem is solved by calling forth solutions based on already known knowledge or logic. The subject often is seeking a known solution to a problem. By contrast, divergent thinking is the ability to generate unusual yet appropriate responses or response patterns when solving the problem and therefore represents creative thinking.

Research into the relationship of creativity and intelligence has shown that there is some correlation between the two. Apparently, however, the mode of thinking is more important to creative thinking than is the amount of intelligence.

EXAMPLE 9.10.   In attempts to measure creativity, psychologists have generated many different types of tests. One involves presenting the subject with a minimal visual cue and asking the subject to complete the drawing. For example, the subject might be shown drawing (*a*) in Fig. 9-1 and asked to complete it. A response such as drawing (*b*) would be judged much less creative than would a response such as drawing (*c*).

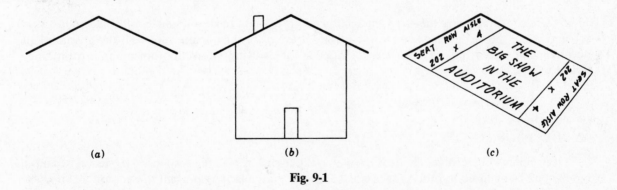

(*a*)   (*b*)   (*c*)

Fig. 9-1

Insight.   *Insight* is the term used to describe the phenomenon in which a problem is posed, followed by a period of no apparent progress in solving the problem and then a sudden solution. The key characteristic of insight is the suddenness of the solution, a swift determination of a hypothesis that can be confirmed. Insight seems to be very personal and is difficult to describe as a psychological process, but it seems to involve reconceptualizing the problem to find the solution or strategy that will solve the problem. (*Note*: Gestalt psychologists viewed insight as understanding how different parts of a problem fit into a cohesive whole. The suddenness of the solution is accounted for by the "instant recognition" of how the pieces fit together.)

Variables Affecting Problem Solving.   Problem solving is a kind of performance and is subject to some of the same influences that affect other types of behavior. Two variables that influence problem solving are motivation and past experiences.

Motivation.   Very low levels of motivation are likely to yield poor problem-solving performance. An individual with insufficient motivation to continue the problem-solving sequence is unlikely to complete that sequence. In addition, a particular motivation may influence a person's attention, directing the person to certain problems or aspects of the environment and away from others.

Past Experience.   Previous experience may predispose a person to respond in a certain manner when trying to solve a problem. In discussing this phenomenon, psychologists usually try to distinguish between a *habit*, which implies a long-term tendency to respond in a certain manner, and *set*, the temporary tendency to respond in a certain manner (see Section 5.5). Some psychologists describe set as an example of an *anchoring heuristic*, in which currently available information is used as the reference point for making a judgment. This is similar to the effect noted earlier in Section 8.6 and Example 8.27 of specific wording on eyewitness testimony.

EXAMPLE 9.11.   If you have been *trampled*, causing you to become *rumpled* and you have *sampled* a very *disgruntled* moment, are you *misled* by the last italicized word? If indeed you mispronounced the last italicized word because the previous four prepared you for a certain form of pronunciation, you have illustrated set, the temporary tendency to respond in a certain manner. In other settings, your habit of pronouncing the word correctly as "miss-led" would be likely to dominate.

A form of past experience that has been studied extensively is called *functional fixedness*. This occurs when a person is unable to see any other use for an object except its normal or usual one even though a novel response might be both useful and appropriate for solving the problem at hand.

EXAMPLE 9.12.   At an outdoor concert that had been threatened by rain, the sun broke through and the temperature rose rapidly. One patron, clutching her furled umbrella, was heard to say, "I'd be okay if I just had some shade." Obviously, she illustrated functional fixedness, being unable to envision opening the umbrella to create the needed shade.

Note also that *negative transfer* (see Section 8.5) is thought to be a possible influence on problem solving. When the techniques learned for solving previous problems interfere with the possibility of developing or employing new or different strategies for a solving a current problem, negative transfer is said to have occurred.

9.3   DECISION MAKING

Decision making involves choice. Given alternative sets of possible responses, the individual must opt for one as opposed to others. Two variables seem particularly important in decision making: the utility of each possible outcome and the probability that each outcome may occur. In addition, the limits of short-term or working memory often affect the decision-making process.

The *utility* of each possible outcome refers to the value the individual places on the outcome. This sometimes is called "weighing one's choices," judging the relative value of each possibility involved in the decision.

EXAMPLE 9.13.   Decision-making utility is easily observed in circumstances where time, expense, or other variables allow for only one of several choices to be carried out. For example, if one must choose between buying a dog and spending the money on a class trip, questions of how enjoyable the trip will be versus how much long-term pleasure the dog will bring must be weighed. Both positives such as those above and negatives such as how bad will you feel if all your friends are on the trip and you are not, compared to how unhappy you will be if you do not have the dog, must be evaluated.

The probability that the actual outcome will occur is also important in decision making. Each decision involves judging the odds of various possible outcomes. Misestimations of probability are certainly part of the explanation for incorrect decision making, such as decisions which lead to an unwanted pregnancy or a sexually transmitted disease.

When the decision involves a relatively complex situation, the limits of short-term storage or working memory (see Section 8.2) also may influence the process. Inability to hold sufficient information in working memory may cause the decision maker to ignore some aspects of the situation and base a choice on a few relevant bits of information. What is considered relevant can be manipulated, as in advertising "pitches" to sell a product.

EXAMPLE 9.14.   Weight-conscious individuals are swayed by advertising that features words associated with being lean or slender. In selling some yogurt products, for example, emphasis is placed on "low-fat" considerations but no mention is made of the relatively high calorie count in many of these products. Consumers buy these products, ignoring some of the available information because of the distraction of other, relevant (if possibly misleading) information.

Humans do not make the "best" decision in all instances. One explanation for this has been called *satisficing*, the selection of the first alternative encountered that appears to be good enough. Rather than investigate all alternatives, evaluating the gains and losses associated with each one, people are more likely to make decisions that simply meet their minimum criteria.

EXAMPLE 9.15.   At least one organization has been very successful by providing reports for consumers that supposedly *have* weighed all the possible alternatives and considered the possible benefits and costs associated with each one. The magazine provided by this organization has great popularity, although evidence indicates that even when such information is available, many people do not use it but instead exhibit satisficing.

Reasoning.   A more formal evaluation of thinking and decision making is the study of *reasoning*, the drawing of conclusions from information or evidence. It must be recognized that conclusions drawn from reasoning will be correct only if the information on which the conclusions are based was correct to begin with. Faulty premises can lead to incorrect decisions even when the logic of the reasoning process is without error.

Inductive reasoning is the process of reaching a conclusion based on specific cases. This is a process of reaching summation, using available information to get to a general rule. *Deductive reasoning* uses general principles to reach specific conclusions. Inductive reasoning is similar to bottom-up processing, while deductive reasoning is similar to top-down processing (see Section 5.5).

One other kind of reasoning that has been studied extensively is *analogical reasoning*, thinking that takes an *a* is to *b* as *x* is to *y* format. This type of reasoning is popular in clinical and counseling practice in employing information gathered from case histories. Based on what has been successful in the past, the therapist makes decisions for the current resolution of a problem.

9.4   LANGUAGE

Language is a major area of cognitive studies. Psychologists who investigate this area are called *psycholinguists* and are interested in the relationships between an organism and its language. *Psycholinguistics* covers the acquisition, structure, and use of language. Several general considerations apply to understanding language acquisition.

Signs versus Symbols.   Signs and symbols are both signals, stimuli that can be used for communication. They differ in that a *sign* has meaning because of its very nature, while a *symbol* has meaning because a number of people (or other organisms) have chosen to accept that meaning. Any agreed upon designation (a word, drawing, gesture, etc.) may serve as a symbol.

EXAMPLE 9.16.   If you made a noise like the squeal of a pig, you would be using a sign, a stimulus that has meaning because it corresponds (at least somewhat) to the sound naturally made by a pig. Writing or saying the word "oink," however, would be using a symbol. The word "oink" does not duplicate the naturally occurring event but has come to have a meaning that is generally accepted.

Written versus Spoken Language.   The development of language in humans generally takes at least two different forms: written and spoken language. Written language depends on the visual presentation of words, while spoken language depends on the production and reception of sounds.

In general, word usage in written language differs somewhat from that in spoken language. Words are used with different frequencies, are arranged differently, are repeated more often in spoken language, and generally take a more casual form in spoken language and a more formal form when written.

Expressive versus Receptive Language. *Expressive language* is defined as words that convey a message. *Receptive language* defines what is understood from the words used. Expressive and receptive language may not be the same thing; the message producer may wish to convey one message, while the message receiver may interpret the same words in a different manner.

EXAMPLE 9.17.   Multiple meanings for words may make it particularly difficult for communication to occur. For example, the word "bad" at one time had at least two meanings: it meant both misbehaving and something judged to be really good. When a message producer said, "He's bad!" the receiver could understand the message in at least two ways.

Word Development and Usage.   The construction and usage of words has been studied in great detail. These investigations have resulted in the development of the following terms and findings.

Phonemes.   The basic sound components of spoken language are called *phonemes*. Young children seem to have the ability to produce the phonemic patterns of many languages but soon learn to limit their patterns to those appropriate to the language being learned. Most analyses suggest that English has about 42 to 45 phonemes. Other languages vary from as few as 15 to as many as 85 phonemes.

Syllables.   While phonemes are the basic units of speech, they are not what is "heard" or concentrated on by the producer or receiver. Instead, concentration is given to *syllables*, which are composed of one or more phonemes.

Morphemes.   *Morphemes* are defined as the smallest meaningful units of a language. Not all syllables are morphemes, because not all syllables have meaning when they stand alone. A morpheme may contain one or more syllables. The entire set of morphemes in a language is called the *lexicon*.

EXAMPLE 9.18.   The words "wing" and "planting" can be used to illustrate the difference between a syllable and a morpheme. "Wing" is a single-syllable word that is also a morpheme. The word "planting" has two syllables, but the "ing" syllable cannot be considered a morpheme because it does not have meaning by itself.

Words.   Phonemes, syllables, and morphemes may be considered the structural components of *words*, the symbols used in a language. The collection or repertoire of words an individual knows and uses is called the *vocabulary*.

Phrases, Clauses, and Sentences.   Word combinations build phrases, which in turn may be developed into clauses or sentences. Sentences may have several clauses, but when they do, the receiver's typical pattern is to treat each clause separately.

Grammar.   The words in phrases and clauses are arranged according to rules of the language that describe how thoughts can be expressed. These are called the rules of *grammar*. How words and phrases can be combined into sentences is referred to as *syntax*. Syntax begins with the study of grammar. The meaning of words and sentences is studied as *semantics*. When sentences are considered, the ideas expressed are referred to as *propositions*. Note also that it is possible to create arrangements of words that fit the rules of grammar yet convey little or no meaning.

EXAMPLE 9.19.   The words "dog," "Cathy," "the," and "bought" must be arranged according to the rules of grammar and syntax to form a comprehensible and sensible statement. It is possible to generate more than one meaningful sentence from these words—"Cathy bought the dog" and "The dog bought Cathy"—although the "idea unit" of the first arrangement makes much more sense than does that expressed in the second arrangement.

Surface Structure and Deep Structure.   Another way to express this concern with the difference between the arrangement of words and the meaning conveyed by words and sentences is to distinguish between surface structure and deep structure. The arrangement of the words has been called the *surface structure* of the language, while the meaning being transmitted is called the *deep structure*.

EXAMPLE 9.20.   Two sentences such as "Glenn took the test" and "The test was taken by Glenn" have the same meaning or deep structure, although their surface structures differ. One could alter the meaning of the second sentence by substituting the word "purse" for "test," so that it would read, "The purse was taken by Glenn." This would leave the surface structure almost the same but alter the deep structure considerably.

Note also that the social context of each statement may affect the way in which the meaning is interpreted. The study of the social rules that help determine the structure (and understanding) of language has been called *pragmatics*. Context often establishes the form with which an individual expresses an idea and enables interpretation by the receiver.

EXAMPLE 9.21.   When a parent asks a child, "Are you going to clean your room this week?" it may be a direct request for information or, perhaps more likely, a teasing or sarcastic remark intended to prompt action by the child. Both the context and the particular inflection of voice will help the child understand the message being conveyed by the parent.

Language Acquisition.   Studies have revealed universal patterns of language acquisition. Almost all children with normal abilities begin by cooing, producing all known phonemes. Cooing is followed by *babbling*, the production of sounds that match the phonemes of the child's primary language. As the child advances from the babbling stage, one-word utterances are followed by *two-word utterances* and then what has come to be called *telegraphic speech*. Telegraphic speech represents the beginning of the production of sentences, but only the words crucial to conveying the message are included. By about age 4, a child begins to produce sentences that more closely approximate those used in normal adult speech in the primary language.

Other common patterns noticed as sentences are developed have been called *overgeneralization* and *overextension*. In overgeneralization, children apply the rules of a language more widely and inflexibly than is appropriate, leading to errors such as applying the *s* or *es* rule for plural words to create ideas such as "foots." Overextension occurs when a child uses an exemplar more widely than is appropriate, such as calling all beverages "milk."

EXAMPLE 9.22. Early speech patterns often incorporate several of the patterns described above. For example, a child in the telegraphic speech stage may say, "Daddy runned," referring to the sight of his father running toward something. Only basic concepts are expressed, and the past tense rule is misapplied. An older child might say, "I saw my daddy run toward the water."

Special Concerns of Language. A number of interesting research areas have arisen from the study of language. While it is beyond the scope of this book to consider each one in detail, brief descriptions will give the reader a sense of the extent to which language influences the study of behavior and mental processes.

The Nature-Nurture Debate. As with many other topics in psychology, the question of whether a behavior develops as a result of inherited characteristics (nature) or from the effects of learning (nurture) has been raised with regard to language. The conclusion most psychologists accept is that both are important in language acquisition. There is evidence for a nature interpretation in that children throughout the world seem to have a *critical period*—a period when learning must occur if it is to occur successfully—for learning language. Children also go through the same stages of language development (see above), create unique statements without the benefit of reinforcement or imitation, and learn appropriate syntax even though they are not corrected by their parents or others on a regular basis.

However, there also is evidence that children produce sounds that are appropriate to the language of the parent or caregiver and are reinforced for having done so. The principle of shaping (see Section 7.2) leads to successive approximations of the desired responses so that the child eventually speaks as well as the adult. Regional differences in pronunciation and phrasing illustrate how different patterns are reinforced in different areas.

Bilingualism. People who speak two languages are called *bilingual*. Evidence indicates that being bilingual may be beneficial or detrimental to overall mental functioning, depending on how well established each of the languages has become. In instances where both languages have been learned well, such as when one is well established before the other is introduced, a bilingual person seems to profit. Circumstances where one language is in effect replacing another seem to produce decreased cognitive functioning. (*Note*: People who speak more than two languages are called *multilingual*.)

Slips of the Tongue. Another intriguing area, well known because of Sigmund Freud's interest in such patterns, has come to be called *slips of the tongue*, in which inadvertent errors of speech production generate changed meaning for the thought being expressed. Freud believed these were expressions of hidden or subconscious motivations.

EXAMPLE 9.23. One college instructor was known to have told the students that they would be divided into groups in a "random passion" rather than a "random fashion." That statement certainly qualifies as a slip of the tongue.

Language for Animals. Extensive research on language development in lower organisms (especially the chimpanzee) has shown that while lower organisms have little success learning written or spoken language as humans know it, they can be taught to communicate using American Sign Language or other symbolic forms. Rather extensive vocabularies have been developed, along with some grammatical understanding. Communication using specially trained symbols has occurred between lower organisms and humans and has been attempted between one member of the species and another (e.g., one chimpanzee and another).

Solved Problems

9.1   Perhaps one of the most difficult problems psychologists have is to define the concept of thinking. What makes the definition of thinking so hard to achieve?

The greatest problem is that thinking is essentially an internal or "hidden" process. It cannot be observed directly but must be inferred from other, measurable behaviors. Although it often is attributed to activity of the mind (mental processes), no direct record of the mind can be achieved.

We cannot observe mental processes directly, but we can make inferences about thinking on the basis of subsequent performance. Thinking is thought of as a mediational process, bridging the gap between stimulus and response through the use of symbols, images, or concepts. (*Note*: The input-processing-output analysis mentioned in Section 8.1 seems to apply here. Thinking falls in the processing stage, and computer programming can be used in attempts to simulate the events that occur during thinking.)

9.2   Consider the words "San Francisco" and "city." Which word is a symbol, and which is a concept?

In this problem, "San Francisco" is a symbol because it is a one-of-a-kind label for a particular city in California. The word "city" is a concept because it can be used to summarize or describe many places, including San Francisco. In general, concepts are symbols that represent common characteristics shared by events or objects that are otherwise different.

9.3   Individuals who are deaf often use means of communication other than speech. Explain how their patterns of communication are comparable to the use of symbols in speech.

A symbol is simply an agreed upon designation that has come to stand for an object, event, action, or idea. The gestures of American Sign Language (ASL) are symbols just as much as written or spoken words are. A similar example is Braille, which is used by many blind people; the raised dots are symbols of letters or numbers. The key characteristic of a symbol is that it has accepted meaning, not that it has a particular form.

9.4   Take a moment to think of a list of fruits. Having done this, consider which ones you listed first and which came later. Now really try to stretch your recall to include as many as you can. Were the fruits you first thought of ones that are fairly common? Did you find that you could add to the list after you tried again? What principle is illustrated by your performance? What does it mean?

If you are like most people, you first named fruits you consider common and could add more to the list when you tried. Your performance showed what is called a concept hierarchy. In a *concept hierarchy*, the associations between the concept and the items given at the beginning of the list are very strong, while those toward the end of the list are much weaker. Thus, you were more likely to think of "orange" or "apple" early in the list rather than "kumquat" or "pomegranate."

9.5   A visitor from Germany was taken to see her first baseball game. Her American host believed he had ample knowledge to explain the game. During the course of the evening, the host realized how difficult it was to explain what seemed to be very simple concepts. For example, the host described a strikeout by saying, "Well, three strikes and the batter is out." When asked to describe a strike, the host had a great deal more trouble. Why?

The concept "strikeout" is a simple concept, while the concept "strike" is a disjunctive concept (a kind of complex concept).

"Strikeout" is a simple concept because any combination of three strikes results in a strikeout. However, the definition of "strike" is much more complicated. A strike may be a missed swing, an umpire's decision about a pitch not swung at, a foul ball if there are fewer than two strikes, a foul tip held by the catcher if there are two strikes, or a foul bunt if the batter has two strikes. These are all mutually exclusive events that are represented by a single disjunctive concept; that is, the concept requires that the action need satisfy only one of these criteria to qualify as a strike.

9.6   Think again about the situation described in the previous problem. A base on balls, or walk, occurs when the batter gets four balls. Explain how "base on balls" is a simple concept while "ball" is a conjunctive concept.

"Base on balls" is a simple concept because any combination of balls adding to four means the batter may go to first base. However, "ball" is a conjunctive concept because it requires more than one criterion to be satisfied. The pitch must be judged by the umpire as being outside the "strike zone" *and* must not be swung at by the batter. If either criterion is not satisfied, the pitch cannot be called a ball.

9.7   We often use phrases such as "heavier than," "shorter than," and "more muscular than" in attempting to distinguish between two people. What kind of concept do these phrases illustrate?

Any relationship between two aspects of a situation may be described as a *relational* concept. The important consideration is that there is a comparison of a common characteristic that they share. Thus, both people have some weight but one is judged to be heavier than the other.

9.8   Explain why the concept *short* is probably better thought of as being fuzzy rather than well defined.

The concept of *short* is a fuzzy one because it depends on the context in which it is used. What is short for adults, for example, may be tall for children. Fuzzy concepts usually require examples to set the context in which they are used.

9.9   Create a mental image of a *farm*. What was included in your image? Why?

If you responded by including, for example, a farmhouse, a barn, and some livestock, you are likely to think of these items as *prototypes* for a farm. Prototypes gain high agreement among people who are asked to designate examples that are representative of the category. (*Note*: You can try this with several friends to find what examples seem to be prototypical for *farm* or any other category you choose.)

9.10   Suppose you are preparing a special dinner and have just put a cake in the oven. You then step outside to cut some fresh parsley from the garden. When you return to the door, you find you have locked yourself out. Obviously, you have a problem. According to the analysis of problem solving, what sequence of events is likely to occur now?

Most problem solving seems to follow a fairly standard sequence. In this case, there may be a brief interlude before problem solving begins while you express the emotion of anger, but once you get past that, the progression may be as follows: (1) define the problem accurately, (2) consider which concepts are most relevant for solving the problem, (3) create hypotheses about how to solve the problem, and (4) test and confirm (or disconfirm) which hypothesis best solves the problem. Thus, your thinking could be as follows: (1) This door is locked. (2) Are all the doors locked? How about the windows? Does anyone else have a key? Will I have to break in? (3) My guess is that there is something unlocked and I'll be able to get it open and get in, or I'll go next door and call my wife. (4) Well, let's try these ideas and see what happens.

9.11 Compare algorithms and heuristics as ways to solve problems, citing the advantages and disadvantages of each.

An algorithm is a procedure or set of actions that guarantees that if a solution to the problem exists, that solution will be found. Usually, algorithms try all possible solutions, noting those which work. Algorithms are relatively inefficient and expensive. Heuristics are "rules of thumb" or shortcut strategies that focus on the most likely solutions. Heuristics cannot guarantee a solution even if one does exist but often are relatively efficient.

9.12 Carrying two shopping bags full of holiday presents, Sandy sees a group of teenage boys approaching on the sidewalk. Worried that the boys might steal the presents, Sandy crosses to the other side of the street, only to be amazed when the boys stop and begin to sing a song of the season. Explain Sandy's behavior in terms of problem solving.

Sandy illustrated the availability and representativeness heuristics, remembering reports of other shoppers having packages snatched from them by teenage boys and judging that these boys fit that category of "package-stealing boys" well. Sandy's amazement occurs when the boys show behaviors not at all expected, failing to confirm the hypotheses she acted on.

9.13 Is convergent thinking always noncreative? Is divergent thinking always necessary for creativity? How important is intelligence to creativity?

Convergent thinking is often noncreative, but it may be used as a "gathering" device to collect information that will be used eventually in a creative solution. Divergent thinking, in which various thoughts are generated and arranged in novel patterns, does seem to be a crucial aspect of creativity.

It is interesting to note that a minimum of intelligence is probably necessary for successful creative thinking, but there does not appear to be a strong correlation between intelligence and creativity. The types of thinking an individual shows seem more important than the level of intelligence.

9.14 Suppose you are given the sequence of numbers 2, 2, 4, 12, 48 and are asked what numbers will follow. You may find that reasoning does not produce a solution immediately. Then, suddenly, after continued study of the sequence, you get an "Aha!" feeling as you spot the principle involved. How do psychologists describe this type of mental process?

This "Aha!" experience is called *insight*, the sudden discovery of a hypothesis that can be confirmed. Such an insight can be described to others, but the actual process of having an insight appears to be a personal experience that is not easily taught to others.

(*Note*: The sequence is based on the following: the first number, *2*, is multiplied by 1; that result is multiplied by 2, the next result is multiplied by 3, and so on.)

9.15 Can a person's expectations affect the way he or she goes about solving a problem?

Some problem-solving attempts follow relativelly rigid or unchanging formats from one situation to to the next. Other attempts respond to changes in the current environment. For example, did you notice there were *two* errors in the first sentence of this answer? Previous experience with textbooks has created a *habit* or expectation that such books are written in grammatically correct English, an expectation that current events typically reinforce. However, having been tricked, you are likely to develop a *set*, or temporary tendency to respond, so that another similar error probably will be caught. The set will dissipate over a period of time, and the stronger habit once again will affect the likelihood of spotting any errors.

9.16 Given a flowerpot, a stick, a banner, and two thumbtacks, Fred was asked to make a flag that would stand up straight. After much puzzling, he finally admitted that he could not accomplish the task. His best effort looked something like Fig. 9-2.

Fig. 9-2   **Fig. 9-3**

Joyce took one look at the problem and said, "You're missing the obvious!" She simply turned the pot over and used the drainage hole in the bottom to support the flag, thus making the flag stand perfectly straight, as shown in Fig. 9-3. What principle explains Fred's failure to solve this problem?

Fred's inability to solve this problem is explained by the principle of *functional fixedness*, a special type of set that makes the person unable to "see" alternative uses for an object. Fred could only envision using the pot right side up, while Joyce, apparently not troubled by functional fixedness, used it upside down as a stand or pedestal.

9.17 Lamar's grandparents give him money toward buying a car as a graduation gift. When he begins to look at the available choices, he finds he can buy an old, low-gas-mileage, somewhat beat-up but really sporty model or a much newer, boxy, rather boring, but economical sedan. If the probability of buying either car is equal in that both are available for purchase at about the same price, what is likely to lead to Lamar's decision?

Two variables are thought to be most important in the decision-making process: the probability that each outcome may occur (which in this case is designated as being equal) and the *utility* of each possible outcome. For Lamar, utility will be the factor leading to a decision. He will have to judge the relative value of each choice, weighing these values to make his final choice. Some considerations, for example, would include how important the look of the car is compared to the reliability, how much work Lamar might have to put into making the car look acceptable, and how important the cost of fuel will be over the life of the car. Lamar is likely to base his choice on some but not all of the possible considerations, with those weighing most heavily or most dramatically being the ones that will sway his decision.

9.18 Rhonda and Ron are shopping for a new television set. As they look at sets in the size which interests them, Rhonda sees one with a good picture and says, "There, that one. That's good enough." What principle explains Rhonda's response?

Rhonda is illustrating *satisficing*, the selection of the first alternative encountered that meets the minimum criteria that were established. In this case, it may be that the set is the right size, has a good picture, and is in an acceptable price range. Looking at other sets and trying to find the "best" set are not undertaken when satisficing occurs.

9.19 Darnell is convinced that all dogs have fleas. His friend, Connie, adopts an abandoned dog from the pound. When she calls and tells Darnell, "I have a new pet," his response to finding out that the pet is a dog is that "it'll have fleas!" Explain how Darnell's response is an example of reasoning and then comment on the premises he has used.

Darnell's response is an example of reasoning because he has drawn a conclusion from the information given to him. His reasoning is possibly faulty because he has started with a premise that is unlikely to be correct: *all* dogs have fleas. One can exercise the steps of reasoning in a fully appropriate manner and still reach an invalid conclusion if at least one of the premises used is in error.

9.20   Does Darnell's reasoning in Solved Problem 9.19 provide evidence for inductive or deductive reasoning? Explain.

   Darnell illustrated deductive reasoning, reaching a conclusion by using a general principle. His general principle—all dogs have fleas—may have been formed from inductive reasoning if there were several instances in his past where he encountered dogs that did have fleas. Inductive reasoning involves basing a conclusion on specific cases.

9.21   At the end of the first week of college, David tells his parents that his roommate's interests are as much like his as "black is to white." What form of reasoning has David shown?

   David's statement is in the form of an analogy. Analogical reasoning takes the format of *a* is to *b* as *x* is to *y*, or "David" is to "roommate" as "black" is to "white."

9.22   Why is the smell of an onion classified as a sign, while the word "onion" is classified as a symbol?

   Both a sign and a symbol are signals and as such may be used for communication. A sign has acquired meaning because its inherent characteristics establish a relationship between it and a naturally occurring event. In this case, the odor of the onion and the presence of that particular vegetable are related. A symbol has meaning only because that meaning is agreed upon. There is no reason why an onion *has* to be called an onion. The letters might be rearranged to spell "ninoo," and if accepted or agreed upon generally, "ninoo" would become the symbol representing that vegetable.

   It should be noted that while written and spoken words are the most commonly used symbols for communication, other symbols exist. For example, the gestures of American Sign Language (ASL) used by persons with hearing handicaps, the Braille alphabet used by blind persons, and international traffic signs are all used for communication.

9.23   In what ways do written language and spoken language differ?

   The most obvious difference is that written language uses letters while spoken language uses sounds, but many other differences exist. Different words are used, they are arranged differently, and a person's spoken vocabulary is usually more limited and more repetitive than her or his written vocabulary. The messages conveyed by the two forms often differ in both content and intent. Spoken language tends to be more casual and direct, while written language often is more formal and more carefully regulated by grammatical conventions.

9.24   A student was assigned the project of developing a psychological test that could be used to measure retention skills. The student chose to test 8-year-old children for their memory of certain designs. The student would show the children a design for a specified length of time, and then remove it and have the children attempt to draw what they had seen. The student's instructions to the children were, "Study the design carefully. When I take it away, take your pencil and make a facsimile of the design." Many of the children did not understand what was expected of them. Explain why.

   Most 8-year-olds do not understand the word "facsimile." While the student apparently thought the word was descriptive, the children did not. The student's intent was to produce expressive language, that is, words that convey a message. In this case, the key word chosen did not convey the message to the children.

9.25   An English-speaking person probably will have no difficulty pronouncing the word "jolly," but a Spaniard is very likely to see that word and say "hoy-yee." Why?

Not all languages make use of the same phonemes. As the basic components of spoken language, phonemes allow linguists to distinguish between one language and another or among speech patterns within the same language. The Spanish language does not make use of sound comparable to the sounds represented by *j* and *ll* in English. In fact, such sounds may be virtually unpronounceable for a Spaniard not trained in English.

9.26   Morphemes and syllables are slightly different. What distinguishes the two?

Syllables are the basic units to which people attend when they hear a spoken language. Syllables often are combinations of phonemes and serve as the smallest speech pattern normally produced. Not all syllables are meaningful by themselves. Linguists have developed the concept of morphemes to represent the smallest *meaningful* units of language. Morphemes are made up of one or more syllables but cannot be separated into smaller units and maintain their meaning.

9.27   Consider the following sentences: "Kraig drove the car," "The car was driven by Kraig," and "The grommavitz was vreebelphritzed by Graik." How are these sentences similar? How do they differ? What terms do linguists use to describe these similarities and differences?

The first two sentences have the same meaning but are constructed differently. Linguists would say that both sentences have the same deep structure or semantic intent but different surface structure or syntax. In the second sentence, substitute the word "at" for "by," making the sentence read, "The car was driven at Kraig." Notice how the surface structure remains about the same but the deep structure changes considerably.

Now consider the third sentence. The surface structure is almost identical to that of the second sentence, yet the idea expressed (the sentence's proposition) is nonsense. Proper grammar is not enough to assure that a message is being conveyed.

9.28   Language often is structured according to social rules or conventions. What is this called? Create an example.

The study of the influence of social rules or conventions on language structure is called *pragmatics*. A sentence as simple as "Do you know what time it is?" can convey quite different meanings depending on the social context, being a simple request of one person to another while passing on the sidewalk or a parent's exasperated comment to a child lazing in bed on a school morning.

9.29   A bright 4-year-old has learned the plural of the word "mouse." It intrigues the child that there are not several "mouses" but several "mice." One day, this child hears her mother referred to as her father's "spouse." Later, she asks her parents if they are "spice." Her behavior illustrates what aspect of language development? Is this comparable for all languages?

Language acquisition begins with the learning of single words and advances to combining words, modifying words, and developing the rules of the language. While the rules of various languages differ considerably (for example, in the placement of adjectives or the gender of words), children seem to learn the appropriate rules for their particular languages at about the same time in approximately the same sequence. In this case, the child's question, which illustrates the principle of *overgeneralization* because she has applied a rule more widely than is appropriate, indicates that rule learning is taking place but is not yet complete.

9.30   At what point do children begin to form sentences?

Parents might say that one-word utterances are sufficient to be treated as sentences, such as when a child says the word "doll" with differing inflections that convey messages including "Pick up my doll," "Hand me my doll," and "Where is my doll?" Linguists usually identify sentences when more than one word is linked in an attempt to convey a message. Telegraphic speech, where only words crucial to conveying the message are used, is thought to be the first evidence of sentence production.

9.31 Many educators think that second-language learning should begin before a child reaches puberty, believing there is a critical period for language learning. Explain this concept.

A critical period is a period when learning must occur if it is to occur successfully. In this case, the evidence argues against a critical period in that second-language learning *can* be done by someone who has passed puberty. However, evidence also indicates that second-language learning is more easily accomplished by children who have not yet reached puberty, and so there is support for starting early.

9.32 In a bilingual family, what has to occur for a child to benefit from knowing both languages?

Children seem to benefit from living in a bilingual family if both languages become well established or well learned. By contrast, when one language appears to replace another, there seems to be a decrease in cognitive functioning.

9.33 In a famous incident, a radio announcer described an advertised product as "the breast in bed" rather than the "best in bread." What is this called? What might Freud have said about this?

The error is called a slip of the tongue or a Freudian slip. Freud believed slips of the tongue represented hidden or subconscious motives and might have interpreted the announcer's error in that way.

9.34 Early research attempting to teach chimpanzees to speak proved almost totally fruitless. Later, attempts to teach American Sign Language and other symbolic codes were judged quite successful. Why the difference? Were the later successes truly representative of teaching language to lower organisms?

The difficulty with the early studies was that researchers were trying to use a mode of communication that could not be accomplished by the chimpanzees, perhaps for physiological reasons. When later investigators switched to a more compatible system, language learning progressed fairly rapidly.

The latter studies did represent teaching language to lower organisms. The format did not involve the use of written or spoken words, but as was mentioned before, ASL and other symbolic codes are forms of language and may be used for communication.

Key Terms

Algorithm.   A procedure or set of actions that guarantees a solution to a problem.

Anchoring heuristic.   A problem-solving procedure in which currently available information is used as the reference point for making a judgment.

Backward search.   A heuristic which begins at the end point of a problem and works backward to the initial point.

Bilingual.   The term used to describe someone who speaks more than one language.

Concept.   A symbol that summarizes or generalizes the attributes of objects, events, actions, or ideas that are otherwise dissimilar.

Conjunctive concept.   A complex concept based on the simultaneous presence of two or more stimulus properties.

Convergent thinking.   Thinking aimed at finding a known solution to a problem.

Creativity.   In problem solving, an original, productive, and unusual approach to a task.

Deductive reasoning.   Using general principles to reach specific conclusions.

Deep structure.   The meaning transmitted by the words used in a language.

Disjunctive concept.   A complex concept that is based on the simultaneous consideration of two or more stimulus properties but in which the presence of any one stimulus property is adequate to qualify the stimulus as an instance of the concept.

Divergent thinking.   Thinking devoted to finding a new or different (previously unknown) solution to a problem.

Expressive language.   Words that convey a message.

Functional fixedness.   A type of set in which a subject is unable to use an object in a novel manner.

Grammar.   The rules of language describing how thoughts can be expressed.

Habit.   A long-term tendency to respond in a certain manner.

Heuristic.   A problem-solving strategy that reduces the complexity of a problem and focuses on the solutions most likely to be successful.

Inductive reasoning.   The process of reaching a conclusion based on specific cases.

Insight.   In problem solving, the phenomenon in which a subject knows the problem, has a period of no apparent progress, and then suddenly finds a solution.

Means-end analysis.   A heuristic which compares a current position with the desired end and then tries to find ways to get from the current position to that end.

Morphemes.   The smallest meaningful units of a language.

Overextension.   In language, when children use an exemplar more widely than is appropriate.

Overgeneralization.   In language, when children apply the rules of language more widely and more rigidly than is appropriate.

Phonemes.   The basic sounds or inflection components of a spoken language.

Problem solving.   The recognition and establishment of a goal, followed by attempts to reach that goal.

Propositions.   The ideas expressed by sentences.

Psycholinguistics.   The study of the relationship between organisms and their language; concerned with the acquisition, structure, and use of the language.

Reasoning.   Attempts to solve a problem by combining two or more aspects from past experience.

Receptive language.   What is understood from the words that are used.

Relational concept.   A complex concept based on the relationship between two features of a stimulus situation.

Satisficing.   In problem solving, the selection of the first alternative that appears "good enough" to solve the problem.

Semantics.   The meaning of words and sentences.

Set.   The temporary tendency to respond in a certain manner.

Sign.   A signal that has inherent meaning because its characteristics are related to naturally occurring events.

Slips of the tongue.   Inadvertent errors of speech production that result in a changed meaning of the thought being expressed.

Surface structure.   The arrangement of words in a language.

Syllables.   The smallest speech units to which the receiver usually attends.

Symbol. Any specified stimulus which has become a commonly accepted representation of an object, event, action, or idea.

Syntax. How words and phrases are combined into sentences.

Telegraphic speech. The beginning of the production of sentences; only words crucial to conveying the message are used.

Thinking. A personal process of symbolic mediation; often attributed to the mind.

CHAPTER 10

Motivation and Emotion

In this chapter, both the situations that provoke behavior and the feelings aroused by many behaviors are considered. *Motivation* is defined as the conditions which initiate, guide, and maintain behaviors, usually until a goal has been reached or the response has been blocked. *Emotion* is a complex state of the organism that generally is characterized by a heightened state of arousal, personal feelings, and expression of what is being experienced.

10.1 THE MOTIVATION CYCLE

Some motives appear in cycles. The *cycle of motivation* follows a three-part repetitive chain: (1) A *need* creates a *drive*, (2) *operant responses* are made as attempts to reach a goal to satisfy the condition, and (3) once the goal has been reached, *relief* from the motive condition follows. Often, the relief is only temporary and the cycle starts again.

EXAMPLE 10.1. An obvious illustration of the motivation cycle is the sequence of hunger, finding and eating food, temporary relief, hunger again, and so on. The repetitive nature of the motivation cycle can be shown for many different motive conditions, although the time span for the cycle may vary.

Variables Affecting the Motivation Cycle. While the motivation cycle seems simple, it may be altered or modified by several types of variables.

Assessment of Motivation. The strength and quality of a motive condition may be estimated in one of two ways. First, an estimate of the strength of motivation can be made by determining how long it has been since the motive was last satisfied. This period of time represents the *deprivation* the organism experiences. In experiments, psychologists manipulate deprivation to influence the subject's motive condition.

A second means of estimating the strength of motivation is to observe particular behaviors and infer from them the subject's motive condition. This method depends on naturalistic observation and requires that the observer have some previous knowledge that associates a certain kind of behavior with a particular motive condition.

172

EXAMPLE 10.2.   The parents of a young child are able to estimate when the child is hungry by finding out how long it has been since the child was last fed. They also may estimate the child's hunger by observing certain behaviors (such as crying) that are associated with hunger.

Adaptation of Response.   Many motives produce nonproductive responses which do not lead to a goal. In many cases, the organism will have to make a behavioral adjustment so that different operant responses are made and the cycle can be completed.

EXAMPLE 10.3.   A young child may find that banging on the table with a spoon or shouting at a parent does not get the parent to bring food. The child may have to adjust his or her behavior—perhaps by learning to ask politely for food—to satisfy the motive condition.

Goal Specificity.   Not all satisfiers (*goals*) are viewed as equally desirable. An organism that prefers a certain goal to others—even when the others would satisfy the motive condition adequately—is exhibiting *goal specificity.*

EXAMPLE 10.4.   Parents feeding a very young child may find that the child expresses preferences very noticeably, even when communication by language has not yet developed. For example, the child may spit out the carrots but gulp down all the green beans.

10.2   PRINCIPLES OF MOTIVATION

It is difficult to determine how many different types of motives exist. It is sometimes impossible to make a simple distinction between unlearned motive conditions and those which are learned. Furthermore, it is sometimes impossible to determine the origin of motives. Despite these difficulties, certain terms and principles seem to apply to many, if not all, motive conditions.

Terminology.   Several terms have widespread use in describing motive conditions. *Instinct* refers to an innate condition that regularly provokes a specific, complex response from all the members of a certain species when a distinctive stimulus pattern is presented. A *need* often is described as a deficit or imbalance. A need may be physiological (such as a need for warmth) or psychological (such as a need for achievement). *Drives* are the internal, psychological states that arise from needs. *Arousal* is thought to be the physiological activation that accompanies drive. Finally, *incentives* refer to external conditions or things that "pull" an organism's activity toward them.

EXAMPLE 10.5.   A holiday meal helps illustrate the differences among these terms. There are no patterns of response for humans that seem to be instinctive. While the hunger motive is certainly important, the patterns that satisfy it vary greatly. However, when deprived of food for some time, people *do* experience a need for food and drive arises, prompting both the psychological state and the physiological arousal leading to appropriate responses to satisfy the motive condition. Eating at a holiday meal often involves "overdoing" so that when the host offers, for example, more turkey, mashed potatoes, dressing, and vegetables, the response is, "I can't. I'm stuffed!" Interestingly, the person making that response may find himself tempted when the pies are brought in. The pies have incentive value even when the internal drive has been satisfied.

Note: The concepts of need, drive, and incentive have been combined in a single approach called *utility theory*, which combines the ideas of how much a person believes he or she needs something (the strength of the drive) with how appealing that thing is (the incentive strength). Each overall judgment, called the *expected utility*, links an estimate of the usefulness of a goal object with an estimate of the probability that a particular behavior will lead to that goal. This theory emphasizes the subjectivity involved in understanding motive conditions.

The Hierarchy of Needs.   The psychologist Abraham Maslow (1908–1970) developed an ordering of needs that came to be known as the *hierarchy of needs*. The basis of what has come to be called the *humanistic theory* of motivation, Maslow's hierarchy emphasizes that lower-order needs must be satisfied before higher-order needs can be considered. For Maslow, the most rudimentary needs are *physiological needs*, such as needs for food, fluids, and warmth. Next come *safety needs*, those assuring one's security, followed by needs for *love and belongingness*. *Esteem needs* such as seeking respect or approval are fourth in the hierarchy, while at the top comes *self-actualization*, the attempt to reach one's full potential.

EXAMPLE 10.6. Actual actions sometimes contradict the hierarchy of needs. Soldiers, police officers, and fire personnel have been known to protect others by facing very endangering situations, seemingly in direct contradiction to the preeminence of safety needs.

Functional Autonomy. Some responses to a motive condition may persist even after the original motive condition ceases to exist. In such a case, the response itself becomes a motive. This is called *functional autonomy*.

EXAMPLE 10.7. Ask almost any "confirmed" smoker if smoking was enjoyable when it was first started. Very few people started smoking because they found it truly pleasurable. Instead, they smoked at first because it brought social approval of some kind. However, smoking becomes self-motivating, to the extent that an individual eventually may smoke even when it is socially disapproved.

Relationship of Motivation to Performance. The general relationship of motivation to performance is shown by the graph in Fig. 10-1.

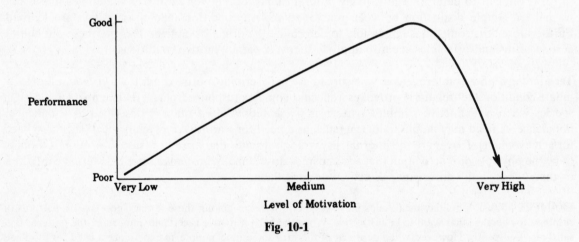

Fig. 10-1

This relationship frequently is described as identifying an *optimal level of arousal* for any task. The exact maximum level of motivation that will yield best performance varies from task to task. In general, the more difficult the task, the lower the optimal level of arousal for performing that task. Note, however, that the performance will be poorer if the motivation level is too low *or* too high.

EXAMPLE 10.8. Students are familiar with the effects of motivation on performance. A student who does not care at all about a course often does poorly. A student who cares but keeps it under control does well. A student who cares too much (and "clutches") often does poorly.

Theories of Motivation. In addition to the *humanistic theory* of motivation mentioned earlier, arousal serves as the basis for the *activation-arousal theory* of motivation, which proposes that any organism has a typical, normal, appropriate level of arousal and that behavior will be directed toward trying to maintain that level. This means that if environmental stimulation is too high, behaviors will occur to try to reduce arousal; if stimulation is too low, an increase of arousal will occur.

EXAMPLE 10.9.   A possible explanation of why a person might seek the anxiety-arousal of a skydiving situation may be found in this theory. This person may have a typically high level of arousal and use activities such as skydiving to keep arousal near or at that norm.

Sigmund Freud is given credit for the *psychoanalytic theory* of motivation. Freud viewed motivation as largely unconscious and frequently as an expression of aggressive or sexual desires. These desires might be expressed openly or in a symbolic form such as dreams or "slips of the tongue."

Social learning theory suggests that previous learning is a major source of motivation. The success or failure of particular responses leads to an understanding of what will produce positive or negative consequences and a desire to repeat successful behaviors. Personal experience is not mandatory for social learning to occur; observing another person succeed or fail may be sufficient to produce motive conditions. Moreover, rewards or punishments may be either external or internal.

10.3   TYPES OF MOTIVES

Motives often are divided into categories of *primary* or *unlearned motives* and *secondary* or *learned motives*. Psychologists have classified many motives using these designations but have found that some motives appear to result from the combined effects of unlearned and learned characteristics, while others cannot be classified as either unlearned or learned and have origins that remain matters of debate.

Unlearned motives. Some unlearned motives are called *survival motives* because they must be satisfied for an organism to continue to live. The list of survival motives is short: hunger, thirst, the need for air, the need to maintain body temperature, the need to relieve fatigue, and the need to eliminate body waste products. The responses that satisfy these motives are eating, drinking, breathing, sheltering, sleeping, and eliminating.

An additional motive condition, that of pain, appears to be unlearned but is *not* a survival motive. It is possible to live without relief from pain for many years, while relief of any of the other unlearned motives must occur relatively quickly or death will follow. In the case of the survival motives, the time span may vary from minutes to weeks, depending on which motive is involved. However, relief is essential in all cases, while it is not for pain.

Homeostasis.   Many of the body processes that operate to satisfy unlearned motives are automatic in nature. The body regulates itself in an attempt to maintain an internal physiological balance. This balance is called *homeostasis*.

EXAMPLE 10.10.   A weight-reduction diet makes use of the body's tendency to make homeostatic adjustments. When individuals who are overweight reduce their food intake, they create an energy deficit. To make up for this deficit, the body will burn stored fats. This will lower the person's weight and thus make the diet successful. (*Note*: You are always on some kind of diet. The question is whether the diet is a good or a bad one for you.)

Hunger.   The most thoroughly researched unlearned motive is hunger. Theories trying to explain hunger suggest that levels of sugar (glucose) in the blood or levels of fat (lipids) signal the need for food. Using both theories and other physiological evidence, psychologists have developed *set-point theory* which proposes that each person has a preset body weight that is determined at birth or soon afterward and is based on factors such as the number of fat cells in the body, the body's metabolic rate, and levels of certain neurochemicals in the brain. The tendency of the body is to return to that set point, although there is evidence that the number of fat cells in the body can increase over time.

EXAMPLE 10.11.   Weight-reduction diets fail in more than 90 percent of cases. Set-point theory would predict that this is inevitable. When one diets to lose weight, the size of the fat cells is reduced, but body adjustments allow more of the lower caloric intake to be processed and therefore create conditions that return the body to its set point. Most effective for weight loss seems to be the combination of exercise and careful eating.

Careful studies of the hypothalamus have shown considerable involvement of that portion of the brain in hunger and related eating behaviors. If the *ventromedial nucleus* is destroyed, an animal will become *hyperphagic* and overeat. If that region is activated, a hungry animal will stop eating at once. When the *lateral hypothalamic area* is destroyed, an animal will become *aphagic* and refuse to eat at all. If that area is activated, the animal will eat even when completely satiated.

Not all hunger motivation can be attributed to physiological factors. Evidence indicates that *context* plays an important role in affecting hunger; that is, the setting for eating and the style of presentation of the food influence eating behavior. This varies by culture so much that external stimuli appear to be able to override the physiological set point, often leading to behaviors identified as eating disorders.

Eating Disorders.   Weight levels at extremes often signal eating disorders. Someone who is exceptionally overweight (20 percent or more over one's appropriate body weight) is said to be *obese*. Obesity is common in the United States, and its frequency has increased in recent years. Explanations for obesity focus on both physiological and contextual stimuli, suggesting that obese individuals may have particularly high set points and that many also may be especially sensitive to external stimuli such the availability, sight, smell, and taste of food.

At the other pole, extremely underweight individuals often are suffering from *anorexia nervosa*, a refusal to eat accompanied by denial that the behavior and the resultant appearance are in any way unusual. Anorectics are literally starving to death. Women from the teenage years to middle age are most likely to become anorectic. A related eating disorder, *bulimia nervosa* is characterized by binge eating followed by some form of purging, such as self-induced vomiting or the use of laxatives. A bulimic usually maintains fairly normal weight but may suffer from a chemical imbalance because of the binge-purge cycle.

Learned Motives.   *Learned motives* often are called *social motives* because they develop from social (environmental) interactions. In many societies, they become the predominant motives because survival motives are satisfied readily and easily. Learned motives generally develop as a result of societal rewards and punishments and include motive conditions such as the need for achievement, the need for friendship or affiliation, the need for dominance or power, and the need for relief from anxiety. None of these conditions is necessary for survival or seems to have an unlearned component, yet all may be very important determinants of behavior. (*Note*: Needs such as those described above probably exist because of a psychological deficit, but direct demonstration of these needs has not been accomplished.)

It should be kept in mind that the list of learned motives given in this section is illustrative but incomplete. A complete list of all learned motives would be exceedingly long. For example, other learned motives include needs for play, approval, autonomy, and aggression.

Need for Achievement.   One of the most extensively researched learned motives is the *need for achievement*. Individuals who set a very high standard for themselves probably have internalized achievement as a personal goal. However, they probably developed the need to achieve because of the social approval of success or the punishment of failure.

Much research on achievement needs has been conducted by using the *Thematic Apperception Test (TAT)* or another, similar projective task. (See Chapter 11.) A person taking such a test is confronted with a series of ambiguous pictures and asked to describe them or tell stories about them. These stories or descriptions are supposed to reveal the subject's motivations, including perhaps the subject's need for achievement. Most of the early studies were conducted with male subjects, although recent investigations have tried to identify achievement and fear-of-success motives in women as well.

EXAMPLE 10.12. In an early investigation of gender differences in attitudes toward achievement, male subjects were asked to respond to a statement describing a man who was the top student in his medical school class and female subjects were asked to respond to a statement describing a woman who was at the top of her medical school class. Almost all the men responded favorably to the top male student; that is, they said the man's achievements would result in positive aftereffects. By contrast, the majority of women indicated that the woman's success would lead to difficulties, particularly loss of femininity and social rejection. Subsequent research has questioned this result and shown changes in social standards for both men and women, but techniques such as this for studying achievement motivation continue to be fruitful.

Interestingly, the difficulty of tasks undertaken by individuals can be predicted from knowledge of each person's need for achievement. In general, people with a high need for achievement choose moderately difficult tasks, avoiding those which are too easy and therefore unsatisfying and those which are too difficult and sure to produce failure. By contrast, individuals low in the need to achieve select very easy or very difficult tasks, assuring success or guaranteeing that no blame will accrue to them if the task is not completed.

Need for Dominance. The *need for dominance* or *power* is satisfied by being able to direct others' behaviors. This may be accomplished by persuasion, suggestion, command, or other means. No matter what technique is employed, successful control over others' responses is the intended goal. The choice of careers such as management and teaching, membership in organizations and office seeking within those groups, and collecting possessions that reflect power are all characteristics that have been found to be correlated with the need for dominance.

Need for Affiliation. Another highly researched learned motive is the *need for affiliation*, the need to experience attachment to others through friendship, sociability, or group membership. Closely related to the need for affiliation is the motive for *dependency*, that is, reliance on others. Affiliation and dependency appear to correlate with a number of other behaviors, including performance in testing situations and reactions to anxiety.

EXAMPLE 10.13. In one research study, college students were observed as they waited to receive an electric shock. During the waiting period, the students showed signs of anxiety and a marked tendency to prefer to wait with others rather than wait alone. Apparently, the need for affiliation grows as the need to relieve anxiety increases.

Need to Relieve Anxiety. Social learning may create problems which in turn create anxiety until the problems are solved. The need to relieve such anxiety may serve as a motive condition, causing a person to seek responses that will reduce the anxiety and solve the problem. Rather than seeking something positive, an anxious person is motivated to get away from something negative.

Other Variations of Motive Conditions. Psychologists have found that some motives result from the combination of unlearned and learned characteristics. Other motives cannot be classified as either learned or unlearned; their origins remain matters of debate.

Sexual Motivation. Probably the best example of a combination motive is *sexual motivation*. Some aspects of sexual development and sexual response, such as the onset of puberty and the time needed for recovery between one orgasm and the next, are physiologically determined. Other aspects of sexuality, such as standards of attractiveness and acceptable sexual practices, are a function of social learning. As a result, any individual's sexual motivation results from a combination of physiological and social influences. (*Note*: Sexual motivation is *not* classified as a survival motive. Survival of the species depends on sexual activity, but the survival of an individual does not.)

Research on sexual responding has shown that women and men experience very similar patterns. Initial *excitement* is followed by an aroused *plateau* stage that culminates in *orgasm*. After orgasm, there is a *refractory period* during which sexual responding cannot take place. Women are more likely to be able to have multiple orgasms, experiencing shorter refractory periods than do men.

The cognitive processes accompanying sexual motivation have been described as *sexual scripts*, mental representations of ways in which sexual behaviors should be enacted. Cultural norms are found for many sexual behaviors, such as masturbation, incest, homosexuality, and modesty.

Contact Comfort.   The apparent need of the young to have soft, warm, cuddly things to which they may cling is called *contact comfort*, a motive with origins that remain matters of debate. It is impossible to know whether this need is an unlearned, inborn reaction or the result of associating such stimuli with rewarding activities such as feeding.

EXAMPLE 10.14.   A "special" blanket or stuffed animal may provide a young child with contact comfort. The reasons why the blanket or animal is so special, however, are not clearly defined. (It is possible that this motive also influences some adult behavior, although examples usually are given for children.)

10.4   CONFLICT

More than one motive condition may be operating at any given moment. Sometimes the motive conditions are compatible with each other, but often they are incompatible. Psychologists call the latter situation a *conflict*. Several different types of conflict situations exist.

Approach-Approach Conflict.   One of the milder and more easily resolved conflicts is the *approach-approach conflict*, a situation in which a person must choose between two or more positively valued persons or objects. A conflict arises because only one of several possible positive responses can be chosen.

EXAMPLE 10.15.   Suppose you are in a restaurant where dessert is included in the price of the dinner. You can choose only one dessert from the list of chocolate parfait, lemon meringue pie, strawberry shortcake, and a hot fudge sundae. If you like more than one of the desserts listed, you are experiencing an approach-approach conflict.

Avoidance-Avoidance Conflict.   An *avoidance-avoidance conflict* exists when a person is confronted with a choice between two or more negatively valued persons or objects. Occasionally the person will withdraw entirely from the situation rather than choose.

Approach-Avoidance Conflict.   An *approach-avoidance conflict* occurs when a person is confronted with a single person or object that has both positive and negative qualities. The relative strengths of these opposing qualities must be weighed before a resolution can be reached. *Multiple approach-avoidance conflicts* are found in situations where there is more than one stimulus and each has positive and negative values.

EXAMPLE 10.16.   Suppose someone on a weight-reduction diet is confronted with the menu described in Example 10.15. This person may see each choice of a dessert as both positive (how good it will taste) and negative (how many calories it has). The menu thus creates a multiple approach-avoidance conflict for the dieter.

10.5   GENERAL CHARACTERISTICS OF EMOTIONS

Emotion is a complex state of an organism that generally is characterized by a heightened state of arousal and personal feelings. The judgment of emotion is largely a subjective matter. (This is true both for a person experiencing an emotion and for someone else who is judging that person's experience.)

Stimulus Identification.   Because so much subjectivity may be involved in judging someone else's emotions, it usually is necessary to identify the stimulus that generated the response in order to make an accurate evaluation of the emotion being expressed.

EXAMPLE 10.17.   Suppose you are looking at a picture of a 35-year-old man. You can see only his head, neck, and shoulders, and tears are streaming down his cheeks. Are the man's tears an emotional response? If so, what emotion do they represent? If the man is chopping onions, this probably is not an emotional response. If the response is emotional, however, it may be a reaction to a sad event or to a very happy one. Without seeing the stimulus, it often is difficult to distinguish the type of emotion being expressed.

Emotion as a Motivator.   The emotional reactions a person experiences may provoke additional responding. When this occurs, emotion serves as a motivator. The chain of response becomes (1) an emotion-producing stimulus leading to (2) an emotional response, which in turn (3) acts as a motivating stimulus, resulting in (4) some expression of the emotion being experienced.

When emotion is considered as a motivator, the same principles discussed for motivation (see above) apply to emotion. Particularly, the relationship between level of emotional state and performance is likely to conform to the inverted-U pattern illustrated in Fig. 10-1.

EXAMPLE 10.18.   Imagine that you are working on a term paper for a class. When you go to the library to locate a particular reference for your paper, you find that someone has cut and removed the pages you need. This is frustrating (an emotion-producing stimulus), and you feel angry (an emotional response). Your reaction may vary with the strength of your anger. If the missing article is not too important, you probably will look for others. If it is fairly important, you may flush somewhat and mutter about the situation but then get on with your work. If it is very important and no substitute will do, you may slam the book closed and go into a rage, yelling at the librarian and forgetting about working on your paper.

Indicators of Emotion.   Several different indicators frequently are used to identify the emotion expressed and the level of arousal and feeling being experienced. These indicators include the personal reports of the person, the observed behaviors of that person, and the physiological reactions that accompany the emotion. Personal reports often include written or spoken descriptions of feelings, while observed behaviors such as gestures, postures, and facial expressions also may be used to help understand the emotion being expressed. Changes in heart rate, blood pressure, breathing patterns, pupil dilation, and electrodermal activity (EDA; formerly known as galvanic skin response, or GSR) are measures often interpreted as indicators of emotions.

EXAMPLE 10.19.   Imagine an actor about to go on stage. Stopped by the director and asked, "How do you feel?" the actor might respond, "Okay. Relaxed" or "Pretty nervous." This personal report might be confirmed or disconfirmed by observations made by the director: Is the actor smiling or frowning, breathing normally, or flushed and sweaty? The director might interpret all these indicators—spoken, observed, and physiological—and then decide how the actor really feels.

Anthropomorphism and Parsimony.   Two cautions about observing or interpreting emotions should be kept in mind. First, one should not interpret the behaviors of lower organisms in terms of human emotions. Attributing human characteristics to lower organisms is known as *anthropomorphism*. This should be avoided, especially when another explanation of the organism's behavior is sufficient.

EXAMPLE 10.20.   When a dog is given food, it often will wag its tail. In psychology, it is more appropriate to say that the dog has responded with tail wagging than to say that the dog is "happy."

The second caution about observing emotional behavior is that if a simple, or *parsimonious*, explanation is adequate for a situation, one should use it in preference to a more complicated explanation. This is a general caution that applies to all aspects of the discipline.

10.6 BASIC TYPES OF EMOTIONS

Most languages contain many words and descriptive phrases associated with emotions. However, when attempts to classify emotions into basic categories have been made, consensus has been hard to reach. Part of the difficulty arises from cultural differences that have been identified. Psychologists generally agree that emotions can be classified on the dimensions of pleasant-unpleasant and mild-extreme, but the number of labels for general categories has ranged from as few as three to eight or more. This section presents classifications that have found some general agreement.

Fear. *Fear*-producing stimuli seem to change in importance as a person grows older. What is sudden, unexpected, and perhaps frightening to a child may not be at all fear-provoking to an adolescent or adult. By contrast, some fear-producing stimuli that affect adolescents and adults, particularly in social settings, may not provoke fear in a young child.

EXAMPLE 10.21.   A 2-year-old in a nursery may have little worry about burping in front of the other children. However, an adolescent with a little gas may dread such an event occurring in front of peers.

Psychologists often distinguish between fear and anxiety on the basis of the specificity of the stimulus that provokes the response. Fear is thought to arise from a fairly well defined stimulus, while anxiety generally is a response to an unspecified threatening stimulus.

Occasionally fears become so severe that they take on irrational but compelling properties. When this happens, fear is called a *phobia*. Phobias often are established in a manner comparable to classical conditioning (see Chapter 7).

EXAMPLE 10.22.   Suppose an individual is involved in an accident that takes place in a small, enclosed space. That type of space may become associated with pain, resulting in the person becoming claustrophobic (that is, fearful of enclosed spaces). Virtually all the enclosed areas that the person encounters after the accident will be perfectly safe, but the previous experience will produce intense fear reactions and therefore an avoidance of such spaces.

Anger.   The emotional reactions associated with *anger* may vary from being modestly "worked up" to being bitter, enraged, or infuriated. Such reactions are provoked by displeasing or frustrating stimuli that block the successful attainment of a goal. They usually are stronger if the activity generating the anger is thought to be intentional rather than accidental. Interestingly, research has shown that rather than relieving anger, the expression of anger may intensify the reaction.

Grief or Sorrow.   In a manner similar to anger, grief or sorrow reactions are provoked by stimuli that are frustrating. The difference is that the stimuli often involve involuntary, permanent separation from a loved one or an irreconcilable mistake or hurt. Milder forms in this category often are labeled as *sadness*.

Pleasure.   Pleasure ranges from simple reactions of delight or fun to ecstatic experiences of joy or love. In general, pleasure reactions are generated by the presence of favorable or approach stimuli that lead to desired goals. Subsequent expressions of pleasure may take such diverse forms as smiling, laughing, and hugging and kissing.

Variations and Combinations. Many emotional situations can be described as variations or combinations of more basic emotions. Indeed, many psychologists believe that any attempt to designate basic emotions is a wasted effort and prefer to investigate cultural and other situational variables to label the circumstances observed. A rich vocabulary representing emotional situations has arisen in an attempt to specify explanations for the many situations observed.

EXAMPLE 10.23. Consider the behavior of a person labeled as "exasperated." The upset and disgust, accompanied perhaps by bullying or blustering behavior, may be the result of anger (from some frustration), fear (of exposure of social inadequacy), and/or pleasure (derived from getting someone else to "give in").

10.7 THEORIES OF EMOTION

Despite the difficulties associated with trying to label emotions, psychologists have proposed several theories to explain emotional behavior. The focus differs from one to the next, but all seem to contribute to the understanding of emotional situations.

The James-Lange Theory.   An early proposal, the *James-Lange theory*, is named for William James and Carl Lange, who independently developed the same basic ideas at about the same time. They proposed that stimuli produce bodily changes that in turn generate felt emotions. This theory thus suggests that stimuli are keyed to physical reactions that only afterward are interpreted as emotions.

The Cannon-Bard Theory.   Both Walter Cannon and Philip Bard recognized that identical psychophysiological states logically could not cause the differing emotions that are associated with them. The *Cannon-Bard theory* suggests that when an emotion-producing stimulus is received in the brain, centers in the thalamus and hypothalamus send out simultaneous signals to both external muscles and internal organs and back to the cortex. The muscles and organs make the physiological reactions to the emotion, while the cortex interprets the signal as emotion. Thus, this theory proposes that physiological and psychological reactions occur at the same time.

(*Note*: Current psychophysiological attempts to explain emotion have looked at activity of the autonomic nervous system and the role of the endocrine system and hormones.)

Cognitive and Attribution Theories of Emotion.   More recent investigations into emotions have stressed the interaction of cognitive (intellectual) and physiological (bodily) influences. For example, the *two-factor theory of emotion* developed by Stanley Schachter and Jerome Singer had physiological arousal as the first component and the labeling of that arousal as the second. Criticized because the same kind of arousal could be associated with a number of different emotional reactions, this kind of theory prompted additional suggestions that incorporated both physiological reactions such as emotion-specific patterns of activity in the autonomic nervous system and investigations of *cognitive appraisal*. Richard Lazarus distinguished between two kinds of appraisal: *Primary appraisal* is an initial assessment regarding how the event occurring may affect personal involvement and well-being, and *secondary appraisal* allows for an evaluation of the resources and options available for responding in the situation.

EXAMPLE 10.24.   A person might explain anger or depression as a result of not sleeping enough, not being able to visit close friends, or not getting a raise when one was expected. In each case, the symptoms might be very similar but the emotion is attributed to different causes. Secondary appraisal may lead to varying reactions. Rearranging one's personal schedule might take care of the difficulties experienced with either of the first two instances but would have no effect on the third. Other options would have to be investigated to resolve the emotions associated with employment.

Robert Zajonc and his colleagues have argued that emotion and cognition are separate processes and that appraisal is *not* necessary for experiencing emotion. Instead, emotion is thought to be a basic process inherent in people and other organisms. It is unlikely that any single theory of emotion is going to be accepted without question.

10.8   SPECIAL TOPICS IN EMOTION

Research on emotions has led to several intriguing areas of investigation.

The Facial Feedback Hypothesis.   The universality of facial expressions that reveal emotions has led researchers to investigate the link of such expressions with the feelings being experienced. In general, findings have shown that facial expressions of emotion contribute to the initiation or modification of emotional experiences. This has been called the *facial feedback hypothesis*.

EXAMPLE 10.25.   One study tried to force subjects to show specific facial expressions. The subjects were asked to hold a pen in their teeth (forcing a kind of smile) or with their lips (forcing a nonsmiling expression). While doing this, the subjects were asked to rate cartoons on how funny they were. In general, those forced to "smile" rated the cartoons as funnier than did those who maintained the nonsmiling expression.

Lie Detection.   A practical application of the study of emotions has been the attempt to develop dependable lie detection techniques. Research has substantiated the idea that emotion-producing situations often can be detected by measuring physiological responses such as heart rate, respiration rate, and electrodermal activity even when personal reports or observed behaviors do not give any indication of emotion.

The theory of lie detection depends on the thesis that a person who is telling a lie is in an emotion-producing situation. Thus, physiological indicators of emotion shown by a *lie detector* can be used to judge whether a person is telling the truth. It must be realized that interpretations of the results from such tests must be made very carefully because many situations other than telling lies may be emotion-producing. So far, research studies have not been able to establish distinct patterns of physiological indicators associated with precise emotional states.

Note: Another technique for trying to identify lies is the use of voiceprints. Supposedly, changes in vocal inflections reveal when a person is lying. Because of the unreliability of lie detection techniques, evidence obtained from such tests usually is not admissible in court proceedings.

Learned Helplessness.   In certain kinds of unpleasant, emotion-producing situations, some individuals may come to believe that an unpleasant consequence is inescapable or inevitable. In such cases, these people may accept what are considered unalterable consequences and demonstrate the kind of behavior psychologists have labeled *learned helplessness*. It may be possible to continue to work against the situation, but the believed certainty of the result keeps these people from making serious attempts to help themselves.

EXAMPLE 10.26.   A person who was abused as a child and was unable to counter the actions of the abuser may continue to fail to make a response even after attaining adult status. The helplessness of the previous period "carries over," and appropriate responses are not made even when they are possible and would succeed in countering the abusive behavior.

Psychosomatic Illnesses and Somatoform Disorders.   Physical problems associated with stress, conflict, or other emotional situations have been classified in two ways. *Psychosomatic illnesses* are real physical problems (such as ulcers) that are linked with psychological components such as stress and conflict. *Somatoform disorders* are characterized by the presence of one or more symptoms of a physical dysfunction for which no organic cause can be found.

EXAMPLE 10.27.   A touch of nausea before an important exam may be psychosomatic in nature. The need to attract or maintain attention may generate a skin rash. Both of these instances reveal possible psychosomatic conditions, although the reactions could be the result of having the flu or suffering from an allergy. It is necessary to determine the cause before making decision. By contrast, a soldier who suddenly becomes paralyzed from the waist down, making him unable to go into combat, but who shows no organic cause for that condition appears to display a somatoform disorder. (This particular condition is called a *conversion disorder*.)

Solved Problems

10.1 Your child's teacher calls one afternoon and tells you that your child has been "acting up" in class. Apparently, your child continues to misbehave until the teacher has to stop whatever else is being done with the rest of the class. The teacher asks why the child persists in misbehaving. Having just studied this chapter, you answer, "It's just an example of the motivation cycle." The teacher asks you to explain. How do you describe the motivation cycle?

The motivation cycle starts with an initial need or drive. This usually is followed by an operant (goal-seeking) response, and if the motive condition is strong enough, the responding continues until the goal is reached. Once the goal is achieved, there is relief. This relief often is only temporary; when the motive strength again builds, the cycle may begin once more.

Perhaps in this case the child needs attention or social recognition from the teacher. If this is lacking in everyday activities, the need continues to grow until the child *has* to find a way to get attention. Disruption is the operant response; the goal is satisfied (temporarily) and does not reappear until the motive strength has increased again.

10.2 Why does the child in Solved Problem 10.1 misbehave rather than do something else to get attention?

Very simply, because it works. Generally, most organisms are able to make adjustments or adaptations to conditions to allow the satisfaction of a motive condition. In this case, apparently, bad behavior gets attention when good behavior does not; the child has adjusted to acting in the manner that works.

10.3 The other children in the class in Solved Problem 10.1 try to stop your child's misbehavior, but the misbehavior continues until the teacher says or does something. Why is that?

The misbehaving child is showing goal specificity. Just as in most cases not any food will satisfy a hunger drive, not any form of attention appears to work in this situation. The child seems to want the *teacher's* attention.

10.4 How can one estimate whether a motive exists and how strong it is?

Estimates of motivation can be made in two ways. One way is to determine how long it has been since the motive was last satisfied; this period of time represents the deprivation the subject has experienced. The other way of assessing motivation involves observing behavior and estimating what the motive must have been that provoked that behavior. This method involves naturalistic observation of the subject and inferences from such observation.

10.5 Does deprivation automatically create a motive condition?

In some cases deprivation automatically creates a compelling motive condition. For example, if you were deprived of air, you would have a very strong motivation to try to correct the situation. However, other kinds of deprivation do not create motive conditions. If you were deprived of a trip to Buffalo, you might not feel deprived or motivated. In other words, deprivation does not necessarily create a motive condition.

10.6 *Instinct*, *need*, *drive*, *arousal*, and *incentive* are all used to describe motivational situations. What does each of these terms mean?

An *instinct* is defined as an inborn condition that regularly triggers specific complex behaviors from all the members of a species when a particular stimulus is present. A *need* is not automatic, but rather is described as a deficit or imbalance that may be physiological or psychological. A *drive* is viewed as the psychological state resulting from the physiological or psychological deficit or, more generally, as a desire to reach a goal. *Arousal* refers to the physiological excitation that accompanies a drive. An *incentive* is an external condition or thing that "pulls" an organism toward it.

10.7   Several years ago fights broke out in toy stores because parents argued about who would take possession of and be able to buy that year's "fad toy." Explain this behavior in terms of utility theory.

Utility theory combines the concepts of need, drive, and incentive. The theory proposes an estimate of how much one believes something is needed, linked with how appealing that thing is. In this case, the fights indicated that a very strong drive ("My child *really* needs that toy") was linked to a strong appeal or incentive ("That's the cutest toy of the season"), producing very emotional behavior.

10.8   Imagine a person opening the door of an apartment and greeting another person who is a new acquaintance. The person who opens the door is looking forward to the visit from someone who may turn out to be a good friend. What need does this person have, and where in Maslow's hierarchy of needs does this need seem to fall?

The person's need is for affiliation, which would be approximately in the middle of Maslow's hierarchy of needs. The person's physiological and safety needs apparently are not uppermost at the moment; affiliation or belongingness holds current importance. Also, at this moment the person does not seem to be trying to satisfy the need for self-esteem or self-actualization.

10.9   What is functional autonomy?

On occasion, a response is first made as an operant response to try to satisfy a motive condition. As the response is made repeatedly, the person comes to appreciate the response for its own sake. When the response becomes motivating in and of itself, functional autonomy has occurred. An example of this might be jogging, which is first done to try to get in better physical condition but later is appreciated for the pleasure it brings.

10.10   Suppose a tennis player says to her coach, "I was so 'up' for that match that I played very poorly." What principle of motivation is the athlete describing?

In general, it seems that a person's performance will improve as the person's motive level increases, but only up to a point. When the level of motivation passes that point, the person's performance can be expected to deteriorate. The tennis player in this example may have been overmotivated. Her performance might have been better if she had not been so "up" for the match and instead had been nearer the optimal level of arousal.

10.11   Leah is a calm, studious, thoughtful 18-year-old. Her sister, Daylynn, seems to go a "mile a minute" every moment of the day. Use the activation-arousal and social learning theories of motivation to explain these differences in behavior.

The activation-arousal theory of motivation suggests that each person has a typical, normal, and appropriate level for his or her motivation and that behavior will be geared to maintain something approaching that level. In this case, Leah would have a much lower typical level than Daylynn, but both would be acting in keeping with the personal arousal needed. If social learning theory is used, the suggestion would be that Leah has learned that being calm will lead to satisfactions, while Daylynn has learned that being very active will produce satisfactions. Thus, they both repeat behaviors that have been successful for them in the past.

10.12   What motive conditions must be satisfied for people to survive?

The unlearned, so-called *survival motives*, each of which must be at least partially satisfied for a person to continue living, are hunger, thirst, the need for air to breathe, the need to maintain body temperature, the need to relieve fatigue, and the need to eliminate waste products from the body. To survive, a person must satisfy each of these motives, some very quickly and others with less immediate demand. (For example, a person cannot survive without air for more than a few minutes but can live several days without sleep and several weeks without eating.)

10.13 Describe some of the adjustments the human body makes automatically to satisfy the survival motives. What name is given to the physiological state the body attempts to maintain?

When the body gets too warm, it perspires to cool off. When the body is too cold, it shivers to warm up. If a person needs liquid and has ingested none for some time, the body's stored liquids are used and dehydration begins. When fatigue becomes intolerable, sleep is inevitable, such as in a state of exhaustion. All these processes represent the body's attempts to maintain *homeostasis*, or internal physiological balance. (*Note*: The motive condition is described as a need or drive, while eating, drinking, sleeping, eliminating, breathing, and sheltering are the responses made to satisfy those motives.)

10.14 All the survival motives are unlearned. Which other motive is unlearned but is not classified as a survival motive?

The need to relieve physiological pain is unlearned but is not included in the list of survival motives. This is the case because one *must* satisfy the survival motives within in some time period or die, while it is possible to live with pain for an entire lifetime.

10.15 Patrick has tried to lose weight by following several different diets over a period of time. No matter how he adjusts his eating behavior, the losses he manages to attain seem to last for only a relatively short period and then his weight goes back to where it was. What theory of hunger seems to explain Patrick's situation?

The set-point theory of hunger proposes that the body has a particular weight that is preset and that that weight level is based on factors such as the number of fat cells in the body, the metabolic rate, and the levels of certain neurochemicals in the brain. The guiding principle of the theory is that the body will adjust itself in attempts to maintain a particular weight regardless of the diet imposed. In Patrick's case, this seems to be happening.

10.16 Hunger is thought to be a function of both internal and external signals. What evidence supports this conclusion?

Research on the involvement of the hypothalamus has shown that hunger (or eating behavior) can be "turned on" or "turned off," depending on which part of the hypothalamus is stimulated or damaged. However, research also has supported the conclusion that the context and presentation of food will influence food consumption. For example, if green food coloring is added to mashed potatoes, it has no effect on the actual palatability of the food, but the color will cause many people to reject the potatoes as inedible.

10.17 What are the similarities and differences between anorexia nervosa and bulimia nervosa?

Anorexia nervosa and bulimia nervosa are both classified as eating disorders. Anorexia is characterized by a refusal to eat and the accompanying denial that such behavior and the resulting loss of weight are at all unusual. Typically, bulimics maintain fairly normal body weight. However, their behavior is characterized by binge eating followed by some form of purging, such as self-induced vomiting or the use of laxatives.

10.18 Are learned (social) motives more important in modern developed societies than they are in underdeveloped societies?

Probably. Most people in modern developed societies do not have to worry much, if at all, about the unlearned (survival) motives; these people have adequate food, drink, shelter, and sleep and the opportunity to breathe and to eliminate body waste products. As a result, learned behaviors, which are influenced by societal rewards and punishments, become predominant in a person's life. In a society that does not offer satisfaction of the basic survival motives (particularly for food and liquids), learned motives may not predominate.

10.19   Why was achievement sometimes called a "masculine" characteristic?

There are two reasons for this. The first is that most of the research in the first 25 years of studies of achievement was done using men as subjects. The second reason is that initial research using female subjects concentrated on the idea that women feared success. (It was believed that a woman showing high achievement risked social rejection and/or loss of femininity, while success motives in men were seen in a more favorable light.) More recent research has indicated that these results may be situation-specific rather than exclusively related to gender.

10.20   Dominance, affiliation, and relief of anxiety have been classified as learned motives. What conditions might lead to the development of such motives?

It is possible that these motives are be necessary for survival; for example, you might want to affiliate yourself with a person who would protect you in a dangerous situation. It is much more likely, however, that these motives result from social pressures. Dominance over others may lead to rewards, affiliation with others may give a person an "in-group" feeling, and relief from anxiety is frequently relief from society-produced problems, getting away from difficulties and establishing a more tolerable condition.

10.21   Is sex a survival motive? Explain your answer.

The best answer is "yes and no." If one is talking about the survival of the species, the answer is yes. However, the survival of an individual does not depend on sexual activity.

10.22   Don't humans have unlearned sexual responses? Why shouldn't sex be classified as un-learned?

Sexual response is unlearned to some extent. Certain physiological processes are relatively automatic and appear if an appropriate stimulation starts the responses. However, learned variables also strongly influence human sexual activity. These variables, which often are referred to as sexual scripts, may differ from one group to another, depending on a society's standards of things such as beauty and sexual morality.

10.23   How does the pattern of sexual responding differ between women and men?

In almost all regards, there are no differences between the sexual responses of women and those of men; the pattern of response for both men and women is seen to be initial excitement, followed by a plateau stage of arousal, then orgasm, and finally a refractory period during which additional responding cannot take place. About the only difference that has been noted is that in general, women experience shorter refractory periods than do men, giving women the possibility of having multiple orgasms in a relatively short period of time.

10.24   A college athlete achieved all-America status in both football and baseball. Professional teams in both sports tried to sign him to a contract. Confronted with two lucrative offers, he could not decide which one to take. What psychological term describes this athlete's situation? What resolution might be expected?

The athlete is faced with an approach-approach conflict in which both possible choices are attractive (or positively valued). The resolution would be to choose the sport that seemed to be most favorable—perhaps football because of the immediate membership on a major league team or perhaps baseball because a longer career in the sport could be expected.

10.25 Name two other common forms of conflict and give examples of each one.

Two other common conflicts are avoidance-avoidance conflicts and approach-avoidance conflicts. *Avoidance-avoidance* involves two unpleasant choices, such as when a person must spend Saturday morning either cleaning house or doing the laundry. *Approach-avoidance* conflicts exist when a single choice has both pleasant and unpleasant possibilities. Studying may result in good grades, but it is also hard work and may keep a person from doing other, more pleasant activities. (In addition, a person may face a multiple approach-avoidance conflict in which there are several choices and each has both positive and negative aspects. For example, when one is buying a car, each one looked at may have positive features such as good looks and good mileage, but each also may have negative features such as a high price and a high insurance payment.)

10.26 How are conflicts resolved?

In general, the resolution of all conflicts is essentially the same: The most dominant motive "wins out," and the person chooses accordingly. However, in the case of an avoidance-avoidance conflict, the person sometimes may choose a third alternative, that of "leaving the field." The person in Solved Problem 10.25 might spend Saturday morning sleeping rather than cleaning or laundering, thus withdrawing altogether from the conflict situation.

10.27 Suppose that the members of the hiring committee of a firm are discussing the candidates they have interviewed. One of the committee members comments about a particular candidate by saying, "Well, that one certainly seemed very emotional." What kind of information probably was used in making this judgment?

Three different kinds of information might have led to this committee member's remark: (1) The candidate might have given a personal report of experiencing emotion, (2) the committee member might have observed behavior that appeared to be the expression of emotion, or (3) there might have been physiological indicators that indicated that the candidate was in an emotional state.

10.28 One committee member responds by saying, "Gee, I didn't think that at all. Can you be more specific?" The response is, "Didn't you see how the nervousness showed? All those little gestures, the strange movements—that guy was really emotional!" Explain why the two members of the committee differ in their interpretations of the candidate's behaviors. What seems to be the most important factor in making *any* decision about whether an emotion has been expressed?

Judgment of emotion is largely *subjective*. What is considered emotional gesturing or movement by one person may seem perfectly calm or normal to another. Additionally, the context of the actions is very important. The most important factor in judging emotional expression is to know the stimulus that provoked the reaction being observed.

10.29 Emotions are said to produce a state of arousal. What kinds of physiological indicators are used to measure this type of arousal?

Several physiological indicators may be used to measure arousal. They include heart rate, blood pressure, respiration rate, electrodermal activity, and pupil size.

10.30 People often say that someone "gets angry" or "gets scared" when something occurs. These phrases suggest that emotions are responses. However, people also say things such as, "I couldn't do anything because I was so scared!" The implication of this kind of remark is that emotion was a stimulus that prevented responding. Can these two different views of emotion—as a response and as a stimulus—be reconciled?

The explanation comes by realizing that there is a stimulus that keys the emotion; thus, getting scared occurs because a stimulus provokes the fear reaction. This fear in turn may stimulate additional responding. The emotion is a response that may then serve as a motive condition, which is a stimulus.

10.31 Are the effects of emotions comparable to the effects of other motive conditions?

In general, emotions affect behavior in the same manner as other motive conditions and the completion of the motivation cycle can be expected. Additionally, the inverted-U curve predicted for the relationship between motivation and performance can be expected when emotion is considered to be the motivator.

10.32 Suppose a dog barks, jumps, spins, and generally shows a high level of activity when you begin to open a can of dog food. Is it correct to claim that the dog is "happy"?

Psychologists must guard against anthropomorphizing, or attributing human characteristics to lower organisms. To say a dog is happy is to attribute a human emotion to the dog; psychologists prefer simpler explanations. Perhaps a psychologist would view the dog's behavior as a conditioned response. (See Chapter 7.)

10.33 Consider the dog's behavior in Solved Problem 10.32. What principle would psychologists use in choosing the simpler explanation rather than the more complicated one?

In psychology, the generally accepted approach is to use the most economical interpretation of an event that will account for the phenomenon observed. This is referred to as the law of *parsimony*, and it applies here.

10.34 A young child often shows fear of strange objects or events, especially if they are unexpected. The young child, however, seldom shows fear of embarrassment or rejection. The opposite may be true of older children and adults. Explain these differences in emotional reactions.

Two variables appear to be important in determining these differences in emotional responding. In the young child's situation, much perceptual learning (understanding) has not yet been accomplished. Sudden, unexpected stimuli may produce fear because they are not understood. Adults too may be frightened by unexpected events or strange objects, but adults generally have had much more experience with such events. However, experience also has taught the adult or older child about social embarrassments and rejections that may occur if inappropriate behaviors are shown. For example, fears concerning body odor and similar factors may be quite compelling for an adult but have little or no effect on a child.

10.35 Shawon is so terrified of dogs that even watching canine cartoon characters produces a feeling of fear. What is the likely explanation of Shawon's behavior?

Shawon appears to have a *phobia*, an intense, compelling, but irrational fear. One likely cause for Shawon's phobic behavior is that classical conditioning occurred: A previously neutral stimulus (a dog) was paired with a fear-producing stimulus, and the learned behavior has generalized to most dog-type stimuli.

10.36 What are the similarities and differences between anger and grief?

Both anger and grief seem to be provoked by stimuli that are frustrating, ones that block the attainment of a goal. The major difference between the two emotions is that a frustrating stimulus that produces grief is likely to have a finality about it; that is not true of a stimulus that produces anger.

10.37 Why is it that when people finish singing a difficult song, hear a joke, or observe a young child trying to learn to ride a bicycle, they may smile or laugh?

The reaction is one of pleasure, outwardly expressed by smiling or laughing. The basis of the emotion of pleasure seems to be the attainment of a goal. In each of these situations, some motive has been satisfied—perhaps achievement for the song, social acceptance for the joke, and affection or pride for the child.

10.38 Envy often has been used as a label for an emotional reaction. Show how the concept of envy may be viewed as a variation and combination of some "basic" emotions.

Envy implies an emotional state in which a person wishes to have what someone else has. This may have resulted from fear of never being able to attain that goal or frustration and the resultant anger from wanting something that is unobtainable. Furthermore, envy might provide pleasure by allowing the person to express such thoughts and thus achieve a reinforcement or goal such as social support from others who feel the same way.

10.39 Imagine walking out of a theater, turning the corner, and being confronted with a very tall individual who is wearing a gorilla costume and screaming at you. Interpret your probable reaction according to the James-Lange theory of emotion.

The James-Lange theory proposed that stimuli (the gorilla suit and scream) automatically trigger bodily changes (perhaps jumping back, gasping, or running) and that the perception of these bodily changes is the emotion you feel.

10.40 What interpretation would be given to the situation in Solved Problem 10.39 if the Cannon-Bard theory of emotion were employed?

The Cannon-Bard theory of emotion states that the felt emotion and the physiological reaction to the stimuli are triggered simultaneously. Thus, the sensory stimuli received by the individual are interpreted by the cortex, and a signal is sent out to activate lower brain areas (the hypothalamus and limbic system). At the same time, messages also are transmitted to the internal organs and the muscles, producing the physiological reactions to the emotion.

10.41 Donyelle has been feeling depressed. When asked why she feels that way, she comments about an unchallenging job, a breakup of a relationship of long standing, and her mother's illness. Create primary and secondary appraisals of Donyelle's emotions.

The primary appraisals would be very similar: Donyelle has symptoms of depression that are associated (she says) with all three of the situations mentioned. Secondary appraisals would be quite different. Evaluation of the resources and options available for dealing with the three components probably will lead to three different conclusions. For example, Donyelle might begin to look at job advertisements for employment that would be more stimulating and might join a local club in an attempt to find a new companion, but she could find that she has neither resources nor options that can change the status of her mother's health.

10.42 Several years ago the popular phrase "Don't worry, be happy" was accompanied by an illustration of what came to be called a "smiley face." Many people did smile when they saw this illustration or heard the phrase. What would the facial feedback hypothesis say about these people?

The facial feedback hypothesis proposes that facial expressions contribute to the initiation or modification of emotional responses. In this case, the hypothesis would suggest that the people who smiled indeed would feel happier; the facial expression "leads" the reaction experienced.

10.43 Explain the theory of lie detection and then explain why the techniques are not thought to be very reliable.

Lie detection is based on the premise that telling a lie is an emotional activity and therefore will be revealed by the physiological reactions that accompany the emotions being felt. In some instances, this is the case. However, evidence indicates that many people are capable of telling a lie without experiencing any noticeable emotion, meaning that the physiological reactions at the time of lying match those shown when the person tells the truth. Most lie detection evidence is not admissible in court.

10.44 Karl suffered a stroke that caused paralysis in his right hand. He started therapy immediately but while doing the therapy switched to writing with his left hand. When the effects of therapy began to correct his problem, Karl continued to use his left hand for writing even though he might have used his (previously natural) right hand. What principle might explain Karl's behavior?

Karl appears to be showing evidence of *learned helplessness*. Having previously suffered from the physical affliction which prevented his making the natural right-handed writing response, Karl continues to fail to make that response even after the disorder has been corrected. The helplessness of the previous period "carries over," and Karl continues not to make the response even when it is again possible.

10.45 Bobby has asthma. His breathing difficulties seem to be associated particularly with feathers. His parents take care to avoid exposing Bobby to feathers in any form, such as trips to the zoo, feather pillows, and pets in the home.

One day Bobby is taken to the art museum on a school trip. Passing a marble sculpture of several birds, Bobby suddenly has a severe asthma attack. Does this incident provide evidence for interpreting Bobby's asthma as a psychosomatic illness?

Psychosomatic illnesses are actual physical problems that are thought to be provoked by psychological situations such as stress and conflict. The immediate evidence indicates that Bobby's reaction is psychosomatic because it was provoked by sculptured marble feathers that could not possibly contain allergens. It is likely this may be a generalized response that originated from a conflict Bobby had previously experienced in the presence of feathers.

Key Terms

Activation-arousal theory of motivation.   The proposal that an organism has a typical or normal level of arousal and attempts to maintain that level.

Anger.   Thought to be a basic emotion; a response of heightened arousal in the class of rage or hostility.

Anorexia nervosa.   An eating disorder marked by a refusal to eat, denial of such behavior, and extreme loss of weight.

Anthropomorphism.   The attribution of human characteristics to objects or nonhuman organisms.

Approach-approach conflict.   A situation in which a subject must choose between two stimulus situations, which both have positive values.

Approach-avoidance conflict.   A situation in which a subject must decide whether to go toward or away from a single stimulus situation that has both positive and negative values.

Arousal.   The physiological activation that accompanies a drive.

Attribution.   A way of ascribing causes to the acts of other people or oneself.

Avoidance-avoidance conflict.   A situation in which a subject must choose between two stimulus situations, which both have negative values.

Bulimia nervosa.   An eating disorder marked by binge eating followed by purging.

Cannon-Bard theory of emotion.   A theory proposing that emotion consists of simultaneously occurring physiological and psychological reactions to the emotion-producing stimulus.

Conflict.   A situation in which two or more incompatible motive conditions are operating at the same time.

Contact comfort.   The need of many young organisms to have something warm and soft to cling to; apparently a combination motive.

Cycle of motivation.   A proposal explaining many motive situations as a sequence of need, operant response, goal, and relief; the cycle often repeats itself.

Deprivation.   Doing without; in motivation, often measured in terms of the time since the motive was last satisfied.

Drive.   The internal, psychological state resulting from need.

Emotion.   A complex state of organism that usually is marked by a heightened state of arousal and the feelings that accompany the condition.

Facial feedback hypothesis.   The proposal that facial expressions contribute to the initiation or modification of emotional experiences.

Fear.   Thought to be a basic emotion; a response in the general class of anxiety or dread.

Functional autonomy.   A situation in which a response which was made originally to satisfy a motive becomes motivating in and of itself.

Goal.   In motivation, the satisfier of a motive condition.

Goal specificity.   The desire to satisfy a motive condition with a particular reinforcement rather than with any reinforcement that would satisfy.

Hierarchy of needs.   A proposal by Abraham Maslow that arranges motives in an order of importance; those lower in the hierarchy must be satisfied before the higher ones can be satisfied.

Homeostasis.   A state of physiological balance.

Incentive.   External conditions that compel activity from an organism; a "pull."

Instinct.   An innate (inborn) condition that regularly provokes specific, complex responses from all the members of a species when a distinctive stimulus pattern occurs.

James-Lange theory of emotion.   A theory proposing that emotion-producing stimuli generate physical reactions which then are perceived as felt emotions.

Learned helplessness.   The acceptance of what seem to be the unalterable consequences of a situation even if a change may be possible.

Learned motives.   Conditions that result from experience and initiate, guide, and maintain behaviors; often called *social motives*.

Lie detector.   A device that measures physiological reactions such as heart rate and electrodermal activity; these reactions supposedly reveal whether the responder has lied.

Motive.   A condition that initiates, guides, and maintains behaviors until a goal is reached or the response is blocked.

Multiple approach-avoidance conflict.   A situation in which a subject must choose between two (or more) stimulus situations, each of which has both positive and negative values.

Need.   A deficit or imbalance; may be physiological or psychological.

Parsimony.   Economy of explanation; a parsimonious explanation is preferred to a more complex one if both explain the situation equally well.

Phobia.   An intense, irrational, but very compelling fear.

Psychosomatic illness.   A real physical problem linked to a psychological precipitator such as stress or conflict.

Self-actualization.   In Maslow's hierarchy of needs, the highest level; the attempt to reach one's full potential.

Set-point theory.   A proposal that each person has a preset body weight and that the body tends to return to that level if an imbalance occurs.

Sexual scripts.   Mental representations of ways in which sexual behaviors should be enacted.

Somatoform disorder.   The presence of one or more symptoms of physical dysfunction for which no organic cause can be found.

Thematic Apperception Test (TAT).   A projective test that involves responses to ambiguous pictures; used to evaluate motivation.

Unlearned motives.   Conditions that are inborn or innate and that initiate, guide, and maintain behaviors; sometimes called *survival motives*.

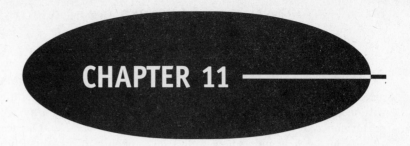

CHAPTER 11

Psychological Testing and Individual Differences

One of the first applications of psychological principles was in the development of *psychological testing* to predict things such as school success and mental fitness. For example, Alfred Binet and others developed the first standardized intelligence tests in the early 1900s.

This chapter is concerned with the important characteristics of a good test, the uses and abuses of tests, and the ethics of testing. It also looks at some basic forms of psychological tests that have been developed. The construction and use of tests to measure aspects of behavior is referred to as *psychometrics*.

11.1 CHARACTERISTICS OF A GOOD TEST

Psychologists have identified several characteristics that seem most important for a good test. Among these are reliability, validity, standardization, and objectivity.

Reliability.   *Reliability* refers to the consistency with which a result will be obtained when identical or supposedly equivalent forms of a test are used. In testing, perfect consistency cannot be expected, but a high degree of reliability is essential. It is impossible to make accurate or meaningful predictions from the results of an unreliable test.

Two common methods for assessing reliability often are used. *Parallel form* reliability calculates the correlation between the results from two forms of a test that are supposed to be equal in difficulty. When only one form is available, the items are divided in half and the correlation between results obtained for the two halves measures *split-half* reliability.

Validity.   *Validity* means that a test measures what it claims to measure; that is, a valid test predicts what it intends to predict. A test may have several validities, for example, a high validity for the prediction of scholastic success in literature courses but a much lower validity for predicting success in mathematics courses. It is very important to identify what a test *does* measure. Improper use of tests may lead to inaccurate predictions and therefore faulty counseling or advice.

Validity is assessed in several ways. In *criterion validity*, a correlation between test results and the measurement of another standard of the behavior under consideration is calculated. When this is done with measures that currently exist, it is called *concurrent validity*; when the results are correlated with performance at a later time, the label is *predictive validity*. On occasion, validity is estimated when experts in the field judge how well a test appears to measure the areas being tested; this is called *content-related validity*.

Note: A test may be highly reliable but invalid. This occurs when a test measures something consistently but does not measure what it claims to measure. However, a test that is valid must be reliable, for if it measures what it claims to measure, it has to do so consistently or it will not predict accurately.

EXAMPLE 11.1. Suppose you are shown the "Keen Test of Intellectual Skills," which involves summing the following three physical measurements: (1) the circumference of the subject's head, (2) the length of the subject's nose from tip to eyebrow, and (3) the distance separating the centers of the subject's eyes. You probably realize this test will have very high reliability but is unlikely to be valid. This example is purposely absurd, but the principle it illustrates is important: It is possible for a number of people to take specified measurements from one subject and obtain the same results (measurements), thus showing the test's reliability. However, such measurements may be completely inappropriate for the purposes stated and thus have no validity. Test developers constantly guard against the possibility that their tests may be unreliable or invalid.

Standardization. *Standardization* refers to how testing is conducted. All aspects of the testing procedure, including the administration of the test, the scoring, and the evaluation of the results, should follow the same pattern each time. If the testing procedure is not standardized, differences among the performances of the subjects may be the result of variations in test procedures, not accurate indicators of differences among subjects.

Norms. One way to standardize test results is to establish *norms*, which are scores obtained from groups of people who have taken the test. Once norms have been determined, the performances of others taking the test in the same manner can be compared to the norms.

EXAMPLE 11.2. College students who expect to go to graduate school often have to take the Graduate Record Exams (GRE) or a comparable test and submit the scores along with their applications. A copy of the scores is sent to each student, along with the norms for the test. Thus, the students know what their absolute GRE scores were and how those scores compared to those obtained by others taking the same tests. Often these are reported as *percentile* values. (A *percentile* is the point below which a certain percentage of the population falls. For example, a person who scored in the sixty-fifth percentile has done better than 65 percent of the people who took the test.)

Possible Problems with Norms. Norms are frequently helpful in interpreting the results of psychological tests but on occasion may be misleading. In such cases, it may be better to use a *criterion*, or absolute standard, to evaluate a person's performance.

In addition, because norms are established on the basis of test results and often are reported as statistics, they sometimes take on a "ring of truth" for a naive reader. They can be misinterpreted, as test results and the norms based on them *may* be typical of any one person, but the norm does not provide any assurance that this is so.

EXAMPLE 11.3. Consider a child who attends a special "magnet" high school academy for mathematics, sciences, and the humanities. It is known that students in this school in general score far higher than does the typical high school student on standardized tests in all three areas. Thus, compared to the norms for the overall population, these students are likely to be above average. However, if the norms for only the academy itself are used, someone who has a value higher than average for the overall population may be found to be in a very low percentile for the school. Care must be taken in reporting the norms being used. In addition, the possibility of stereotyping on the basis of norms certainly exists. The reasoning might be something like this: (1) The students attend an academy where all the children are bright, (2) students at that academy get high scores on standardized tests, and so (3) the norms for that group apply to any student who is a member of that group. The statistics alone cannot assure that every student will have high scores in all three areas emphasized by the school.

Objectivity.   *Objectivity* means that an observer's or measurer's biases or prejudices play no role in observation, measurement, or assessment; that is, all measurements are made in a neutral or dispassionate fashion. Observers who allow bias to influence their judgment or measurement are described as exhibiting *subjectivity* rather than being objective.

EXAMPLE 11.4.   In some cases the person administering, scoring, and evaluating a psychological test is not told why the subject is being tested. This is done so that person will not form preconceptions. It is inappropriate, for example, for a teacher who has complained about a student's behavior in class to give a personality test to that student. Instead, the test should be given by someone who is neutral and will proceed in an objective fashion.

11.2   MEASURING INTELLIGENCE

Because of interest in predicting the academic success of schoolchildren, the first standard measurements of intelligence were developed in Paris in the early 1900s by Alfred Binet and his colleagues. Binet's test was later revised by Lewis Terman of Stanford University for use with children in the United States and was released in 1916 as the Stanford-Binet Intelligence Test. A revised form of this test is still in use.

Definition of Intelligence.   Since 1916, a number of different *intelligence tests* have been created, but no single definition of intelligence has gained dominance in the field. Phrases commonly found in current definitions of *intelligence* include "goal-directed," "adaptive behavior," and "ability to understand the world," characteristics that allow problem solving, thinking rationally, and using resources effectively. Some psychologists, avoiding the difficulty of choosing any single definition, simply say that intelligence is what intelligence tests measure.

Mental Age.   The Stanford-Binet makes use of the concept of *mental age* (*MA*). If it is passed, each subtest in the Stanford-Binet receives two months' credit, with six subtests specified for each year level. Mental age is determined by totaling the number of months' credit accumulated by the subject.

EXAMPLE 11.5.   Ike passes all six subtests at the 7-year level, five subtests at age 8, three at age 9, three at age 10, one at age 11, and none at age 12. In this testing situation, Ike's *basal age* (the highest age at which all six subtests are passed) is 7, his *ceiling age* (the age at which no subtests are passed) is 12, and his mental age is 9 years: MA = $(7 \times 12) + (12 \times 2) = 108$ months, or 9 years. If Tina is tested and obtains a mental age of 108 months (9 years), she and Ike have the same mental age regardless of their actual ages. They both can be expected to perform at a level comparable to that of the average 9-year-old.

Intelligence Quotient (IQ).   Because not all subjects who achieved the same mental age value on a test were the same age, a ratio was developed to try to express the differences implied by the observed performances. This ratio was called the *intelligence quotient (IQ)* and was equal to the value of the MA divided by the *chronological* (or actual) *age* (*CA*), multiplied by 100.

$$IQ = \frac{MA}{CA} \times 100$$

EXAMPLE 11.6.   In the previous example, both Ike and Tina obtained an MA of 9 years (108 months). Ike is 9 years old, while Tina is 6 years, 9 months old. Using these chronological age values, Ike's IQ is 100, while Tina's is approximately 133. Calculations of these values are as follows:

$$\text{Ike's IQ} = \frac{9}{9}\left(\text{or } \frac{108}{108}\right) \times 100 = 100$$

$$\text{Tina's IQ} = \frac{9}{6.75}\left(\text{or } \frac{108}{81}\right) \times 100 = 133$$

Ratio versus Deviation IQ. The concept of an intelligence quotient was developed on the basis of work with the Stanford-Binet test, in which IQ was defined as the ratio of mental age to chronological age. However, difficulties with using this ratio arose as subjects approached adult status; there was no way for the Stanford-Binet to measure mental age in a way that could take into account the ever-increasing chronological age of a subject.

As a result, David Wechsler proposed the idea of *deviation IQ*, basing the reported IQ value on the normal probability curve (see Chapter 2). The Wechsler tests of intelligence have a mean IQ of 100 and a standard deviation of 15. When the subject has completed the test, the administrator determines IQ by comparing the subject's performance to the norms from that subject's age group to establish the percentile and IQ scores for the subject.

EXAMPLE 11.7. Using the generally accepted standard deviation and mean values for intelligence tests, a person scoring 115 is found to be in the eighty-fourth percentile compared to the total population, while the percentile value for someone scoring 70 is two and one-half. (See Chapter 2 if this example seems difficult.)

Exceptional Subjects. Arbitrarily, persons who obtain scores which differ from the mean by two or more standard deviations have been designated as *exceptional subjects*. People two or more standard deviations below the mean often are referred to as *mentally retarded* subjects, while those two or more standard deviations above the mean are called *gifted* subjects.

Mentally Retarded. Simply designating a subject as being mentally retarded because the obtained IQ value is two or more standard deviations below the mean has not proved to be an adequate description of a subject's capabilities. As a result, subgroups within the category of *mental retardation* have been developed. These subgroups, along with their IQ cutoff points, are as follows:

70–50: Mildly retarded (educable)
49–35: Moderately retarded (trainable)
34–20: Severely retarded (minimal skills)
19–0: Profoundly retarded (custodial care)

Retardation may be the result of environmental and/or hereditary factors. Inadequate nutrition and ingestion of toxins are examples of prenatal environmental influences that may lead to subsequent mental retardation. Postnatal trauma, such as brain injury from an accident, also may produce retardation. Extra chromosomal material can produce *Down syndrome*, a genetic syndrome marked by retardation, while the interaction of environmental and hereditary factors is shown in the effects of *phenylketonuria (PKU)*, a hereditary disease that leads to retardation if appropriate postnatal dietary (environmental) interventions do not take place.

In the United States, recent legislation has stipulated that retarded children be educated in the *least restricted environment*. This often has been referred to as *mainstreaming*, the integration of retarded individuals into the regular classroom as much as possible.

The Gifted. Exceptional subjects classified as gifted are not divided into further subgroupings. Some studies have shown that subjects with very high measured intelligence (IQ values of 180 or more) may have adjustment difficulties because they are misunderstood by parents or peers. However, most research indicates that the gifted as a group are better adjusted and healthier than are people of average intelligence.

Heritability Coefficient.   Genetic effects that lead to individual differences in measured intelligence are represented by the *heritability coefficient*, with possible values ranging from 0, meaning that heredity has no effect on the variation among people, to 1, which indicates that the variation among people on measured intelligence could be attributed exclusively to heredity.

The most common ways of estimating heritability coefficients have been to study identical twins who were reared apart or make comparisons between commonalities shown by identical twins versus fraternal twins. Psychologists also investigate relationships between birth parents versus adoptive parents with the characteristics of adopted children. Estimates of heritability coefficients have ranged from 0.3 to 0.8 depending on the study undertaken, but many possible explanations continue to influence the interpretations of these results.

EXAMPLE 11.8.   Studies of identical twins placed in separate homes must take into account the fact that placing agencies often try to pick homes that are comparable in several qualities. It is very likely that environmental influences in both homes are very similar, meaning that attribution of a relatively high heritability coefficient between identical twins who have been reared apart primarily to heredity may be a misrepresentation of the actual effects.

11.3   COMPOSITION OF INTELLIGENCE

The composition (or structure) of intelligence has been described in several different manners. A common approach has been statistical analysis, while other proposals have attempted to organize intelligence according to developmental stages or have employed information-processing approaches.

Factor Analysis.   The statistical technique most often used to determine aspects of intelligence is *factor analysis*. The study of various problem-solving tasks and their solutions allows psychologists to identify characteristics of intelligence that seem to be correlated.

General Factors.   Early research using factor analysis showed that many different tasks appeared to share a common base. Charles Spearman called this the *g factor*, or *general intelligence factor*. L. L. Thurstone accepted the concept of a general factor but proposed that it served to link seven basic characteristics of intelligence he identified by using factor analysis. Those characteristics were as follows:

Verbal comprehension: definition and understanding of words
Word fluency: being able to think of words rapidly
Number: being able to do arithmetic problems
Space: being able to understand spatial relationships
Rote memory: being able to memorize and recall
Perceptual: being able to grasp rapidly the similarities, differences, and details of objects or stimuli
Reasoning: being able to understand the principles or concepts necessary for problem solving

EXAMPLE 11.9.   In testing the spatial factor, the subject may be asked to try to find a figure "hidden" within a more complex figure. See Fig. 11-1, where drawing (*a*) is embedded in drawing (*b*).

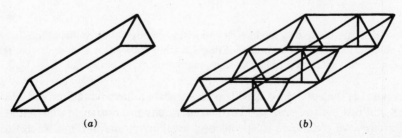

(*a*)   (*b*)

Fig. 11-1

Some years later, Raymond Cattell suggested that there are two general intelligence factors he called *fluid intelligence* and *crystallized intelligence*. Fluid intelligence is marked by the ability to reason abstractly, think creatively, or understand complex relationships and seems to be influenced by hereditary characteristics. Crystallized intelligence represents what a person has learned and retained from experiences and thus indicates the influences of environment on intelligence.

EXAMPLE 11.10.   Being able to solve word usage problems such as fill-in-the-blank definitions requires reliance on previous learning and thus the use of crystallized intelligence. However, solving anagram problems requires both knowledge and flexibility and thus fluid intelligence. Completing the sentence "Wearing apparel for the foot is called _____" requires crystallized intelligence, while recognizing that the letters in the word "shoe" can be found in the word "honest" requires more mental flexibility, or fluid intelligence.

Piaget's Stages of Cognitive Growth.   The developmental sequence of cognitive growth proposed by Jean Piaget (discussed in detail in Section 4.4) has been used as an approach to understanding intelligence. It has been proposed that an individual's intelligence can be estimated by comparing the particular characteristics of that person with the sequence proposed by Piaget.

Multiple Intelligences.   Several proposals have suggested that there may be a number of types of intelligence. Howard Gardner proposed eight types of intelligence, noting that any task might involve several of these working together:

Musical intelligence: skills in performing tasks related to music
Bodily kinesthetic intelligence: skills in using the body to solve problems
Logical-mathematical intelligence: skills in scientific thinking and problem solving
Linguistic intelligence: skills in the production and use of language
Spatial intelligence: skills concerning spatial relations
Interpersonal intelligence: skills in interacting with others
Intrapersonal intelligence: skills in assessing one's own feelings and emotions
Naturalistic intelligence: skills in making distinctions in the natural world

Robert Sternberg developed a *triarchic theory of intelligence*. Sternberg calls the three major aspects of intelligence *componential*, *experiential*, and *contextual*. The componential aspect refers to abilities used in analyzing information to solve problems. Experiential intelligence represents how previous learning is used to solve problems, while contextual intelligence shows how intelligence is used to face environmental demands and often is thought of as *practical intelligence*.

More recently, Sternberg modified his position to propose the concept of *successful intelligence*, stressing that the concept of intelligence needs to be considered more broadly and to account for more than just academic successes. For Sternberg, successful intelligence is defined in terms of one's ability to achieve success in life according to both personal standards and the sociocultural context in which one lives. Sternberg emphasizes analytical, creative, and practical skills as ways to adapt to environments, shape environments, and select environments. A further element of successful intelligence, according to Sternberg, is the ability to capitalize on one's strengths while both correcting and compensating for weaknesses.

EXAMPLE 11.11.   Tests are being developed to try to assess contextual or practical intelligence. Respondents are asked to indicate how likely different choices of responses might be given a situation that requires analysis of everyday circumstances such as a job problem in sales, management, or personnel.

Another proposal is that of John Carroll, who suggests a hierarchical model of cognitive, rather than intellectual, abilities. At the base of Carroll's hierarchy are *narrow abilities* that are acquired in response to environmental pressures. In the second level are *broad abilities*, such as learning, verbal fluency, perception, and memory, that are thought to result from an interaction of environmental and hereditary influences. At the top of the hierarchy is *g*, or *general cognitive ability*, which is attributed primarily to genetic influence only.

11.4 ASSESSING PERSONALITY

Personality tests are designed to determine what is typical of an individual or what a person usually does. Generally, these tests are related to a theory regarding the structure of personality and therefore attempt to measure the traits or characteristics specified by that theory. (The basic principles of personality are considered in depth in Chapters 12 through 14.) There are several different ways to evaluate personality, including self-report tests, projective tests, behavioral assessments, and techniques such as interviewing.

Self-Report Tests.   Questionnaires containing statements to which the individual can respond with answers such as "yes, maybe, no" or "true, false, cannot say" are *self-report tests*. Perhaps the best known of these tests is the *Minnesota Multiphasic Personality Inventory-2 (MMPI-2)*, which consists of 567 items sampling areas such as opinions, mood, and physical and psychological health. Interpretation of the MMPI-2 is based on the pattern of responses shown and yields 10 scales, plus three checks for the validity of responses (including a "lie scale" that indicates when a respondent falsifies responses in an attempt to make the pattern look more favorable). Another form of self-report testing is the adjective checklist, from which the respondent picks those he or she feels are self-descriptive.

Projective Tests.   In *projective personality tests*, the subject usually is presented with a series of ambiguous stimuli and asked for a description of or a story about each. The theory of these tests is that a person will reveal some personality characteristics by introducing them into (or projecting them onto) the stimulus provided.

The two most widely known projective tests are the *Thematic Apperception Test (TAT)*, which uses a series of 20 monochrome pictures, and the *Rorschach test*, which uses 10 inkblots, some of which have color. Scoring techniques have been developed to help maintain some objectivity when using these tests.

EXAMPLE 11.12.   The "inkblot" shown in Fig. 11-2 is not taken from the Rorschach test but is similar to the types of figures used in that test. The subject is shown the figure and asked, "What could this be?" or "What does this remind you of?" After responding to the entire set of figures, the subject goes back through the cards and points out what part of each inkblot determined the response.

Fig. 11-2

Other Personality Assessments.   Two other general categories of personality evaluation deserve mention. They are *behavioral assessments* and *interviews*.

Behavioral assessments may be done in a naturalistic setting such as home, work, or school. Some, however, are conducted in previously planned situations, in which the subject reacts to controlled conditions established by the psychologist. The responses made by the person are evaluated as a means of determining personality characteristics.

Interviews are face-to-face encounters between people. They may be conducted to gather the same information that may be obtained by using a self-report inventory but often give the interviewer an opportunity to expand on the questions or probe the answers the subject gives.

EXAMPLE 11.13.   Years ago, a popular situational test incorporated into an employment interview situation consisted of offering the candidate a cigarette and a light but not providing an ashtray. The reactions of the candidate to the growing length of ash and the lack of a place to dispose of it were observed in an attempt to determine something about the candidate's personality. As might be imagined, there are serious doubts about the reliability and validity of such "one-shot" tests of a personality.

It should be noted that psychotherapy (see Chapter 14) might be considered to be a special form of personality assessment through interviewing. Freud employed *free association* (letting each thought simply lead to the next) as a means of assessing inter- and intrapersonal issues.

11.5   OTHER TESTING AREAS

Although testing in psychology frequently has focused on intelligence and personality, tests for selection in academic and vocational settings also have gained popularity. In addition, psychologists have tried to find ways to evaluate creativity apart from intelligence.

Achievement versus Aptitude Tests.   Tests designed to measure what a person has accomplished up to that time are called *achievement tests*. Tests intended to predict what a person may accomplish in the future are designated as *aptitude tests*. Both types of testing are based on the concept of *ability*, a person's potential for acquiring a skill. Achievement tests show how well a person has acquired the skill up to the point of testing, while aptitude tests indicate how well a person may acquire the skill in the future.

Note: In a sense, *all* ability tests are achievement tests, showing only how well a person does on the given test at a particular time. However, the purposes of achievement and aptitude tests differ. Psychologists often try to design aptitude tests that measure basic skills that do not require specific knowledge.

Aptitude tests frequently are divided into two categories. *Scholastic tests* are intended to predict future success in academic pursuits, and *vocational tests* are intended to estimate future success in employment situations.

EXAMPLE 11.14.   Scholastic aptitude tests based exclusively on vocabulary skills predict quite well how a student may react to additional academic training. However, such a test might be almost totally inappropriate for checking physical proficiencies or psychomotor abilities, for which tests of muscular strength, manual dexterity, or coordination should be used. The psychologist has to design a testing program that is suited to the particular task being evaluated. (*Note*: Tests of physical proficiencies sometimes are referred to as tests of *noncognitive* abilities. Both cognitive and noncognitive abilities sometimes are tested when a person applies for a job such as package delivery, which involves both cognitive abilities such as map reading and physical abilities such as lifting.)

Interest versus Screening Tests.   Tests related to employment also may be categorized as *interest tests* or *screening tests*. Interest tests propose careers consistent with what intrigues the person, the individual's likes (or dislikes). Screening tests are intended to identify applicants who show the "best fit" for the job. There may be anything from high to no correlation between these two types of tests, depending on the job being evaluated.

Creativity.   A *creative act* is one which is novel or original, purposeful, useful, or worthwhile and represents a unique solution to a problem. Creative thinking often is referred to as *divergent thinking*, attempts to use exceptional or novel responses to solve problems. Divergent thinking often leads to responses that are viewed as creative acts, while *convergent thinking* leads to problem-solving responses that are correct but are considered routine or common. However, even divergent thinking does not necessarily predict creative thinking; being able to generate many different ideas to solve a problem probably is part but not all of *creativity*. Note also that when the solution finally is picked and implemented from among the many that are generated, convergent thinking is likely to be exhibited.

While measured (academic) intelligence may be related to creativity, several other characteristics seem to better differentiate creative people from noncreative people. In general, a creative person is quite flexible in thinking patterns, is interested in complex ideas, and shows a fairly complex personality pattern. Additionally, a creative person tends to be aesthetically sensitive, is interested in the unusual or novel, and shows a relatively higher willingness to take risks.

Measures of creativity have in common the aim of evaluating unique or novel solutions to problems that might reveal the characteristic. Among such tests are the following:

Unusual uses tests: Present an object and determine how many unusual uses the subject can generate for it.
Remote association tests: Present several stimulus words and determine if the subject can "find" the associate common to all.
Anagram tests: Present a stimulus word and determine how many and what smaller words can be created by using the letters of the stimulus word.
Drawing completion tests: Present a partial stimulus and ask the subject to finish the drawing.

EXAMPLE 11.15.   In a drawing completion test, the administrator may present a stimulus such as the one in Fig. 11-3(*a*) to the subject and ask the subject to "complete" the drawing in any way he or she wants. Response (*b*) might indicate a lack of creativity, while response (*c*) would be considered more creative.

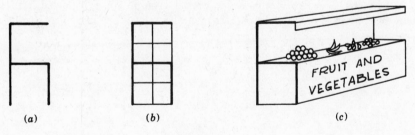

(a)   (b)   (c)

Fig. 11-3

11.6   TESTING CONCERNS

Several variables must be taken into consideration in using psychological tests. Some of the most important are discussed in this section.

Ethics of Testing.   The use of psychological tests has become very important in our society. Accompanying this increase in importance has been concern about ethical administration, scoring, interpretation, and reporting of the results. Perhaps most serious has been the concern for privacy, that is, to whom the results should be made available. Privacy is invaded if the results of an individual's test are revealed without that person's knowledge or consent.

EXAMPLE 11.16. Laws have been enacted to protect a person's privacy. For example, it is illegal to "post grades" in any manner that allows the members of the class to be identified and their results revealed. Comparable restrictions apply to almost all other evaluations based on psychological tests.

Test Fairness. Attempts have been made to try to develop culture-free or culture-fair tests, but success has been limited. Thus, psychological tests may be misused if they are administered to a subcultural group for which they are inappropriate. In addition, psychologists must realize the limitations of test scores and not rely on them exclusively when making decisions about individuals.

EXAMPLE 11.17. In an attempt to dramatize lack of test fairness, a "ghetto" test was developed several years ago. Based on the slang language of a particular subcultural group, the test showed how results could vary widely, depending on the language used in the test and the backgrounds of the people being tested.

Test Batteries. Psychologists sometimes combine information from more than one test when making assessments. This is referred to as using a *test battery*.

Group versus Individual Tests. Many forms of psychological tests, including intelligence tests, can be administered either to individuals or to groups. *Individual tests* are thought to be more sensitive than *group tests* and are used frequently when subjects' motivation is suspect. However, individual tests are more expensive to administer, require more training of the administrator, and require more time for the collection of data from a large group of subjects.

Cross-Sectional versus Longitudinal Investigations. Psychologists often need to compare the performances of subjects in various age groups. There are two basic ways to make such comparisons. *Cross-sectional investigations* are tests of different individuals in each of the age groups being studied. Data collection can take place fairly quickly, but matching samples from one age group to another may be difficult or impossible. *Longitudinal investigations* test the same subjects throughout the study, and thus matched samples are unnecessary. However, longitudinal studies take much longer to complete and tend to have a higher probability of subject loss because of the waiting period between one testing session and the next.

EXAMPLE 11.18. Suppose a psychologist wants to test the motor skills of children ages 2, 4, 6, 8, and 10. In a cross-sectional study, matched groups of children in each age group could be tested in a matter of days. A longitudinal study, by contrast, would require a testing period stretched out over eight years.

Solved Problems

11.1 Dr. Smith claims to have developed a short test that can measure musical talent. The test consists of five measurable tasks, including how frequently the subject can tap on a table in three seconds and how much pressure the subject can exert when clenching his or her fist. How reliable and valid do you think the Smith Test of Musical Abilities will be?

The test is likely to be quite reliable but not valid. It is reliable because the responses obtained from subjects probably would be consistent; the strength of a person's grip or the ability to tap on a table are not likely to change drastically from one test to the next. However, it is also safe to assume that hand strength or speed cannot be correlated directly to musical talent. Thus, the test would measure quite consistently but not measure what it claimed to measure.

11.2 What are common ways to assess the reliability and validity of a test?

Reliability can be determined by calculating the correlation between the administration of a test and the administration of a comparable form of the same test (parallel form reliability) or by dividing the test into two halves and calculating the correlation between the results obtained (split-half reliability). Validity is assessed in a number of ways. When a correlation is calculated between the test results and another standard of the behavior being measured, *criterion validity* is employed. When experts in the field judge how well the test appears to measure the areas being tested, this is called *content-related validity*.

11.3 Another characteristic of a good test is standardization. What does this term imply about a test?

In a sense, everything about a test that can be standardized should be standardized. The administration of the test and the scoring and evaluation of the results should be done in the same manner every time the test is used. Variations in any of these procedures may yield test results that are not attributable to characteristics of the subjects taking the test but instead to the way in which the testing was conducted.

11.4 What is the most common way to establish norms for a test?

Norms typically are established by testing representative populations, collecting the results, and then presenting the mean (average) scores for the groups. For example, on intelligence tests, norms for each age group are determined by finding what the "typical" person of that age will score on the test and setting that score as 100 (mean value) for that age.

11.5 How can the establishment of norms lead to stereotyped descriptions of individuals?

Statistics sometimes exert undue influence on an observer's interpretations. (You may have encountered people who believe that anything established statistically *must* be right.) Using a norm as the basis for an assertion may lead to statements such as "The average _____ does such-and-such or so-and-so." This in turn is followed by the stereotypical judgment: "Well, you *are* a _____, and they do such-and-such or so-and-so, and so you must do these things also." One must remember that norms reveal what groups of people have done. Norms are thus a collective report of behavior and do not necessarily indicate anything about what any individual will do.

11.6 What does it mean to say that norms often are reported as percentile values?

A percentile is the point below which a certain percentage of the population falls on a given test. Group norms frequently are presented with percentile values attached so that the results of any respondent can be compared to the pattern established by the population. For example, someone having a score that is one standard deviation below the mean on a test falls in the sixteenth percentile. This means that 16 percent of those taking the test have scores that are lower than that of this person or that 84 percent have higher scores.

11.7 Students sometimes complain that two people in a class can give the same answer to an essay question and the instructor will score one answer higher than the other. If students are correct in saying that the two answers are basically the same, what characteristic of a good test has the instructor failed to satisfy?

If previous work by the instructor has shown that the essay questions used on this exam were valid and reliable and could be graded in a standardized manner, the instructor probably has failed to satisfy the criterion of objectivity. Apparently, some bias or prejudice has caused the instructor to make two different evaluations of the same answer. (*Note*: In defense of the instructor, perhaps bias was not involved but fatigue or boredom with grading caused the discrepancy.)

11.8 What was the original purpose of intelligence tests?

The original, and perhaps still the best, use of intelligence tests was to predict how well students could profit from being in school. In the early 1900s, Alfred Binet and his colleagues were asked by the Paris school system to develop such a test. By 1916, Lewis Terman of Stanford University had revised Binet's successful test to suit children in the United States. The latter test came to be known as the Stanford-Binet test and, in a revised form, is still used today.

11.9 A psychometrist who is administering a Stanford-Binet Intelligence Test finds that a child is able to pass all the tests at age 4; some at age levels 5, 6, 7, and 8; but none at age 9. The total number of tests passed in ages 5 through 9 is 10. What are the basal age, ceiling age, and mental age of the child?

Basal age is the highest level at which all tests are passed, in this case, age 4. Ceiling age is the level at which no tests are passed; here it is age 9. Mental age is determined by calculating the months' credit accumulated by the child. Each test is worth two months' credit, and thus the child's mental age is equal to $4 \times 12 = 48$ (credit for the basal age years) plus $10 \times 2 = 20$ (credit for the tests passed), or a total of 68 months' credit, for a mental age of 5 years and 8 months.

11.10 Using the formula originally proposed, what would be the value of the IQ for the child in Solved Problem 11.9 if that child's chronological age was 4 years and 3 months?

The child's IQ can be calculated by dividing the mental age (MA) by the chronological age (CA) and multiplying by 100. In this case, the MA is 68 months and the CA is 51 months. By dividing the MA by the CA and multiplying by 100, we get the child's IQ, which is approximately 133.

11.11 The intelligence quotient given in the previous problem is called a *ratio IQ*. Why have such calculations been discarded in favor of *deviation IQ*?

The difficulty with a ratio IQ is that as a person grows older, there is no way to show a continuing growth of MA to correspond equivalently to the ever-increasing value of CA. If a ratio IQ were used as a measure for adults, those people would almost certainly receive lower and lower IQ values with increasing age.

David Wechsler developed the deviation IQ to overcome this problem. The raw scores of intelligence tests are statistically transformed and distributed on a normal probability curve. This curve has a mean of 100 and a standard deviation of 15 for all age levels. The deviation IQ is now the accepted standard for presenting and interpreting intelligence test scores.

11.12 Using 100 as the mean and 15 for the standard deviation, what levels of intelligence have represented the exceptional subjects tested?

IQ values that are two standard deviations above or below the mean of 100 are considered exceptional. Thus, subjects with scores of 130 or higher (gifted) and subjects with values of 70 or below (retarded) are labeled exceptional.

11.13 How are the mentally retarded defined and classified? Are the mentally retarded capable of learning?

Subjects whose intelligence scores are at or below the -2 standard deviation point on a normal probability distribution arbitrarily are defined as mentally retarded. Those with values between 50 and 70 are called *mildly retarded* or *educable*. Those whose IQs range from 35 to 49 are called *moderately retarded* and are considered *trainable*. Those with IQs from 20 to 34 are designated as *severely retarded*, while any score under 20 represents *profound retardation*.

The mildly retarded often are able to function at an adolescent level but require supervision.

Moderately retarded persons function at a mental age of about 4 to 7 years. The severely retarded can at best develop minimal personal skills, such as those necessary for hygiene and feeding. The profoundly retarded are unable to learn anything but the simplest responses and require constant custodial care.

11.14 In the United States, what policy has been adopted for educating the mentally retarded?

Legislation has mandated that retarded children be educated in the least restricted environment possible. In many cases, this means mainstreaming, the inclusion of a retarded child into a regular classroom as much as possible.

11.15 Explain why retardation is thought to result from environmental and/or hereditary causes.

Evidence has been gathered that shows both environmental, hereditary, and combined causes for mental retardation. For example, an improper prenatal environment such as the ingestion of toxins by a pregnant woman, a postnatal trauma such as head injury from an accident, a hereditary pattern such as Down syndrome, and the link of dietary (environmental) intervention with phenylketonuria, a hereditary disease, are all explanations for why retardation may occur.

11.16 The mentally retarded can be classified in four subgroups. Are there comparable subgroups for the exceptionally intelligent?

Some investigators have attempted to establish subgroups or categories (such as "genius") for the exceptionally intelligent, but the choice of IQ cutoff points has been arbitrary and has not been tied to observable behaviors. The little research that has been done has shown that persons with extraordinarily high IQs (perhaps 180 or higher) may be more likely to have adjustment difficulties because of being misunderstood by parents or peers, but no special label has been used to classify such people or others in this very high range.

11.17 If a researcher found an exceptionally high heritability coefficient, what conclusion might be reached regarding the behavior being investigated?

A heritability coefficient estimates the effect hereditary factors have on the variation in measured responses. The higher the value of this coefficient is, the more the variation can be attributed to heredity rather than environmental factors.

11.18 Can intelligence be defined concisely?

No. Defining intelligence is very difficult. A simple solution, but one that is not very helpful, is to define intelligence operationally—to say that intelligence is what intelligence tests measure. A better but less clear solution is to define intelligence as the relatively enduring mental characteristics a person can put to use in solving various types of problems. Still another way to view intelligence is to separate intelligence into (1) inherited potential and (2) demonstrated levels of understanding and performance. Intelligence has been defined in terms of general factors, specific factors, multiple intelligences, and even factors leading to success in one's life pursuits. Obviously, the variety of these definitions suggests that no single choice has been dominant.

11.19 Intelligence has been defined as a set of characteristics helpful in problem solving. What statistical technique has been used to identify these characteristics?

The technique is the statistical procedure called *factor analysis*. Subjects are presented with a number of problem-solving tasks, which are later analyzed to determine which are correlated with each other because they require the same type of responding. All these characteristics then are given labels that indicate how they seem to be linked together.

11.20 An early multifactor interpretation of intelligence was developed by L. L. Thurstone. In one of Thurstone's tests, a subject might be given the following incomplete couplet:

> To keep from feeling any pain,
> The boy made sure to _____

and asked to produce as many rhyming solutions as possible in 30 seconds. Which of Thurstone's factors most likely is being tested by such an exercise? What other factors of intelligence did Thurstone propose?

The two factors most likely to be tested here are verbal comprehension (especially the size of vocabulary) and word fluency (the ability to think of words quickly). Other factors proposed by Thurstone were numerical facility, reasoning ability, perceptual speed, rote memory, and the ability to handle spatial relations.

11.21 Would solving the rhyming exercise in Solved Problem 11.20 require fluid or crystallized intelligence?

Solving novel problems seems to require the use of fluid intelligence, and creating rhymes can be considered this type of a problem. Crystallized intelligence is used when one applies what already has been learned. Crystallized intelligence is more likely to be habitual, while fluid intelligence is more apt to be flexible.

11.22 Suppose Catherine is 9 years old. If she has average intelligence, according to Piaget's proposals, what stages of cognitive development has she passed through? Where is she now? What is yet to come?

According to Piaget's description of cognitive growth, Catherine has passed through the sensorimotor and preoperational stages and should be in the concrete operational stage. She has the formal operational stage to complete, beginning at about age 11. Catherine already has learned about sensations and perceptions, language, conceptualization, and some logic, and she is able to develop coordinated series of ideas. However, she has not yet developed understanding of abstract logic and generalizations. (Review Section 4.4 for a more thorough discussion of cognitive development.)

11.23 A famous jazz group once recorded an album in which many of the songs involved intricate rhythms, such as two players performing music containing four beats to each measure while the other two simultaneously played music involving only three beats to each measure. Using Howard Gardner's proposal for multiple intelligences, select those you think might have been shown in this accomplishment. What other types did Gardner propose?

At least three of Gardner's suggested types of intelligence appear to apply to this recording session. Certainly musical intelligence is important. In addition, the intricacy of the rhythms probably involves logical-mathematical intelligence, while the interactions necessary among the players would require interpersonal intelligence. Gardner also suggested bodily kinesthetic intelligence (which might be involved here in the actual playing), linguistic intelligence, spatial intelligence, intrapersonal intelligence, and naturalistic intelligence.

11.24 In Sternberg's triarchic theory of intelligence, which of the three major aspects of intelligence is thought to represent practical intelligence?

Of the three, contextual intelligence—how intelligence is used to face environmental demands—is thought of as practical intelligence. The other two aspects of intelligence, according to Sternberg, are componential and experiential intelligences.

11.25   What recent proposal by Sternberg has modified his approach to understanding intelligence?

Sternberg believes that intelligence should be thought of as *successful intelligence*, which he defines as one's ability to achieve success in life according to both personal standards and the sociocultural context in which one lives. This proposal stresses far more than just academic success, the behavior that formed the basis for many of the earlier proposals regarding intelligence.

11.26   Explain Carroll's hierarchical model of cognitive abilities in terms of environmental and hereditary influences.

Carroll's hierarchy of cognitive abilities has narrow abilities learned in response to environmental pressures as its base. The middle level is called *broad abilities*, skills that are thought to arise from an interaction of environmental and hereditary influences. The top level of the hierarchy is labeled *g*, representing general cognitive ability thought to be primarily hereditary only.

11.27   Valerie applies for a job, and when she arrives for the interview, she must take some tests. One is a self-report personality test; she is told there are no right or wrong answers and she is to respond as she usually would. How will the person evaluating Valerie's responses know whether she has complied with these instructions?

Although there is no absolute assurance that Valerie has complied with the instructions and given what might be called her *typical performance*, many self-report tests include measures of response validity. If Valerie responds in ways that are intended to "make her look good" even though the responses are not accurate indicators of her usual pattern of behaving, the built-in indicators (sometimes called "lie scales") may spot her attempts and invalidate her overall score.

11.28   After taking the personality test, Valerie asks the administrator why there were no inkblots or pictures. What answer is she given?

Valerie was given a self-report (paper-and-pencil) test, not a projective test. Self-report tests generally require a person to make choices among the answers provided or to check a list of adjectives he or she believes are self-descriptive. Some personality tests measure both normal and abnormal characteristics, while others are concerned only with normal characteristics. In projective tests, a person is presented with a series of ambiguous stimuli and asked to tell a story about or give a description of each. It is thought the person's responses reveal personality characteristics that are projected onto the ambiguous stimuli.

11.29   What measures of personality besides self-report and projective tests are used?

The evaluation of a person's personality sometimes is made through an interview. The advantage of this evaluation technique is that it gives the interviewer an opportunity for additional probing and observation. Subjects can be observed directly as they respond, and the interviewer can "steer" the interview toward points of special interest as they arise.

Less common is the technique known as *behavioral assessment* or *situational testing*, in which a subject is brought into a naturalistic setting or a predetermined environment established by the psychologist and then observed as she or he reacts. The responses are interpreted by the observer.

11.30   When Fred is interviewed for a job, he is told that he also is expected to take several tests. He asks what kind, and the company representative replies, "Oh, some noncognitive ones." Fred is confused by this answer and asks what the word "noncognitive" means. What answer is he given?

The company representative explains that they are interviewing Fred for a job that requires both scholastic (or cognitive) abilities *and* noncognitive (or vocational) aptitude. By checking his school records and the recommendations he has received, they are satisfied he has sufficient cognitive skills for the job. However, the company needs to make certain Fred has the perceptual-motor abilities and physical proficiencies necessary to do the job, and the noncognitive (vocational) aptitude tests are designed to measure those qualifications.

11.31 For counseling purposes, psychologists sometimes combine both scholastic and vocational tests into a series that measures several different aptitudes. What is this series of tests called? What kinds of results are reported at the end of such a series?

The series of tests often used for counseling purposes is called a *test battery*. The results obtained from the various tests are summarized by plotting what is called a *profile* of scores. By using these test batteries, counselors frequently can guide students or others in making educational or vocational choices that best suit their abilities.

11.32 What are the similarities and differences between achievement tests and aptitude tests?

Achievement tests are intended to measure performance development up to the time of testing. Aptitude tests are supposed to predict performance in the future. In reality, achievement and aptitude tests often are very much alike; they reveal what skills and abilities a subject has at that time. However, their results are used differently.

11.33 How do interest and screening tests compare with aptitude and achievement tests?

Interest tests simply identify areas related to possible educational concentrations or occupations that intrigue the person making the responses. The fact that someone shows interest in a particular field, however, gives no assurance that that person will have skill in that area. Screening tests are in effect aptitude tests. Such tests are used to try to identify individuals who have best fit for a job.

11.34 What are the important characteristics of a creative person?

The research on this issue may be subject to question, but the characteristics that show up for creative people include a preference for complexity and the less ordinary, independence, openness, aesthetic sensitivity, and emotional and social sensitivity. Measured intelligence (especially academic intelligence) also seems to be related to creativity, as does a willingness to take risks.

11.35 What is a creative act? What are some of the ways creativity is tested?

The creative act is considered purposeful and productive and makes use of unusual solutions to problems. This means a creative act is both original and somehow useful or worthwhile.

Tests of creativity may measure how many unusual uses someone may be able to generate for some object or how well a person can determine the remote associations that exist among several divergent stimuli. Drawing-completion tests and anagram tasks also are sometimes used to measure creativity.

11.36 Tests such as those mentioned in Solved Problem 11.35 frequently focus on the difference between divergent and convergent thinking. What is this difference?

Convergent patterns of thinking are revealed by responses that are considered correct but conventional or unoriginal. Divergent thinking is characterized by the subject's ability to produce a variety of responses, many of which are unique or original. Divergent thinking is more often thought to be representative of creativity, although the ability to produce many different responses is not sufficient to be judged creative. The responses produced must be unique or "new."

11.37 By its very nature, is a psychological test an invasion of privacy? Who should have access to the results of such tests?

In and of itself, a test is not an invasion of privacy. Only abuses of testing or the misuse of the results of tests can be considered invasions of privacy.

The rights of an individual must be protected, and coercion must not be used to force someone to take a test. Information on test results should be available to the person being tested and should be distributed to others only after that person or a guardian has given permission. Great care must be taken to guarantee that psychological tests are not used to threaten individuals or coerce them into doing what they otherwise would not do.

11.38 The answer to Solved Problem 11.37 implies that a person should have a choice of whether to be tested. Why, then, should anyone ever choose to be tested?

A psychological test may help someone make life choices and in a way is no different from using a physical test to help make medical decisions or dietary choices.

11.39 Many colleges require candidates for admission to take some form of standardized test so that the basic scholastic skills of all the applicants can be compared. Why are these standardized tests almost always group or computerized tests? When might a student be asked to take an individual test?

Group or computerized tests usually are selected to survey large numbers of people (such as all candidates for admission to a college in a given year) because they are relatively inexpensive, can be given to many people simultaneously, and are fairly easy to administer and evaluate. It is difficult, however, to assure the effort or motivation of each person taking the test.

A student might be evaluated with an individual test if that student had particular difficulties with classwork, had particular physiological problems, or was so exceptional that she or he asked for admission into a special program or asked to be given advanced placement. Such an individual test is generally more expensive because of the need for a specially trained administrator and/or scorer. However, an individual test may yield much more information about a subject's special qualities, and the person administering the test may have an opportunity to observe the subject's effort and motivation.

11.40 What are the supposed properties of culture-free or culture-fair tests?

In a culture-free test, the questions or tasks supposedly are selected so that cultural differences will not play a role in influencing the subject's response. In culture-fair tests, the questions or tasks are expressed in terms understandable to members of the subject's culture. Unfortunately, the results of culture-free and culture-fair tests have shown that these tests do not produce results significantly different from those produced in standard psychological testing; that is, at present there probably is no such thing as a truly culture-free or culture-fair test.

11.41 A high school student did not do very well on the nationwide test he took, yet the college he wanted to attend accepted him but did not take a student who had better scores on the same test. Why would the college ask for such scores and then apparently ignore them?

Test results are very seldom used as the sole basis on which admission decisions, or any other kinds of decisions, are made. Other information is available and may be important. In this case, things such as class records and letters of recommendation would be used in conjunction with the test scores to make the admissions decisions. In addition, some decisions are made on an intuitive basis rather than a statistical one. Test results are not meant to be taken as absolute indicators of ability. A personal interview with the candidate or an essay he wrote may have signaled to an admissions officer a special quality the student possessed.

11.42 Suppose the high school student in Solved Problem 11.41 was *not* accepted by his "first-choice" school and complained that the test was unfair. What response can be given to such a complaint?

Most psychologists are willing to accept the conclusion that no test is entirely culture-free, culture-fair, or even conclusive. However, psychologists also realize that test results seldom are used as the only basis for selection or admission. Tests will not predict academic success perfectly but still can be used as *one* indicator of ability among many.

11.43 Suppose several investigators wanted to study the relationship of age to intelligence. What would be some of the advantages and disadvantages of both cross-sectional and longitudinal studies in this investigation?

Cross-sectional studies have the advantage of allowing the investigators to collect data very quickly at a relatively low expense. Cross-sectional studies have limitations, however. For example, it may be difficult to match samples at the different age levels being tested: The educational opportunities may have been significantly better for those in the younger age groups, and the scores obtained may be incorrectly interpreted as a decline in intelligence with increased age.

Longitudinal studies have the advantage of testing the subjects throughout the study. Thus, differing educational opportunities that might have influenced the results in a cross-sectional investigation would not be an important factor. However, data collection in a longitudinal study is a *very* slow process, and there is a chance that many subjects will drop out over the course of the investigation.

Key Terms

Ability.   A person's potential for acquiring a skill.

Achievement test.   A test that measures what a person has accomplished up to the point of testing.

Aptitude test.   A test designed to predict what a person may accomplish in the future with additional training.

Basal age.   The highest year level at which a subject passes all the subtests in an intelligence test.

Ceiling age.   The year level at which a subject fails to pass any subtests in an intelligence test.

Convergent thinking.   Problem-solving responses that are correct but follow routine or common patterns.

Creativity.   Original, purposeful, worthwhile, and unique approaches to problem solving and other activities.

Criterion.   An absolute standard used to evaluate a person's performance on a test.

Cross-sectional investigations.   Investigations in which a psychological test is administered at the same time to subjects in different age groups.

Crystallized intelligence.   Intelligence used in the application of already learned materials; usually considered to be routine or unchanging.

Deviation IQ.   The value of intelligence established by using the normal probability distribution of scores obtained for various age levels.

Divergent thinking.   Problem-solving responses that have unique or novel patterns.

Exceptional subjects.   Subjects whose scores are more than two standard deviations from the mean of an intelligence test.

Fluid intelligence.   Intelligence that can adjust to new situations; usually considered flexible or adaptive thinking.

Gifted subjects.   Subjects whose scores are above the +2 standard deviation point on the normal probability distribution of intelligence scores.

Group test.   A psychological test administered to more than one subject at the same time.

Heritability.   Genetic effects that lead to individual differences among people in measured intelligence.

Individual test.   A psychological test given by an administrator to only one subject at a time.

Intelligence.   The enduring characteristics that allow an individual to solve problems, understand or adapt to the world, think rationally, use resources effectively, or reach goals; one of the most difficult concepts in psychology to define.

Intelligence quotient (IQ).   The ratio obtained by dividing mental age by chronological age and then multiplying by 100.

Intelligence test.   A test designed to measure intelligence; usually consists of a series of aptitude tests most likely to predict academic ability.

Interest tests.   Tests that determine a person's likes and dislikes; often used to propose careers compatible with the results found.

Longitudinal investigations.   Investigations in which a psychological test is administered to the same subjects at different times, often with fairly long periods of time between testing sessions.

Mainstreaming.   Integrating retarded individuals into the regular classroom as much as possible.

Mental age (MA).   A measurement of a person's performance on an intelligence test; the basis for measurement is the chronological age at which people typically pass tests.

Mental retardation.   Arbitrarily established as a characteristic of a person who scores below the -2 standard deviation point on a normal probability distribution of intelligence scores.

Norms.   The scores, obtained by a representative group taking a particular test, that serve as the standard against which an individual's score can be compared.

Objectivity.   Refers to conduct or evaluation that is free from bias or prejudice.

Percentile.   In a distribution of scores, the point below which a certain percentage of the population falls.

Personality tests.   Tests designed to determine attributes that are unique, enduring, and typical of a particular individual.

Projective personality tests.   Personality tests in which ambiguous stimuli are presented to a subject who is asked to describe or tell a story about each one; supposedly, the reactions reveal personality characteristics the individual has projected onto each stimulus.

Psychological testing.   The use of a measurement technique to assess a behavioral characteristic.

Psychometrics.   The construction and use of tests to measure aspects of behavior.

Reliability.   The consistency of results when a psychological test or another measuring technique is used more than once.

Rorschach test.   A projective test using 10 inkblots as stimuli.

Scholastic tests.   Tests used to predict future success in academic pursuits.

Screening tests.   Tests used to identify individuals who "best fit" an occupation or another situation.

Self-report tests.   Questionnaires containing statements to which the respondent can choose answers such as "yes, maybe, no," or "true, false, cannot say."

Standardization.   The process of testing with a consistent pattern and the establishment of norms.

Subjectivity.   Conduct or evaluation that is influenced by bias or prejudice.

Test battery.   The combination of several different psychological tests into a series presented to the subject.

Thematic Apperception Test (TAT).   A projective test using 20 monochromatic, ambiguous pictures as stimuli.

Validity.   The capacity of a test to measure what it claims to measure or predict what it claims to predict.

Vocational tests.   Tests used to predict future success in employment situations.

Personality Principles

An individual's *personality* consists of the enduring attributes that are representative of his or her behavior. These attributes may be acquired because of the person's unique experiences or because of experiences shared with others. They also may result from the influence of heredity or the interaction of heredity and environment.

Several theories have been proposed to explain the acquisition of personality and describe personality. After a brief review of the general factors that influence personality, these theories will be discussed below.

12.1 GENERAL FACTORS INFLUENCING PERSONALITY

Regardless of the theory proposed to explain personality, two general factors are seen to influence personality development: a person's experiences within the environment and that person's hereditary background.

Environmental Experience. A person's experiences within the surrounding environment may have major effects on the development of personality characteristics. These experiences may be *unique* to one person only or *common* to many people.

EXAMPLE 12.1. Imagine a man who lives in a fishing village and works on a fishing boat. The experiences of living in the village can be thought of as shared experiences common to many of those who live there. Suppose, however, the man in question once spent several hours alone in the open sea after falling out of a boat. In this respect at least, his experience is unique. The experience of being adrift may influence his personality in ways that differ from the influences of the village experiences he has shared with other people.

Hereditary Effects. The particular genetic pattern established at the moment of conception influences the personality characteristics a person will develop. In very obvious forms, inherited brain damage or birth defects may have a pronounced influence on a person's behavior. Additionally, somatic (body) factors such as height, weight, skin coloration, and the functioning of sense organs may affect personality development.

EXAMPLE 12.2. The gender of an individual is established at the moment of conception. Regardless of interests, both women and men have certain physiological characteristics that are unchangeable and affect their behaviors. For example, women can be impregnated and men can impregnate; neither sex, however, can duplicate exactly the experiences of the other.

Interaction of Heredity and Environment. As has been mentioned in several other contexts, the combined effects of heredity and environment appear to influence many personality characteristics. In most cases, it is difficult or impossible to assign percentages of importance to hereditary and environmental influences, but it is easy to see that the two do interact.

EXAMPLE 12.3. Diet provides a good example of the interaction of hereditary and environmental influences at the many stages of human development. The mother's diet may affect the uterine environment, thus influencing the expression of hereditary characteristics in the embryo or fetus. Later, a person's diet may affect weight gain or loss and thus personal appearance. This in turn may dispose the person to act in certain ways or lead others to react to the person in a particular manner.

Psychologists have attempted to determine the relative effect of heredity and environment in the development of personality. As with other characteristics (for example, see Chapter 11 regarding intelligence), the closer the relationship of two people is, the more likely it is that their personality characteristics will be the same. However, this tendency is affected by environmental circumstances. Thus, identical twins reared together are more likely to show similar patterns than are identical twins reared apart, but even twins reared apart are more similar than siblings who are not twins.

12.2 FREUD'S THEORY OF PERSONALITY

The best known theory of personality developed from the work of Sigmund Freud, a Viennese physician. In his approach, Freud emphasized on the concept of mental illness and the use of psychotherapy to help people with problems. (See Chapters 13 and 14 for discussions of abnormal personality patterns and therapies.) A theory of personality emerged from Freud's attempts to develop successful therapeutic techniques.

Very important in Freud's approach was his emphasis on the influence of the unconscious on behavior. The theory emerging from his work has come to be known as a *psychodynamic* theory, emphasizing that personality and its development are the result of events within the mind. The *unconscious* was thought to be an internal structure of the mind, the activity of which was outside normal cognition or awareness. The unconscious differed from the *conscious* or *preconscious*, which contained thoughts of which one is aware or thoughts that one can readily bring to awareness. Activities of the unconscious frequently influence behaviors despite the lack of ready awareness of these unconscious effects.

EXAMPLE 12.4. Freud believed that influences of the unconscious often revealed themselves in a *symbolic* manner. Thus, slips of the tongue (often called "Freudian slips") and awkward behaviors, such as when an announcer misspoke, referring to a product as the "breast in bed" rather than the "best in bread," were thought to represent the influence of unconscious motivations.

Structure of Personality. Freud believed the personality had three basic components: the id, the ego, and the superego. The personality was motivated throughout life by the fundamental drive called *libido*. Libido provided the psychic energy that was devoted to the achievement of goals. Freud emphasized the underlying sexual nature of libido and believed that many of the goals people sought could be explained as the pursuit of pleasure.

The Id. According to Freud, the *id* is the most primitive or instinctive part of the personality. The id operates according to the *pleasure principle*, that is, seeking pleasure and avoiding pain regardless of societal beliefs or restraints. This means actions generated predominantly by the id are likely to be unsuppressed or unrestricted. The behavior of young children often shows control of the id.

The Ego. In Freud's approach to personality, the *ego* is the problem-solving part of the personality, which operates according to the *reality principle*. The ego seeks pleasure and avoids pain in rational ways that society approves. The ego thus seems to take the demands of the id and determine how to satisfy them in an acceptable manner.

The Superego.   The third component of personality, according to Freud, is the *superego*. The superego reminds the person of what would be ideal behaviors and what behaviors are totally unacceptable. The *conscience* is found in the superego.

EXAMPLE 12.5.   Shopping in a supermarket, Louise, her teenage son, and her 1-year-old daughter stop in an aisle beside the fruit display. Each is occupied, and so none of them is watching the others. The daughter sees an apple, reaches and grabs it, and begins munching happily; she simply seeks pleasure and satisfies the motive, having no idea she is doing something that might be considered wrong. The son spots some grapes, thinks to himself that everybody "rips off" the store a little, and takes a small handful and starts eating. Louise sees some peaches she would really like to have but feels they are too expensive. Momentarily, she considers having a few weighed and priced and then putting some more in the bag after the grocery clerk has gone on to the next customer. However, she realizes this would be dishonest and decides to do without the peaches. Louise's actions represent superego influence, her son seems to have been under ego control, and her daughter was under the control of motivation from the id.

Development of Personality.   Freud proposed that the development of personality advanced through several *psychosexual stages*. In each of these stages, the libidinal energy found a particular focus. If the individual progressed through each stage without serious difficulties, a mature adult expression of libidinal energy eventually could be achieved. However, disturbances in the form of frustration or excessive gratification at one of the stages could lead to *fixation* at that stage, meaning that some of the libidinal energy of the adult would have to be used to satisfy responding appropriate to that stage rather than responding appropriate for an adult. A truly adult pattern of personality reflects the successful completion of all the stages.

The Oral Stage.   The first psychosexual stage is called the *oral stage*. Libidinal energy centers on oral activities, particularly feeding and weaning. This stage lasts from birth into the second year of life. Fixation at this stage means that a high level of oral activity may be shown by an adult.

EXAMPLE 12.6.   Fixation at the oral stage may be represented by activities such as smoking, excessive gum chewing, fingernail biting, talking, and eating. These behaviors are thought to occur because a person was satisfied too much during the oral stage or did not have enough satisfaction during that stage.

The Anal Stage.   The second psychosexual stage is the *anal stage*, where the focus of libidinal energy centers on the external conflicts created for a child who is being toilet trained. The way the parents or other significant adults conduct toilet training affects adult personality characteristics. Fixation at this stage may result in adult difficulties with the giving or withholding of love or approval, stubbornness, and conflicts between neatness and sloppiness.

The Phallic Stage.   In the *phallic stage*, the source of libidinal pleasure is the genitalia. Characteristic behaviors at this time include exploration of the genitals, infantile masturbation, and interest in the anatomic differences between the sexes. Inability to achieve adult sexuality and responsiveness may result from fixation at this stage.

Freud believed this was the period when what he called the *Oedipal complex* (for boys) and the *Electra complex* (for girls) had to be resolved. Freud proposed that a child has sexual desires for the parent of the opposite sex and feels rivalry with the parent of the same sex. However, fear of punishment causes the child to identify with the parent of the same sex and adopt similar behaviors. According to Freud, failure to complete this identification process may result in incomplete gender identity and possibly affect responses in situations involving authority (an underdeveloped conscience) or sex-role-appropriate behaviors.

The Period of Latency.   At the end of the phallic stage (about age 5 or 6), Freud believed a child entered a *latency stage*, when preoccupation with sexual concerns is very much reduced. During this period, libidinal energies are weak and most behaviors center on interaction with same-sex peers.

The Genital Stage.   With the onset of puberty, a person goes into the final stage of development. When one enters adolescence, libidinal energies are rearoused and the individual attempts to achieve adult sexuality. If there have been difficulties at earlier stages, the giving and receiving of adult (mature) love may be difficult or impossible to achieve.

EXAMPLE 12.7.   Suppose a person experiences considerable frustration during the period of toilet training. It is possible that the residual fixations will cause the person to be stingy, stubborn, or extremely fussy. All these characteristics might prevail against the mature expression of giving or receiving love.

Ego Defense Mechanisms.   Freud proposed that actions or events that offend the superego and damage one's self-image result in anxiety in the ego. To keep this damage and anxiety to a minimum, a person develops and uses *ego defense mechanisms* as ways to protect the self. Some examples of ego defense mechanisms follow.

Repression.   The first step in all defense mechanisms (and thus the most prevalent step of all) is *repression*, which occurs when the individual "forgets" anxiety-producing memories or keeps unacceptable desires from surfacing in the conscious. Sustained repression requires psychic energy, and so if the repressed material is especially anxiety-producing, the individual may devote a large portion of available energy to it. This may result in an abnormal personality pattern. (See Chapter 13.)

Rationalization.   A person who acts for a reason that is considered unacceptable may account for that action by claiming it was done for some other, acceptable reason. A person who behaves in this way is showing *rationalization*, thus alleviating potential anxiety.

EXAMPLE 12.8.   Imagine a surgeon who really enjoys cutting the patient's flesh. Admitting this to herself or to others could damage the surgeon's self-image. When asked, "Why did you go into surgery?" the protective (rationalizing) answer might be, "I really think I can help people, and I like to make money."

Projection.   People who attribute their own unacceptable feelings to others are demonstrating *projection*. Projection allows a person to express sentiments or beliefs that would produce anxiety if they were accepted as his or her own. (This concept also provides the basis for projective personality tests such as the Rorschach test and the Thematic Apperception Test. See Chapter 11.)

Displacement.   When aggressive reactions are directed toward an "innocent" stimulus rather than the one actually producing the anger, *displacement* is said to have occurred. This is done because a direct attack on the hostility-producing stimulus is viewed as too stressful or dangerous, yet relief is desired.

Sublimation.   Sometimes described as a form of displacement, *sublimation* involves diverting unwanted impulses into socially approved behaviors. Freud thought sublimation was healthy and socially acceptable, for example, when a person diverts sexually inappropriate desires into socially approved creative work.

Regression.   A person who adopts an attitude that is appropriate to a younger age level may be showing *regression*. Adopting a more childlike attitude may allow a person to avoid responsibilities yet not "lose face."

EXAMPLE 12.9. An older child often resorts to "baby talk," thumb sucking, or other age-inappropriate behaviors after the birth of another child in the family. A direct attack on the new baby would be inappropriate, but the regressive behavior may attract the parents' attention and thus help the older child maintain a feeling of self-worth.

Denial. When one keeps anxiety-producing thoughts or feelings from affecting consciousness by refusing to accept or acknowledge them, the defense mechanism is called *denial*. This often occurs after a tragic event.

12.3   OTHER PSYCHODYNAMIC THEORIES

Freud was the first person to popularize a psychodynamic (or *psychoanalytic*) theory of personality, but several other theories were developed by his associates or by psychologists who came later (sometimes called *neo-Freudian* theorists). The theories of Jung, Adler, and Erikson are examples of other psychodynamic approaches. A more recent approach is called *object-relations theory*.

Carl Jung's Theory.   An associate of Freud, Carl Jung accepted many of Freud's explanations of personality but differed with him in several important aspects. In comparison to Freud, Jung placed more emphasis on current events than on childhood experiences and on social motives than on sexual drives. Jung's *analytical psychology* also emphasized spiritual needs and thoughts for the future.

Another major difference between Jung and Freud was Jung's conception of the unconscious. Jung proposed that there were (1) a *personal unconscious*, similar to the unconscious proposed by Freud because it contained memories and repressed desires, and (2) the *collective unconscious*, which contained personality characteristics inherited from ancestors. The latter kind of unconscious carried tendencies that Jung called *archetypes* which had developed over many generations to become typical of all people within different cultures.

EXAMPLE 12.10.   The descriptions of human figure plastic toys provided to children display the influence of what Jung would think of as an archetype concerning sex roles. Although the sizes and shapes of the figures are very similar, those bought for girls are called "dolls" while those purchased for boys are referred to as "action figures." Such labels are thought to reflect the effects of many generations' distinctions between boy- and girl-appropriate behaviors that have become ingrained in the collective unconscious.

Alfred Adler's Theory.   Alfred Adler also stressed social motivation rather than sexual drives. For Adler, the key to personality was a striving for superiority. Adler felt a person would recognize deficiencies, feel inferior, and then work to compensate for this inferiority. He also recognized that, unfortunately, society sometimes reinforces these felt deficiencies. Adler believed that when this happened, the person might develop an *inferiority complex*.

An intriguing aspect of inferiority was that it might be *real*—that is, an actually existing deficiency—or *imagined*—a felt deficiency that does not exist. Either type of inferiority may motivate a person to try to compensate and seek superiority.

EXAMPLE 12.11.   Recall the eating disorders described in Chapter 10. Using Adler's conceptualization of inferiority, a person who is grossly obese and concerned about it may be viewed as having a real inferiority, while an anorectic may be classified as being motivated by an imagined inferiority.

Erik Erikson's Theory. Erik Erikson tried to combine Freud's emphasis on sexual drives with the emphasis on social motives stressed by other theorists. The result was an eight-stage theory characterized by a *crisis* that had to be resolved at each stage. The stages, along with the crises faced, are as follows:

Oral-sensory stage: trust versus mistrust
Muscular-anal stage: autonomy versus doubt
Locomotor-genital stage: initiative versus guilt
Latency stage: industry versus inferiority
Puberty and adolescence: identity versus role confusion
Early adulthood: intimacy versus isolation
Young and middle adulthood: generativity versus self-absorption
Mature adulthood: integrity versus despair

In each crisis, the successful resolution of the conflict will affect the ultimate psychological activity.

EXAMPLE 12.12.   In Erikson's second stage, a child may have the opportunity to use and control musculature, for example, when feeding herself. If these attempts are successful, the child develops a sense of independence, adequacy, and self-control. However, if the attempts are limited or are labeled as failures, a sense of inadequacy and a lack of autonomy may develop. The feeling that develops then carries over to affect later psychological development.

Object-Relations Theory.   Theory that combines a focus on the ego with an emphasis on social relations has come to be called *object-relations theory*. *Object* refers to the people with whom an infant forms attachments, especially the mother. Personality development is thought to be influenced by how a child relates to others in ways that satisfy emotional needs. Attachment and subsequent separation are believed to be important determinants of personality development.

12.4   DISPOSITIONAL THEORIES OF PERSONALITY

Some early attempts to describe personality focused on classifying a person according to a single category or *type*. Most psychologists realized that a single label did not adequately portray the personality and, with the notable exception of trying to use Jung's concept of an *introversion-extraversion* continuum, abandoned efforts to type people.

Labels, however, have remained popular ways to try to categorize personalities. Identifying the stable, dominant, and enduring personal qualities of an individual has been the basis of many theorists' efforts and has led to what have been called *dispositional* or *trait theories* of personality. These theories categorize personality on the basis of several observed behavioral characteristics, with each particular combination of traits producing a unique personality pattern.

The decision regarding which characteristics to use often is made on the basis of statistical analysis, using *factor analysis* (see Chapter 11). Note, however, that the selection of the original items used in the factor analytic technique (perhaps questions or adjectives to be checked) is crucial, because the resulting factors depend on the material used.

Allport's Trait Theory.   Gordon Allport spent most of his career studying the words people use to describe themselves and others. Although he found thousands of possible labels, he realized that most descriptions focus on one or only a few general categories. Allport classified the labels according to the degree to which they applied in differing circumstances, proposing three levels of traits.

Allport called a single characteristic that determines behavior in almost all situations a *cardinal trait*. This type of trait appears to control almost everything a person does, unifying and integrating the person's behavior. *Central traits* are not as broad as cardinal traits but are relatively general and apply in many situations. Less consistent and less generalized, *secondary traits* apply in limited circumstances.

EXAMPLE 12.13.   Casual conversations often reveal the differences Allport tried to identify. It is not unusual to hear someone describe a public figure such as Martin Luther King, Jr., with an adjective meant to apply to almost all circumstances, for example, by saying Dr. King was "dedicated to the cause." King's devotion to civil rights advocacy can easily be thought of as a cardinal trait, influencing almost all of his behaviors. In contrast, describing a person as "happy-go-lucky, outgoing, and yet competitive" is likely to be an attempt to identify central traits, several characteristics that apply in many but not all situations. Talking about a boss who is "a nice guy on Fridays" may represent a secondary trait, one that applies in limited circumstances.

Cattell's Personality Factors.   Another attempt at identifying traits that describe personality is represented by the work of Raymond Cattell. From a large list of descriptive adjectives, Cattell used factor analysis to identify what he called the 16 primary or *source traits* of personality. He developed a test, popularly known as the "16-PF," to measure an individual's expression of each of these traits.

The "Big Five."   A combination of new research and reanalysis of older work has shown that people in different cultures, age groups, and occupations consistently tend to use five major categories or traits to describe personality. These categories have been called personality's "big five" and are as follows:

> *Extraversion:* social activity, outgoing, affectionate, fun-loving—not shy
> *Agreeableness:* trusting, helpful, cooperative—not hostile or self-centered
> *Conscientiousness:* dependable, responsible, organized—not careless or impulsive
> *Openness to experience:* imaginative, curious, flexible—not conforming or rigid
> *Neuroticism:* anxious, insecure, unstable—not calm or well-adjusted

Biological Dispositions.   Another dispositional approach has been to focus on biological influences on behavior. Researchers have investigated possible predispositions that exist because of things such as the configuration of the nervous system, the activity of the endocrine glands and their associated hormones, and the production of neurotransmitters. Many psychologists accept the concept of *temperament*, a basic or innate biological disposition that predisposes mood and activity levels.

EXAMPLE 12.14.   A recent news account portrayed a elderly man who, after a very active work career, retired, only to take up skydiving for the first 20 years of his retirement. Only when he had a hip replacement did he stop this activity. Psychologists might describe this high-activity individual as someone with a temperament or biological disposition high in sensation seeking.

12.5   LEARNING THEORIES OF PERSONALITY

Many psychologists attribute the acquisition of personality characteristics to learning. Early attempts emphasized how classical conditioning and operant conditioning were influential in establishing personality characteristics, while more recent approaches have looked at observational learning or modeling and cognitive viewpoints. (See Chapter 7 to review learning principles.)

B. F. Skinner's Reinforcement Approach.   Perhaps the most radical early learning explanation of personality was that of B. F. Skinner, who proposed that personality was nothing more than the sum of learned behavior patterns made in response to environmental contingencies. If a particular pattern of responding (for example, acting "cute") is reinforced consistently, the person repeats that pattern and develops that kind of personality. Cues in the environment, responses to those cues, and the reinforcement or lack of reinforcement of the responses determine the personality pattern established.

Social-Cognitive Theories.   As the emphasis on cognitive psychology grew in the 1950s and 1960s, work such as that of Julian Rotter emphasized cognitive interpretations and expectancies as major contributors to patterns of personality. Rotter reasoned that a person's interpretation of an event affected how that person responded and that the response made then affected the interpretation of the event.

In Rotter's theory, special importance is given to *locus of control*, the generalized expectancy that behaviors are determined by one's own efforts (*internal locus of control*) or that behaviors are determined by environmental factors beyond one's control (*external locus of control*). The scale Rotter developed to measure these expectancies is often called the I-E Scale.

EXAMPLE 12.15.   A person with an internal locus of control is likely to think that hard work, perseverance, and personal skills make job success a possibility. A person with an external locus of control attributes job success to factors such as whether the boss seems friendly, how others in similar jobs behave, and good luck or fate. The personality patterns underlying such beliefs are quite different.

Albert Bandura also has studied cognitive and social influences on personality. Bandura stresses the effects of modeling, imitation, and observational learning on personality patterns, believing that much of what develops as a person's personality pattern is the result of what that person has observed and copied.

Two concepts reflect Bandura's approach. *Reciprocal determinism* refers to the interaction of (1) behavioral variables (what people actually do), (2) environmental variables (the setting in which the behavior occurs), and (3) personal/cognitive variables (how the person thinks about, perceives, or expects events to occur). Much of what happens in interactions is determined by *self-efficacy*, the feeling of competence associated with any particular setting. In general, people with higher feelings of self-efficacy are likely to expect to and therefore actually complete tasks successfully.

EXAMPLE 12.16.   Trying to learn a second language can be used to illustrate Bandura's principles. Actually enrolling in a class interacts with variables in the setting, such as the skill of the instructor, the timing of the class, and the difficulty of the materials assigned. The person's interpretations of the choice to enroll and the setting affect subsequent activity; for example, if the initial learning seems to go well and the instructor is thought to be terrific, expectations for future learning are enhanced. In addition, if the initial experiences are positive ones, the person's feelings of self-efficacy are likely to be increased and subsequent attempts to continue such learning are likely to go well.

12.6 HUMANISTIC THEORIES OF PERSONALITY

Humanistic theories of personality emphasize studying the whole human being and helping people achieve their full potential. Subjective experience is considered as important as objective reports, and the unusual or exceptional is studied as well as the general or usual. Humanistic theories stress *personal responsibility*, including the ability to plan and choose the responses one will make and how a person feels about what happens to him or her.

The work of Abraham Maslow forms much of the basis for humanistic approaches to personality. His hierarchy of motives (see Chapter 10) culminated with self-actualization, the state in which people reach ultimate fulfillment. Self-actualization is thought by those accepting a viewpoint informed by *humanism* to be the driving force in personality.

Rogers's Self Theory.   Carl Rogers, a leading proponent of humanistic psychology, developed a *self theory* which stressed that the basis of personality is the person's wish to realize potentialities. Full realization would mean that individuals would be living in perfect accord with themselves and others. But full realization of potentials depends on the atmosphere in which one grows up. Rogers hoped this atmosphere would reflect an attitude of *unconditional positive regard*, in which individuals are loved, valued, and respected simply for what they are. Unfortunately, Rogers found that most people seemed to be raised in an atmosphere of *conditional positive regard*, in which approval and respect are given for some but not all parts of behavior.

EXAMPLE 12.17.   Consider a college student who truly wants to be a physical education teacher but is told by his parents, "We will love and support you as long as you pursue a major in business and intend to join the family company after you graduate." Rogers would say the family is providing conditional positive regard rather than accepting and loving the son for who he is.

According to Rogers, personality maladjustment occurs when a difference develops between a person's self-image and the reality of the situation. When a person is unable to incorporate new experiences into his or her self-image, anxiety may result and lead to the development of defenses against seeing the truth of the situation. Rogers would hope the person would have a more flexible self and be able to adjust to situations as they occur, thus avoiding personality maladjustment.

12.7   CROSS-CULTURAL DIFFERENCES IN PERSONALITY

Psychologists generally agree that personality is the result of the totality of experiences and attributes an individual possesses. Many believe that because this so, there is no way to make comparisons across different cultural settings either within one country or among different countries. Experiences and inherited attributes are thought to differ so much that comparison of personality patterns from one culture to another is fruitless.

Other psychologists try to separate general and specific patterns of personality, suggesting that there are general patterns that cross cultural boundaries but other characteristics that depend on the particular environment in which a person is raised. This is an area where much additional research will be needed before any conclusions are widely accepted.

EXAMPLE 12.18.   The area most frequently studied when cultural differences in personality are explored is that of individualism versus collectivism. It is suggested that cultures such as that in the United States (and viewpoints such as humanism) place great emphasis on the maximizing of self or individual potential, while other cultures emphasize group, cooperative activities and frown on excesses of individualism. The personality patterns that emerge in the different societies are said to reflect these cultural differences.

Solved Problems

12.1   During the years when he was in middle school, Manuel had a blood disease that kept him at home much of the time. The doctor told him to remain quiet, but Manuel was bored doing nothing and began sewing to fill the time. When his classmates learned about his sewing, many laughed and teased him about his "sissy" interests. However, when they saw the clothes Manuel made, they realized he was quite talented.

As an adult, Manuel became a respected fashion designer. When interviewed about his development, he described this period and attributed the development of many of his personality characteristics to that time. Explain how this period provided both common and unique experiences that helped form Manuel's personality.

Common experiences are those shared by all the members of a culture or subculture. In Manuel's case, the attitudes toward gender roles apparently included the belief that males should not pursue sewing, which was labeled a "sissy" interest. However, another aspect of this culture was to admire talent and creativity. Manuel's disease represented a unique experience not generally shared by others in his culture or subculture. It created the circumstances that led to his time-filling task of sewing, which in turn led to the development of his interest.

12.2   Bonnie and Becky were identical twins who because of family difficulties were raised in separate households. By chance, as adults, they happened to meet and were amazed by their similarities and differences. They decided to attend a "twin convention."

While at the convention, Bonnie and Becky were able to compare their similarities and differences to those of other pairs of twins. Based on past research findings, how should Bonnie and Becky compare to identical twins reared together and to fraternal twins?

Using research findings as the basis for prediction, the general expectation would be that Bonnie and Becky would show more differences than identical twins raised together but more similarities than fraternal twins. The particular similarities and differences would depend on the interaction of the characteristics they inherited and the environments in which they were raised.

12.3   Many psychologists envision Freud's description of the mind as being similar to an iceberg. What does this mean?

An iceberg has most of its bulk hidden below the surface. In the same manner, Freud emphasized that much of what forms a person's personality resides in the unconscious, an internal structure of the mind whose activity is usually not readily accessible to awareness. What is available is the conscious (the portion above the surface) and the preconscious (that portion just below the surface that is readily called into consciousness).

12.4   Brent and Mimi have had a "marital spat." Brent storms out of the room and heads for the kitchen, only to trip on the dining room rug, start to fall, and then save himself from falling by grabbing the table. In doing so, he knocks Mimi's treasured cut-glass candy dish from the table. The dish smashes on the floor. Interpret Brent's behavior from a Freudian symbolic viewpoint.

Someone who accepts the concept that unconscious motives can express themselves in a symbolic manner might say that Brent really wanted to hurt his wife, knew he could not do this in a direct manner, and therefore unconsciously but intentionally tripped at exactly the right moment so that the dish would be dislodged and broken. (*Note*: This example also can represent displacement, the release of anger against an innocent or neutral object rather than the person who provoked the anger.)

12.5   When the family gathers for Thanksgiving dinner, the grandparents are thrilled to have Katie, age 15 months, sitting in her high chair right beside the table. As the meal progresses, there is a moment when the conversation pauses, and at that moment Katie burps. The family is at first somewhat surprised but then laughs and goes on with the meal. According to Freud's theory, Katie's behavior was a result of control by which part of the personality?

Katie's behavior apparently was controlled by the id. In general, behaviors under the control of the id operate according to the pleasure principle, that is, seeking pleasure and avoiding pain regardless of social sanctions. Loud burping is not considered socially acceptable in adults, but Katie has not yet learned this and cannot be expected to do so for a while.

12.6   Later, the grandfather in Solved Problem 12.5 finds himself with the same need to burp but does so in a muffled, polite manner. Using Freud's theory, explain the difference between the grandfather's response and Katie's response.

The grandfather, having long since learned what is socially approved or disapproved, muffles his burp to be polite. His behavior shows control by the ego part of the personality, operating according to the reality principle, which means seeking pleasure and avoiding pain according to what society accepts. The difference between the grandfather's behavior and Katie's lies in acting according to societal standards.

12.7   While working on his income tax return, Peter realizes he has the opportunity to "hide" some income and not pay taxes on it. He considers what others in his society might do but finally decides that such behavior simply is not right. He declares the money and pays the taxes. According to Freudian theory, which part of the personality structure probably was operating when Peter made this decision?

It appears that Peter made this decision according to the ideal standards he has learned or perhaps the desire not to feel guilty if he did cheat. Such a decision is a function of the superego, which, according to Freud, houses the conscience and ideal standards for behavior.

12.8   The fundamental drive motivating the personality was given a particular label by Freud. What was it? What were the general properties of this drive?

The fundamental drive motivating the personality was called the *libido* by Freud, who believed this motivation operated from birth until death. The essential feature of the libido was that it had a sexual quality which, because of societal restrictions, could not be expressed directly. Instead, the libido had to find release in substitute or indirect fashions. These expressions begin in the first year of life but change radically as a child matures and passes through what Freud called the *psychosexual stages*.

12.9   Not too many years ago, a famous actor had to undergo surgery for lung cancer. In publicity releases it was revealed the actor had been smoking five packs of cigarettes a day. How might Freud have explained this extremely heavy smoking?

Freud proposed that disturbances during childhood psychosexual stages could tie up libidinal energy so that as an adult the individual is fixated at a particular psychosexual stage. A fixated adult might then show behaviors appropriate to the childhood stage rather than mature or adult behaviors. In this case, the proposal would be that the actor was fixated at the oral stage, which occurs in the first two years of life, and expressed this through the very heavy smoking pattern.

12.10   After the oral stage, Freud proposed two additional childhood psychosexual stages. What were these stages called? What was the center for libidinal expression in each one? What followed these stages?

After the oral stage, the two remaining childhood psychosexual stages were called the *anal stage* and the *phallic stage*. In the anal stage, pleasure resulting from the excretion or retention of body waste products was the dominant characteristic. The phallic stage was characterized by libidinal expression generated by excitation of the genital areas. Freud proposed that a period of latency, or a quiet period for libidinal energies, followed the three childhood stages.

12.11   Is it possible that fixation at one of the childhood psychosexual stages will limit adult expression of libidinal energy?

Freud proposed that libidinal energy was "reawakened" with the onset of puberty. If the individual had progressed through the initial stages without significant disturbances, it was expected that mature, adult expression of libidinal energy could be achieved. However, fixation at one of the earlier stages would mean that some of the libidinal energy would be drained off to satisfy the fixation, thus leaving the individual with incomplete adult relationships.

12.12   Mr. Brewster had a bad day. The alarm clock did not go off, he was late for work, and his boss yelled at him during the day. Later, he came out of his office to find that someone had hit and damaged his car without leaving a note or identification.
          As Mr. Brewster pulled his car into the driveway, the family dog, Abby, ran to greet him. When Mr. Brewster stepped out of the car, he kicked the dog. His son, Gerald, happened to see

this and ran toward his father saying, "Daddy, why did you *kick* Abby?" Brewster's response was, "She tried to bite me." He then turned and went into the house.

In terms of the ego defense mechanisms proposed by Freud, what explanation might be given for Mr. Brewster's actions?

It is likely that Mr. Brewster built considerable frustration and aggressive tendencies during his bad day but had no opportunity to release them. When he arrived home, Abby happened to provide a good target, and Mr. Brewster illustrated *displacement*, releasing his aggression toward an innocent object rather then the hostility-provoking stimuli.

When his son asked him why he did this, Brewster illustrated a second defense mechanism, *rationalization*, behaving as he did because of one set of motives but attributing his behavior to another motive.

12.13 A psychologist finds that a new client presents a very strong "I'm fine!" attitude but sees problems in the behaviors of many others around her. For example, although she professes to have no personal difficulties, she indicates that she and her father do not get along because "he's always angry at me." What kind of ego defense mechanism is this person probably using?

These responses may indicate *projection*, or seeing in others the motives that dominate the self. In this case, the woman may feel hostile toward her father but feel that it is inappropriate to admit this. However, she finds she can talk about anger by projecting it onto the behavior of others, thus protecting her self-image while satisfying her need to discuss the topic.

12.14 Some adults discussing politics at a party begin to argue. Finally, one of the group turns to Phyllis and asks, "How do you feel about that?" Phyllis responds by giggling and saying, "Oh, you don't want to ask that of a little girl like me!" The others in the group laugh and then go on with the discussion. Phyllis continues to smile but does not participate. Her response to the direct question probably represents which ego defense mechanism?

Phyllis's need to protect her self-image may have led her to show a form of *regression*, the adoption of a childlike attitude. She is unable to answer the question and unwilling to admit that, and the giggle and the remark allow her to escape from a possible confrontation or disagreement.

12.15 Which ego defense mechanism was thought by Freud to be a potentially positive one?

Freud believed that *sublimation* was a potentially positive ego defense mechanism. A person diverts unwanted impulses into socially acceptable behaviors, often making a contribution to the community by doing so. For example, a couple may avoid marital discord by choosing to join a community action group and sharing a high level of involvement while helping within the community.

12.16 In some people a conflict may be so painful or anxiety-producing that it is blocked entirely from conscious memory. What did Freud call this? What may result?

Freud called this blocking from conscious memory, or motivated forgetting, *repression*. A repressed conflict may persist, providing motivation from the unconscious and causing an individual to respond to it even though the source of motivation is not recognized at a conscious level.

12.17 Sitting together in the park, two mothers watch their children play. The children's game involves a good deal of "make-believe" fighting, shooting, and falling. One of the women turns to the other and comments, "I certainly wish they wouldn't play those awful shooting games."

The second woman responds, "Well, it's not fun to watch, but I really think that's just part of growing up. I think all children in every generation must play like that at some time." How would someone who had studied Jung's theories interpret the latter remark?

Jung expanded on Freud's theory of the unconscious, dividing it into a personal unconscious (based on one's own experiences) and a collective unconscious (which consists of primitive experiences shared throughout history). The second woman's remark seems to show a belief that this collective unconscious exists and serves as the motivational source for the aggressive games played by each succeeding generation.

12.18 Although others respected his skills and felt he was a very good speaker, Karl did not agree. He therefore enrolled in special speech-training classes, where he worked diligently to overcome what he felt were his shortcomings. How might Alfred Adler interpret Karl's behavior?

One of Adler's major concepts was to emphasize the social factors in personality development. A second important topic was the inferiority an individual might feel, either real or imagined. In this case Karl apparently has imagined his inferiority in speaking, but this has served as motivation to make him seek special training. Adler would interpret this as a compensation performed to try to overcome the perceived inferiority and satisfy Karl's striving for superiority.

12.19 As a class exercise, Dr. Lindquist asks all his students to respond to an adjective checklist by rating items they think are descriptive of themselves. The completed lists are then turned in anonymously. Dr. Lindquist then uses these response sheets to show the students how a factor analysis can be conducted. What does he say?

Dr. Lindquist's description of factor analysis shows the class two basic principles. First, the analysis is based on correlations between items on the list. That is, if students rated one item high, did they also rate another, similar item high? If they did not rate the first one high, did they not give a high rating to the second? When such correlational checks are complete, common factors or traits can be identified.

Second, a factor analysis is only as complete as the items in it. For example, if Dr. Lindquist purposely left out all adjectives related to extraversion, he can show the class that the factor analysis totally missed that personality characteristic.

12.20 "It doesn't matter what the situation is, he is honest!" Using Allport's trait theory, label the trait identified in the preceding sentence. What other labels did Allport suggest for traits?

Allport would call honesty a *cardinal* trait for this person. Cardinal traits are ones which determine behavior in almost all situations, no matter what the circumstances. Allport also suggested that there are *central* and *secondary* traits. Central traits are relatively general and apply to many situations, while secondary traits are thought to be fairly specific, less consistent, and less generalized.

12.21 People in different cultures appear to use "the big five" descriptors for personality. Name these five categories and then create a "person" by using a feature from each category.

The "big five" categories for describing personality are extraversion, agreeableness, conscientiousness, openness to experience, and neuroticism. In that order, an imaginary person might be affectionate, helpful, responsible, curious, and low in anxiety, traits that are common throughout many different cultures.

12.22 If you hear a conversation in which someone says, "Well, that family is just like that; it runs in the family, I think," while talking about a particular personality characteristic, what explanation can account for such a statement?

This comment seems to indicate a belief in biological dispositions as determiners of personality. Many psychologists refer to a predisposition for activity or mood levels as *temperament*, a basic, innate biological characteristic of a person.

12.23 "Rachel is such a brat when she is put to bed. She cries and whines; why, sometimes we have to go in three or four times to get her settled down." What would Skinner say about Rachel's personality and behavior?

Skinner believed that personality was learned from behaviors that were reinforced. Rachel apparently has found a way to get her parents' attention and gets reinforced repeatedly for crying and whining: They reappear and spend more time with her. She develops that personality pattern because it "works." (*Note:* Rachel's parents can break this pattern by letting her cry herself to sleep for a few days. This is called extinction of the response; see Chapter 7.)

12.24 Amanda claims that it doesn't matter what she does; her life is controlled by her parents, her husband, her boss, the weather, and even fate. How would Julian Rotter describe Amanda's personality?

Rotter proposed a social-cognitive theory that emphasized *locus of control*. Amanda appears to believe that forces outside her control determine what her life will be like, making her an "external" person according to Rotter's theory. By contrast, people who believe they can determine their own fates are called "internals."

12.25 What is the concept of self-efficacy? How does self-efficacy appear to affect behavior?

Albert Bandura stressed the concept of self-efficacy in his social-cognitive theory of personality, noting that self-efficacy is the feeling of competence associated with a particular setting or task. In general, research has shown that the greater the feeling of self-efficacy, the greater the likelihood of success in that circumstance. Self-efficacy varies according to the circumstances being confronted.

12.26 Using Bandura's concept of reciprocal determinism, analyze a situation where a person is learning how to water-ski.

Bandura's concept of reciprocal determinism presents the interaction of behavioral, environmental, and personal/cognitive variables. In this situation, behavioral variables include the choice to try to learn to water-ski and the responses made to try to accomplish this, such as finding a friend with a boat and equipment and persuading that person to take one along on a trip to the lake. Environmental variables refer to the setting in which the behavior occurs. These variables might include the weather on the day the trip occurs, the temperature of the water, the power of the boat, and similar concerns. The personal/cognitive variables refer to expectations and perceptions of the situation. The person may have strong feelings of self-efficacy in this situation, for example, and fully expect to learn quickly and well. Bandura might propose that the interaction of these various concerns would produce the particular behavioral patterns shown; for example, the person might undertake this, even if the weather was cold and rainy and the boat was less than powerful, because the commitment was so strong and the expectation of success so great. Someone else might back out because of the discomfort associated with the same circumstances. Reciprocal determinism says that all three aspects are important and interact with one another in determining what occurs.

12.27 In a family where all the male members have been physicians and attorneys for several generations, Alan has decided he wants to become a forest ranger. Although his relatives claim to love him, they express great disappointment with and disapproval of Alan's choice. Using the terminology developed by Carl Rogers, describe the attitude shown by Alan's family.

Carl Rogers distinguished between *unconditional positive regard* and *conditional positive regard*. The former means that all the individual's actions will be respected and accepted, while the latter means that the response to some of the individual's actions will be warm and valued but other actions will be disapproved. Alan's family represent the latter case. They love Alan but disapprove of his choice of career. Rogers believed that an atmosphere of unconditional positive regard is necessary for a person to realize fully his or her potentialities. Thus, in this situation, Rogers might say that it would not be possible for Alan to realize his full potential, or self-actualize.

12.28 Margie is experiencing a conflict between what she feels is her self-image and the criticisms her father is leveling at her. She believes she loves her parents, yet because of her father's attitude toward her style of dress, she is experiencing many feelings of hostility. According to Rogers, what are the two courses of action Margie may adopt as a result of this situation?

   Rogers proposed that the individual either may incorporate new experiences into an ever-changing and flexible view of self or perceive feelings as a threat to self-image, deny those feelings, and create a gap between reality and self-image. Margie may recognize her feelings of hostility, admit them, and adjust her self-image to include those feelings, or she may deny the feelings and, according to Rogers, become maladjusted because of the discrepancy between her self-image and the reality of the situation. Rogers would prefer the first choice, believing that well-adjusted people are able to have an ever-changing self.

12.29 After several weeks of living with the host family, an exchange student talks with his host "brother," commenting, "People here seem to be out for themselves even if it means upsetting others in the family. That would never happen in my country." Discuss the student's remarks in terms of cross-cultural differences in personality.

   The exchange student appears to be emphasizing the importance of cultural values for personality characteristics, noting that the host culture where he currently lives is far more individualistic than his home culture, which stresses collective or group behavior. The differences between individualistic and collective societies have been the most studied differences in investigations of cross-cultural variables. There remains much debate about whether personality variables are universal or are limited by culture.

Key Terms

Anal stage.   In Freud's theory of personality, the period when libidinal energy is expended to satisfy the conflicts created by being toilet trained.

Archetypes.   In Jung's theory of personality, behavioral tendencies carried in the collective unconscious that have been inherited from preceding generations.

Cardinal trait.   In Allport's theory of personality, a single characteristic that determines behavior in almost all situations.

Central trait.   In Allport's theory of personality, relatively general characteristics of an individual that apply to most circumstances.

Collective unconscious.   In Jung's theory of personality, the part of the personality that holds behavioral characteristics inherited from ancestors.

Conscience.   In Freud's theory of personality, the part of the superego that reminds a person of what is not acceptable behavior.

Denial.   Refusal to accept or acknowledge anxiety-producing thoughts or feelings.

Displacement.   The process of directing aggressive tendencies toward an innocent object rather than the one that produced the aggressive feeling.

Ego.   In Freud's theory of personality, the problem-solving part of the personality; operates according to the reality principle.

Ego defense mechanisms.　Actions or techniques that allow an individual to protect her or his self-image or cope with anxiety.

Factor analysis.　A statistical technique involving the use of correlations to determine common factors or traits.

Fixation.　In Freud's theory of personality, the carryover of effect from one of the psychosexual stages to the adult personality so that the adult's libidinal energy must be expended, at least in part, to satisfy motives appropriate to the earlier stage.

Humanism.　An emphasis on positive, constructive human capacities; the basis of humanistic psychology.

Id.　In Freud's theory of personality, the most primitive or instinctive part of the personality; operates according to the pleasure principle.

Inferiority complex.　In Adler's theory of personality, the concept that a person may experience feelings of deficiency and be reinforced in those beliefs by others in the society.

Introversion-extraversion.　Proposed by Jung, the continuum representing how responsive an individual is to stimuli within or outside the self.

Latency stage.　In Freud's theory of personality, the period extending from the end of the phallic stage to the onset of puberty; during this period, libidinal energies are quiet.

Libido.　In Freud's theory of personality, the fundamental drive that provides psychic energy; has a basically sexual nature.

Locus of control.　In Rotter's theory of personality, the generalized expectancy that behaviors are controlled by one's own efforts (*internal locus of control*) or by environmental factors beyond one's control (*external locus of control*).

Object-relations theory.　A personality theory that combines a focus on the ego with an emphasis on social relationships.

Oedipal complex.　In Freud's theory of personality, a child has sexual desire for the opposite-sex parent and rivalry with the same-sex parent; successful resolution occurs when the child identifies with the same-sex parent; sometimes called the *Electra complex* in discussing girls.

Oral stage.　In Freud's theory of personality, the period from birth into the second year of life, when libidinal energy is expended primarily to satisfy mouth-oriented activity.

Personality.　Enduring characteristics that are representative of a person's behavior; may be developed from unique or common experiences and the effects of hereditary and environmental influences.

Personal unconscious.　In Jung's theory of personality, the part of the personality that holds memories and repressed desires.

Phallic stage.　In Freud's theory of personality, the period when libidinal energy centers in the genitalia; the period of the Oedipal complex.

Pleasure principle.　In Freud's theory of personality, seeking pleasure and avoiding pain regardless of social dictates; a property of the id.

Positive regard.　In Rogers's theory of personality, the concept of acceptance by others; may be unconditional (unrestricted) or conditional (restricted).

Preconscious.　In Freud's theory of personality, thoughts that are not currently conscious but can be brought to conscious awareness easily.

Projection.　Attributing one's own motives to others; seeing in others the motives that dominate the self.

Psychosexual stages.　In Freud's theory of personality, a series of phases in the development of personality.

Rationalization.　Acting because of an unacceptable motive while crediting that action to an acceptable motive.

Reality principle.   In Freud's theory of personality, seeking pleasure and avoiding pain in a socially acceptable manner; a property of the ego.

Reciprocal determinism.   In Bandura's theory of personality, the interaction of behavioral, environmental, and personal/cognitive variables.

Regression.   Acting in a manner appropriate to someone of a younger age.

Repression.   The use of psychic energy to keep anxiety-producing memories from conscious recognition; motivated forgetting.

Secondary trait.   In Allport's theory of personality, characteristics of the individual that are relatively inconsistent, are not generalized, and apply in limited circumstances.

Self-efficacy.   Feelings of competence associated with a particular setting.

Source trait.   In Cattell's theory of personality, 16 primary characteristics of personality.

Sublimation.   Sometimes thought of as a form of displacement; diverting unwanted impulses into socially approved behaviors.

Superego.   In Freud's theory of personality, the part of the personality concerned with ideal behaviors and what is not acceptable (ego ideal and conscience).

Temperament.   A basic or innate biological disposition that predisposes mood and activity levels.

Trait theory.   An attempt to categorize personality by using the presence or absence of *several* characteristics.

CHAPTER 13

Abnormal Personality Patterns

In psychology, one of the most difficult areas to define accurately is that of abnormal personality patterns. While it is recognized that the word "abnormal" means "away from the norm," these difficulties have arisen because it is difficult to determine what norm or norms to use.

13.1 DEFINITION OF ABNORMAL PERSONALITY PATTERNS

Behaviors that produce significant and often persistent discomfort or upset for a person or for others in that person's society are described as *abnormal personality patterns*. The personal and social settings to a great extent determine whether a pattern is considered abnormal.

EXAMPLE 13.1. A famous television star had a reputation for being insulting. His remarks often were rude and outrageous. However, he made those remarks in the context of his "act" or performance, and as a result, no significant societal upset occurred. If the same remarks had been made in a different social context, such as in a business meeting or a classroom, a totally different interpretation might have been made and the pattern easily could have been judged as being abnormal.

Other terms used to describe abnormal personality patterns have included "mental illness" and "emotional disturbance." Some psychologists prefer to avoid such terms because the terms imply characteristics that are not necessarily present in an abnormal response.

Properties of Abnormal Personality Patterns. Some actions that are temporarily upsetting for a person or that person's society may not be interpreted as abnormal. Because such interpretations are relatively subjective, both the *quantity* and the *quality* of the behavior must be considered in judging whether the behavior is abnormal. In other words, both the frequency and the intensity of the behavior should be considered.

EXAMPLE 13.2. Practically everyone experiences anxiety at some time; anxiety can be considered a normal part of anyone's personality. However, if the frequency and intensity of the anxiety seriously affect a person's actions, the anxiety may be considered abnormal. For example, temporary anxiety about making a public speech would be considered normal, while constant anxiety about life in general probably would be classified as abnormal.

Predisposing and Precipitating Factors.   The onset of abnormal personality patterns seems to be the result of an interaction between a person's background and that person's current environment. The background factors, which include hereditary patterns and childhood experiences with parents, peers, and others, are called *predisposing factors*. The stimuli that finally initiate the abnormal pattern are called *precipitating factors*. In a few instances, such as the case of brain damage, it may be impossible to distinguish between predisposing and precipitating factors.

EXAMPLE 13.3.   A person's childhood experiences could predispose that person to show an abnormal pattern of personality later in life. Parents who show an inordinate amount of concern for cleanliness in their children, for example, could predispose those children to have abnormal anxieties about dirt and disorder. This predisposition, once it was well established as part of the child's personality, could create serious anxieties later in life.

DSM-IV.   In recent years, the definition of abnormal patterns has been established by using the *Diagnostic and Statistical Manual of Mental Disorders, Fourth Edition (DSM-IV)*, published by the American Psychiatric Association. Using five separate dimensions, or *axes*, DSM-IV provides a means for evaluating behaviors in more than 200 separate diagnostic categories. DSM-IV is primarily descriptive; that is, it does not try to specify a cause or reason for a problem behavior but simply provides a way to identify or label that behavior. Although disagreements arise over some of the categories, DSM-IV has become the most widely accepted way to identify abnormal personality patterns. The discussions of abnormal personality patterns that follow are based on those in DSM-IV.

13.2 PERSPECTIVES ON ABNORMAL BEHAVIORS

Attempts to understand why people behave abnormally have led to several different models of abnormal behavior.

The Biomedical Model.   *Biomedical models* emphasize the influence of bodily functions on personality patterns. Disease, genetic inheritance, or the condition of a person's nervous system may be seen as the sources of abnormal behavior, and some abnormal patterns of behavior are easily associated with actual physical problems. However, one of the problems with biomedical models is that a great demand is placed on psychiatrists, who are expected to give medical treatment for problems that may not have medical solutions. Another problem is that patients who consider themselves sick may not accept responsibility for their actions, making treatment more difficult. Therapies based on biomedical models of personality often make use of drugs or surgery.

The Psychodynamic Model.   Psychologists who base their approach to personality on the work of Freud and his associates believe that abnormal behaviors that cannot be directly attributed to a physical problem are likely to result from conflicts arising in the unconscious (the *psychodynamic model*). As was discussed in Chapter 12, unconscious sources of motivation are thought to arise from repressed conflicts resulting from fixation that occurred at one or more of the childhood stages of development. Therapies based on the psychoanalytic model stress becoming aware of the unconscious processes and thus resolving the conflicts.

The Behavioral Model.   Another model that emphasizes conditions outside the control of the person experiencing the abnormal behavior is the *behavioral model*, which attributes abnormal patterns to learning. Abnormal responses are acquired because of reinforcement, observation, and imitation. Therapies based on this model may make use of the principles of classical conditioning, operant conditioning, and modeling.

The Humanistic Model.   In contrast to the models presented above, the *humanistic model* stresses a person's control of and responsibility for behavior even if that behavior is abnormal. The humanistic model sees each person as rational and social and as attempting to interact with others. Abnormal patterns arise from conflict between a person's self-image and the reality of the situation. Therapy based on this model focuses on helping a person understand and find ways to reach the self-image that allows interaction with others in the environment.

The Cognitive Model.   As the name implies, the *cognitive model* focuses on the thoughts or beliefs that are central to a person's abnormal behaviors. Cognitive theorists look at beliefs and biases related to a person's feelings of self-worth, view of the world, and conceptualization of the future, stressing the idea that abnormal patterns often result from negative approaches to one or more of these factors. Therapy based on the cognitive model tries to change the client's thinking by teaching new, adaptive patterns of responding.

Some abnormal personality patterns may be best explained by making reference to more than one of these models, and most psychologists have come to realize that each model makes an important contribution to the understanding of abnormal personality patterns. As a result, acceptance of several models has been quite widespread and the use of combinations of two or more models is not uncommon.

13.3   ANXIETY DISORDERS

When a person's daily behavior is affected noticeably and in a prolonged manner by the occurrence of anxiety that appears to have no obvious external cause, that person is said to suffer from an *anxiety disorder*. The several categories of anxiety disorders that have been identified are discussed in this section.

Panic Disorders.   Characterized by sudden, unexplained attacks of fear that last up to several hours, *panic disorders* often are very intense. People with panic disorders may experience nausea, numbness, dizziness, difficulty with breathing, chest pain, sweating, trembling, and even the fear of dying or "going crazy." Sufferers often experience a sense of imminent catastrophe associated with a panic disorder. Panic disorders are more common in women than in men, and there is evidence that hereditary biological factors may be involved.

Phobic Disorders.   *Phobias* (*phobic disorders*) are intense, compelling fears of a specific situation or object. The fears usually are much more intense than the circumstances warrant. Phobias have been explained as the result of classical conditioning or as the result of displacement, in which the fear of one thing is actually a symbolic fear of something else.

EXAMPLE 13.4.   Claustrophobia, the fear of being in enclosed spaces, is a fairly common phobia. The desire to avoid severe overcrowding—or the danger of being trapped or suffocating in a small space—can be considered reasonable. A person with severe claustrophobia, however, may go to unreasonable lengths to avoid being in an enclosed space. Thus, someone who walked up 15 flights of stairs to avoid having to use an elevator would be showing an abnormal behavior.

Obsessive-Compulsive Disorder.   Some people find themselves thinking thoughts or performing actions in a repeated and disturbing fashion. Such thoughts (called *obsessions*) and actions (called *compulsions*) may be unwanted by the individual, but she or he may not be able to prevent them. Often, obsessive thoughts are linked to and seem to produce compulsive behaviors (*obsessive-compulsive disorders*).

EXAMPLE 13.5. Obsessive-compulsive behavior can be seen in a person who is plagued by worries that the doors to the office have not been locked at the end of the day and must return repeatedly to check. The thoughts are intrusive, and the behaviors accompany the thoughts.

Generalized Anxiety Disorder. A person experiencing a *generalized anxiety disorder* has long-term, persistent anxiety without being able to identify the cause of that anxiety. This person worries about something but cannot identify what it is. Freud called this *free-floating anxiety*. This kind of anxiety often leads to disorganized behavior and frequently produces physiological symptoms such as muscle tension, headaches, dizziness, and insomnia.

13.4 DISSOCIATIVE DISORDERS

Dissociative disorders involve a disturbance of personal memories or identity. The term "dissociative" indicates that part of the self seems to split from the remainder in one of several ways. Dissociative disorders are thought to be attempts to escape from anxiety-producing situations.

Dissociative Amnesia. The partial or total forgetting of some past experiences, usually after a stressful event, is called *dissociative amnesia*. The cause is psychological rather than organic, for example, when someone witnesses a traumatic accident and then is unable to remember that event or any of the activities that followed. Some psychologists believe that the "forgotten" material is still in memory but cannot be recalled.

Dissociative Fugue. *Dissociative fugue* is characterized by "walking away" from one's life for periods of time that may range from hours to years. The individual often assumes a new identity and, if subsequent recovery occurs, remembers nothing about the fugue period.

EXAMPLE 13.6. Troubled by an unpleasant marriage and family circumstance, one man went fishing after work and never came back. Discovered in another city several years later, he remembered nothing about his previous life and refused to believe he had been married to the woman who was his wife.

Dissociative Identity Disorder. Popularly referred to as *multiple personality*, this disorder involves a person who has more than one well-defined and separate personality and thus is said to show *dissociative identity disorder*. Some people with this relatively extreme form of dissociation have been known to have 10 or more distinct personalities. Transition from one personality to another usually occurs rapidly, with changed voice, gestures, and expressions. One personality may know of another personality even to the point of "friendship" or "rivalry."

EXAMPLE 13.7. Although thought to be fairly rare, dissociative identity disorders have received much public recognition because of books and movies such as *The Three Faces of Eve* and *Sybil*. These cases show how, when faced with anxiety-producing circumstances, an individual switches to another personality that is better able to cope with the situation.

13.5 SOMATOFORM DISORDERS

When an individual has symptoms of a physical dysfunction for which no identifiable organic cause can be found, that person is said to show a *somatoform disorder*. Somatoform disorders differ from *psychosomatic disorders*, which are real physical problems arising, seemingly in part but not exclusively, from psychological causes.

EXAMPLE 13.8. Research on the causes of ulcers prompted investigations of psychosomatic illnesses. Current beliefs are that ulcers result from both stress and a particular strain of bacteria. Regardless of their cause, psychosomatic disorders reveal actual physical problems.

Hypochondriasis.   A person who actually has minor symptoms and interprets them as evidence of a major illness or life-threatening disease is showing *hypochondriasis*. Hypochondriacs are seldom actually physically ill but, when given clearance from medical tests, often will not accept the results and go to another physician to have additional tests. Even with repeated reassurance, hypochondriacs find little relief from their anxieties.

Conversion Disorders.   The term *conversion disorder* comes from the idea that a psychological problem can be converted into a physical problem. People showing *conversion disorders* have symptoms of physical distress, such as paralysis or blindness, for which no organic cause can be found. Somewhat paradoxically, persons who display such reactions may show little anxiety, probably because there is relief from the anxiety-producing situation that initiated the reaction.

EXAMPLE 13.9.   A college instructor worried about having to teach a large lecture section class for the first time awakens the day of the first class to find that she is paralyzed from the waist down. This illustrates conversion disorder. The paralysis means she can no longer be expected to teach that class, and anxiety thus is reduced.

13.6   MOOD DISORDERS

When affective or emotional states reach levels severe enough to interfere with daily living, a person is said to be experiencing a *mood disorder*. While everyone experiences mood swings, people who exhibit mood disorder have symptoms that are more intense and longer-lasting and interfere with normal functioning.

Depressive Disorders.   The symptoms of *depressive disorders* often include loss of energy, inability to concentrate, agitation, significant weight change, feelings of worthlessness, and thoughts of suicide or death. Using categories established in the DSM-IV, psychologists distinguish between *major depression*, which is characterized by periods of great sadness or despair that last two weeks or more, and *dysthymia*, a particularly severe form of depression that usually is labeled as chronic. In dysthymia, the person seldom experiences any relief from the depressive symptoms for more than short periods of time.

Suicide.   Sometimes labeled "the only fatal mental illness," severe depression often is linked with suicide attempts or actual suicide. The strongest predictors of suicide are stressful events in a person's life linked with feelings of hopelessness or depression. Three times more men than women kill themselves, although three times more women than men attempt suicide.

Bipolar Disorders.   In a minority of mood disorders, depression is accompanied by occasional periods of mania, a condition characterized by a high energy level, increased activity, elation, and expansiveness. When this occurs, it is referred to as *bipolar disorder*. Extreme levels of mania often lead to behavior described as totally out of control, behavior as frightening as that experienced in a depressive state. The frequency of each state varies among individuals, with some showing a very rapid change from mania to depression, others experiencing longer bouts of each state, and some interspersing periods of relatively normal behavior between the two extremes.

13.7   SCHIZOPHRENIC DISORDERS

The group of disorders characterized by disturbed thought processes and emotions and by pronounced distortion of or detachment from reality are referred to as *schizophrenic disorders*. Although *schizophrenia* means "split mind," schizophrenic disorders should not be confused with dissociative identity disorder (see Section 13.4). The split referred to here is that of separating from reality rather than forming multiple personalities.

Symptoms of schizophrenia include *delusions*, which are irrational beliefs that persist even in the face of overwhelming evidence to the contrary; *hallucinations*, the perception of something that does *not* exist, such as hearing voices that are not really there; flattened affect or blunted emotional responding; and bizarre behavior. Schizophrenics often show disturbed motor responses, disturbed perceptions, disturbed emotions, disturbed relationships, and/or a disturbed sense of self.

Disorganized Schizophrenia. Characterized by profound disintegration of personality and psychological disorganization, *disorganized schizophrenics* frequently experience delusions and hallucinations and often manifest extremely incoherent speech patterns. They also are likely to show inappropriate emotional expressions, such as giggling when there is no stimulus to provoke that response.

Catatonic Schizophrenia. The most noticeable expression of *catatonic schizophrenia* is unusual motor behavior patterns. Catatonics show excessive and sometimes violent motor behavior or lapse into a stupor or immobility. There is an apparent complete detachment from reality.

Paranoid Schizophrenia. Most commonly, individuals with *paranoid schizophrenia* report delusions of grandeur, persecution, or both. They trust no one and sometimes attempt to retaliate against their supposed persecutors. (*Note:* Paranoid schizophrenia is distinguished from paranoid personality disorder. See Section 13.8.)

EXAMPLE 13.10. A woman who hears voices instructing her to take control of the school where she teaches is also convinced that there is a plot to keep her from accomplishing this mission. The plot is attributed to the other teachers, the principal, the school board, and some community politicians. This pattern of behavior reflects paranoid schizophrenia.

Undifferentiated Schizophrenia. Although this is a general label, the diagnosis of *undifferentiated schizophrenia* means an individual shows delusional behavior, hallucinations, and incoherence but does not meet the criteria of the other categories listed above. In some cases the person may show symptoms associated with more than one of the patterns previously presented.

13.8 PERSONALITY DISORDERS

Characterized by behaviors that deviate markedly from the expectations of an individual's society and seem to be inflexible and ingrained, *personality disorders* typically cause more distress for the people around than for the person manifesting the symptoms. In this sense, personality disorders differ from the patterns described above, where distress is more noticeable for the person afflicted. Several examples are discussed below.

Antisocial Personality Disorder. Unconcerned with the rights of others or the rules of society, persons with an *antisocial personality disorder* (also sometimes called *psychopathic* or *sociopathic* personalities) are not troubled by actions that may bring great pain to others. Often seemingly charming, bright, and socially facile, these individuals have difficulty forming attachments and typically are manipulative and deceptive.

EXAMPLE 13.11. Antisocial behavior often is associated with a "con man." Several years ago one person "bought" a house by making a down payment and then rapidly "sold" that house six times in less than a week, collecting six down payments from the "buyers." All six families arrived at the same house on the same weekend, only to learn of the deception accomplished by the "seller."

Narcissistic Personality Disorder. People with a *narcissistic personality disorder* have a very exaggerated sense of self-importance and are likely to seek special treatment or admiration constantly. They are unlikely to have much regard for the needs of others, focusing only on themselves.

Dependent Personality Disorder. Characterized by lack of self-esteem and a need for others to make important decisions, *dependent personality disorder* also is marked by lack of responsibility for major areas of one's life. This type of individual is likely to lack self-confidence and be extremely sensitive to criticism.

Paranoid Personality Disorder. A *paranoid personality disorder* is similar to paranoid schizophrenia in that feelings of persecution and mistrust of people are common. The differences are a matter of degree: Paranoid personality disorder seems to operate in the "real world" in that the beliefs associated with the persecution and mistrust are focused on real situations and do not involve delusional or hallucinatory behaviors. Although they are sure they are "right," people with paranoid personality disorder often can maintain relatively normal lives and avoid hospitalization even when they are fairly isolated from normal daily activity.

EXAMPLE 13.12. A design consultant who developed a package for a product was extremely disappointed when it was rejected by an interested company. Soon afterward, the consultant became very suspicious and began to believe that a conspiracy within the company was the reason for the rejection. This belief grew stronger after several other companies rejected the proposal, and finally, the consultant believed that the industry in general had conspired in not recognizing a "great" design. Eventually the consultant called the Better Business Bureau to report this major conspiracy.

13.9 CONSIDERATIONS FOR DIAGNOSIS OF ABNORMALITY

The categories identified by DSM-IV provide standards for making decisions about abnormal personality patterns. However, many factors appear to influence the decision-making process. Several are presented in this section to show the difficulties in making such decisions.

Diagnosis and Gender. Disorder rates differ between women and men. Although there is considerable debate about why this happens, it appears that certain categories are thought to be more "appropriate" or "fit better" for one sex or the other. For example, women are thought to be more likely to show anxiety or depression than are men, while men are more often diagnosed as having antisocial personality disorder than are women.

Diagnosis and Culture. Psychologists have gathered evidence that indicates that DSM-IV categories do not necessarily apply to or cover all the circumstances in different cultures. Moreover, even when the category does seem appropriate for different cultures, the actual expression of the abnormal personality pattern may take a very different form. These differences appear to arise from differing cultural values, such as individualism versus collectivism, as was noted before.

EXAMPLE 13.13. Symptoms of depression identified in the United States typically focus on lack of self-esteem, hopelessness, and similar behaviors. In many Asian cultures, depression is identified by using somatic (physical) symptoms. Diagnosis is related to the values of the culture in which the individual lives.

Psychologists must be careful to account for characteristics such as gender and cultural background when making diagnoses. Misdiagnosis can lead to inappropriate treatment, especially with drugs, and subsequent problems are likely to result.

Legal Insanity. The requirements of the courts differ from the categories presented in DSM-IV in regard to determining *legal insanity*. The criteria applied are that the individual committing the act lacks the capacity to distinguish that the act is wrong or is unable to act in accordance with the requirements of the law. Several states have instituted a verdict of "guilty but mentally ill," apparently reasoning that declaring someone innocent because of legal insanity continues to put society at risk.

Solved Problems

13.1   What is abnormal behavior? Is it always a reason for concern?

When someone shows behavior noticeably different from the average, it may be called *abnormal* (away from the norm). This behavior may be of concern when it creates personal discomfort or difficulties for others in that person's society. Often, both the quantity and the quality of the behaviors must be evaluated before a decision is made regarding whether attempts should be made to modify or correct the abnormal pattern.

13.2   What kind of abnormal behavior patterns might not be a cause for seeking help or change?

Some of an individual's behavior patterns could be abnormal but not upsetting to either the individual or society at large. For example, suppose a man who jogged every day always stopped in the middle of his running sessions to do push-ups, sit-ups, and stretching exercises at the side of the road. Such behavior might be considered pretty far from the norm, but it would not necessarily signal that the man needed help. However, if that man insisted on doing his exercises in the middle of an intersection, disrupting traffic and endangering himself, the pattern probably would need modification.

13.3   How do psychologists decide whether a person's personality pattern is abnormal enough to require treatment? What are some of the basic causes of the abnormal personality patterns a psychologist might look for?

A psychologist's decision about a subject's personality pattern would be based on a number of factors, including the subject's ability to show good judgment, the kinds of activities the subject pursues, the subject's ability to plan and control her or his own behavior, and even the subject's attention span. If any one or a some combination of these factors creates personal discomfort or problems with society, the subject could be labeled as abnormal and have treatment recommended.

In examining a subject with a possible abnormal personality pattern, a psychologist may look for predisposing and precipitating factors that caused the pattern. It is very possible that something in the subject's background combined with a particular recent event to set off the abnormal pattern.

13.4   Give examples of predisposing factors from a person's past that might lead to an abnormal personality pattern.

Predispositions generally refer to any hereditary tendency or past experience that plays a significant role in the subsequent development of an individual's personality. An experiential factor psychologists have studied is called the *self-fulfilling prophecy*. A self-fulfilling prophecy is often the result of repeatedly expressed expectations for behavior. A person for whom the constant expectation is to act abnormally may accept abnormality as the usual mode of behavior.

13.5   Is it always correct to say that a person showing an abnormal personality pattern is "sick"?

No. Some abnormal personality patterns result from physiological problems, but many do not have physical causes. The term *mental illness* implies that the person is sick but probably is not a good term to use because it confuses the issue.

Some other terms, such as *emotional disturbance* and *behavioral disorder*, also are not very descriptive. For example, emotions are not always involved in abnormal personality patterns, nor are disturbances as such always apparent.

13.6　Describe the most widely accepted means for identifying and labeling abnormal personality patterns.

Most psychologists and psychiatrists accept the *Diagnostic and Statistical Manual of Mental Disorders, Fourth Edition* (DSM-IV) as the means for identifying and labeling abnormal personality patterns. DSM-IV provides categorization for more than 200 diagnoses. It is primarily descriptive and generally does not specify the cause of the problem being observed.

13.7　Name and briefly describe the models or perspectives used to explain abnormal personality patterns.

Five perspectives have gained general acceptance. They are as follows:

Biomedical model: Emphasizes bodily functions such as disease, genetic inheritance, and nervous system malfunction.
Psychodynamic model: Abnormal patterns not directly attributable to physical disorder are believed to result from conflicts arising in the unconscious.
Behavioral model: Abnormal patterns of responding are learned.
Humanistic model: The person has control of and responsibility for behaviors even if they are abnormal.
Cognitive model: Abnormal behaviors arise from negative thoughts associated with self-worth, worldview, or expectations about the future.

13.8　Name a similarity and a difference between panic disorders and phobic disorders?

Both panic disorders and phobic disorders are classified as anxiety disorders, in which a person's daily behavior is affected noticeably by the occurrence of anxiety. They differ in that panic disorders describe situations in which the intense and sudden attacks of fear last for a period of time but are unexplained, while the anxiety of phobic disorders may be equally intense but usually is tied to a particular situation or object.

13.9　Phobias have been described as intense, compelling fears. Consider a phobia such as fear of darkness. How could classical conditioning serve as an explanation of the development of such a phobia? How could the phenomenon of displacement also be used to account for the phobia?

If it can be assumed that darkness is the original neutral stimulus that then is paired with a fear-producing stimulus (for example, a sudden, loud, unidentifiable noise), this coupling may be looked at as a combination of a conditioned stimulus and an unconditioned stimulus and the conditioned response would be fear produced by the darkness (the conditioned stimulus).

Displacement might occur when a child has an intense dislike of a parent but is afraid of expressing this dislike because doing so would be socially unacceptable. The fear may then be displaced to a more acceptable stimulus, in this case, darkness. This becomes the symbolic expression of the fear of the parent, perhaps because the child links the parent with the darkness associated with being put to bed.

13.10　Over a period of time, Ramona has developed a pattern "requiring" her to take a fresh tissue every 15 minutes, blow her nose, and then discard the tissue immediately. When asked about this, she explains that it prevents infections from starting. Would Ramona's behavior be classified as obsessive or compulsive? What distinguishes the two?

Ramona's behavior represents a compulsion, an act that intrudes repetitively on her behavior. It is called a *compulsion* because it is an overt act. An obsession refers to a thought that intrudes repeatedly on a person's consciousness. The possibility that obsessive thoughts accompany Ramona's compulsive actions is quite high. Often, persons are identified as having obsessive-compulsive disorder because of the close correspondence between their continually repeated thoughts and actions. (*Note*: Ramona may realize that her behavior is unreasonable yet feel compelled to carry out the repetitive ritual anyway.)

13.11 When the teacher asks her student, "What's wrong?" the student's response is, "I don't know. I'm worried all the time. In fact, I even worry about being worried." How might a psychologist classify a response such as the one given by the student?

The student's response may represent generalized anxiety disorder. When there is long-term or persistent anxiety that cannot easily be attributed to a particular source (does not fit any of the other classifications within anxiety disorders), it is referred to as a generalized anxiety disorder.

13.12 Arthur witnesses his sister, Catherine, suffer a disfiguring accident. When asked about this years later, he responds, "You know, I can't remember. I think I was there when it happened, but I just do not recall exactly what occurred." What form of dissociative disorder does Arthur seem to be displaying?

Arthur appears to be experiencing dissociative amnesia. The forgetting of a past traumatic experience, one usually caused by a particularly stressful event, is thought to be amnesia. Usually, the event itself and whatever occurred immediately afterward will be blocked from recall.

13.13 A famous case history describes a young man walking into a police station and telling the desk sergeant he knows the murderer who has been terrorizing the college town. When asked to give the name, the young man replies with an identity of one of his other personalities! How is this possible? What do psychologists call this disorder?

In the relatively rare cases where an individual expresses more than one personality, it is possible that one of the identities knows about the others. Psychologists call this circumstance *dissociative identity disorder*; more popularly, it is called *multiple personality*. Evidence indicates that one of the identities can know about the others, sometimes to the point of developing friendship or rivalry with them.

13.14 Ernest's posture at his computer causes him to suffer back cramps. Ernest believes the pain he is experiencing is evidence of a cancerous tumor. He has gone to several physicians and, although he has received clearance from each one, continues to persist in his belief and look for other diagnoses. How would a psychologist interpret Ernest's behavior?

Ernest's responses represent hypochondriasis, the interpretation of relatively minor symptoms as representing major, life-threatening illness. Even with the repeated clearance from a series of physicians, Ernest persists in believing there is something seriously wrong; this is characteristic of hypochondriasis.

13.15 A woman was admitted to a hospital with paralysis of both arms. Careful examination indicated there was no physiological cause for the paralysis, and so other variables were investigated. It was found that the woman was working to put her husband through college. The day before the onset of her paralysis, her husband had left to "go home" to visit his parents, leaving her to continue working and take care of their 1-year-old child.
The woman's reaction is called a *conversion disorder*. What is this? How does it differ from an actual illness? How does it differ from a psychosomatic disorder?

A conversion disorder is a physical reaction that allows a person to escape from an anxiety-producing situation. It differs from a physical illness in that there is no apparent precipitating physiological or biological cause. (In this case, for example, there was no apparent damage to the spinal column or the arms. However, the physical symptoms were present.)

Conversion disorders are thought to differ from psychosomatic disorders in that psychosomatic disorders generally are accompanied by actual physiological damage to a body organ or malfunctioning in an organ system; this is not usually true of conversion disorders.

13.16 Research evidence shows that most attempted suicides involve people who are considered seriously depressed; in fact, profound depression has been called the only "fatal" abnormal personality pattern. Depression is considered to be representative of what kind of disorder? What other behavior pattern fits in this category?

Depression is classified as a mood disorder, a situation in which affective or emotional states reach a level severe enough to interfere with daily living. The other mood disorder is called *bipolar disorder*, in which an individual cycles between depression and mania, with the latter being a state of heightened energy, activity, and elation.

13.17 Describe the usual characteristics shown by a schizophrenic. Why is the term *schizophrenia* often misinterpreted?

The general characteristics associated with schizophrenic behavior include disturbances of perceptions, emotions, motor responses, and relationships with others and a disturbed sense of self. Schizophrenics often experience hallucinations and delusions and show bizarre patterns of responding.

The term *schizophrenia* means "split mind" but does not refer to dissociative identity disorder or multiple personality. Rather, the split referred to by this term indicates a splitting from reality; a schizophrenic is thought to have lost reasonable contact with the reality of his or her environment.

13.18 Anwar "hears voices" and often giggles or cries when no stimulus seems to provoke such a response. Which category of schizophrenia seems to fit Anwar's behavior?

Anwar probably would be classified as a disorganized schizophrenic. This disorder is characterized by extreme psychological and personal disorganization. As a disorganized schizophrenic, Anwar also might experience delusions and show extremely confused speech patterns.

13.19 Locked in apparent physical immobility, Clarice shows almost complete detachment from reality. Which type of schizophrenia best describes Clarice's behavior?

Clarice is classified as a catatonic schizophrenic. Catatonic schizophrenics show unusual motor behavior, sometimes making excessive or violent movements or, as Clarice is doing, slipping into almost total immobility. They are uncommunicative and appear unable to interact with the "real world."

13.20 "I know the fuzzy orange guys are there. They hide in the walls, but when no one is around, they come out and try to steal my things. They even tried to take my dog. I have to be on constant watch to keep them from winning." These comments are representative of what kind of schizophrenic reaction?

Delusional comments that focus on feelings of persecution are most likely to indicate paranoid schizophrenia. A paranoid schizophrenic trusts no one and typically is convinced there is a plot against her or him, such as the one involving the fuzzy orange guys.

13.21 A number of years ago a young man was convicted of first-degree murder. He had been hitchhiking, and a family stopped to give him a ride. When he asked for a cigarette and found that none of them smoked, he killed them all. The man was asked if he knew that killing was considered wrong. He said that he did know this but persisted in explaining his actions by saying that no one in the family had any cigarettes. This pattern of behavior is representative of what kind of abnormal personality pattern?

Several labels have been used to describe this type of behavior. In DSM-IV this is called *antisocial personality disorder*, but it also is known popularly as *psychopathic* or *sociopathic behavior*. No matter what label is used, this type of personality disorder is characterized by a persistent failure to act according to the rules of society. It seems that those who show antisocial personality disorder believe that special sets of rules apply only to them and seldom have anxiety about such a feeling.

13.22 Really mad at her boyfriend, Jane Ann screams at him, "You don't care about me. All you care about is yourself and your clothes and your car and how good everything looks. The only time you think about me is to see if I look okay, so you'll look better to others!" If Jane Ann's statement is accurate, what type of personality disorder is she attributing to her boyfriend?

Jane Ann thinks her boyfriend is a narcissist. People with narcissistic personality disorder have an exaggerated sense of self, worry little about the needs of others, and often expect special treatment or adoration. However, narcissists typically have fear of failure and are sensitive about being criticized.

13.23 How would a person diagnosed with a paranoid personality disorder differ from the individual described in Solved Problem 13.20 who "knew" that fuzzy orange guys were plotting against him?

Someone diagnosed as showing paranoid personality disorder is likely to have feelings of persecution and not trust others. However, the expression of these or other symptoms of paranoia are likely to be less severe than those of a schizophrenic, and the individual will have relatively good contact with reality. Persons showing paranoid personality disorder frequently lead relatively "normal" lives and do not manifest delusional or hallucinatory behaviors.

13.24 A persistent question about abnormal personality patterns has been whether certain groups of people are more likely to show certain patterns compared with others. Is it possible to point to any variables and say there are well-established relationships between those variables and abnormality? What kinds of results have been obtained?

Several variables show fairly strong correlations with abnormal personality patterns, although this may not indicate that causal relationships exist. Two that are frequently mentioned are gender and culture. There is evidence indicating that certain patterns of abnormality are more likely to be shown by women than by men and vice versa. There also is evidence that certain patterns are found far more frequently in some cultural groups than in others. Other variables that have been considered include age, marital status, social class, and ethnicity.

13.25 The young man described in Solved Problem 13.21 was found guilty of murder and executed. Many people would say that his behavior seemed "crazy." How was it that he was found legally sane and taken to trial? What have some states done about individuals who have committed heinous crimes but have been found to be insane?

The young man was found legally sane because he knew what societal standards described as "right" and "wrong." The fact that he chose to ignore these standards because he did not believe these rules applied to him did not change the judgment of legal sanity.

In instances where the individual fails to meet the standards of legal sanity, being unable to distinguish between right and wrong or unable to act in accordance with the requirements of the law, some states have instituted a verdict of "guilty but mentally ill." This enables continued confinement of the individual rather than allowing the individual's release back into society because of actions committed while legally insane.

Key Terms

Abnormal personality pattern.   Behavior that produces significant personal discomfort or creates problems for others in a person's society.

Antisocial personality disorder.   Sometimes called *psychopathic or sociopathic disorder*; characterized by manipulative or deceptive behaviors and lack of concern with the rights of others or the rules of society.

Anxiety disorders.   Any of a number of patterns in which a person's daily activities are affected noticeably by the occurrence of anxiety.

Behavioral models.   Proposals that attribute abnormal personality patterns to learning.

Biomedical models.   Proposals that emphasize the influence of bodily functions on personality patterns.

Bipolar disorder.   A mood disorder characterized by alternate periods of depression and mania.

Catatonic schizophrenia.   A pattern of schizophrenic behavior characterized by extremes of cooperation and activity; the best-known example is total withdrawal accompanied by complete muscle rigidity.

Cognitive models.   Proposals that focus on a person's thoughts or beliefs as explanations for abnormal personality patterns.

Conversion disorder.   The term used to describe a physical problem that results from (is converted from) a psychological problem.

Delusion.   An irrational belief that persists even in the face of overwhelming evidence to the contrary.

Dependent personality disorder.   An abnormal personality pattern characterized by lack of self-esteem and lack of responsibility for major areas of one's life.

Depressive disorders.   Mood disorders characterized by loss of energy, inability to concentrate, feelings of worthlessness, and possible thoughts of suicide.

Dissociative amnesia.   The partial or total forgetting of some past experiences, usually after a stressful event.

Dissociative disorders.   Abnormal personality patterns involving disturbance of personal memories or identity.

Dissociative fugue.   A dissociative disorder characterized by "leaving" one's life and assuming a new identity.

Dissociative identity disorder.   Also called *multiple personality*; an abnormal personality pattern in which an individual has two or more well-defined and separate personalities.

DSM-IV.   The *Diagnostic and Statistical Manual of Mental Disorders, Fourth Edition*; published by the American Psychiatric Association, it provides means for evaluating abnormal personality patterns in more than 200 separate categories.

Dysthymia.   Particularly severe depression, usually labeled as chronic.

Generalized anxiety disorder.   Long-term, persistent anxiety for which there is no identifiable cause; sometimes called *free-floating anxiety*.

Hallucination.   The perception of something that does not exist; a false sensory experience.

Humanistic models.   Proposals that stress a person's control of and responsibility for behavior, including abnormal patterns.

Hypochondriasis.   An abnormal personality pattern marked by the misinterpretation of minor physical symptoms as being a major or life-threatening illness.

Mania.   An abnormal personality pattern characterized by excessive energy, activity, elation, and expansiveness.

Mood disorders.   Abnormal personality patterns involving affective or emotional states that reach levels severe enough to interfere with daily living.

Narcissistic personality disorder.   An abnormal personality pattern characterized by an exaggerated sense of self-importance and little regard for the needs of others.

Obsessive-compulsive disorder.   Repetitive thoughts (obsessions) or actions (compulsions) that are unwarranted and disturbing for the individual.

Panic disorder.   Sudden, intense, and unexplained attacks of fear that may last several hours.

Paranoid personality disorder.   An abnormal personality pattern characterized by feelings of persecution and mistrust of others; generally thought to be less severe than paranoid schizophrenia.

Paranoid schizophrenia.   A schizophrenic pattern characterized by delusions of grandeur, persecution, or both.

Personality disorders.   Abnormal personality patterns characterized by behaviors which deviate markedly from the expectations of an individual's society and typically cause more distress for others in the society than for the person showing the behaviors.

Phobic disorder.   Intense, compelling fear of a specific situation or object; usually irrational.

Precipitating factors.   Stimuli that actually initiate behavioral patterns.

Predisposing factors.   The background characteristics of a person that influence personality patterns.

Psychodynamic models.   Proposals that emphasize the work of Freud and his associates for understanding personality patterns.

Psychosomatic disorders.   Physical problems which arise, seemingly in part but not exclusively, from psychological causes.

Schizophrenia.   Abnormal personality patterns characterized by disturbed thought processes and pronounced distortion of or detachment from reality.

Somatoform disorders.   Abnormal personality patterns characterized by symptoms of a physical dysfunction for which no organic cause can be found.

CHAPTER 14

Therapies

Psychologists are interested not only in the identification and diagnosis of abnormal behaviors, but also in developing techniques to treat these problem behaviors. This chapter discusses some of the therapies that have been developed.

14.1 GENERAL OVERVIEW OF THERAPY

The overall purpose of therapies is to help individuals overcome problems such as those described in Chapter 13. Individuals may receive help from a number of different types of therapists.

In general, therapies can be divided into two major groupings: biomedical therapies and psychotherapies. *Biomedical therapies* involve physical or medical procedures such as the use of drugs or surgery. *Psychotherapies* are nonmedical techniques used to help a patient overcome a problem. There are several different types of psychotherapy, but the concept of psychotherapy probably is best viewed as originating from the work of Sigmund Freud, whose theory of *psychoanalysis* emphasizes personality conflicts and unconscious motivations.

While varying estimates have been made of the percentage of the American population showing abnormal personality patterns that may require therapy at some time, a fairly well agreed upon ratio is one in two. Included in any one year are 10 to 15 million people who abuse alcohol or other drugs, over 2 million who have major depression, and over 1 million who are actively schizophrenic. It should be noted that the frequency of such behaviors differs in other cultures and that many of the people exhibiting these behaviors do not seek treatment.

Types of Therapists. There are a number of different types of therapists. Probably the best known are psychiatrists and clinical psychologists. Psychiatrists are medical doctors who receive specialized training after the completion of medical school. Clinical psychologists usually obtain a Ph.D. or Psy.D. degree, along with specialized training in therapeutic techniques.

Other types of therapists include *psychoanalysts* (usually psychiatrists with specialized training in Freudian therapeutic techniques), psychiatric nurses, psychiatric social workers, counseling psychologists, and some paraprofessional personnel. (*Paraprofessional* personnel are often volunteers with limited training who work for organizations such as crisis intervention centers.)

EXAMPLE 14.1. Ready access to supportive personnel may be crucial in helping a person overcome a crisis. In recent years, many different kinds of agencies and organizations that specialize in providing initial support have been established. These include crisis or suicide prevention centers, drug or alcohol rehabilitation centers, and call-in services for runaways. Frequently, the paraprofessional personnel in these organizations are minimally trained but capable of helping a person overcome a temporary problem and then guiding the person to a more thoroughly trained individual for additional help.

Trends in Treatment. Therapies for treating abnormal personality patterns generally have not become so rigidly standardized that the people who administer them are unwilling to change techniques as new developments occur. As a result, the therapeutic techniques discussed in this chapter may find differing interpretations and uses as therapists adjust to changing trends in treatment. What is safe to say is that many therapists employ *eclectic* approaches, combining aspects of several different therapies in dealing with any one situation.

Several other trends are noticeable. Perhaps the greatest change has been the increased use of *psychotropic drugs*, substances that act on a person's mental or psychological state. Drug therapy has led to a decrease in the hospitalization of persons with abnormal personality patterns and a decreased length of stay for those who are hospitalized.

Greater community involvement has produced the development of *community psychology* as a field, the branch of psychology based on the premise that a better community attitude can help prevent abnormal behaviors. This involvement has led to increases in the number of agencies and organizations that specialize in providing support for people with abnormal patterns and the extension of community values and social standards into the hospital setting in what is called *milieu therapy*. One result of increased community involvement has been *deinstitutionalization*, the trend to transfer treatment from inpatient mental hospitals to outpatient community-based facilities.

Additionally, greater knowledge and better techniques in physiology and biology have led to increased genetic counseling, so that parents can better know the probability of whether a baby may be born abnormal.

EXAMPLE 14.2.   The probability of forms of mental retardation such as Down syndrome can be identified while the mother carries the fetus. During pregnancy, it is possible to consult with the parents, explain the chromosomal upset and describe the effect it could have on the child, and the courses of action available. In some cases this may lead to a choice of a therapeutic abortion. In other cases the parents may decide to carry the child, but they certainly will be better prepared for the behaviors to be expected than they would be if the information were not made available.

14.2   BIOMEDICAL THERAPIES

Physical procedures used to treat abnormal personality patterns are called *biomedical therapies*, or *somatic therapies*. By far the most frequently used procedure is drug therapy, while psychosurgery and electroconvulsive therapy are used occasionally in certain specialized circumstances.

Drug Therapies.   The most prevalent biomedical therapy today is *drug therapy*, the use of psychotropic drugs to change brain functioning and, as a result, modify abnormal personality patterns. Two advantages of drug therapies are that (1) there is no tissue destruction as in psychosurgery and (2) the patient allegedly can be made more open to therapeutic influence.

EXAMPLE 14.3.   Patients with mood disorders often are treated with drug therapy. Manic patients may be given a tranquilizer to reduce agitation, while depressive patients may be given antidepressants such as Prozac (fluoxetine) and Elavil (amitriptyline). In such cases, it is hoped that the resultant behavior pattern will be closer to the norm and make the patient more amenable to other forms of treatment.

Several cautions are appropriate: While drug therapy may relieve the symptoms of abnormal patterns, this relief may last only as long as the use of the drug continues. Once a patient stops using the drug, the symptoms may return. Additionally, the patient may become psychologically dependent on the drug. In many cases, it is essential to have other forms of therapy accompany the drug therapy if an eventual cure is to be expected.

Electroconvulsive Therapy (ECT).   Also known as *shock therapy*, *electroconvulsive therapy (ECT)* involves placing the patient in a bed, administering a short-lived anesthetic and a muscle relaxant, and then restraining the patient while a brief electric current in the range of 70 to 130 volts is passed across the temples, producing convulsions of the body muscles. It is believed that ECT may cause the release of the neurotransmitter beta-endorphin, which somehow contributes to relief from severe depression.

ECT is not used with great frequency but often is employed when other techniques for treating severe depression have not been successful and there is fear that the patient will commit suicide. There is some possibility of memory loss, although the loss is generally not permanent. ECT produces only transient effects, meaning there is a fairly high relapse rate. Nevertheless, ECT is used when no other treatment appears viable.

Psychosurgery.   Techniques involving surgical removal of brain tissue are classified as *psychosurgery*. The initial form of psychosurgery, the *prefrontal lobotomy*, involved destroying tissue linking the frontal lobes and the thalamus, with the intent of reducing emotionality and abnormal patterns in the patient. Although occasionally successful in accomplishing this purpose, this type of surgery has been abandoned almost completely because of the many drastic side effects, including severely changed personality patterns, inappropriately changed emotional states, and in some cases death.

Current techniques are far more sophisticated, involving the destruction of very small portions of brain tissue, but are used only when all other possibilities have been exhausted. It should be noted that more routine brain surgeries, such as removal of a brain tumor, also may affect personality patterns and thus might be classified as psychosurgery.

14.3 PSYCHODYNAMIC THERAPIES

The bases of psychodynamic therapies were developed by Freud, who believed it was the therapist's responsibility to help and guide the client, providing direction during the therapy sessions. The goal was seen as having the patient achieve *insight* into the underlying causes of the abnormal behavior. Several aspects of the client's responding during the sessions were considered most important.

Developing out of what Freud and his partner Breuer called the "talking cure," a major aspect of therapy is the process of *free association*. Free association means the client is expected to say whatever comes to mind regardless of the distastefulness or apparent irrelevance of a statement.

As the therapy progresses, the client often demonstrates what Freud called *transference*, the development of an emotional relationship with the therapist. Freud believed this relationship represented a reenactment of the association the person had with a parent during childhood. Freud also warned against the possibility of *countertransference*, in which the therapist develops inappropriate affection for the client.

When the client develops trust in the therapist, it becomes possible to explore more of the conflicts that have created the client's problem. The therapist directs the sessions to encourage the person to recognize and evaluate these conflicts. However, as the crucial causes of the problem come to be expressed, a client often may exhibit *resistance*; that is, the client is unwilling to discuss the topic. If the resistance can be overcome, the therapy may be successful.

Freud felt that one way to generate ideas and explore desires within the therapeutic setting was *dream analysis*. To Freud, dreams represented thoughts and wishes the client held but was unable to express consciously. Often, even the content of the dream did not express the message directly but did so through symbolic representation. Freud distinguished between the *manifest content* of a dream, which showed the actual content of the dream, and the *latent content*, which held the symbolic meaning of that dream. (*Note*: Symbolism in dreams has created problems of interpretation because more than one interpretation often can be suggested.)

EXAMPLE 14.4. The client may start a therapy session by relating the content of a recent dream. The therapist may pursue this in different manners, perhaps exploring the meaning of the dream or using the dream material as the initial step in a free association series of thoughts. The therapist needs to recognize the possibility that the dream's content may be symbolic and not something that can be taken at face value.

Modern approaches to psychodynamic therapy have included *ego analysis*, in which there is less concern with unconscious conflicts arising from childhood (id) experiences and more of an emphasis on having clients develop problem-solving skills (ego) that are adaptive. Therapists also have tried to find briefer forms of psychodynamic therapies that adhere to the format proposed by Freud but shorten the time involved by being more direct.

14.4 HUMANISTIC THERAPIES

Another approach to psychotherapy is classified as *humanistic therapy*, which focuses on personal growth or self-actualization. The therapist's responsibility is to help the client understand or become aware of feelings and perceptions, guiding the client toward the self-actualization of individual potential. Humanistic therapists believe that the problems they deal with originate from unreasonable "conditions of worth," in which the client is trying to conform to expectations that are inconsistent with personal potential. Several variations of humanistic therapies have become popular.

Client-Centered Therapy. Carl Rogers was the leading advocate of *client-centered therapy*, proposing that a therapist make no judgment about a client's behaviors but instead offer *empathy*, *genuineness*, and *unconditional positive regard*. In effect, the therapist serves as a role model for the client, showing openness and understanding rather than imposing standards that conflict with the client's perceptions of the world. Client-centered therapy often is referred to as *nondirective therapy*, with progress depending on the ability of the client to verbalize and then work through his or her problems. The therapist typically plays a minimal role in "steering" the client through the expression and resolution of conflicts. This type of therapy seems to work best with clients who are highly verbal.

Gestalt Therapy. As its name implies, *Gestalt therapy* is based on the idea that personality must be treated as an organized whole. A Gestalt therapist encourages a client to make use of inner resources to gain more control and become more active and responsible for his or her actions. The client's aim is to overcome behaviors such as passivity, irresponsibility, and a poor self-concept and open blocked potentials for growth. Gestalt therapy often involves various kinds of exercises to help the client accomplish these goals.

EXAMPLE 14.5. If a client starts a therapy session by saying, "Today has been a bad day," a Gestalt therapist's initial reaction might be to ask the client to rephrase that statement. The therapist, for example, might respond by commenting, "Gee, today for me has been a really great one. Will you think about what you just said and try again?" The client in this situation learns to take responsibility for her or his actions and might rephrase by saying, "I have had a bad day today."

14.5 BEHAVIOR THERAPIES

Based on principles developed in the study of learning, *behavior therapies* try to deal directly with the symptoms of abnormal personality patterns. Typically, behavior therapies are short-term, directive, and based on a scientific model.

Classical Conditioning Techniques. Some forms of behavior therapy rely on the classical conditioning format. A correctional experience (serving as an unconditioned stimulus) is paired with a conditioned stimulus that appears to provoke maladaptive responding. The unconditioned stimulus (US) experiences may be pleasant or unpleasant (positive or aversive), depending on the type of behavior change being attempted.

Systematic desensitization relies on the use of relaxation (a positive experience) paired with various forms of the anxiety-producing situation. This step-by-step procedure or hierarchy of stimuli is designed so that each conditioned stimulus (CS) comes closer to the one that is most anxiety-provoking. The therapist's task is to monitor each experience, providing effective relaxation cues and maintaining a moderate pace throughout the hierarchy.

EXAMPLE 14.6.   If a patient has an intense, compelling fear of the dark, systematic desensitization may be used to help overcome these symptoms. At first the patient may be asked to read stories about or descriptions of dark places. While this occurs, the patient is reassured and helped to experience relaxation. Successive steps following this might include observing a movie about people going into caves, then actually seeing someone else in a dark room, and finally entering a dark room. Each step pairs relaxation (the new US) with images or experiences of the dark (the CS) until the person is able to confront the dark without feeling intense anxiety.

A different way of confronting an anxiety-provoking stimulus occurs in *implosion therapy*. The patient is asked to imagine the very worst possible version of the anxiety-producing stimulus and experience all the attendant anxiety. However, this is done in a totally reassuring environment and the patient is made to see that nothing has happened and that the imagined anxiety-producing stimulus produces no harm or injury.

An even more direct version of this therapy is called *flooding*, in which the client is brought in direct contact with the anxiety-provoking situation and made to see that nothing actually happens. In both implosion therapy and flooding, the idea is that extinction and counterconditioning will occur, for when the patient once again confronts the anxiety-provoking situation, the memory will be that nothing did happen and that coping is possible.

Aversion therapy is a technique used with patients who show self-destructive or otherwise inappropriate behaviors. The therapist pairs painful or unpleasant stimuli as unconditioned stimuli in the situations that induce the maladaptive behavior. The patient learns that responding in the inappropriate way leads to aversive stimuli, and the frequency of such maladaptive responding decreases.

EXAMPLE 14.7.   Aversion therapy sometimes is tried with clients who abuse alcohol. By taking a drug that will produce nausea if alcohol is ingested, the client comes to learn that even the slightest use of alcohol will produce very unpleasant reactions. Used in conjunction with other therapy, aversive conditioning can help modify an alcoholic's behavior.

Operant Conditioning Techniques.   Changing behavior patterns by using operant conditioning techniques concentrates on reinforcing responses that are appropriate and lead to desirable goals while also attempting to extinguish maladaptive responses. It is necessary to have a very consistent reinforcement pattern, because even an occasional reinforcement for the maladaptive response may make that response very resistant to extinction. (This is the partial reinforcement effect; see Chapter 7.)

One application of operant conditioning in modifying behavior is called a *token economy*, which is used mostly in institutional settings. The patients are able to earn tokens (such as poker chips or tickets) which, when accumulated, can be traded for privileges or rewards. The tokens are awarded for adaptive responses and withheld when maladaptive patterns are shown.

EXAMPLE 14.8.   The sophistication of the token economy can advance with the increasing abilities shown by the patient. At first, tokens (and eventually rewards) may be given for behaviors as simple as maintaining personal cleanliness, caring for one's possessions, and showing good manners toward others. As these behaviors are achieved, they continue to be reinforced, but additional responses can be added to the behavior repertoire. For example, rewards may be given for the acquisition of job skills. Eventually, it is hoped the patient will be able to return to normal functioning.

One version of operant conditioning has been called *behavior (contingency) contracting*, in which the therapist and the client establish a contract specifying the behaviors that satisfy the goals of the therapy and therefore, when shown, will be rewarded. Behavior contracting has the advantages of delineating the responsibilities of both the therapist and the client and establishing the criteria for success of the therapy. The contract also may specify punishments to be administered if the goals are not met.

Modeling Techniques.   The basic principles of modeling also can be used in modifying maladaptive behaviors. By observing someone who is coping successfully with an anxiety-provoking situation, the patient can discover and perhaps imitate responses that will be adaptive in that situation.

EXAMPLE 14.9.   Consider again the description of desensitization in Example 14.6. Some of the later steps in that process incorporate modeling techniques. Both the movie and the actual observation of another person would serve not only as conditioned stimuli to be paired with relaxation but also as models of appropriate or adaptive responding. (*Note*: It is not uncommon for several behavior therapy techniques to be combined.)

14.6   COGNITIVE THERAPIES

While also focusing on learning, *cognitive therapies* try to change the way clients think rather than change the observable symptomatic behavioral patterns. Because of the link with learning, these therapies sometimes are referred to as *cognitive-behavioral therapies*. The premise of cognitive therapies is that behaviors can be changed if the cognitions underlying those behaviors are changed.

Rational-Emotive Therapy.   Developed by Albert Ellis, *rational-emotive therapy* tries to help a client recognize the irrationality of the beliefs that control her or his behavior and then practice new ways of thinking and behaving that are more rational. Rational-emotive therapists usually play a very active role in the therapeutic process, challenging dysfunctional patterns of thought and suggesting alternative patterns of thinking and acting that will be more adaptive and rational.

EXAMPLE 14.10.   A client claims, "I'm no good. I flunked my biology exam. I just am no good!" A rational-emotive therapist may confront this kind of reaction directly by asking, "Why does flunking one exam make you have no good characteristics?" The client is forced to see the irrationality of the conclusion reached and then is given guidance for developing new patterns of responding.

Cognitive Therapy.   Aaron Beck developed *cognitive therapy*, a less confrontational form than rational-emotive therapy. Cognitive therapists who follow Beck's suggestions act more like teachers, trying to help the client learn information that will allow a change from distorted and illogical thinking to patterns that are more logical and adaptive. Cognitive therapy often is used with chronic depressive patients and appears to be about as successful as other techniques (e.g., drugs) in alleviating depression.

Stress-Inoculation Therapy.   Another form of cognitive therapy is called *stress-inoculation therapy*. In this technique developed by Donald Meichenbaum, the client first prepares for change by developing an understanding of the beliefs and concerns associated with stressful situations and then acquires and rehearses adaptive, coping self-statements, applies them in the controlled therapy setting, and finally practices and is reinforced for using those strategies in real-life situations.

14.7   GROUP THERAPIES

In *group therapy*, more than one client is involved in the therapeutic setting at the same time. The belief supporting this technique is that the group provides a social setting where resolution of problems, which often are first developed in a social setting, may be achieved.

Groups may include several patients from differing backgrounds or may be composed of people sharing similar characteristics, such as the same problem (e.g., alcohol abuse), family membership, or marital status. Usually, group therapy is less expensive than individual therapy. A group may provide strong support for the individuals within the group and at the same time exert pressure to change maladaptive behavior patterns. Disadvantages of groups include a loss of focus on one's specific problems, less individual attention for the individual client, and less effective responding on the part of the therapist because of the multiple demands created by the group.

14.8   OTHER CONCERNS WITH THERAPY

Several other considerations are important in discussing therapy. This section presents some of the most critical.

Ethical Issues.   No matter what form of therapy is being used, ethical issues are always important. A therapist is in a position of power and must always take care not to abuse that standing. The basic premise of any therapy is to do no harm. In addition, a major consideration is the confidentiality of the activities that take place within the therapeutic setting.

EXAMPLE 14.11.   Although rare, the best known abuse of the therapy setting occurs when a therapist takes sexual advantage of a client. Any documented instance of this kind of ethical breach is certain to lead to expulsion of the therapist from professional organizations and may lead to legal difficulties for the therapist as well.

Cultural Sensitivity.   Related to ethical issues is concern with cultural sensitivity. Therapists often must deal with gender, ethnicity, sexual preference, or race as part of the therapeutic process and should be careful to understand the attributes and values associated with these cultural patterns. Failure to be cognizant of those patterns may affect the therapy process adversely.

Self-Help.   Many persons showing what could be diagnosed as abnormal personality patterns do not seek the help of a professional therapist in attempting to overcome these difficulties. Instead, they turn to self-help techniques, including many "*pop*" (for *popular*) therapies found in books, magazines, and Web sites. It is almost impossible to evaluate these techniques because no research or professional writing is associated with most that are proposed. It is true, however, that some people report successfully changing their behavior patterns after reading and adopting the premises of some self-help programs. Whether the program was the reason for this or whether there was *spontaneous remission* of the symptoms or perhaps a *placebo effect* involved is almost impossible to determine.

Effectiveness of Therapy.   There is no easy way to determine the effectiveness of therapy. Several considerations are important; for example, the type of therapy used in relation to the symptoms presented may determine the ultimate effectiveness of the therapy. In addition, the expectations brought to the therapeutic setting by the client and/or the therapist may have a pronounced effect on the success of the technique. Evidence indicates that therapist bias that is incompatible with the biases of the client in regard to characteristics such as ethnicity, religious beliefs, and sexual orientation may have negative effects on the success of the therapy. Nevertheless, most research indicates that a majority of clients claim benefit from having been in therapy. Not all do; at least one study indicated that approximately 10 percent of those assessed reported no improvement or even deterioration in the problem being treated.

Solved Problems

14.1 Distinguish between biomedical therapies and psychotherapies. Why can the latter be thought to have arisen from the former?

Biomedical therapies involve physical or medical procedures, including the use of drugs, surgery, and electroconvulsive shock. Psychotherapies are nonmedical techniques used to help a patient overcome problems. Psychotherapies are thought to have developed from the work of Sigmund Freud, who was a practicing medical doctor when he explored these nonmedical approaches.

14.2 What professionals besides medical doctors are involved in the treatment of individuals with abnormal personality patterns?

Psychiatrists and some psychoanalysts are medical doctors. Some of the other professionals involved in treatment are clinical psychologists, who usually have a Ph.D. or Psy.D. degree. Other people who help treat individuals with abnormal personality patterns are psychiatric social workers, psychiatric nurses, counseling psychologists, and paraprofessional personnel. People in the last group often are volunteers, many of whom need only limited training for the jobs they do.

14.3 What percentage of the population of the United States can be expected to show behaviors that could be classified as abnormal personality patterns at some time in their lives? What are the most common forms observed?

It is estimated that one in every two people in the United States shows behavior at some time that could be classified as an abnormal pattern. The categories showing particularly high frequency are substance abuse and depression.

14.4 What are some of the recent trends in the treatment of individuals with abnormal personality patterns? Can these trends be expected to continue in the future?

It is difficult to predict future developments accurately because we never know what might be learned or discovered and thus provide a major breakthrough. However, there are some recent trends that have been identified.

One is that the rate of hospitalization or custodial care for people with many forms of abnormal personality patterns is dropping. Most likely, this change can be attributed to the increased use of psychotropic drugs to alleviate or control patterns that previously required the patient to be hospitalized. It also may be the result of other improved therapeutic techniques or of a more tolerant and understanding attitude in the population in general.

Other noticeable trends include greater community involvement, with community psychology and crisis intervention centers becoming more common. There has been an increase in "halfway houses" to ease the transition for patients who have been hospitalized or imprisoned and are returning to the larger society. Milieu therapy—the attempt to bring many of society's functions and demands into the custodial or hospital setting by incorporating the social standards of the culture or community into the therapy being used—is another development. In addition, there has been a trend toward increased genetic counseling, which allows an estimate of the probability that a baby will be born abnormal. This information may lead to a choice of a therapeutic abortion.

Finally, therapy providers have been seen to adopt more eclectic approaches, often combining aspects of several different techniques in any one situation.

14.5 What are psychotropic drugs? What are the advantages of using drug therapy to treat abnormal personality patterns?

Psychotropic drugs are substances that act on a person's mental or psychological state. One advantage of using drugs for therapy is that no tissue destruction is involved, as occurs, for example, in psychosurgery.

In addition, drug therapy is thought to make patients more open to other forms of therapy, and the combination of therapies is likely to alleviate the problem.

14.6   Drug therapy does not cause tissue damage, but it may create a different type of problem for the patient. What is this problem? What *should* be done in conjunction with drug therapy?

There seem to be two problems related to the same source. Because drug therapy often produces noticeable and rapid changes in behavior, the patient may develop a dependence on the drug as a means of alleviating the problem rather than develop alternative patterns of responding. In a similar vein, the persons in charge of these patients may come to rely on and be satisfied with drug therapy and not make an effort to help a patient develop alternative behavior patterns. Frequently, the symptoms will return if the patient stops using the drug. In instances such as these, drug therapy should be combined with psychotherapy, with the drugs being phased out as more adequate behaviors are developed.

14.7   In a popular movie about a mental hospital, several of the patients were "treated" with electroconvulsive therapy (ECT). In one instance, ECT was used to keep a patient docile, although the ECT did not appear to be the appropriate therapeutic treatment for the circumstances. Was this a common occurrence? What treatment is now far more likely? What example can you give of an appropriate use of ECT?

Opinions vary as to the extent to which ECT was used to "create" docile patients. There is evidence that some serious abuses of the treatment did occur. With the development of effective psychotropic drugs, the use of ECT has declined considerably. A continued appropriate use of ECT, however, has been in treating severely depressed patients who do not seem to respond to other forms of treatment and seem to be at risk of committing suicide. Even in such cases, ECT often appears to produce only transient effects.

14.8   Psychosurgery is another form of biomedical therapy. How commonly is it used? What are the potential benefits of and difficulties with psychosurgery? What other type of therapy often is substituted for psychosurgery?

Psychosurgery has been used less frequently in recent years. The potential uses of psychosurgery remain valuable in certain instances, for example, when a tumor creates hallucinations because of unusual stimulation of the visual cortex. However, the practice of performing prefrontal lobotomies to control certain abnormal patterns has proved inconsistent and frequently dangerous, occasionally leading to seizures or death. With increased research, the use of drugs has taken the place of psychosurgery in almost all cases.

14.9   Is there more than one kind of psychotherapy?

There are many different kinds of psychotherapy, including psychodynamic, humanistic, behavior, cognitive, and group therapies. It probably is reasonable to think that all these therapies should give some credit to Freud, because the psychotherapeutic movement originated from his work. However, many other people have made major contributions to the development of the different techniques. Freud's influence is still seen, particularly in the psychodynamic and psychoanalytic approaches.

14.10   What is free association, and what role does it play in the therapeutic situation?

Free association is a technique in which the patient in a psychodynamic therapy setting lets each thought lead to the next without restriction. The purpose of free association is to get the patient to consider all the different factors that may be creating problems. Speaking what comes to mind without forethought is supposed to facilitate the release of information from the unconscious. It is hoped the person will express even things that seem objectionable or irrelevant, thus revealing fears or conflicts that cannot be reached through ordinary rational discourse.

14.11 Some patients in therapy find themselves unwilling or unable to make use of free association. What is this phenomenon called, and what are the possible explanations for it?

This unwillingness is one aspect of what Freud called resistance. Presumably, the patient is in therapy because of painful conflicts that persist in the unconscious, and it stands to reason that the patient may resist exposing such conflicts even through free association. In addition, the patient may be unable to remember certain anxiety-laden events (repression), showing resistance at an unconscious rather than a conscious level. Much of the therapist's work may involve helping the patient overcome these resistances, recognize the sources of anxiety, and learn to cope with them.

14.12 When asked how therapy is going, patients have been known to say, "I just love my therapist!" Some people do not recognize that this may actually be true and an important part of the therapeutic situation. What is this called? Why might it be important in the therapy setting?

This situation represents transference, the transfer of attitudes about one person to another person. From the psychodynamic point of view, this transference is thought to be the reenactment of a child-parent relationship, with the therapist substituting for the parent. In this case, the situation illustrates positive transference, which often helps the patient overcome resistance. A patient who shows an aggressive or hostile attitude toward the therapist may be experiencing negative transference. Even this may help the therapist and patient understand what the difficulties are.

14.13 What is the situation called when the therapist develops an inappropriate affection for the client? What resolution should be sought in such circumstances?

When a therapist becomes enamored with a client, countertransference is occurring. The best resolution for such a circumstance is to reassign the client to another, noninvolved therapist.

14.14 Therapists have been known to interpret dreams as evidence of wish fulfillment. What does this mean? How does the manifest content of a dream differ from the latent content?

Freud believed that thoughts which were too anxiety-provoking or threatening to be expressed directly, even in dreams, might be disguised and symbolically represented in a dream. Thus, he distinguished between the actual event reported in the dream—the manifest content—and what he called the latent content, or the symbolic meaning of the dream. If the symbols can be interpreted correctly, they reveal particular urges that the person would like to fulfill. Thus, the concept of wish fulfillment represents what a person is able to accomplish symbolically in dreams but not in actual behavior.

14.15 What have been the modern trends in psychodynamic therapies?

Two trends are most noticeable in modern psychodynamic therapies. First, there is more of an emphasis on the problem-solving skills associated with ego functions and less concern with trying to identify childhood conflicts arising from the id. (See Chapter 12 for a review of ego and id functions.) In addition, therapists have tried to find briefer versions of psychodynamic approaches, reducing the total time the patient must remain in the therapeutic situation.

14.16 After several therapy sessions, Arthur is perplexed. He expected the therapist to take an active and guiding role but instead has found that he does most of the talking himself. The therapist listens and gives relatively little direction. Finally, Arthur "gets up his nerve" and asks the therapist why there isn't more guidance. Using the different descriptions of psychotherapy given in this chapter, pick the one that best seems to fit this circumstance and then describe the answer the therapist might give Arthur.

This situation seems to be an example of *client-centered therapy*, sometimes called *nondirective therapy*. The client's role in this therapy is to explore very actively the various possibilities that may help explain the problems being experienced. The therapist attempts to create a permissive atmosphere, usually keeping interpretations and advice to a minimum.

In this case, the therapist might tell Arthur that this type of therapy is being used because Arthur is doing so well without a lot of direction. With a client like Arthur, who is quite verbal and can express feelings freely, it is not always necessary for a therapist to take a guiding, active role.

14.17   If a therapist is *not* adopting an active or guiding role in client-centered therapy, what characteristics should the therapist be showing?

Proponents of client-centered therapy expect the therapist to offer empathy, adopt a truly genuine manner, and provide unconditional positive regard. This means the therapist shows openness and understanding and does not impose any standards that conflict with the client's perceptions of the world. The client, by having such support, is expected to work through the perceptions and come to understand which need to be modified in order to overcome the difficulties being experienced.

14.18   If the client starts a therapy session by saying, "What a lousy world this is. People just stink, you know?" how might a therapist employing a Gestalt therapy approach respond?

Gestalt therapy emphasizes the client's responsibility for actions, including the interpretations given to one's environment. The therapist might respond by asking the client to rephrase this interpretation and continue to "push" until the client says something such as, "I am not happy in my world. Most of the people I interact with are people with whom I don't get along."

14.19   Brent is disturbed by a very compelling fear of cats, and so he decides to consult a psychologist. The psychologist sets out an eight-step procedure for Brent, starting with reading stories about cats and eventually ending with Brent actually handling a cat. Brent is told he should relax at each successive stage, and when anxiety does arise, the therapist helps him become calm. The procedure involves only several short sessions over a period of several weeks, but Brent's fear of cats finally is eliminated. What is the name of this technique? Explain the principles of this technique as they apply to Brent's situation.

Brent has been guided through a procedure of *systematic desensitization*. The basis of this procedure is that relaxation and anxiety are incompatible. Therefore, if Brent can remain relaxed at each successive stage of exposure to cats, he will not experience anxiety. Basically, this is a counterconditioning procedure, pairing relaxation with the stimuli while extinguishing the anxiety that previously existed.

14.20   Suppose the psychologist Brent visited believed in the use of implosion or flooding therapies rather than systematic desensitization. How would the procedure employed differ from the one described in Solved Problem 14.19?

Implosion therapy involves having the client imagine the worst possible situation, while flooding therapy actually places the client in a very anxiety-provoking situation such as, in this case, a closed room containing a number of cats. Both techniques have the client experience the strongest anxiety produced by the feared stimulus. The therapist, however, makes certain that Brent actually has nothing untoward happen to him. The theory of implosion and flooding is that when Brent does not experience actual harm or injury, the subsequent recognition that involvement with cats does not hurt him should help him overcome his fears.

14.21   By age 6, Nathan was showing increasing levels of self-destructive behaviors. For example, he might knock his head against a wall several hundred times in one day. Tranquilizers and other drugs had proved ineffective. In an attempt to reduce and eventually eliminate these behaviors, a therapist strapped a small device to Nathan's body that could deliver an electric shock. (The device could be activated by a remote control transmitter.) Nathan's behaviors were monitored constantly, and each time he hit himself, a shock was administered. What type of therapy was Nathan given? Explain the principle that applies to Nathan's case.

This procedure is called *aversion therapy*. The principle is simple: Something unpleasant is associated with the undesirable response. The result hoped for is that the stimulus situation (whatever it may be) that provokes the undesirable response will instead come to be aversive and no longer generate the abnormal response pattern.

14.22 The director of a home for teenage girls with behavioral problems decides to institute a "ticket" system. The girls are instructed that responses that are positive (that is, appropriate to the social setting) will be rewarded with "tickets" that may be used for things such as clothing, special food, attendance at movies, and the use of the telephone. Girls who make negative responses will not receive tickets and may even have tickets taken away. A list of appropriate and inappropriate responses, along with their ticket values, is posted and discussed. Name and describe the technique used in this situation.

The plan the director has created is called a *token economy*. The girls' responses are rewarded or punished through the use of secondary reinforcers, the tickets. The girls will be likely to learn very quickly that reinforcements and punishments are contingent on certain types of behaviors and thus will learn which responses to make and which to avoid.

14.23 If the director in the Solved Problem 14.22 had chosen to use behavior (contingency) contracting, how would the procedure have differed?

Behavior or contingency contracting involves establishing a contract specifying the behaviors that will satisfy the goals of the therapy and therefore will be rewarded. The contract also may specify instances where punishment will be administered. Behavior contracts have the advantage of establishing the criteria for success in the setting and establishing the responsibilities of both the clients (the girls) and the therapist (the director).

14.24 Consider again Brent's fear of cats (Solved Problem 14.19). Suppose the therapist decided to use a modeling procedure in the treatment Brent received. How might this be done? Why?

Modeling involves having a client observe someone who is coping successfully with what is an anxiety-provoking situation for the client. Brent would be given the opportunity to observe a person (model) handling a cat and petting and playing with it with no fear. The belief here is that the patient can learn simply by watching the behavior of others. Brent should be more able to cope with cats by having seen what kinds of successful responses toward cats can be made.

14.25 How do cognitive therapies differ from other therapies based on learning principles?

Cognitive therapies try to change the way a client thinks, while other learning therapies focus on the actual symptoms being shown. For example, if the patient is a pedophiliac (an adult who is sexually attracted to children), a behavior therapy such as aversion therapy might be employed to alter the person's symptomatic behavior (pairing exposure to attractive pictures of children with an electric shock), while a cognitive therapy might focus on the maladaptive thought patterns (e.g., "I know an adult wouldn't be attracted to me, but I can control a child and satisfy myself that way") and try to change them.

14.26 The client says, "I know I'll never find another husband. My marriage failed. I failed. I just can't seem to make things work." How does a rational-emotive therapist respond to this?

Because rational-emotive therapists stress recognizing the irrationality of beliefs, the initial reaction is likely to emphasize the fact that one failed relationship does not mean that no relationship can be successful. The therapist might encourage the client to attempt new contacts, using new ways of thinking such as "I'll try this out and try to make it good." The idea of rational-emotive therapy is to replace dysfunctional thinking with patterns that are rational and adaptive.

14.27 A client is having trouble coping with the unexpected death of a spouse. He is depressed and finds himself unable to participate in routine daily activities. He talks with a therapist who suggests trying stress-inoculation therapy. What kind of pattern is attempted?

In stress-inoculation therapy, the client is first helped to understand the nature of the stress along with the concerns and beliefs he or she has about the situation. The therapist then helps the client develop and practice adaptive self-statements that can be used in facing the stress-producing stimuli (e.g., "Okay, stay calm when someone expresses sympathy"). Next, the client actually tries such statements in the controlled setting of the therapeutic situation as the therapist evokes mild, controlled levels of the stress. Finally, when the self-statements are well practiced, the client uses them in real-life circumstances. Assuming they work, the client experiences reinforcement and finds that he or she is able to cope with the anxieties associated with the situation.

14.28 A fairly well known book about psychotherapy deals with the experiences of a therapist attempting to help three patients, each of whom believes he is Jesus Christ. The therapist arranges to have all three meet and interact, with the hope this might help the men eliminate their delusions. What is the name given to such a therapeutic approach? What does this approach try to accomplish? Are there other varieties of this approach? What are the advantages and disadvantages of this approach?

Bringing several patients together in a therapeutic setting is called group therapy. The purpose of group therapy is the same as that of any other therapy: to help each client overcome a particular problem or problems. The rationale of group therapy is that if problems develop in a social setting, they also may be resolved in a social setting.

Other types of group therapy include family therapy and marital therapy. Group therapies typically are less expensive than individual therapy and often provide a setting of both support and pressure that helps the members resolve their problems. The disadvantages of group therapy include loss of focus and lack of attention for both the patients and the therapist.

14.29 What does it mean to say that a therapist should not abuse the power inherent in the therapeutic situation?

Because the therapist is in effect "in charge" while therapy is going on, the therapist holds a position of power over the client. If the therapist takes advantage of that power, the client may experience harm. This creates an ethical violation that is inappropriate in any therapeutic circumstance. The key concept of therapy ethics is to do no harm.

14.30 Explain what is meant by saying that a good therapist will show cultural sensitivity.

The concept that a good therapist will show cultural sensitivity indicates that the therapist must take into account characteristics such as gender, ethnicity, race, and sexual preference as variables that may govern the patterns of behavior shown by the patient. The attributes and values associated with such cultural patterns may play important roles in determining the observed behaviors and, if ignored by the therapist, may affect the therapist's ability to help the patient.

14.31 Why are "pop" psychologies almost impossible to evaluate?

"Pop" psychologies are referred to in this manner because they are popular, often found in books, magazines, and Web sites that are readily accessed at a very low cost. These approaches are difficult to evaluate because almost no research or professional writing has been devoted to them. Without controlled research, the effectiveness of these techniques is judged on the basis of anecdotal rather than scientific reports.

14.32 Why is it often difficult to determine the effectiveness of various therapies?

The effectiveness of therapies is debated for several reasons. First, the accuracy of the data collected is suspect because much of that information, especially for psychodynamic therapies, comes from case histories, which may contain biases and probably have been judged against varying criteria. Second, there is a possibility that some people show spontaneous remission (that is, they recover, but not because of the therapy). Finally, there is evidence that a placebo effect may exist for certain therapies. In such cases, it is probably the enthusiasm or determination of the client, rather than the therapy itself, which effects the cure.

Key Terms

Aversion therapy. A behavior therapy that pairs a painful or unpleasant stimulus with the inappropriate behavior.

Behavior contracting. Also called *contingency contracting*; behavior therapy in which the therapist and the patient create a contract specifying behaviors that will be rewarded.

Behavior therapies. In psychotherapy, techniques based on learning principles that deal directly with symptoms and typically are short-term and directive.

Biomedical therapies. Also called *somatic therapies*; in the treatment of abnormal behaviors, the use of physical or medical procedures.

Client-centered therapy. Proposed by Rogers and often called *nondirective therapy*; techniques that emphasize empathy, genuineness, and unconditional positive regard for the client rather than judgments of the client's behaviors.

Cognitive therapies. Also called *cognitive-behavioral therapies*; in psychotherapy, techniques that try to change the way a patient thinks rather than changing observable, symptomatic behavioral patterns.

Community psychology. A branch of psychology based on the premise that a better community attitude and greater community involvement can help prevent and/or treat abnormal behavior patterns.

Countertransference. In psychodynamic therapies, occurs when the therapist develops a strong emotional attachment (often inappropriate affection) to the client.

Dream analysis. In psychodynamic therapies, the procedure of interpreting the meaning of dreams reported by a patient.

Ego analysis. In psychodynamic therapy, an emphasis on having clients develop problem-solving skills that are adaptive; usually briefer in duration than traditional Freudian psychodynamic therapy.

Electroconvulsive therapy. Also called *shock therapy*; a medical therapy that involves passing an electric current through the patient's brain, producing convulsions of the body's muscles.

Flooding. A behavior therapy that forces the client to experience an anxiety-producing situation, pairing it with no harmful outcome, in an attempt to alleviate the symptoms associated with that situation.

Free association. A psychodynamic therapy technique in which the client says whatever comes to mind, letting each thought lead to the next.

Gestalt therapies. Psychotherapies that emphasize the patient's responsibility for behavior; based on the idea that the personality must be treated as a whole.

Group therapy. Any therapy in which more than one patient is present in the therapeutic setting at the same time.

Humanistic therapies. Psychotherapies that focus on personal growth or self-actualization.

Implosion therapy. A behavior therapy that pairs imagining the worst possible version of an anxiety-producing situation with a reassuring and secure environment in an attempt to alleviate the symptoms associated with the anxiety.

Latent content. In dream analysis, the symbolic meaning of a dream.

Manifest content. In dream analysis, the actual content of a dream.

Milieu therapy. A type of therapy that attempts to incorporate the social standards of the community into the hospital or therapeutic setting.

Paraprofessional. The designation of a person with relatively little training who works (often as a volunteer) to help individuals confront personal problems.

Placebo effect. An effect that occurs when a technique for therapy works only because the patient believes it will.

Prefrontal lobotomy. The initial form of psychosurgery, involving destruction of tissue in the frontal lobes and thalamus; thought to reduce emotionality and abnormal symptoms.

Psychiatry. A speciality of medicine concerned with the diagnosis and treatment of abnormal behaviors.

Psychoanalysis. The theory and form of therapy proposed by Freud; emphasizes personality conflicts and unconscious motivations.

Psychoanalyst. A person (usually a psychiatrist) trained to use the therapeutic techniques developed by Freud.

Psychosurgery. In the treatment of abnormal behaviors, techniques involving surgical removal of brain tissue.

Psychotherapy. In the treatment of abnormal behaviors, the use of psychological methods.

Psychotropic drugs. Substances that act on a person's mental or psychological state.

Rational-emotive therapy. A form of cognitive therapy developed by Ellis that emphasizes recognizing of irrational thinking and practicing new ways to behave or think that are more rational.

Resistance. In psychodynamic therapies, the phenomenon in which the patient does not wish to discuss a certain topic.

Spontaneous remission. Recovery from abnormal personality patterns without any therapy.

Stress-inoculation therapy. A sequential cognitive therapy developed by Meichenbaum that involves the development of strategies, the practice of those strategies in the therapeutic setting, and finally adaptation of the strategies to daily living.

Systematic desensitization. A behavior therapy that pairs relaxation with the anxiety-producing situation.

Token economy. A behavior therapy in which secondary reinforcers (tokens) are given for adaptive responding; when accumulated, these tokens can be traded for privileges or rewards.

Transference. In psychodynamic therapies, the phenomenon in which the patient develops a strong emotional attachment (reminiscent of an earlier emotional attachment) to the therapist.

CHAPTER 15

Social Psychology

Psychology is concerned primarily with the study of individual behavior, but the influence of group membership on an individual cannot be ignored. *Social psychology* is the study of an individual's behavior as it is influenced by membership in a group.

15.1 SOCIAL KNOWLEDGE

Just as in other areas of behavior, individuals are likely to categorize or structure knowledge about social relations. In this process, social categories and social schemas are developed and then influence behaviors. Some of the principles that affect social knowledge are explored in this section.

Social Categories and Schemas.   Attempts to simplify and organize one's social world lead to the development of social categories and social schemas. A *social category* characterizes or groups people in ways that make it easier to understand or explain the social world. When such categories are used, the social world can be organized by creating *social schemas*, which represent feelings and beliefs about the people being considered. Social schemas often foster *social scripts*, or ways of acting based on the schemas that have been created.

EXAMPLE 15.1.   Consider getting on an almost empty bus. You know none of the people on that bus yet walk down the aisle and take a seat next to one of them. It is likely that you have violated the accepted social script for bus riding (and perhaps caused some anxiety for the person you sat beside). The typical social schema for this situation says that adjacent seats are not used by "strangers" until the bus is full enough to warrant this action.

Often, social schemas are formed about oneself. Such *self-schemas* are the components of one's *self-concept*, the beliefs and feelings people have about themselves. Many aspects of self-concept affect daily behaviors. Several have been studied and labeled.

Self-referencing refers to situations in which a person is better able to remember something about someone else if that information relates in some way to himself or herself. One's self-concept is important in affecting not only personal behavior but the ways in which a person relates to others.

The *self-fulfilling prophecy* is another example of self-concept being affected by social influence. The expectations of others about future behaviors lead to a greater probability that the expected behaviors will occur. When the behaviors do occur, *behavioral confirmation* is said to have been shown.

EXAMPLE 15.2.   Imagine two groups of high school students who are given a lengthy word problem in algebra. One group is told that the solution to the problem will be time-consuming but easy because it involves only a rudimentary knowledge of mathematics. (This description of the problem is accurate.) The other group is told that problem is a real "brainteaser" that often is given to graduate students in mathematics. Such descriptions easily could create a self-fulfilling prophecy: The students in the second group are likely to perform less well on the problem than are those in the first group because of the expectations created by the false description.

Attributions.   *Attributions* are attempts to explain the causes of behavior. Three dimensions of causal attributions have been studied extensively. The first is whether the behavior can be attributed to an *internal* (or *personal*) cause or to an *external* (or *situational*) one. The second is whether the behavior can be attributed to a *stable* or *unstable* cause, and the third is whether the behavior can be attributed to a *controllable* cause or an *uncontrollable* one.

EXAMPLE 15.3.   Consider the classic case of getting a bad grade on an exam. An internal attribution would lead to a comment such as "Well, I deserved it. I really didn't study much." By contrast, an external attribution might produce the statement "I didn't have a chance. I was really sick that day with a bad cold." An attribution reflecting stability might take the form of "Math is always tough for me," while an attribution suggesting unstable conditions could create the comment "That was a one-time thing. I know I'll do better on the next exam." Finally, attributing the exam grade to a controllable cause could yield the statement "I had the chance. I just didn't study enough," versus an explanation reflecting lack of control, such as "He wrote the most impossible exam. I could have studied forever and never passed it!"

Attributions determine how people react to themselves and to others. Interpretations based on the internal-external, stable-unstable, and controllable-uncontrollable dimensions produce beliefs and feelings that produce expectations about the future and affect subsequent behaviors.

Attribution Biases.   A number of forms of *attribution biases* serve as interpretations of causes that reveal how people view their worlds. The *self-serving bias* is an excellent example of this: Attribution of one's successes is made to internal or personal causes, while attribution of poor outcomes or failures is made to external or situational events.

EXAMPLE 15.4.   One college administrator was known to comment on any success in his unit by starting with, "Well, I decided that . . ." and then describing the success of the group. When something went wrong in his unit, however, the usual start to his explanation was, "Well, you know, the committee voted that . . ." and the subsequent explanation was attributed to causes external to him.

In Western society particularly, there is an overwhelming tendency to stress internal or personal explanations, especially for the responses of others. This is called the *fundamental attribution error*. The exaggeration of the importance of dispositional or personal causes of behavior, rather than environmental or situational factors, probably results from the availability of information about the person as opposed to information about the situation. The fundamental attribution error often is linked with what is called *correspondence bias*, the tendency to assume that people's behaviors correspond to their attitudes and intentions.

Another variation of attribution bias has been called the *halo effect*. If the initial description of a person is very positive, any subsequent interpretation of that person's behavior is likely to be positive even if there is evidence to the contrary. A reverse pattern, or negative halo effect, can occur when the initial description is very negative.

Attribution bias also is seen in what is called *assumed-similarity bias*, also called the *false consensus bias*. In this case someone else's characteristics are assumed to match one's own even when one is meeting that person for the first time. Similar to the halo effect, assumed similarity or false consensus means that what the other person does will be interpreted according to one's own beliefs or attitudes and that the other person will be expected to act the way the interpreter acts.

Finally, the *actor-observer bias* refers to situations in which the person making the interpretation either is involved in the behavior or simply is watching it. Some of the other biases mentioned above may combine with this as interpretations are made.

EXAMPLE 15.5.   Sitting in the dormitory room and looking out the window, Alphonse notices a fellow student slip and nearly fall on the sidewalk below. His reaction is to say, "Look at Roseanne. What a clumsy clutz she is!" When Alphonse leaves for class the next hour, he also almost falls and immediately responds, "Boy, it's really slippery today!" The difference between observing the behavior and actually performing the response combines with internal or external thoughts to determine what he says. Alphonse's responses also reflect the self-serving bias and probably the fundamental attribution error.

One other form of bias deserves mention. Called *self-handicapping*, it refers to situations where a person actually creates conditions to prevent the successful completion of a task so that there will be a "built-in" excuse for failure.

EXAMPLE 15.6.   Anthony joins many student organizations, spends many hours doing volunteer work, and then attributes grades that are less than he is capable of achieving to "not having enough time to study." While he indeed may not have enough time for studying, he has deliberately chosen to act in ways that have created the conditions that prevent studying. This probably reflects self-handicapping.

Cognitive Consistency and Cognitive Dissonance.   Another aspect of social knowledge has to do with the consistency or conflict associated with social thinking. Many theorists believe that people wish to maintain some *cognitive consistency*, having a social world that is predictable. Actions are based on previous social experiences, with the assumption that those actions will lead to results similar to the ones experienced before.

It is possible that exposure to a particular stimulus may occur under more than one set of conditions. If these conditions differ significantly, the person may learn conflicting attitudes toward that stimulus, resulting in what has been called *cognitive dissonance*. Just as with other conflict situations, a person will try to reduce the cognitive dissonance, often by changing one of the two beliefs to bring it more "in line" with the other. This, of course, will yield better cognitive consistency.

EXAMPLE 15.7.   Suppose Norma has had a great desire to attend a rock concert in a city about 90 miles from her home. She has worked extra hours to save enough money to be able to afford the ticket, transportation, and time off from her job. Finally, the night of the show arrives. However, the featured group is very late, plays poorly, and uses a bad sound system. Furthermore, the weather is rotten. Norma is now quite disappointed.

The next day, when she is asked if the show was worth all the effort she devoted to be able to see it, Norma answers by saying that the show was pretty bad, but she really hadn't made such a special effort to be able to see it. Her "playing down" of her extra labors may be viewed as an attempt to reduce cognitive dissonance. Admitting that the show was poor means that it was not worth much effort. Therefore, Norma reinterprets her previous behaviors to fit better with the result.

It also must be noted that dissonance sometimes produces *justification* in that by acting in a certain manner, a person creates a reasonable explanation for doing so even when the behavior is in conflict with previously held values. The phrase "doing is believing" is used to represent what happens.

EXAMPLE 15.8.   A person who continues to smoke cigarettes despite knowing the possible health risks may justify the smoking behavior by claiming that it helps reduce the stress in her job. She may make comments to herself such as, "I'll just take a cigarette break. It'll calm me down, and I'll be able to work better."

15.2   ATTITUDES

A major aspect of social psychology is the study of *attitudes*, which are learned evaluative reactions to people, objects, events, and other stimuli. This section considers the development of attitudes as well as ways to change attitudes.

The ABC Definition of Attitudes.   An easy way to remember the components of an attitude is to use an "ABC" interpretation. The *A* refers to the *affective component* of an attitude, the feeling or emotional reaction the individual has toward the stimulus. Affective reactions may be positive or negative. The *B* component is the *behavioral* aspect, the actions—either favorable or unfavorable—which the person may take toward the stimulus, while the *C* represents the *cognitive component*, the beliefs, perceptions, or thoughts the individual holds about the stimulus.

EXAMPLE 15.9. The stimulus in question need not be a tangible or visible one, such as a person, group of people, or institution; it may be an abstract stimulus such as the idea of education. It is very possible for a person to develop a positive feeling toward education (affective component) based on the belief that everyone can benefit from education (cognitive component). That person might well make a contribution to a local educational institution (behavioral component). This example pictures a favorable reaction to or attitude about education. It should be recognized, however, that others might hold exactly opposite attitudes that involve a negative feeling, no belief in the benefits of education, and actions that would work against an educational institution. Both types of attitudes would be learned, evaluative reactions to the stimulus.

Attitude Formation.   Attitudes are learned through classical conditioning, operant conditioning, and modeling. Sources of reinforcement and influence include parents, peers, educators, and the mass media. Research has indicated that people tend to seek information that fits with already existing schemas; this is referred to as *confirmatory hypothesis testing*, and in effect it "sets the stage" for attitudes that will be learned and maintained.

EXAMPLE 15.10. Upon retiring, Frank is asked why he is not moving from his current residence to one in a more moderate climate. Frank's response is, "I can handle the winter, but there's lots of dangerous weather in the South. Didn't you hear about that big hurricane in Florida? What about those tornadoes in Texas? It's not safe to live in the South." Frank's selection of information appears to support the idea of confirmatory hypothesis testing; it would be just as easy to present a different set of examples that would make living in the North seem dangerous and living in the South seem safe.

Attitude Change.   Trying to change attitudes has been called *persuasion*. Important variables that facilitate or hinder attitude change have been studied extensively. Four of the most important variables are the source of the message (the communicator), the message itself, the situation in which the message is presented, and the characteristics of the person receiving the message.

One of the most important factors in trying to change a person's attitudes is the source of the message or persuasion. Three factors found to be significant are how *credible* (or *believable*) the source appears to be, how *attractive* and *likable* the source is judged to be, and how much *power* or *prestige* the source seems to have. Maximizing these factors, for instance, by using a source judged to be honest, sincere, expert, and attractive, should lead to a high probability of accomplishing attitude change.

EXAMPLE 15.11. In the early 1960s, President John F. Kennedy combined the three factors of being believable, attractive, and in a position of power. He did this so well, in fact, that many of his followers accepted his statements without criticism. Later historical evaluations have shown that some of his judgments may not have been as good as they seemed at the time, when Kennedy's personality made them completely acceptable to large numbers of people.

Another important factor is the type of message being presented. In general, if the recipient (the person being persuaded) is already in favor of the communicator's message, a *one-sided argument* appears most effective in solidifying or increasing that favorable belief. However, if the recipient appears to have a negative attitude toward the message, a *two-sided argument* may be more effective, presenting both the communicator's position and the one being argued against. A two-sided argument is thought to be successful in such situations because it seems thoughtful and precise. Another consideration is the use of *fear* in a message. Fear-producing messages generally are found to be quite effective as long as the fear produced is not too strong, in which case the message tends to be ignored. Fear messages also work better when accompanied by specific recommendations about how to avoid the dangerous stimulus.

Research also has shown that simply being exposed repeatedly to the desired message or the person or object being considered may be enough to change one's attitude. This has been called the *mere exposure effect*.

Attitude change is a cognitive process. The *elaboration-likelihood model* explains the effects of persuasion by evaluating how people process the information being provided. This model suggests that there are two modes of processing. *Central processing* occurs when messages are carefully examined. The recipient typically is attentive and interested in the message being presented, is analytical and critical, and shows effortful processing. Although creating attitude change is more difficult to accomplish in this manner, the person will be persuaded by a high-quality argument and will be likely to sustain the attitude change over a period of time. In contrast, *peripheral processing* does not involve careful examination of the information being presented. The recipient often is distracted and uninterested, processes the information relatively automatically, and may be more easily persuaded, although the change in attitude is less likely to endure.

EXAMPLE 15.12.   Therapists who work with patients who have eating disorders frequently see the effects of peripheral processing creating attitude change. One therapist reported a group session with young women in which every member of the group, when presented with a picture of Marilyn Monroe, described her as being far too fat, using derogatory terms such as "cow," "pig," and "fatso." The therapist attributed those responses to the repetitive persuasive messages stressing thinness found in the mass media, believing the patients had processed such messages in a careless and automatic manner.

15.3 PREJUDICE

A *prejudice* is a learned reaction that is overgeneralized and unjustified. Although a prejudice may be thought of as a positive or favorable reaction, most research centers on unfavorable or negative attitudes. Prejudices are thought to represent *antisocial* behaviors. This section concentrates on prejudices as unfavorable attitudes or biases.

Note: In discussing prejudice, the term *discrimination* often is used. Psychologists tend to distinguish between the two terms by thinking of prejudice as the thoughts or feelings one holds, while *discrimination* is actual biased treatment of or actions against a group of people.

EXAMPLE 15.13.   Many jokes have prejudices as a basis. "Dumb blonde" jokes, by including all blond women as their targets, are overgeneralized. Because they ignore evidence to the contrary, these jokes are unjustified. A statement such as "Some people make dumb responses" would not be considered prejudiced because it is both limited and justified by evidence.

Developing a Prejudice.   Prejudices are developed and maintained in the same way as other learned responses. It is interesting to note that modeling may be the most important source for learning a prejudice. In other words, a prejudice is likely to be learned from someone who is prejudiced rather than from actual contact with the stimulus against which the prejudice is held.

Once developed, prejudices are supported by occasional reinforcements, thus demonstrating the partial reinforcement effect. Occasional or infrequent support for a prejudice, in the manner of confirmatory hypothesis testing, is enough to make the prejudice very resistant to extinction.

Stereotypes.   The term *stereotype* is used frequently to describe the prejudiced beliefs shown by an individual. A *stereotype* can be defined as an oversimplified and relatively rigid schema applied to a person or group of people. The same characteristics are attributed to all the members of a group regardless of how much variation the members of the group actually show.

EXAMPLE 15.14.   Did you notice in Example 15.13 that the reference to "dumb blonde" jokes also attributed the behavior to women? This is an example of a stereotype, assigning the characteristics to all the members of a particular group. Think about making "dumb blond men" jokes—is there any likelihood of doing so? The stereotype is not only oversimplified but also quite rigid, applying only to women and not to men.

Stereotypes often are expressed in terms of *in-group* or *out-group* affiliation. Groups with which one identifies are called *in-groups*, while *out-groups* are "the others." The formation of in-groups and out-groups changes the attribution process, as does changing membership from one group to the other. Psychologists often designate the attitude expressed toward the out-group as *out-group homogeneity bias*, representing an assumption that members of the out-group are more alike than are members of the in-group. This interpretation helps solidify the attitudes held in a prejudice.

Note: While a stereotype is a generalization about all the members of a group, psychologists usually think of a prejudice as an attitude about an individual, based on that individual's membership in a group.

EXAMPLE 15.15.   Recent health campaigns have created the conditions for in-group and out-group affiliation. "Smokers" and "nonsmokers" frequently use stereotyped remarks to describe the other (out-) group. Moving from one group to the other is accompanied by a change in perception and an accompanying change in the evaluation of each group. Comments such as "Anyone who smokes is just stupid!" illustrate out-group homogeneity bias.

One explanation for prejudice and discrimination is called the *social identity theory*. This theory suggests that group membership supports a sense of pride and self-worth. The accompanying prejudicial behaviors occur when the members of the group seek not just identity but the feeling of being *better* than others. Positive aspects of the in-group are inflated, and negative aspects of the out-group are stressed, so that the out-group ultimately is judged as being inferior.

15.4   INTERPERSONAL ATTRACTION

It is possible to consider interpersonal attraction from either a "like" or a "dislike" position, but this section concentrates on why one person is attracted to (or likes) another. The concept of disliking another person usually is studied as a part of prejudice, the topic dealt with in the preceding section.

Arousal.   Interpersonal attraction appears to be influenced by *arousal*. Typically, higher levels of arousal, such as those produced by physical exercise or an anxiety-provoking situation, lead to a greater possibility of attraction to someone met while one is in that aroused state compared to a nonaroused condition.

Proximity.   *Proximity*, the real or perceived distance between one person and another, has been found to be a very important determinant of interpersonal attraction. In general, the greater the real or perceived distance between two people (or groups) is, the less likely it is that interpersonal attraction will develop.

EXAMPLE 15.16.   The lyrics of a popular song include the line "Love the one you're with." College students often find that this applies to their daily situation: If the companion with whom they have been going out is attending another school, it often is much easier to maintain a relationship with someone who is nearby. Proximity influences attraction and dating; long-distance relationships are hard to preserve.

Similarity.   Repeated research studies investigating the correlation of characteristics shared by friends, married partners, and other people with positive interpersonal attractions have shown that these correlations are fairly high. This means that people with similar characteristics often are attracted to each other. This holds for sociological characteristics (such as socioeconomic status, education, and subcultural group) and physical characteristics (such as height, hair color, and skin color).

Concerns with similarity have been studied as *equity theory* and as *balance theory*. Equity theory suggests that people are attracted to others who "take" at about the same level at which they "give." Attraction or a subsequent relationship will fail when one person feels the other is taking far more than giving. Balance theory proposes that people try to maintain the sense of giving and taking in interactions, that is, act to sustain reciprocity or equity.

Complementarity.   Somewhat the opposite of similarity, *complementarity* occurs when two people have dissimilar characteristics that blend nicely and form the basis for interpersonal attraction. (For example, a dominant person and a submissive person may get along well because each fulfills the other's needs.) It should be recognized that both must agree that the dissimilarity is a good foundation for a relationship.

EXAMPLE 15.17.   A marriage in which the husband believes that the way one does the laundry is to throw dirty clothes on the floor succeeds only if the wife accepts the complementary attitude that she should pick up the clothes, launder them, and put them back in the appropriate places. If she is unwilling to accept that role, changes in attitude and behavior will have to occur for the relationship to continue positively.

Physical Attractiveness.   Another factor that helps determine interpersonal attraction is *physical attractiveness*. People who are judged to be physically attractive frequently are better liked than are those rated as unattractive. This judgment of attractiveness may influence other people to perceive additional positive qualities in the attractive person, an example of the *halo effect*.

EXAMPLE 15.18.   The attractiveness of a person may lead others to expect a certain kind of behavior from that person. Thus, if a man is very handsome, people may expect him to be charming also, and they may perceive such charm regardless of whether it actually is one of the man's characteristics.

Love.   All the variables described above for interpersonal attraction seem to influence the possibility of "falling in love." Psychologists have difficulty defining the differences between attraction and love, but *love* is thought to represent stronger or deeper feelings than mere attraction.

Robert Sternberg has labeled three basic components of love: (1) *intimacy*, or feelings of closeness and connection, (2) *passion*, an intense desire for union with another, and (3) *commitment*, the decision to sustain a relationship over a long period of time. Sternberg proposes that *consummate love*, or complete love, occurs when the individuals involved are high in all three components. Other categories of love show high values for one or two of the three basic components but not for all three. For example, *infatuated love* is high in passion but low in the other two components, while *companionate love* has the opposite values for the three components.

EXAMPLE 15.19.   Loving one's parents usually is described as a companionate relationship. Such love involves closeness and has a long duration but does not include passion. By contrast, infatuation typically involves only desire; it changes to *romantic love* when closeness or connection occurs and intimacy is added to the relationship.

15.5 GROUP BEHAVIOR

It should be recognized that almost every person's behavior is influenced by membership in groups almost all the time. Some of these groups are *formal*, with designated titles and rules. Other groups are *informal*; they are organized casually and have unwritten (and perhaps very flexible) rules. The groups also may be *present*, with members actually physically present in the person's environment, or *absent*, which occurs when other people are not physically present but association with the members remains an important influence on a person's behavior.

EXAMPLE 15.20.   Adam is affiliated with a religion that proscribes the use of any caffeinated beverage. He attends a gathering where he is offered a cup of coffee. He refuses politely. In doing so, Adam is influenced by the beliefs he holds as part of his formal membership in a particular church. The influence of his group membership is important even though other group members are not present at the moment.

Socialization and Cultural Relativity.   As an individual grows up within a given culture, family, school, peers, and the community at large furnish many influences that help establish the values and norms by which the individual lives. This rather general process, which is called *socialization*, seems to result from both modeling and the reinforcement of what are considered appropriate behaviors.

The process of socialization establishes values and norms that affect daily living. However, it must be recognized that the values and norms may be appropriate only for the particular culture or subculture. The principle of *cultural relativity* proposes that behavior must be judged according to the cultural setting in which it occurs.

EXAMPLE 15.21.   One difference between American and certain European cultures can be seen in the ways in which men greet each other. American men typically greet each other with a handshake (which may have several different variations, depending on the subculture involved). In some European countries, men kiss each other on both cheeks when they meet after a long separation. What is considered appropriate and ordinary in one culture may be considered out of the ordinary in another.

Social Facilitation and Social Interference.   The presence of others may influence one's performance of a task. If the presence of others seems to improve performance, *social facilitation* has taken place. *Social interference*, which sometimes is called *social inhibition*, occurs when the presence of others seems to impair performance. Quite frequently, social facilitation will occur when the person is performing a task that is quite well learned, while social interference may be more likely when the person is performing a task that has not been learned well.

EXAMPLE 15.22.   The amount of experience a person has had in teaching often is reflected by the style with which a lecture is delivered. A "rookie" teacher who is comfortable when practicing or rehearsing at home may have difficulties with pronunciation, remembering a sequence of topics, or answering questions when in front of the class. A "veteran" teacher, by comparison, actually may relax in class and be more personable and confident in teaching situations than in nonteaching situations. The new teacher's difficulties illustrate social interference, while the experienced teacher's abilities illustrate social facilitation.

Conformity.   Some behaviors are established by group opinion. A person who behaves according to the expectations of a group shows *conformity*. A person who recognizes the expectations of a group but chooses to act in the opposite fashion shows *nonconformity*. A person whose behavior is not influenced one way or the other by social expectations shows *independence*.

In general, conformity is more likely to occur when the group being followed is attractive to the person being influenced, when the response being made is public rather than private, when the task is ambiguous, and when the group shows unanimity. Conformity is reduced when there is even one *social supporter* who advocates a different opinion that is closer to the one originally held by the person being influenced rather than the opinion of the rest of the group.

EXAMPLE 15.23.   Group opinion often exerts a powerful effect on styles of dress. Some will "catch on" if many people conform to the style of the moment; for example, wearing caps has become very popular. In the fashion industry, financial success depends to a large degree on how many people will conform to a new style or "look." Many manufacturers made large profits by making caps because the level of conformity was so high.

Compliance and Obedience.   For conformity, psychologists usually think of the social pressure as being relatively indirect or subtle. However, when there is direct, obvious pressure to choose a particular pattern of behavior or endorse a particular opinion, *compliance* is expected. Even with compliance, the pressures are not as great as those found in *obedience* circumstances, where the person being influenced is expected to follow a direct command.

Obedience is most likely to take place when the person giving the command is seen as someone in authority who has a legitimate reason for making the command. The surprising results of studies indicate that subjects who believe they have little or no choice in responding (even if they are told they do have a choice) are likely to obey. It seems that if subjects can attribute responsibility for their actions to another person who is judged to be superior or in authority, they will do as they are told even if their actions may be potentially harmful to someone else.

Group Dynamics.   The social interactions that occur within groups have been summarized under the heading *group dynamics*. Research on group dynamics has focused on variables such as the effect of the size of a group, leadership, perceived responsibilities, and loss of personal identity within a group. This section explores some of the variables that have received the most research attention.

Group Size.   Any gathering of two or more people can be thought of as a group. The size of the group appears to affect many of the social interactions that will develop within it. Researchers have found, for example, that when a group consists of three people, the interactions often create a "two-against-one" situation.

Larger groups frequently produce *diffusion of responsibility*, in which any one person takes less responsibility than he or she would assume if acting alone. One form of diffusion of responsibility has been called *social loafing*, which occurs when larger groups produce less than the expected result because each member tends to contribute less than maximum effort to the task at hand. Another form is labeled *bystander apathy*; this involves circumstances where any one individual is less likely to help a victim when others are present, assuming that the others will act.

EXAMPLE 15.24.   The incident that provoked the initial research into bystander apathy was the killing of a young woman in New York City. More than 30 people admitted having witnessed some or all of the incident, yet not one went to the woman's aid or even called the police. When interviewed later, they stated that they felt "someone else" could or would take that responsibility. Research studies under controlled conditions have confirmed that this type of behavior is common in many groups.

Prosocial Behavior and Aggression.   Group dynamics also are looked at in regard to both *prosocial* (helping) *behaviors* and *aggression*, or intentional attempts to harm. The evidence presented above shows that prosocial behavior may be more likely to occur when an individual is acting alone. However, group dynamics also may encourage such behaviors, for example, when one participates with a group having the designated purpose of helping. One form of prosocial behavior has been labeled *altruism*, helping behavior that is beneficial to others but clearly involves individual self-sacrifice with no hope of reciprocity.

EXAMPLE 15.25.   Natural disasters such as hurricanes, tornadoes, and floods often produce evidence of altruism. People volunteer to help those who have been affected, knowing there is no possible payback for the efforts they make.

At least three explanations have been put forth to explain aggressive interactions within a group. One suggests that aggression is instinctual and occurs as an attempt to achieve *catharsis*, or the release of built-up aggressive tendencies. A second proposes that aggression results from experiencing frustration; that is, frustration leads to anger, which in turn produces aggression. A third states that aggression is learned through modeling. Seeing others have seeming successes by being aggressive leads the observer to attempt to make the same kinds of responses.

Group Polarization.   Studies have shown that groups tend to make more extreme decisions than any one member of the group would make if acting alone. This has been called *group polarization* and operates toward both possible types of decisions, either more risky or more conservative. The direction chosen usually reflects the initial position of the group. If it first favors a fairly risky position, the group will be more likely to adopt even greater risk; if the initial position is conservative, the later decisions will be even more conservative.

A relatively extreme version of group polarization has been called *groupthink*. In this case the members of a group create an atmosphere that dominates the thoughts or opinions of all the members.

Characteristically, the members of such a group believe the group's opinions are invulnerable to outside criticism, a situation referred to as an *illusion of invulnerability*. The apparent unanimity of the members' opinions is enough to convince them of their inherent rightness in spite of evidence to the contrary. Evidence opposing their viewpoint may be ignored, and dissenters may be urged to change their viewpoints to conform with that of the group.

EXAMPLE 15.26.   During the early part of World War II, the "groupthink" phenomenon was observed in the behaviors of some Americans of German descent. People who were otherwise firm in their admiration for democracy and justice would meet to extoll the virtues of the changes taking place in Germany. They also tried to encourage other German-Americans to accept those beliefs and became upset with the ones who did not. As more information about the conduct of the war became available, these people simply could (or would) not believe the reports. It was not until late in the war, when the evidence was overwhelming, that they were persuaded to change their thinking about the Nazi regime.

Deindividuation.   Psychologists have investigated why individuals in groups act in manners they would never adopt if asked to act alone. This loss of individuality and reduction of constraints against unacceptable behaviors has been termed *deindividuation*. Although this usually is thought to involve negative forms of social behavior, there are studies showing that more positive responses also are produced in certain forms of deindividuation.

EXAMPLE 15.27.   When asked if they really wanted to see the person jump from the building and commit suicide, many individuals who had participated in chanting "Jump, jump, jump" while watching in a group on the sidewalk below replied, "Oh, no. Of course not." Being in the group apparently created a sense of deindividuation and prompted participation in the chanting even though the values expressed were contrary to personal belief.

Solved Problems

15.1   How is social psychology related to sociology and to other aspects of psychology?

Social psychology is the study of an individual's behavior as it is influenced by membership in a group. Sociology typically studies the behaviors of groups as units. Other aspects of psychology look at individual behaviors but often study those behaviors as independent from the influences of others.

15.2   Distinguish between social categories and social scripts. Then explain how both relate to social schemas. Give an example that illustrates these topics.

A social category is a way of classifying a group of people. Social scripts are patterns for behavior used in the social environment. Social categories often form the basis for social schemas, the feelings and beliefs held about the people being classified. Social schemas establish the conditions by which social scripts are formed.

"Teenage punks" is a social category employed by some people to characterize groups that wear certain clothes, "decorate" themselves with body piercings or tattoos, and listen to certain types of music. The reaction to these people may be positive or negative, forming a social schema for the observer. Based on that schema, the observer may approach the group if the reaction is positive or avoid interactions with the group if the reaction is negative.

15.3   Mitchell is a very bright 10-year-old. He has been encouraged by his teachers to pursue special classes related to art, being told, "You're really a good drawer. You can be a great artist." What principle describes why, if Mitchell hears such remarks repeatedly, he will be likely to show success in the field of art?

Psychologists explain Mitchell's situation by referring to the self-fulfilling prophecy, in which the expectations of others lead to a greater probability that the expected behaviors will occur. The more Mitchell hears people say he will do well in art, the more likely it is that he will, and his excellent drawings will provide behavioral confirmation of those expectations.

15.4   What is self-referencing? Create an example that illustrates this principle.

Self-referencing refers to the finding that a person often is better able to remember something about another individual if that information relates to the first person in some way. Asked if she remembers a classmate from high school, Karen responds by saying, "Do I remember Diane? You bet. She's the one who forced a cop off the road one day in driver's education. I thought we were going to crash, and I was really scared. Diane was *not* the best driver."

15.5   Called at home one evening, Vernon's parents are asked to come to the police station to get their 14-year-old son, who has been arrested for drinking alcoholic beverages. The next morning Vernon's school principal asks the parents, "Why did Vernon go drinking?" They respond, "Well, it's really not his fault. The other guys got hold of some booze and talked him into it. He doesn't do stuff like this." Using your understanding of attributions, analyze the response the parents gave.

Attributions are attempts to explain the causes of behaviors. Vernon's parents attribute Vernon's behavior to the influence of others, claiming that this was so strong that Vernon had no choice and that his drinking was unlikely to be a repetitive pattern. This attribution would be classified as being external (not Vernon's internal characteristics but the influence of the group), uncontrollable (so strong that he had no choice), and unstable (not a typical pattern but a one-time thing).

15.6   Suppose, rather than drinking with the guys, Vernon had called his parents and asked them to come get him, thus avoiding being arrested. When asked the next morning how Vernon made such a good decision, what kind of response might his parents give if their response illustrated the self-serving bias?

The self-serving bias attributes good results to internal or personal variables, while attribution of poor results is made to external or situational events. Vernon's parents might comment, "We taught Vernon to be responsible, and he showed that he learned our lessons. We're really proud of the boy." Vernon's actions are attributed to the personal variables of the parents when they make such a response; credit for a good action is taken to be a function of their personal values.

15.7   When she heard that Bob's house had burned to the ground the night before, Alicia's initial comment was, "Probably just careless. You know how careless Bob can be. He's always leaving things in dangerous places." Alicia is embarrassed later when she finds out that an electrical short caused the fire. What principle explains Alicia's original comment?

The overwhelming tendency to attribute the behaviors of others to internal or personal characteristics is called the *fundamental attribution error*. Particularly common in Western societies, this tendency is likely to result from having more information about the person than about the circumstances. That is the case here, where later investigation provides an external or situational explanation for what happened.

15.8   Vernon, who was introduced in Solved Problem 15.5, has always been on the A/B Honor Role in school. Teachers and the parents of his classmates have described Vernon in "glowing terms," often using him as a model for others to copy. If, after he is arrested for drinking, Vernon is still described in positive terms, what principle appears to apply?

Continuing to describe Vernon in positive terms even when there is evidence to the contrary is explained by the halo effect. In such circumstances, it may take the accumulation of quite a bit of negative evidence before descriptions of Vernon will change.

15.9   Explain the concept of actor-observer bias. How is this frequently linked with the fundamental attribution error?

Actor-observer bias refers to whether the person making the attribution is participating in the event being considered or is merely watching someone else's actions. Differing attributions seem to arise depending on how much involvement in the situation the person has. Quite often, if the person *is* involved, the attribution will be to external or situational causes. If the person is only observing, the attribution is more likely to reflect interpretations of the personal characteristics of the person being observed. This pattern is a common one in Western societies and has been described as the fundamental attribution error.

15.10   Standing on the first tee, Sandy complains about the "horrible work schedule" that has kept him from practicing for the last two weeks. "I probably have no chance to play well," he says. How do Sandy's comments provide evidence for self-handicapping?

Self-handicapping refers to situations where an individual actually creates conditions that prevent the successful completion of a task. It may be that, knowing this big golf game was coming up, Sandy intentionally planned a very busy work schedule for the preceding weeks, providing a ready excuse for why he will not be able to play well.

15.11   Mark has had heart trouble. He believes that drinking beer is bad for him but likes beer very much. On occasion Mark has a glass of beer with dinner. Explain what it means to say that Mark experiences cognitive dissonance when this occurs. What resolution to that cognitive dissonance might take place?

Mark is experiencing conflicting attitudes toward the same stimulus: beer. Such conflict is described as cognitive dissonance, that is, having two contrasting beliefs about a single stimulus. In this case, if he continues to drink beer despite his heart ailment, Mark probably will try to reduce the dissonance by thinking, "I'm not really *that* ill," or "An *occasional* beer can't hurt."

15.12   What does it mean to say that attitudes are explained "as easily as ABC"?

A simple way to remember what psychologists say about attitudes is to use an ABC explanation. *A* refers to the affective component of attitudes, the feelings or emotional reactions a person has about the stimulus or event being considered. *B* identifies the behavioral component, the favorable or unfavorable responses the individual makes to the stimulus or event. The *C* component is the cognitive one, representing the beliefs, perceptions, or thoughts the person has toward the stimulus or event.

15.13   Why is it that attitudes about new stimuli or events seem to match attitudes already held?

Most people tend to seek information that fits with already existing schemas. Called *confirmatory hypothesis testing*, such behavior creates the conditions for the attitudes to be learned.

15.14   Using the four factors described as being important in persuasion, create the conditions that are most likely to bring about a change in attitude.

To create "ideal" conditions for persuasion, conditions would have to maximize each of the following: (1) The communicator presenting the message should be credible or believable, attractive and likable, and a person in a position of prestige or power, (2) the message should be geared correctly to the audience receiving it—one-sided if the audience already holds a similar position but two-sided if the recipients appear to hold a negative attitude about the topic being considered, (3) the situation should be arranged to be neither too restricted (allowing careful analysis of the message) nor too distracting (preventing reception of the message), and (4) the person should be processing the message in a manner most consonant with the persuasion desired (see also Solved Problem 15.16). The closer one can come to these conditions, the more likely persuasion is to occur.

15.15 Camp directors often arrange housing for the campers so that children from different backgrounds live with each other. This is done with the hope that the children will learn to get along with each other. What principle of persuasion supports such decisions?

The principle applied here is the mere exposure effect. Simply being exposed to people with differing backgrounds may be enough to change one's attitude about the group or groups represented by those people. The camp directors are likely to produce understanding and harmony within the camp merely by creating groups that mix campers with different backgrounds.

15.16 The answer to Solved Problem 15.14 mentions processing the message in a manner most consonant with the persuasion being sought. What model deals with the processing of persuasive messages? What are the general principles put forth by this model?

The explanation of persuasive message processing is found in the elaboration-likelihood model. The model suggests two modes of processing: central and peripheral. Central processing refers to careful, analytical, effortful processing that is likely to produce an attitude change that will endure. Peripheral processing is casual, often distracted, relatively automatic processing that may lead to relatively easy momentary persuasion that does not endure.

15.17 What is similar about prejudice and discrimination? What is different?

Although positive reactions could be occurring, prejudice and discrimination typically are thought to depend on negative or antisocial attitudes. Prejudice refers to the thoughts or feelings an individual holds about a person or group of people, while discrimination refers to actual biased treatment or actions an individual makes against that person or group.

15.18 Pulling into a parking space, Scott and Kellie see a teenage girl in a nearby car throw a wad of gum onto the pavement of the parking lot. Disgusted, Kellie turns to Scott and says, "Gum chewers are really slobs, aren't they?" Scott, who chews gum occasionally, replies, "I chew gum sometimes, and I'm not a slob, am I?" How does Kellie respond? Explain your answer by using principles related to stereotyping.

Kellie might answer, "Well, you are the exception to the rule!" Her answer actually may be the reverse of what is correct. Most gum chewers may dispose of their gum in tidy ways, but Kellie focuses on the relatively few instances that support her belief. This is an example of the partial reinforcement effect, and it means that her belief is likely to be very resistant to extinction. The stereotype she holds is oversimplified and relatively rigid, attributing the same characteristics to all the members of the group (gum chewers) no matter what the evidence shows.

15.19 Create an in-group/out-group example that supports the social identity theory as an explanation of prejudice and discrimination.

Social identity theory suggests that prejudice and discrimination occur because the individual feels a need to be part of a group that is *better than* some other group. The in-group with which the individual identifies is evaluated as having characteristics that are superior to those of some other group, the out-group. In-group membership thus can be a source of pride and a means of establishing self-worth.

Gang membership often is interpreted in this manner; joining a gang lets the member take pride in that membership and devalue the members of other, rival groups.

15.20 Joanne's mother has tried to encourage her to date Dennis, a young man who lives in the next community. Joanne is more interested in Tony, who lives nearby. A very simple but very important principle seems to explain Joanne's preference for Tony. What is it?

Joanne's choice of Tony rather than Dennis may reflect the principle of proximity, or nearness. In general, people are more attracted to those who live near them as opposed to those who live at a greater distance. This principle holds for both actual distance and "perceived" distance, perhaps because proximity allows greater familiarity, which in turn leads to attraction.

15.21 Two old-fashioned sayings are "Birds of a feather flock together" and "Opposites attract." Both may sound sensible, but they are contradictory. Which one is correct? Are they both correct? What principles explain these sayings?

Both sayings may be correct. Interpersonal attraction may be a result of similarity of interests ("Birds") or of complementarity ("Opposites"). The latter principle is like the story of Jack Spratt, who would eat no fat, while his wife would eat no lean. They matched perfectly because what one did not like, the other did.

15.22 Physical attractiveness has been recognized as an important variable affecting interpersonal attraction. Describe at least two ways in which attractiveness may influence interpersonal attraction.

Physical attractiveness itself appears to be important in determining interpersonal attraction. In general, better-looking people are liked more than are less attractive people (according to whatever standards of attractiveness are current in a culture or subculture).

There is also the possibility that physical attractiveness may create what has been called a *halo effect*; that is, people may perceive in an attractive person characteristics that they normally associate with physical attractiveness, even if that judgment is not warranted.

Additionally, attractiveness may be affected by the preconceived notions the observer holds. This in effect is an example of a self-fulfilling prophecy; the observer may expect the person to be attractive and thus perceive the person as being attractive in spite of evidence to the contrary.

15.23 Using Sternberg's three basic components of love, distinguish between romantic love and consummate love.

Sternberg proposes that love depends on the three components of intimacy, passion, and commitment. In distinguishing between romantic love and consummate love, Sternberg suggests that romance involves both intimacy and passion but that commitment has not yet developed. Consummate, or complete, love adds the third component of commitment to the other two.

15.24 Identifying the affiliations Lauren maintains includes mentioning the church youth group to which she belongs and the fact that she "hangs out with a group of buddies from school." Both affiliations appear to influence Lauren's behaviors. What labels are used to describe the group memberships Lauren has? Explain.

Lauren has both formal and informal group memberships. The church youth group is described as a formal group, one with a designated title and probably certain rules for participation. The group of buddies is an informal group with no specific title or rules. Lauren's behaviors may be influenced by her membership in each of these groups whether she actually is interacting with some of the members or finds herself alone. Groups that are present have direct influence in that others can react to Lauren's behaviors as they occur. Even when they are not present, however, Lauren may still consider what the others "might think" about what she plans to do and be influenced by the absent group.

15.25 The values Lauren has learned by being in her groups, whether formal or informal, are attributed to a rather general process of development. What is this process called? How is it affected by where Lauren lives?

The values and norms by which an individual lives are established by what has been called socialization. Family members, peers, schoolteachers, and many others have both reinforced Lauren's behaviors and provided models for her to copy. In general, socialization depends on the culture or subculture in which a person lives. Customs differ from one group to another, and the values and norms associated with the particular set of sources will affect the values Lauren learns. This is called *cultural relativity*.

15.26 A track coach is concerned because one of the high jumpers on his team has shown an unusual pattern of behavior. In practice, the jumper is capable of clearing seven feet. When a meet is held, his best jumps are always lower. It seems the athlete's performance is impaired by the presence of other jumpers and spectators. What principle explains the fact that as the size of the meet and the number of spectators increase, the athlete's performance deteriorates?

The athlete's jumping seems to be affected by the number of people watching. Indeed, in this case, there appears to be a strong correlation between the size of the crowd and the quality of performance. The athlete seems to show the effect of social interference, which occurs when the mere presence of others makes performance more difficult (and poorer) than it might otherwise be.

Note: In some cases, the presence of others may help performance rather than hinder it; this phenomenon is called *social facilitation*. This athlete's performance is unusual in that the presence of others usually facilitates a well-learned behavior. Typically, it is recently learned behaviors that suffer most from the effects of social interference.

15.27 For years the residents of Belknap Acres have had an unwritten policy of keeping all the backyards open so that children and pets can play wherever they wish. However, when the Brune family moved in, they immediately began constructing a fence around their property. Although several of the neighbors discussed the neighborhood "rule" with the Brunes, the Brunes chose to continue with the construction. The Brunes' behavior illustrates what pattern of responding? Is this type of behavior fairly common?

The building of the fence in spite of the neighborhood pattern illustrates nonconformity. The Brunes recognized the social expectations operating in the environment but chose to act in an opposite fashion. Nonconformity is not as common as conformity, the tendency to go along with group opinion. (The additional category of independence exists when a person ignores or does not recognize the social norms and acts without the influence of such standards.)

15.28 Once the Brunes have started their fence, suppose the Cannyons also start building a fence. The Cannyons have lived in Belknap Acres for many years. What explains the change in their behavior?

Conformity is reduced when there is even one social supporter for a nonconforming pattern. Once the Brunes begin building the fence, the Cannyons can feel they are "not the only ones" and build a fence of their own rather than continue to match the opinion of the others in the development.

15.29 Wanting very much to be initiated into a high school "secret society," Rosalie has begun to go through a "pledge period." One day, after walking to school with her friend Edna, Rosalie is taken aside by some members of the group and told they would prefer that she (Rosalie) not hang around with Edna anymore. When Rosalie protests that Edna is her friend, the other girls say, "You let us worry about that. If you want to be one of us, you may want to listen to what we're saying." Rosalie stops seeing Edna. Explain her behavior in terms of compliance versus obedience.

Rosalie's choice to stop seeing Edna probably best represents what psychologists think of as compliance. Compliance occurs when there is direct and obvious pressure to respond in a certain manner and a person endorses it or chooses to do so. Compliance is thought to differ from obedience only in that while the pressure is indeed direct and obvious, there is no direct command. Obedience is thought to be the response to a specific command that usually is given by someone in authority.

15.30 What is the general finding regarding effort expended by the members of a group as the size of the group increases?

In general, as the size of a group increases, any single member of the group becomes less likely to expend maximum effort. At least two kinds of research support this finding. Studies of social loafing indicate that larger groups produce less than expected results because each member of the group tends to give less than maximum effort to the task at hand. Studies of bystander apathy show that any one individual is less likely to help a victim (someone in need of help) when others are present, assuming that the others will act. The principle explaining this has been called *diffusion of responsibility*.

15.31 What characteristics of a group seem to help overcome diffusion of responsibility, leading instead to action on the part of group members?

If a group has as its stated purpose the intent of acting in some manner, the group purpose seems to overcome possible apathy or reduced participation on the part of the members. Groups such as Habitat for Humanity and the Red Cross were founded with the intent of helping; thus, people joining such groups have an expectation of contributing effort to the purposes stated by the group, and there is a reduced likelihood of diffusion of responsibility and diminished effort.

15.32 Distinguish between prosocial behavior and altruism.

Prosocial behavior is the more general label used to describe helping behaviors. Altruism is an instance of prosocial behavior but is given a separate label because the helping behavior is done without any hope of reciprocity, involving self-sacrifice rather than the hope that there will be some sort of payoff for having helped.

15.33 "That group got ugly, didn't it?" This phrase often is used to describe a group of people showing aggressive behaviors. What is aggression? What explanations are given for aggressive behaviors by individuals or groups?

Aggression is behavior that has the intent of causing harm. Explanations for aggressive behavior include the possibility that such behaviors are instinctual, representing attempts to produce catharsis, or the release of built-up aggressive tendencies. Another explanation is that aggression occurs as the by-product of the anger produced when an individual or group experiences frustration. Modeling also is proposed as an explanation for aggression; the observation of others' aggressive behaviors serves as the exemplar for one's own aggressive actions. The group's ugly behaviors may be the result of any one or a combination of these possibilities.

15.34 A group gathers to discuss a possible business venture. After the discussion, it occurs to several members that they are embarking on a hazardous and possibly even ruinous course. What principles seem to explain such group decision making, in which the group as a whole is willing to take risks that none of the members would take alone?

The group's decision reflects what has been called *group polarization*. The best explanation of such behaviors seems to be the role of arguments presented during the group's discussion. If the arguments favor a liberal or risky decision, the group decision will tend to be risky. However, if a conservative decision seems to be favored in discussion, the group's decision will tend to be very conservative. Either way, however, the decision of the group will tend to be more extreme than the decision that would be expected from the individual members acting separately, without the effects of group discussion.

15.35 Based on their knowledge of the group polarization phenomenon and what has been called *groupthink*, political scientists have expressed fears that national planning agencies or councils may create potentially dangerous situations while acting in good conscience. Explain why this conclusion may be a very reasonable one.

Group polarization predicts that a group decision may be more risky than the decision that would be reached by the individuals if they had not had a group discussion about the topic. Furthermore, studies of groupthink situations have shown that the members often view the group as invulnerable and correct and act unanimously when forming decisions. As a result, evidence contrary to the decision made can be ignored and unfair pressure can be exerted on those who might try to dissent.

When they consider the combination of these two phenomena, political scientists predict that national planning agencies or councils may make potentially dangerous decisions even while believing a decision is both reasonable and appropriate.

15.36 While attending Mardi Gras festivities, college females are tempted by passersby to expose their breasts for a reward of Mardi Gras beads. Many do, but one group found pictures of themselves doing so on an Internet site the week after spring break. They were upset and embarrassed. What principle explains why these young women would act in a manner quite different from what they typically show in their day-to-day circumstances?

Being part of a large group often leads to deindividuation, the loss of individuality and reduction of constraints against normally unacceptable behaviors. In this case, the young women acted in a manner encouraged by the large, festive group, even though any one of them would be very unlikely to act in a similar manner if asked to act alone in a different setting. Although usually associated with inappropriate or negative behaviors, deindividuation sometimes produces more positive behaviors than might be expected in certain situations that favor such behavior.

Key Terms

Actor-observer bias.   Basing a judgment or interpretation on whether the action being evaluated is being observed or is part of one's own behavior.

Aggression.   Behavior with the intent to do harm.

Altruism.   Prosocial (helping) behavior that clearly involves self-sacrifice and no hope of reciprocity.

Assumed-similarity bias.   Also called the *false-consensus bias*; assuming that someone else's characteristics match one's own even when no evidence for that assumption exists.

Attitudes.   Learned evaluative reactions to people, objects, events, or other stimuli.

Attributions.   Attempts to explain the causes of behavior.

Balance theory.   Similar to *equity theory*; a proposal that suggests that people try to maintain equivalent "giving and taking" in personal interactions.

Behavioral confirmation.   Happens when expected behaviors occur, thus satisfying the self-fulfilling prophecy.

Bystander apathy.   A form of diffusion of responsibility; any individual is less likely to help a victim, assuming that others will take that responsibility.

Catharsis.   The release of built-up aggressive tendencies.

Cognitive dissonance.   An evaluative conflict; occurs when the same stimulus situation is followed by two or more contradictory sets of conditions.

Complementarity.   An explanation for attraction; occurs when two people have dissimilar characteristics that blend nicely and fulfill each other's needs.

Compliance.   Performing a particular behavior in response to direct, obvious pressure to do so.

Confirmatory hypothesis testing.   Seeking information that fits with already existing schemas.

Conformity.   Occurs when a person responds in accordance with a group's expectations or opinions.

Correspondence bias.   The tendency to assume that people's behaviors correspond to their attitudes and intentions.

Cultural relativity.   The proposal that social behavior must be judged according to the cultural setting in which it occurs.

Deindividuation.   Occurs when individuals in groups act in manners they would never adopt if acting alone; often marked by loss of individuality and reduction of constraint.

Diffusion of responsibility.   In group behavior, a situation where any one person takes less responsibility than would be taken while acting alone.

Discrimination.   Actual biased treatment of or actions against a group of people.

Elaboration-likelihood model.   A cognitive explanation for attitude change; based on concepts of *central processing* and *peripheral processing*.

Equity theory.   A proposal that suggests that people are attracted to others who "take" at about the same level as they "give."

Fundamental attribution error.   The tendency to stress internal or personal causes for behavior, especially the behavior of others.

Group dynamics.   The social interactions that take place within groups.

Group polarization.   Occurs when a group makes a more extreme decision than any member would make if acting alone.

Groupthink.   An extreme example of group polarization; occurs when a group develops an *illusion of invulnerability*, ignores opposing evidence, and acts with unanimity of decision.

Halo effect.   A form of attribution bias; if the initial judgment of an individual is very positive, subsequent expectations and evaluations remain positive even in the face of contradictory evidence.

Independence.   Refers to a situation in which a person's responses are not influenced one way or another by social expectations or opinions.

Justification.   Acting in conflict with previously held beliefs and then creating a reasonable explanation for doing so.

Mere exposure effect.   The change in one's attitude simply because of repeated exposure to a persuasive message or a person or object being considered.

Nonconformity.   Occurs when a person responds in a manner opposite to a group's opinions or expectations.

Obedience.   Performing a particular behavior in response to a direct command.

Out-group homogeneity bias.   An assumption that the members of an "out-group" are more alike than are the members of an "in-group."

Persuasion.   Trying to change someone else's attitudes.

Prejudice.   A learned reaction to a social stimulus, typically overgeneralized and unjustified; an attitude about someone based on that person's membership in a group.

Prosocial behavior.   Helping behavior.

Self-concept.   The beliefs and feelings one has about oneself.

Self-fulfilling prophecy.   Occurs when the expectations of others appear to lead to or cause the anticipated behavior.

Self-handicapping.   Creating conditions that prevent the successful completion of a task so that there is a ready excuse for failure.

Self-referencing.   Situations in which memory about someone else is better retained because the information is somehow related to oneself.

Self-serving bias.   For an individual, occurs when attribution of success is made to an internal cause or when attribution of failure is made to an external cause.

Social categories.   Ways to categorize or group people that make it easier to understand or explain the social world.

Social facilitation.   Occurs when the presence of others appears to help the performance of a particular response.

Social identity theory.   A proposal that suggests that group membership supports a sense of pride and self-worth; thus, prejudice against others occurs because the members of the group seek to feel better than others.

Social interference.   Also called *social inhibition*; occurs when the presence of others appears to hinder the performance of a particular response.

Socialization.   The general process of learning and establishing values and norms within a cultural setting.

Social loafing.   A form of diffusion of responsibility; occurs when large groups produce less than expected responses because each member contributes less than maximum effort to the task.

Social psychology.   The study of an individual's behavior as it is influenced by membership in a group.

Social schemas.   Ways of organizing the social world based on social categories.

Social scripts.   Ways of acting in the social world based on social schemas.

Stereotypes.   Oversimplified and relatively rigid schemas applied to a person or group of people regardless of the variation among individuals in that social group.

Examination I

For each of the first 25 questions, circle the best answer. (The correct answers appear on page 283.)

1. A psychologist who emphasizes the stimuli that provoke observed responses and tends to avoid the concept of mind was most likely trained in the _____ tradition.

   - (*a*) Psychoanalytic
   - (*b*) Structuralist
   - (*c*) Behaviorist
   - (*d*) Gestaltist

2. Nonscientific influences such as physiognomy and phrenology were important in the development of psychology because they

   - (*a*) accurately answered basic questions about physiology
   - (*b*) provoked study of what is correct rather than what they suggested
   - (*c*) were the sources of methodologies later used in experimental psychology
   - (*d*) were particularly concerned with unconscious motives

3. A student is depressed because he has trouble getting along with his new roommate. His grades have dropped slightly, and he wishes he had someone to talk with about his problem. He would most likely go to which of the following?

   - (*a*) counseling psychologist
   - (*b*) clinical psychologist
   - (*c*) educational psychologist
   - (*d*) social psychologist

4. A psychologist has studied the effects of room lighting on the ability of rats to solve a maze-learning problem. The independent variable in such a study is

   - (*a*) the numbers of errors made in the maze
   - (*b*) the number of subjects tested
   - (*c*) the responses, as measured by the time needed to solve the maze
   - (*d*) the room lighting

5. Although a number of different religious beliefs are held by members of the population in differing percentages, when the subjects are selected from this population, all the members have an equal chance of being chosen for any one of the designated groups. The experimenter used a(n) _____ sampling technique.

   - (*a*) random
   - (*b*) stratified
   - (*c*) accidental
   - (*d*) naturalistic

6. Unknowingly, the experimenter creates conditions that "force" particular responses from the subjects. This form of experimenter bias is called

   - (*a*) extraneous variables
   - (*b*) expectancy effect
   - (*c*) single-blind procedure
   - (*d*) demand characteristics

7. Which of the following is *not* a measure of central tendency?

   (*a*) mean
   (*b*) median
   (*c*) mode
   (*d*) range

8. Which of the following is *not* true of correlation?

   (*a*) It shows the relationship between two variables.
   (*b*) It shows contingency, or a causal relationship.
   (*c*) It may have positive or negative values.
   (*d*) It is represented by a scattergram.

9. The transmission of a signal through a nerve cell is called

   (*a*) excitatory potential
   (*b*) resting potential
   (*c*) action potential
   (*d*) graded potential

10. Which of the following is part of the peripheral nervous system?

   (*a*) the cerebellum
   (*b*) the spinal cord
   (*c*) the autonomic system
   (*d*) the corpus callosum

11. The endocrine system secretes

   (*a*) hormones
   (*b*) blood cells
   (*c*) to the exterior of the body
   (*d*) neurotransmitters

12. The sex of a human child is determined by

   (*a*) the chromosome carried by the male sperm cell
   (*b*) the chromosome carried by the female egg cell
   (*c*) the combination of chromosomes created in the zygote
   (*d*) all 46 chromosomes that form the embryo's cells

13. Given: Father has characteristic *Ff* and mother is *ff*, where *F* is dominant and *f* is recessive. What percentage of children could *pass on* the recessive characteristic?

   (*a*) 25
   (*b*) 50
   (*c*) 75
   (*d*) 100

14. A spontaneous change in the genetic code that creates a permanent and often radical effect is called

   (*a*) crossing over
   (*b*) mutation
   (*c*) vacuum activity
   (*d*) eugenics

15. Suppose research has shown that a particular behavior can be learned only during a limited time period. The concept of _____ seems most appropriate to describe the situation.

    (*a*) nonspecificity
    (*b*) readiness
    (*c*) critical period
    (*d*) cognitive stages

16. A child is able to develop coordinated series of ideas but to do so must relate them to observable events or objects. This child is probably in which of Piaget's stages of cognitive development?

    (*a*) sensorimotor
    (*b*) preoperational
    (*c*) concrete operational
    (*d*) formal operational

17. As a child grows older, the influence of _____ is likely to become more important, while the influence of _____ generally decreases.

    (*a*) peers, significant adults
    (*b*) heredity, environment
    (*c*) prenatal stages, postnatal stages
    (*d*) readiness, critical periods

18. Sensation has taken place when

    (*a*) the signal is picked up by the receptor
    (*b*) the action potential has passed through the sensory peripheral nerves
    (*c*) the signal has been recorded by the brain
    (*d*) a response has been made by a muscle or gland

19. Color vision is best when the image is focused on the

    (*a*) cornea
    (*b*) fovea
    (*c*) rods
    (*d*) cochlea

20. The conversion of a stimulus into an action potential is described by the term

    (*a*) dysfunction
    (*b*) reception
    (*c*) perception
    (*d*) transduction

21. Seeing ◯ as a circle represents

    (*a*) closure
    (*b*) grouping
    (*c*) perceptual constancy
    (*d*) figure-ground relationship

22. If you read the sentence "Sigmund Fraud was a founder of psychology" and do not spot any errors, you have demonstrated the principle of

(a) set
(b) perceptual constancy
(c) subliminal perception
(d) contrast

23. A person who misinterprets a stimulus that actually exists has experienced

    (a) a hallucination
    (b) an illusion
    (c) subliminal perception
    (d) extrasensory perception

24. Most dreams appear to take place during

    (a) stage 4 sleep
    (b) non-REM sleep
    (c) REM sleep
    (d) transcendental states

25. Which of the following is *not* a stimulant?

    (a) cocaine
    (b) caffeine
    (c) nicotine
    (d) alcohol

26. Psychology has purposes that include the prediction and modification of actions or thoughts. How are these alike? How do they differ?

Both prediction and modification are based on the investigations psychologists conduct to learn more about behavior and mental processes. They differ in that prediction usually refers to the psychologist's ability to anticipate naturally occurring events, while modification refers to situations in which a psychologist manipulates the circumstances and therefore the observed responses.

27. One of the students in Mrs. Hodge's class has had trouble "keeping up" with the rest of the class. Mrs. Hodge decides to try to find out why. What kind of psychologist would she ask to help?

Mrs. Hodge would ask a school psychologist to evaluate the student's problems. This might involve psychological testing, diagnosis, and counseling for that student.

28. A psychologist has tested the effects of room color on the activity level of children playing in the room. What kinds of extraneous or irrelevant variables might the psychologist try to control in such an experiment?

The size of the room, the consistency of lighting, the temperature of the room, unusual noises, interruptions, and the like, are all examples of extraneous or irrelevant variables that might affect the results obtained.

29. In some experiments, subjects are temporarily but deliberately misled about the purposes of the investigation. In others, neither the subjects nor the data-collecting experimenters know the intent of the study. Why are some investigations conducted in these manners?

Both techniques are used to try to avoid the influence of biases on the results of the experiment. It is hoped that by employing such procedures, the experimenter can isolate the effect of the independent variable on the dependent variable being measured in the experiment. Preconceptions, demand characteristics, and other influences are controlled when such techniques are used.

30. What is meant when a teacher says, "Well, that test score would fall in the eighty-fourth percentile on a normal curve"?

The normal curve is the graphical representation of the normal probability distribution, an idealized, symmetrical distribution portraying the distribution of scores or values for many characteristics that psychologists study. The normal curve is based on the mean and standard deviation, so that scores that fall one standard deviation above the mean are in the eighty-fourth percentile of the distribution. This means that 84 percent of the people taking the test have scores below the one the teacher is describing.

31. The firing of a neuron has been described by the "all-or-none principle." What does this principle state?

The all-or-none principle describes the response of a neuron to the precipitating stimulus. If the stimulus value is great enough to surpass the threshold of the cell, an action potential is generated and travels the length of the neuron. No signal can start and then "die" partway through the neuron.

32. What explanation is there for human beings' superiority over other organisms in the ability to communicate, generate thoughts, and create ideas?

Researchers have been able to "map" some of the functions of the cerebral cortex. The findings indicate that only a small percentage of the cortex's total area is involved with sensorimotor functions; a much larger area seems to control communications and memory processes. "Lower" animals do not have such a highly developed cerebral cortex.

33. What are the purposes and findings of split-brain research?

Split-brain research has investigated the functioning of the cerebral hemispheres when the connections between the two hemispheres are temporarily disrupted or permanently destroyed. These studies reveal the difference in function for the two hemispheres, allow investigation of hemisphere dominance, and provide information regarding the transfer of information from one hemisphere to the other.

34. Suppose a particular species of bird seemed to develop longer wings over successive generations. What explanation might be given in terms of Charles Darwin's theory?

Darwin believed in natural selection, or "survival of the fittest." Apparently, the birds that develop longer wings are more likely to be able to survive. Thus, over generations, long-wing characteristics are found, while shorter-wing characteristics "drop out."

35. What are the general causes of mental retardation? Are there ways to anticipate the possibility of a baby being mentally retarded?

Mental retardation may result from a genetic imbalance such as Down syndrome or an environmental variable such as excessive ingestion of alcohol by the mother during pregnancy. Testing and subsequent genetic counseling can help prospective parents understand the possibilities of inherited, genetic causes for retardation, while appropriate education can present the possible environmental effects.

36. Why must psychologists be careful in applying concepts such as developmental stages in explaining a particular child's behavior?

Developmental stages have been proposed as indicators of what a typical or average child might do. However, any individual child has particular characteristics unique to her or him, and the individual differences among children must be recognized.

37. What is the proposed "cutoff" age for the sensorimotor stage, infancy, and the oral stage? What argument is made against such designations?

All three concepts propose the completion of the period as occurring at age 2. Piaget's sensorimotor stage progresses to the preoperational stage, infancy changes to early childhood, and according to Freud, the oral stage is followed by the anal stage. Psychologists argue that such arbitrary designations fail to take into account the "seamlessness" of behavior and prefer to look at development as a continuous process throughout life.

38. Even with the arguments against stage proposals, the development of morality has been described as going through three stages. What would the behavior of the third stage be like?

In the third stage, a person accepts standards because of self-understanding and the development of principles and a conscience. This behavior is considered "beyond" moral behavior that occurs simply because of rewards and punishments or because of duty.

39. Why is sensation said to occur in the brain?

Sensations are not registered or "recorded" until the signal has reached the sensory area of the cerebral cortex. A signal is picked up by a receptor, transduced into an action potential, and transmitted through the sensory peripheral nervous system to the cerebral cortex, where it is interpreted as a sensation.

40. Standing at attention during a military review, a soldier notices that it is somewhat difficult to maintain perfect balance. Why?

It is likely that several factors have combined to affect the soldier's balance. The position of attention may have put unusual demands on the kinesthetic senses by having the body held in a rigid position. The soldier's position also may have restricted visual referents and limited touch and vestibular reception. Any or all of these factors might affect balance and help create the soldier's problem. This is an excellent example of how the senses often work together to affect behavior.

41. There are several different kinds of perceptual constancies. All of them, however, share a common principle. What is it?

Perceptual constancies show that an experienced organism's response to stimulation remains the same even when the stimulus is placed in different circumstances. Thus, a square is seen as a square even when it is viewed at an angle, and a yellow car is seen as yellow even in unusual lighting.

42. In a drawing of a golfer striking a drive, the viewer is led to focus on the person. The tee, the trees, the fairway, and other aspects of the drawing surround the person but are not prominent. What principle describes the relationship between the person represented and the other components of the drawing?

This is the figure-ground relationship. The person (figure) is made to stand out from the background (ground), and so the viewer's focus is on the golfer and not on the other parts of the drawing. This can be accomplished by placement of the figure, size, contrast, and many other factors.

43. Suppose in the same drawing the artist includes some double-image lines and "sweep" lines around the arms. What is the artist attempting to accomplish?

These lines would be used to try to give the impression of movement. In a static presentation such as a drawing, the use of apparent movement is an attention-getting device.

44. How are sensory deprivation and sensory overload alike? How do they differ?

Sensory deprivation and sensory overload represent the two ends of the sensation continuum: unusually low and unusually high levels of stimulation, respectively. The response to sensory deprivation often is to try to generate more stimulation. The response to sensory overload often is sensory adaptation.

45. A famous conductor once took responsibility for two orchestras, one in the United States and the other in Europe. Explain why he had considerable difficulty with his sleeping and eating schedules as he flew back and forth to work with those groups.

Each person establishes what are called circadian rhythms, or a biological clock. When the concert schedule demanded frequent moves between the two continents (a six-hour time difference), the conductor had considerable difficulty adjusting. For example, waking in the United States often will occur in the "wee hours," while tiredness and a desire to sleep will set in just when rehearsals should be held. This difficulty has the popular label "jet lag."

Answers to Problems 1-25

1. (c)	6. (d)	11. (a)	16. (c)	21. (a)
2. (b)	7. (d)	12. (a)	17. (a)	22. (a)
3. (a)	8. (b)	13. (d)	18. (c)	23. (b)
4. (d)	9. (c)	14. (b)	19. (b)	24. (c)
5. (a)	10. (c)	15. (c)	20. (d)	25. (d)

Examination II

For each of the first 25 questions, circle the best answer. (The correct answers appear on page 290.)

1. Functional autonomy refers to

   (*a*) the reduction of cognitive dissonance
   (*b*) the principle of homeostasis
   (*c*) the satisfaction of survival motives
   (*d*) the concept of a self-reinforcing response

2. Children at the beach often are seen running toward the waves, only to shy away from the water at the last possible moment. Their behavior probably illustrates

   (*a*) approach-avoidance conflict
   (*b*) approach-approach conflict
   (*c*) avoidance-avoidance conflict
   (*d*) multiple approach-avoidance conflict

3. In the hierarchy of needs proposed by humanistic psychologists, the highest level is called

   (*a*) belongingness
   (*b*) self-actualization
   (*c*) esteem
   (*d*) safety

4. When a person chooses not to vote and says, "My vote doesn't matter; they'll do whatever they want anyway," the principle illustrated is

   (*a*) phobic reaction
   (*b*) autonomic depression
   (*c*) psychosomatic disorder
   (*d*) learned helplessness

5. The use of a lie detector depends on

   (*a*) trapping the subject into making contradictory responses
   (*b*) identifying the lie from changes in physiological processes
   (*c*) spotting nonverbal gestures which reveal the lie
   (*d*) determining the subject's subjective appraisal of arousal

6. "Our dog, Biscuit, was feeling *very* lonely while we were gone." A sentence such as this is an example of

   (*a*) parsimony
   (*b*) set
   (*c*) anthropomorphism
   (*d*) functional fixedness

7. In a classroom demonstration, the instructor has a student sit on the desk in front of the class and hold her head still. A bellhop's bell is sounded and followed by a puff of air into her eye from a quickly squeezed empty syringe. Soon the student begins to blink when the bell sounds. In this example, the US is the

    (*a*) air puff
    (*b*) sound of the bell
    (*c*) desk
    (*d*) empty syringe

8. When tested for a reaction to the word "horse," a subject answers "ride." Later, when tested to the word "pony," the subject again answers "ride." Giving the same response to these two stimuli illustrates

    (*a*) primary stimulus generalization
    (*b*) secondary stimulus generalization
    (*c*) confabulation
    (*d*) spontaneous recovery

9. Forward trace conditioning occurs when the

    (*a*) the CS comes on and stays on until the US goes off
    (*b*) the CS and US come on together
    (*c*) the CS comes on and goes off before the onset of the US
    (*d*) the US comes on before the onset of the CS

10. A coach who tries to get a player to come closer and closer to a particular movement needed in the sport is probably using

    (*a*) respondent conditioning
    (*b*) programmed learning
    (*c*) shaping
    (*d*) punishment

11. A rat being reinforced on a fixed ratio of 15 (FR = 15) is being reinforced

    (*a*) every 15 seconds
    (*b*) for a response after each 15-second period
    (*c*) after a US presented every 15 seconds
    (*d*) for a certain number of responses

12. If the removal of a stimulus strengthens or maintains a response, it probably is correct to say that

    (*a*) punishment has occurred
    (*b*) positive reinforcement has occurred
    (*c*) negative reinforcement has occurred
    (*d*) a noncontingent reinforcer has been established

13. Sandra has found that spraying her skillet with a special preparation keeps food from sticking when cooked. Sandra's response illustrates

    (*a*) an avoidance response
    (*b*) an escape response
    (*c*) an approach response
    (*d*) a punishing response

14. When a person observes not only a response being made but also the consequences of that response, psychologists say that _____ may occur.

     (*a*) vicarious learning
     (*b*) noncontingent reinforcement
     (*c*) distributed practice
     (*d*) negative transfer

15. A child's use of derogatory phrases without any apparent understanding is most likely an example of

     (*a*) overlearning
     (*b*) pure imitation
     (*c*) repression
     (*d*) retroactive interference

16. If Adria has been a bad girl and as a result is not allowed to watch her favorite television show, her parents are using

     (*a*) positive reinforcement
     (*b*) negative reinforcement
     (*c*) positive punishment
     (*d*) negative punishment

17. In a learning curve, a plateau occurs when

     (*a*) the performance has reached a final peak
     (*b*) a level period of performance is preceded and followed by performance improvement
     (*c*) a negatively accelerated performance curve has been obtained
     (*d*) one-trial learning has been observed

18. Which of the following combination of factors should produce the best acquisition of a response in a subject?

     (*a*) overlearning, massed practice, passive attitude
     (*b*) overlearning, massed practice, active attitude
     (*c*) no overlearning, distributed practice, passive attitude
     (*d*) overlearning, distributed practice, active attitude

19. When the learning of one task makes it more difficult to learn the next task

     (*a*) positive transfer has taken place
     (*b*) overlearning has been observed
     (*c*) learning without awareness has occurred
     (*d*) negative transfer has taken place

20. If Robert took 15 trials to learn a list of words and later relearned the same list in 6 trials, his savings was _____ that of Lois, who learned in 20 trials and later relearned in 8 trials.

     (*a*) greater than
     (*b*) the same as
     (*c*) less than
     (*d*) cannot tell from the information given

21. Repression is defined as

     (*a*) an increase in performance after a period of rest
     (*b*) going back to a more childlike attitude

   (*c*) motivated forgetting
   (*d*) proactive interference

22. When the pattern for the experimental group in an experiment is learn task 1, learn task 2, rest, test task 2, _____ probably is being studied.

   (*a*) transfer of training
   (*b*) retroactive interference
   (*c*) proactive interference
   (*d*) the von Restorff effect

23. A popular form of humor relies on referring to people or objects by using very elaborate phrases (for example, a short person might be described as being "height challenged" or "vertically impaired"). These elaborate phrases are illustrations of what level of conceptual thinking?

   (*a*) superordinate
   (*b*) basic
   (*c*) subordinate
   (*d*) hierarchical

24. In problem solving, "shortcut" strategies ("rules of thumb") are labeled as

   (*a*) algorithms
   (*b*) signs
   (*c*) divergencies
   (*d*) heuristics

25. A morpheme is

   (*a*) a phrase's meaning
   (*b*) a phonemic syllable
   (*c*) typically divided into clauses
   (*d*) the smallest meaningful unit of a language

26. Describe the concept of homeostasis and explain how it is related to unlearned motives.

   Homeostasis is defined as internal, physiological balance. The body attempts to maintain this balance automatically. The adjustments which are made by the body are in keeping with unlearned (or survival) needs, for example, perspiring when body temperature begins to get too high or "passing out" when one is exhausted.

27. Why are some motives treated as "combination" motives?

   Research so far has revealed that some motives, such as sex, seem to contain both learned and unlearned components and that other motives, such as contact comfort, cannot be classified as learned or unlearned. Thus, it is necessary to refer to some as combination motives.

28. Suppose Ramon has felt very emotional and has been experiencing "upset stomach" quite frequently. Using the concept of *cognitive appraisal*, explain Ramon's situation.

   Cognitive appraisal of emotions is said to involve two levels of evaluation. The first, primary appraisal, is an initial assessment of how the event or reaction may have occurred and the effect it has on one's behavior. In this instance, Ramon may decide that the upset stomachs are a result of difficulties he is having with his girlfriend and that his well-being is being affected significantly.
   The second level of evaluation, secondary appraisal, allows for consideration of the options available for responding to the situation. Ramon might consider breaking up with his girlfriend, or suggesting that

they both go for counseling, or just "putting up with" the irritation he is experiencing. The option that best relieves the anxiety and the accompanying symptoms is the one he will be most likely to choose.

29. Kathryn has been clothes shopping. She has found everything she set out to get and prepares to leave the mall. As she is passing through the jeans section of the store on her way out, she spots a pair that looks particularly attractive, stops to try it on, and eventually buys it. Explain Kathryn's behavior in terms of need, drive, and incentive.

When she started shopping, Kathryn truly had a need. She had evaluated her wardrobe and found there were certain clothes she should buy to prepare for the upcoming season. This need (psychological) produced a drive (internal state) with accompanying arousal (physiological activation) that prompted her to go shopping. Kathryn bought the items that should have satisfied her need, reduced her drive, and terminated the motive condition. However, incentive refers to an external condition that "pulls" activity toward it. It appears that Kathryn is influenced by the incentive value of the jeans, and she buys them even though she neither needs them nor planned to get any.

30. Describing an incident later, Larry says, "I was so mad, I could have spit nails. I couldn't think of what to say!" Explain this reaction in terms of emotion, motivation, and performance.

The emotion is anger at a very high level of intensity. Larry's reaction is comparable to other behaviors performed under high levels of motivation; that is, performance is poor. (He was unable to speak.) Later, when calmer, Larry probably could think of lots of responses that would have been appropriate.

31. Why is extinction considered both a procedure and a result?

The two aspects of extinction are essentially inseparable. Removal of the reinforcement creates the extinction procedure and leads to the result of the response returning to its preconditioning level.

32. When bending over to smell the flowers, Randy is stung by a bee. How would you test later to see if Randy has become classically conditioned in this situation?

Assuming that the bee sting was painful, a later test for a classically conditioned response would be to have Randy go near the flowers again and observe his reactions to identify any expressions of fear, such as withdrawal and verbal comments. The CS is the flowers, the US is the bee sting, the UR would be the reaction to the pain, and the CR would be a comparable reaction.

33. Faced with a highly exciting situation, a worker is unable to complete a job even though he previously learned it well. In terms of learning, what has happened?

This worker's reaction illustrates the learning-performance distinction. Performance does not necessarily reveal learning. Once again, this is an example of overly high levels of motivation leading to poor performance.

34. "Horse players" often seem to be hooked on gambling. In terms of schedules of reinforcement, explain why.

Betting on horse races is an example of variable ratio reinforcement: The more often a bet is made, the more likely a "win" is. But no gambler wins all the time. The successes and failures represent a partial reinforcement condition, and research has shown that partial reinforcement leads to greater resistance to extinction than does continuous reinforcement.

35. Describe the differences between punishment and escape situations.

Punishment occurs when an aversive stimulus follows a response and a contingent relationship exists. Escape occurs when a response allows a subject to get away from an aversive stimulus; that is, the contingency is between a response and a negative reinforcement.

36. What is the most typical way to measure operant conditioning?

Operant conditioning is measured by determining a cumulative record of responses. This is a record of the number of appropriate responses made during a given time period.

37. Observational learning has some advantages over other forms of learning. What are some of these advantages?

Observational learning is more advantageous than other forms of learning in that it can help prevent dangerous, embarrassing, or otherwise difficult situations from being experienced. Seeing someone else's difficulties (such as slipping on ice and falling, which can be both dangerous and embarrassing) will allow adjustment of one's own responses to avoid experiencing the same kind of thing.

38. If your friend tells you how to bake delicious cookies ("Add two cups of flour, then one teaspoon of vanilla, etc.") and you follow that recipe successfully, you have demonstrated a particular kind of observational learning or modeling. What kind?

This is symbolic observational learning, particularly verbal modeling. Without actually seeing your friend perform any of these steps, you are able to duplicate the performance and make the cookies.

39. At your 10-year reunion, you are asked to recall the name of the couple that began dating as soon as the fellow transferred into the school. In terms of types of storage, trace the pattern of acquisition of the response that allows you to answer immediately, "That was Jack and Grace."

Psychologists usually accept three kinds of storage for information. The first, sensory storage, is extremely brief and consists of nothing more than holding unprocessed information in a sensory form. In this case, sensory storage might have been nothing more than hearing Jack's name for the first time. Initial processing takes place in short-term storage. Pairing the name "Jack" with the face of that person or with a discussion of the school from which he had transferred might represent short-term storage. If additional processing occurs, the memory is held in long-term storage. Long-term storage has unlimited capacity and duration, so that even 10 years later, it is possible for you to remember the names of the couple and respond immediately.

40. What is an asymptote? Why is this term used in describing incremental (step-by-step) learning?

An asymptote refers to a level of performance that appears to be near the maximum that can be achieved for the response. In incremental learning situations, performance generally keeps improving until the asymptotic level is reached.

41. What role might sleep play in the retention of learned materials?

A subject who sleeps after learning avoids the possibility of encountering interfering materials. This means the subject avoids the possibility of retroactive interference, and better retention could result. Furthermore, sleeping may be viewed as a rest period separating periods of learning, and periods of learning alternated with rest periods are more effective than is massed learning.

42. Can a hand gesture be a symbol?

A symbol is any stimulus that has come to have a commonly accepted meaning for something else. Any gesture may be a symbol as long as there is general agreement about what the gesture represents. Sign language used by the hearing-impaired provides evidence that hand gestures have symbolic meaning.

43. Concepts often are described as being ambiguous or "fuzzy." Why are prototypes often used to try to explain what a concept means?

A prototype is an example of a concept that shares many of the features or properties that people usually associate with that concept. Thus, if confusion or "fuzziness" is associated with the concept, using a prototype allows an understanding of what is thought to be typical of that concept.

44. Four-year-old Tara was misbehaving. Her mother, trying to get her under control, told her, "Stand in the corner for the present." Tara quickly ran to the corner of the room and waited happily for quite a while. Finally, she asked, "Mommy, where's my present?" Explain this sequence of events in terms of expressive versus receptive language.

Expressive language is defined as words that convey a message. Tara's mother was trying to convey the message that Tara should slow down and behave better. However, Tara interpreted what her mother said in quite a different manner. Receptive language refers to what is understood from the words used. Because there was ambiguity in what Tara's mother said, the phrase "for the present" was interpreted as meaning a gift was on the way, not as a reference to time.

45. In terms of language structure, explain the difference between the sentences "What Boyd grabbed was glory" and "What Boyd grabbed was gory."

Language structure is evaluated in two ways: Surface structure refers to the arrangement of words, while deep structure refers to the meaning conveyed by the words. In this case, there is only one letter of difference between the two sentences and the surface structure is almost identical. However, that one letter changes the deep structure considerably, and the two sentences have very different meanings.

Answers to Problems 1–25

1.	(d)	6.	(c)	11.	(d)	16.	(d)	21.	(c)
2.	(a)	7.	(a)	12.	(c)	17.	(b)	22.	(c)
3.	(b)	8.	(b)	13.	(a)	18.	(d)	23.	(c)
4.	(d)	9.	(c)	14.	(a)	19.	(d)	24.	(d)
5.	(b)	10.	(c)	15.	(b)	20.	(b)	25.	(d)

Examination III

For each of the first 25 questions, circle the best answer. (The correct answers appear on page 297.)

1. The comparison standards established by testing a group usually are called

    (*a*) reliability
    (*b*) norms
    (*c*) cross-sectional standards
    (*d*) validations

2. The potential for acquiring a skill is called

    (*a*) ability
    (*b*) personality
    (*c*) achievement
    (*d*) criterion

3. Which of the following IQ scores probably would not classify a person as exceptional?

    (*a*) 65
    (*b*) 115
    (*c*) 135
    (*d*) 155

4. Determine the ratio IQ for a child who is 8 years old and scores at the 10-year mental age level.

    (*a*) 80
    (*b*) 100
    (*c*) 125
    (*d*) 133

5. A very creative person probably would show which of the following characteristics?

    (*a*) fluid intelligence, convergent thinking
    (*b*) crystallized intelligence, convergent thinking
    (*c*) fluid intelligence, divergent thinking
    (*d*) crystallized intelligence, divergent thinking

6. For Freud, control of behavior according to societal standards rests in the

    (*a*) id
    (*b*) ego
    (*c*) superego
    (*d*) libido

7. Value and respect for *all* of a person's behavior would be classified by Rogers as

    (*a*) unconditional positive regard
    (*b*) negative regard
    (*c*) conditional positive regard
    (*d*) self-actualization

8. George, a heavy smoker, blames his inability to quit on his upbringing, claiming that he *has* to smoke to satisfy cravings left from when he was a child. George's explanation for his smoking is based on what principle proposed by Freud?

  (*a*) regression
  (*b*) transference
  (*c*) resistance
  (*d*) fixation

9. Furious with his teacher, Lance leaves the classroom and punches the door of his locker. Lance's behavior illustrates

  (*a*) sublimation
  (*b*) projection
  (*c*) displacement
  (*d*) rationalization

10. Which of the following does *not* belong in a list of the "big five" categories for describing personality?

  (*a*) temperament
  (*b*) extraversion
  (*c*) neuroticism
  (*d*) conscientiousness

11. Self-efficacy refers to

  (*a*) being able to perform well in front of others
  (*b*) feelings of competence associated with any particular setting
  (*c*) a sense of freedom from parental influence
  (*d*) personal responsibility for mistakes

12. Jeanette is convinced that the difficulties she is having with her job are the result of a conspiracy organized by her secretary, one of the custodians, and two of the people in the next office. Assuming the conspiracy really does not exist, Jeanette's behavior might be labeled as

  (*a*) paranoid
  (*b*) sociopathic
  (*c*) phobic
  (*d*) autistic

13. Which of the following perspectives probably would classify abnormal behaviors as an "illness"?

  (*a*) cognitive model
  (*b*) behavioral model
  (*c*) biomedical model
  (*d*) psychodynamic model

14. A person who is absolutely certain the slight twinge of pain felt in the hip is a symptom of cancer of the bone most likely will be diagnosed as showing

  (*a*) conversion disorder
  (*b*) hypochondriasis
  (*c*) panic disorder
  (*d*) phobias

15. An individual who shows extremes of mood and activity level is most likely to be diagnosed as having

    (*a*) schizophrenia
    (*b*) psychosomatic illness
    (*c*) narcissistic personality disorder
    (*d*) bipolar disorder

16. Electroconvulsive therapy (ECT) is most likely to be used when a patient shows

    (*a*) severe depressive responses that do not respond to other treatment
    (*b*) noticeable hypochondriasis that is chronic
    (*c*) extreme resistance to psychotherapy
    (*d*) mental retardation in the range below 50 on an IQ test

17. Therapists who emphasize shorter-term therapy in which patients develop problem-solving skills that are adaptive are categorized with the term

    (*a*) client-centered therapy
    (*b*) Gestalt therapy
    (*c*) implosion therapy
    (*d*) ego analysis

18. Token economies are based on

    (*a*) modeling
    (*b*) operant conditioning
    (*c*) classical conditioning
    (*d*) biofeedback

19. A return to "normalcy" without the help of therapy is called

    (*a*) the placebo effect
    (*b*) ego analysis
    (*c*) spontaneous remission
    (*d*) repression

20. If the presence of others seems to make a professional actor perform better than he does in rehearsals, _____ probably has been illustrated.

    (*a*) social facilitation
    (*b*) socialization
    (*c*) social interference
    (*d*) social exchange

21. Warren wears crew-neck sweaters and khaki pants simply because he likes them. Warren's choice of clothes represents

    (*a*) nonconformity
    (*b*) conformity
    (*c*) independence
    (*d*) obedience to group opinion

22. Suppose a couple gets along because one or the other often says things such as, "I'll do the dishes if you'll change the bed." Their behavior might be said to illustrate

    (*a*) complementarity
    (*b*) primary effect
    (*c*) scapegoating
    (*d*) anchorage

23. The most effective attitude changers probably would be

    (*a*) unbelievable—absolutely "wild"
    (*b*) relatively weak—just "one of the group"
    (*c*) quite attractive—pleasing to look at
    (*d*) a combination of all three of these characteristics

24. Jeffrey is best able to remember things about his coworkers by relating the information to things in his own life. Jeffrey's behavior represents

    (*a*) self-fulfilling prophecy
    (*b*) self-referencing
    (*c*) self-serving bias
    (*d*) fundamental attribution error

25. Kathi spills her backpack in a busy classroom. Not one of the other students stops to help her pick up her belongings. Such circumstances illustrate the principle of

    (*a*) social loafing
    (*b*) prosocial behavior
    (*c*) altruism
    (*d*) bystander apathy

26. "The test *must* be valid—I got the same results from her three times in a row!" Explain why this sentence is not necessarily correct.

    The speaker of this sentence has confused the reliability and the validity of a test. Obtaining the same result repeatedly indicates that the test is reliable; that is, the test shows consistency of measurement. A good test will be reliable and indeed must be reliable if it is to be valid. However, a valid test must measure what it claims to measure. In this case, even if the same results are obtained again and again, they may be results that have nothing to do with the behavior that supposedly is being tested. The test could be very reliable and still be wholly invalid.

27. How is a criterion used in evaluating test results? Give an example.

    Using a criterion means that the results are judged against an absolute standard. This standard is established without reference to the performance of those at a particular age level or another group. Unlike a norm, which can change depending on the reference group addressed, a criterion is set and maintained. For example, in grading an examination, the teacher might use a criterion by saying that any score that is 90 percent correct or above receives an A. By comparison, a normative standard might be that any student who scores in the top 10 percent on the exam gets an A. In the latter case, it would be possible to get only 70 percent correct and still receive an A if that score fell in the top 10 percent performance level.

28. Mainstreaming is a concept that has been of interest in educational settings in recent years. What is this concept, and what is being attempted because of it?

Mainstreaming refers to attempts to integrate retarded students into the regular classroom as much as possible. The idea is to give every student an education in the least restricted environment that can be used successfully.

29. Several psychologists have suggested that there are multiple intelligences. Explain what is meant by this.

Rather than accepting the idea of a general or singular interpretation of intelligence, many modern theorists have proposed explanations of intelligence that categorize varying types of intelligence. In effect, these psychologists propose that different kinds of intelligence apply to differing situations and that any individual may have higher or lower abilities in the different categories. In addition, cultural context is considered by some theorists, who suggest that personal standards and the cultural context in which one lives may influence the kind of intellectual behavior necessary for being successful.

30. What purposes are served by trying to design culture-fair tests?

Culture-fair tests try to eliminate unfair biases that may result from being raised in one setting as opposed to another. For example, test items that favor specifically rural or urban knowledge would be avoided or balanced in an attempt to create an equitable test for all.

31. Ratio IQs have been replaced by deviation IQs as the most commonly used form of IQ. Why?

Ratio IQs did not take into account the fact that after a certain number of years, a person's mental age is likely to stabilize while that person's chronological age continues to increase. Thus, if ratio IQs were used, practically all adults would have ever-decreasing IQs.

32. Measured intelligence correlates more highly with school success than does any other variable. However, these correlations are relatively low. What are some explanations for this?

Motivation, social status, financial considerations, the expectations of others, previous successes or failures, and many other factors besides intelligence may affect school success. Thus, the predictions made on the basis of measured intelligence alone often will not be very accurate.

33. Explain why defense mechanisms may be either normal or abnormal.

According to Freud, defense mechanisms protect the ego. In many cases, a person who is coping well within society must defend the ego and employs a defense mechanism in an "acceptable" manner. In some cases, however, the person is not able to cope within the demands of the environment yet hopes to protect the personality structure. In such situations, abnormal adoptions of defense mechanisms may be tried.

34. Why is repression considered the first step in, and therefore the most prevalent of all, defense mechanisms?

Freud believed that defense of the personality started with repression, the "intentional forgetting" of anxiety-producing memories. Repression is thought to keep unacceptable desires from surfacing in the conscious. Other defense mechanisms react to the unconscious but active influences of the repressed memories.

35. Erikson's theory of personality is said to be similar to Freud's, yet they differ in one very significant way. How is Erikson's theory both similar to and different from Freud's?

Erikson accepted the concept of stages of personality development and proposed five stages from birth to adolescence that paralleled those proposed by Freud. The major difference between the two approaches is that Erikson proposed three more stages after puberty and stated that those stages continued through the remainder of one's life. In addition, Erikson suggested there was a primary crisis to be dealt with at each of the eight stages, the resolution of which would determine the personality that developed.

36. What are the "big five" categories that have been used in describing personality? How were they determined?

The "big five" categories or traits used for describing personality are *extraversion*, *agreeableness*, *conscientiousness*, *openness to experience*, and *neuroticism*. These categories have been selected as the traits most often used to describe personality on the basis of a combination of new research and a reanalysis of previous studies.

37. Brought to a clinic by his wife, Henry appears to be very excited, even boisterous, yet his wife says that he frequently becomes very morose and reluctant to communicate. What type of abnormal personality pattern does Henry show?

Henry probably is showing bipolar disorder. This mood disorder is characterized by extreme swings of mood, often in a cyclical pattern. The length of each cycle and the possibility of showing relatively normal behavior between bouts of mania or depression vary from one individual to another.

38. What are the standards applied in determining legal insanity?

Legal insanity is decided if the individual being evaluated appears to lack the capacity to distinguish that the act being performed is wrong or is unable to act in accordance with the requirements of the law. The requirements of the courts differ from the standards presented in *DSM-IV*.

39. Many fewer patients diagnosed with some form of abnormal personality pattern are hospitalized than was the case in previous years. Why?

Although there may be any number of reasons for the reduced hospitalization of people showing abnormal personality patterns, probably the most important is the use of psychotropic drugs. As more drugs have been discovered and developed, outpatient treatment has become more acceptable because symptoms can be controlled with the drugs and the individual can remain in society.

40. What are the benefits and drawbacks of using group rather than individual therapy?

Two major benefits of group therapy are the social setting and the lower expense. The social setting provides a context that may be similar to the one in which the problem first developed and will facilitate achieving resolution of the problem. The reduced cost makes therapy available to more people, many of whom could not afford individual therapy costs.

The drawbacks of group therapy include possibly reduced attention from the therapist to the patient, a possible lack of focus on a person's specific problems, and possible ineffective responding by the therapist because of the multiple demands of the setting.

41. What are "pop" therapies? How are they related to therapy in a clinical setting?

"Pop" therapies are self-help techniques provided by magazines, books, Web sites, and other popular sources. Pop therapies may be based on clinical practices that have been developed and/or researched by psychologists or psychiatrists, or they may be schemes for someone to make money and have no scientific or practice background. There are no ethical limitations on pop therapies that are comparable to the ethical principles under which psychologists and psychiatrists practice.

42. Randy is attempting to learn a new movement in his gymnastics routine. By chance, several people are observing his practice. What effect might this have on his performance?

It is likely that social interference will occur; that is, the presence of others will hinder Randy's performance of the recently learned task. In the case of a well-learned task, the presence of others often helps performance, resulting in what is known as social facilitation.

43. If a person performs one task exceptionally well, others may expect that person to perform other tasks with great skill. Why? Why may that result actually occur?

The expectation that someone who is good at one task is good at all tasks is called the *halo effect*; a "good boy" is always seen as "good," regardless of the circumstances. This actually may happen because the person responds according to those expectations, an example of the *self-fulfilling prophecy*.

44. Raised in Williamsville, Elwood is heard to say, "Amherst High? All the kids there are country clubbers! We have all kinds at WHS." In terms of social psychology, interpret Elwood's remark.

Whether Elwood's remark is meant to be derogatory or not, it is evidence for what social psychologists have called *out-group homogeneity bias*, the idea that the members of an out-group (in this case, a different high school) are more alike than are the members of the in-group. Elwood's comment is stereotypical because it is oversimplified, relatively rigid, and attributed to all the members of the group.

45. Evidence indicates that adult leaders of children's organizations sometimes abuse the children under their direction. Why, even if they have been taught to resist such abuse, are children likely to allow such behaviors to occur?

Research on obedience indicates that demands will be followed if the person giving the command is seen as someone in authority who has a legitimate reason for making the command. The adult leaders of children's organizations have the authority that accompanies such a position and can, in cases such as these, use that authority to command behavior that is inappropriate.

Answers to Problems 1–25

1. (b)	6. (b)	11. (b)	16. (a)	21. (c)
2. (a)	7. (a)	12. (a)	17. (d)	22. (a)
3. (b)	8. (d)	13. (c)	18. (b)	23. (c)
4. (c)	9. (c)	14. (b)	19. (c)	24. (b)
5. (c)	10. (a)	15. (d)	20. (a)	25. (d)

Final Examination

For each of the 50 questions, circle the best answer. (The correct answers appear on page 309.)

1. Although both use many of the same techniques, a major difference between a psychologist and a psychiatrist is that a

    (a) psychologist studies Freudian techniques exclusively
    (b) psychiatrist studies only Freudian techniques
    (c) psychiatrist is medically trained
    (d) psychologist may be a psychoanalyst, while a psychiatrist cannot be one

2. Credit for the start of the science of psychology in _____ is given to _____.

    (a) 1879, Wundt
    (b) 1885, Freud
    (c) 1858, Fechner
    (d) 1913, Watson

3. An experimenter who tests the proposition that the results obtained from an experimental group will not differ significantly from those obtained from the control group is testing

    (a) a molar variable
    (b) a directional hypothesis
    (c) the null hypothesis
    (d) the naturalistic observation

4. One reason for using naturalistic observation as a technique for gathering information is

    (a) the high level of control possible
    (b) the accuracy of clinical records
    (c) the possibility of avoiding "forced" responses
    (d) none of the above

5. The total genetic pattern for any individual is called

    (a) a mutation
    (b) a genome
    (c) zygote
    (d) eugenics

6. Ann and her brother Fred are twins. Their hereditary pattern must be such that they

    (a) developed from the splitting of a single zygote
    (b) resulted from two separate conceptions
    (c) would both show the recessive characteristics of their parents
    (d) would have the same color eyes

7. Until the baby-to-be has become attached (linked) to the mother's system, it is described as

    (a) a fetus
    (b) an embryo
    (c) an infant
    (d) a chromosome

8. The need to collect information about a developmental question in a short period of time probably would be reflected by the use of a

 (*a*) developmental scale
 (*b*) longitudinal study
 (*c*) deprivation study
 (*d*) cross-sectional study

9. In general, the sympathetic system

 (*a*) acts as a unit in active situations
 (*b*) acts only in part in active situations
 (*c*) operates only in quiet situations
 (*d*) operates only after electrical stimulation of the brain

10. A signal may be transmitted from one nerve cell to another when

 (*a*) the absolute refractory period is happening
 (*b*) the cerebral cortex is in a state of resting potential
 (*c*) the transmitter substance passes across the synapse
 (*d*) all of the above are occurring simultaneously

11. An absolute threshold is defined as

 (*a*) a just noticeable difference (j.n.d.)
 (*b*) the level at which correct detection of a stimulus occurs 50 percent of the time
 (*c*) the level at which correct detection of a stimulus occurs 100 percent of the time
 (*d*) the difference threshold of the stimulus

12. The "chemical senses" include

 (*a*) taste
 (*b*) kinesthesis
 (*c*) vestibulation
 (*d*) hearing

13. One binocular cue that affects perception is

 (*a*) subliminal perception
 (*b*) stimulus intensity
 (*c*) perceptual constancy
 (*d*) retinal disparity

14. Many fortune-tellers claim to be able to predict a client's future. If they could do this, they would have what is called

 (*a*) telepathy
 (*b*) precognition
 (*c*) clairvoyance
 (*d*) psychokinesis

15. It is likely that the most widely used psychoactive drug is

 (*a*) alcohol
 (*b*) marijuana
 (*c*) LSD
 (*d*) heroin

16. The attempt to focus on a single sound or object is likely to be part of

    (*a*)   opening-up meditation
    (*b*)   circadian rhythm
    (*c*)   REM sleep
    (*d*)   concentrative meditation

17. Which of the following is typically *not* correct?

    (*a*)   Very low levels of motivation usually lead to poor performance of a task.
    (*b*)   Homeostasis is the body's tendency to maintain an internal "balance."
    (*c*)   Deprivation often is used as the measure of level of motivation.
    (*d*)   Very high levels of motivation usually lead to outstanding performance of a task.

18. If Ruth is thirsty but will satisfy this thirst only with a cola drink, she has demonstrated

    (*a*)   cognitive dissonance
    (*b*)   goal specificity
    (*c*)   functional autonomy
    (*d*)   sensory adaptation

19. To identify the emotion being expressed, it probably is most important to know the

    (*a*)   provoking stimulus
    (*b*)   respondent's social background
    (*c*)   physiological indicants
    (*d*)   level of motivation experience

20. The concept that emotions resulted from perceived bodily changes was the key to

    (*a*)   the James-Lange theory
    (*b*)   the Cannon-Bard theory
    (*c*)   the activation-arousal theory
    (*d*)   the facial feedback hypothesis

21. While walking on the sidewalk, 3-year-old Charles is surprised by the loud blast of an automobile horn. He slips, falls, bumps his knee, and cries from the pain. Later, he is out again and hears another auto horn, and he begins to cry. In this example, the CS is the

    (*a*)   bump on the knee
    (*b*)   crying to the pain
    (*c*)   crying to the sound of the horn
    (*d*)   sound of the horn

22. That evening Charles is watching television, and by chance, the show features a "chase" scene with much honking of automobile horns. Charles starts to whimper. His reaction represents

    (*a*)   primary stimulus generalization
    (*b*)   secondary stimulus generalization
    (*c*)   response generalization
    (*d*)   differentiation

23. Many soldiers returning from the war found that their language was not appropriate for "proper" society. Most were able to extinguish the incorrect responses. However, once in a while, when a

particularly provocative situation occurred, the soldiers might revert to their wartime language. Such a response would illustrate

  (a) stimulus generalization
  (b) response generalization
  (c) spontaneous recovery
  (d) stimulus contiguity

24. Which of the following would lead to the poorest operant conditioning?

  (a) feedback as a reinforcer
  (b) conditioned reinforcers
  (c) delay of reinforcement
  (d) response as reinforcement

25. A practical application of operant conditioning is

  (a) modeling
  (b) behavior modification
  (c) desensitization
  (d) higher-order conditioning

26. Following written directions would be classified as

  (a) verbal modeling
  (b) vicarious learning
  (c) live modeling
  (d) pure imitation

27. An abstract representation of an observed behavior is called a

  (a) conditioned response
  (b) schema
  (c) generalized response
  (d) mnemonic device

28. Lowell needs to go shopping for many items, but he tries to memorize them rather than write a list. Later, he finds he can recall only the first and last items he memorized. This illustrates

  (a) long-term retention
  (b) recognition rather than recall
  (c) paired-associate learning
  (d) the serial position effect

29. The most easily recalled items in a list would show

  (a) high organization and low imagery
  (b) low organization and low imagery
  (c) low organization and high imagery
  (d) high organization and high imagery

30. Suppose the word "murder" is introduced in a long list of fruits and vegetables. The resultant high level of recall of that word in its place in the list would illustrate

  (a) the reminiscence effect
  (b) short-term memory

(c) the von Restorff effect

(d) the TOT phenomenon

31. Jerry learned to play tennis. One winter, he learned to play badminton. When he started to play tennis again the following spring, Jerry found that much of the badminton learning disrupted his tennis game. This is an example of

(a) negative transfer

(b) positive transfer

(c) proactive interference

(d) retroactive interference

32. "If it's blue *or* it's borrowed, I can use it for my wedding." A sentence like this illustrates a

(a) conjunctive concept

(b) disjunctive concept

(c) prototype

(d) relational concept

33. The basic sound or inflection components of a language are called

(a) syllables

(b) phonemes

(c) morphemes

(d) words

34. Prediction of future performance is the intent of

(a) achievement tests

(b) aptitude tests

(c) group tests only

(d) culture-biased tests

35. The results of psychological testing should be released on demand to

(a) only the individual tested and those the individual names

(b) the individual, close relatives, and school personnel

(c) any competent psychologist, relatives, and close friends

(d) anyone with a need for the information

36. The percentage of the population falling between +1 and −1 standard deviations on the normal curve (normal probability distribution) is

(a) 16

(b) 34

(c) 68

(d) 95

37. Which of the following is *not* a measure of central tendency?

(a) correlation

(b) mode

(c) median

(d) all are measures of central tendency

38. The resolution of crises at each stage of personality development was part of the theory of

   (*a*) Jung
   (*b*) Freud
   (*c*) Adler
   (*d*) Erikson

39. According to Freud's theory, if Abner tends to be sloppy and disorderly, it may be because he is fixated at the

   (*a*) oral stage
   (*b*) anal stage
   (*c*) phallic stage
   (*d*) latent stage

40. The highest age at which a child passes all items on that level of the Stanford-Binet Intelligence Test is called

   (*a*) basal age
   (*b*) mental age
   (*c*) ceiling age
   (*d*) chronological age

41. Suppose a child were able to use logical concepts as long as they were tied to observable things. According to Piaget, the child probably would be how old?

   (*a*) less than 2 years
   (*b*) 2 to 7 years
   (*c*) 7 to 11 years
   (*d*) 11 years or older

42. Which of the following probably would *not* be used to measure creativity?

   (*a*) remote association test
   (*b*) anagram test
   (*c*) Thematic Apperception Test
   (*d*) drawing completion test

43. A persistent need to wash one's hands at least once every half hour probably represents

   (*a*) a dissociative reaction
   (*b*) an obsessive reaction
   (*c*) a hysterical reaction
   (*d*) a compulsive reaction

44. An individual who understands society's rules but chooses to ignore them and act according to personal wishes shows

   (*a*) psychosomatic disorder
   (*b*) antisocial personality disorder
   (*c*) mood disorder
   (*d*) autism

45. Which of the following is *not* a biomedical therapy?

(*a*) ECT
(*b*) drug therapy
(*c*) psychosurgery
(*d*) implosion therapy

46. The placebo effect is illustrated best by

(*a*) the use of ECT to overcome chronic depression
(*b*) overcoming resistance in a psychotherapeutic setting
(*c*) the patient's recovery based on the belief that the therapist *must* know all the answers
(*d*) the use of genetic counseling regarding the possibility of birth defects

47. In reading a restaurant menu, trying to choose between two very tasty entrees illustrates

(*a*) approach-avoidance conflict
(*b*) avoidance-avoidance conflict
(*c*) approach-approach conflict
(*d*) cognitive dissonance conflict

48. Suppose four teenagers get together and decide to try smoking marijuana. Alone, none of them would have done this, but as a group they do. This illustrates

(*a*) the quadratic effect
(*b*) group polarization
(*c*) stereotyping
(*d*) catharsis

49. Jack really likes Jill. When asked why, he responds, "Because she gives as much to our relationship as she takes." Jack's comment about Jill illustrates

(*a*) social identity theory
(*b*) balance theory
(*c*) the elaboration-likelihood model
(*d*) equity theory

50. If you believe in the saying "First impressions count," you agree with the principle of

(*a*) the primacy effect
(*b*) the halo effect
(*c*) least interest
(*d*) the recency effect

51. What are the general trends in the development of psychology as a science today?

Several trends appear to be prominent. Psychology has expanded into many new areas in business, the community, and research. In general, psychologists tend to study fairly specific topics rather than large or general areas, and while there are unifying attempts among psychologists and growing cooperation among the different specialities in psychology, there are no longer efforts to explain all of behavior with a single position, as happened at the start of psychology.

52. Although Freud often is mentioned as a very important person in the development of psychology, he is not given credit for starting psychology. Why?

Freud is not given credit for starting psychology because he did not claim to be a psychologist. He was a medical doctor and developed a speciality in psychiatry. Wundt is credited with starting psychology because he claimed to be a psychologist and started the first psychology laboratory.

53. Why is it necessary to write a research report in a form that allows the study to be repeated exactly?

It is possible that the results obtained in any study occurred by chance. If it is not possible to repeat the study, there is no way for other experimenters to check and confirm or revise the findings. Replicability is thus a cornerstone of the experimental method.

54. How do human germ cells (egg and sperm) differ from other body cells?

Germ cells are the only cells in the body that may unite to create a zygote. Moreover, they have only half the number of chromosomes that other body cells possess. (When the egg and the sperm unite, the 23 chromosomes in each germ cell pair to create the 46-chromosome complement in the zygote.)

55. Which of the measures of central tendency is most sensitive to the effects of an extreme score in the distribution?

Assuming there is only one score that differs considerably from the others in the distribution, the mean will be more sensitive to the effects of that score than will the median or the mode. The mean is the average score and incorporates all the scores when it is calculated. The median and the mode may vary slightly because of the addition of one more score to the distribution but will be influenced much less than will the mean.

56. How does the growth rate of a child's head compare with the growth rate of the rest of his or her body?

One trend in physical development is called the cephalo-caudal trend. This means the head area grows more rapidly than do the other portions of the body. In the human developmental sequence, this appears to be necessary to accommodate the rapid development of the brain.

57. Why do children in different cultures learn different languages?

Children in different cultures learn different languages simply because of the models they have. Evidence indicates that all normal children may have the capacity to learn any spoken language and indeed may produce the sounds of all different languages early in life. However, a combination of modeling and reinforcement for appropriate responses helps form the selected language for the children.

58. There are two aspects of the refractory phase for nerves. What are they called, and how do they differ?

The refractory phase is divided into the absolute refractory phase and the relative refractory phase. During the absolute refractory phase, no stimulus, no matter how strong, can cause the neuron to conduct a signal. In the relative refractory phase, a stronger than normal stimulus can generate a signal. Once the refractory phase is complete, a normal signal will fire the neuron.

59. Why is the autonomic nervous system sometimes described as "antagonistic"?

The autonomic nervous system is composed of the sympathetic and parasympathetic systems. In general, these systems work in opposite (or antagonistic) manners, with the sympathetic system stimulating or supporting action and energy expenditure and the parasympathetic system involved with energy conservation and body recuperation.

60. Why is a description of the "basic five" senses misleading?

A description of the basic five senses is misleading because it is incomplete. Evidence indicates that there are at least seven basic senses, with kinesthesis and balance (vestibulation) added to the traditional five. In addition, much evidence indicates that there are distinct subcategories of most, if not all, of these seven senses.

61. Many researchers have tested people for their sensitivity to touch. Most people can tell when there are two points slightly touching their lips or mouth region. However, when the same stimulus is applied to their backs, people show much less sensitivity. Why?

Touch receptors are not distributed equally on the body. The number of receptors and the amount of brain area devoted to touch reception around the mouth are considerably greater than those associated with the back. This means that the region around the mouth will have greater touch sensitivity than will the back.

62. In general, what are the major factors studied in signal detection theory?

Three considerations seem most important for signal detection theory. The first is the motivation experienced by the person being studied, the second is the level of extraneous stimulation ("noise") that is occurring, and the third is the probability of occurrence of the stimulus being investigated. These three factors combine to affect how likely a person is to attend to a stimulus.

63. What is the gate-control theory of pain?

The gate-control theory of pain suggests that there are receptors that can send signals to make a person more or less sensitive to pain. It appears there may be two variants of this: One indicates that when another set of neural receptors is activated, the pain sensation is reduced, while the other suggests that signals sent from the brain close the gate to pain from the injured area.

64. What are the characteristics of a person *least* likely to be hypnotized?

It is most difficult to hypnotize someone who is unwilling to be hypnotized, is relatively rigid in thinking patterns, and does not trust the hypnotist. People most likely to be hypnotized show the opposite characteristics.

65. Why is human sexual behavior not considered a survival motive?

Sexual behavior is necessary for the survival of the species but not for the survival of a single individual. The other survival motives must be satisfied or an individual will die. However, an individual can remain celibate throughout life without influencing his or her chances for survival.

66. Learned motives seem to be predominant in our society. Why?

The reason learned motives appear to predominate in our society is that unlearned (survival) motives are in general easily satisfied. If for some reason survival motives became difficult to satisfy, they certainly would become predominant.

67. What are some of the physiological indications of emotional arousal?

Physiological indicators of emotion include changes in heart rate, respiration rate, blood pressure, electrodermal activity (EDA), glandular secretions, and other bodily processes. These changes sometimes are more revealing than is the expression of emotion through language or gesture.

68. Some physiological illnesses appear to be brought on by psychological causes. What are these illnesses called?

Such illnesses are called somatoform disorders. A considerable amount of research indicates that some actual physical problems result from psychological causes rather than from organic malfunctioning. For example, a person may experience blindness or paralysis (a conversion disorder) yet show no physical problem that could account for the difficulty.

69. In the early stages of a classical conditioning procedure, the subject sometimes responds by turning toward the CS as well as reacting to the US. What is the reaction to the CS called? What usually happens to it?

The reaction to the CS is called the *orienting response*. Usually, as the subject becomes accustomed to the conditioning procedure, the orienting response drops out. (This is comparable to the principle of habituation.)

70. How would a conditioned aversive stimulus be established?

To establish a conditioned aversive stimulus, a previously neutral stimulus would have to be paired with an aversive stimulus a sufficient number of times for the subject to make the association between the two. The previously neutral stimulus would come to take on aversive properties.

71. Behavior modification often is used as a therapeutic technique for autistic children. What is behavior modification? Why might it be particularly useful in the treatment of autistic children?

Behavior modification involves the use of operant conditioning principles to change responding patterns: Appropriate responses are reinforced, and inappropriate responses are extinguished or punished. This treatment is sometimes very effective for autistic children because such children are reinforced for communicating and therefore become more amenable to other therapeutic treatments.

72. What does it mean when one says that retention often is evaluated by using an information-processing approach?

Retention of information that has been learned often is evaluated as the last part of a sequence involving acquisition, storage, and retrieval of that information. With the greater use of computers, a comparable pattern is seen with the computer analogy of input-storage-output, an information-processing approach that can be applied to retention.

73. Why is knowledge of results (KR) often considered to be reinforcing?

Knowledge of results provides information about the success of responding. Assuming that the response has "worked," KR will be judged as reinforcing. This in turn will strengthen or maintain the response, making it more likely the same response will be used in the next similar situation.

74. Why might different measures of retention reveal considerably different values?

The three most commonly used measures of retention—recognition, recall, and relearning—do not measure exactly the same things. In addition, because of the possibility of chance responses, the values which can be obtained vary. (For example, only relearning could yield a negative value.) Thus, when a report of retention is given, the measure used also should be specified.

75. What is comparable in the psychological terms *forgetting*, *habit*, and *ego*?

These three terms (and many other psychological terms) refer to qualities that cannot be measured or observed directly. They are useful explanatory or summary concepts, but they must be used carefully. Terms such as these often are called *intervening variables*, meaning they cannot be observed directly but are "tied to" observable or measurable variables.

76. Given an opportunity to suggest different uses for a chair, Patrick finds he can think of a chair only as something one sits on. What term describes Patrick's limited responding?

Patrick's "block" is a form of set called *functional fixedness*. Functional fixedness means the respondent can think of an object only in terms related to its usual or normal function and is unable to break the set and generate other ideas.

77. Arrange the terms *clause*, *phoneme*, *syllable*, and *sentence* in a hierarchy and explain the order you choose.

The hierarchy for these terms might be (1) phoneme, (2) syllable, (3) clause, and (4) sentence. A phoneme is a sound or stress component of a spoken language. Syllables are composed of one or more phonemes. Words are composed of one or more syllables and are used to form clauses. A sentence may be composed of one or more clauses.

78. Some people like to solve the maze puzzles in the Sunday newspaper supplement by starting at the goal and tracing a pattern back to the start. What problem-solving strategy does this match?

   Starting at the end and working backward is comparable to the heuristic called *backward search*. One begins at the end point of a problem and works backward, a strategy that often helps maximize the possibility of finding a correct solution.

79. Robert Sternberg developed a triarchic theory of intelligence. What were the three components of this theory? Which one of the three was thought to represent practical intelligence?

   The three components of Sternberg's triarchic theory of intelligence are (1) componential intelligence, the abilities used to analyze information in order to solve problems; (2) experiential intelligence, how previous learning is used to solve problems; and (3) contextual intelligence, how intelligence is used to face environmental demands. The last of these components, contextual intelligence, sometimes is thought of as representing practical intelligence, that is, getting along in one's world.

80. What are the differences between a projective test and a behavioral assessment in evaluating personality characteristics?

   Projective tests present ambiguous stimuli such as pictures and inkblots or a written stimulus and ask the subject to respond. The responses are interpreted in an attempt to assess personality. Behavioral assessments present "natural" settings (either actually natural or contrived by the examiner) in which the individual reacts. The person's activities are interpreted in an attempt to understand personality characteristics. Behavioral assessments involve predetermined situations and actual responses, while projective tests evaluate reactions to ambiguous pictures or situational descriptions.

81. What is a regression procedure? How commonly are these procedures used?

   A regression procedure involves making predictions about future behaviors on the basis of past correlations that have been calculated. If one knows the value of a correlation and the values of one comparable variable, predictions about the values of a second comparable variable can be made. Regression procedures are used when the evidence supporting one correlation is sufficient to warrant making the additional predictions.

82. What emphasis did Freud place on the stages of the development of personality?

   Freud felt the first three stages of personality development (oral, anal, and phallic) were more important than the latter stages (latent and genital) in the formation of personality. Fixation at these early stages could carry over and affect adult expression of personality. Freud placed emphasis on the sexual and aggressive aspects of development during these stages.

83. Allport distinguished among three different levels of personality traits. What were these three levels? Which was considered most important in influencing personality?

   Allport distinguished among cardinal, central, and secondary traits of personality. The cardinal trait level was considered the most important; cardinal traits unify, integrate, and control a person's behavior. Central traits also are important in many situations, while secondary traits affect some but not many situations.

84. What is a phobia? Why are phobias explained or interpreted in more than one way?

   A phobia is an intense, compelling fear of a particular situation or type of stimulus. The intensity of a phobia usually is far greater than the circumstances seem to warrant. Several types of explanations are used to try to account for phobias. Some psychologists believe phobias are the result of classical conditioning, where a previously neutral stimulus is paired with a fear-producing stimulus and the previously neutral stimulus comes to be fear-producing. Others suggest that phobias are actually a form of displacement, so that the fear of one thing is actually a symbolic fear of something else.

85. Distinguish between physiological and psychological addictions.

A physiological addiction refers to a dependence on a substance such that if the substance is removed abruptly, a physical illness or distress results. Psychological addiction means the dependence is such that if the substance, object, or support is removed, pronounced anxiety or psychological discomfort will result. In some cases, both dependencies can exist simultaneously.

86. Psychological depression has been called the only "fatal" mental illness. Why? What biomedical therapies often are used to combat chronic depression?

Depression has been called the only "fatal" mental illness because so many people in that condition commit suicide. The most common form of biomedical therapy used for depression is drug therapy. A number of drugs are classified as antidepressants. In instances where even antidepressants do not seem to work, some patients are given electroconvulsive therapy (ECT). ECT seems to alleviate depression and make a patient more receptive to other therapies.

87. Distinguish among delusions, illusions, and hallucinations.

Delusions refer to irrational beliefs that persist even in the face of overwhelming evidence to the contrary. Illusions are misinterpretations of actually existing sensory stimuli. Hallucinations are perceptions of things that actually do not exist.

88. In a situation that requires assisting someone else, when is a person most likely to help?

In assistance situations, a person is most likely to volunteer help when he or she is alone. When a person in need is confronted by a group of people, the responsibility of each person in the group appears to become diffused, and helping behavior becomes less likely.

89. What are the three major components of an attitude?

The three components of attitude can be remembered as "ABC." *A* stands for the affective, or emotional, component; *B* for the behavioral, or action, component; and *C* for the cognitive, or thinking, component.

90. Having just missed several lines in a play, Adrienne comes off stage and says, "It would be hard to remember anything today; the theater is just too darn hot to think straight!" Adrienne's comment can be explained by what principle of social psychology?

Adrienne's response provides evidence for self-serving bias. If she had remembered all her lines, she would have been likely to take personal (internal) credit for doing so. However, having missed several, Adrienne attributes her mistakes to the temperature in the theater (external) instead of a personal characteristic.

Answers to Problems 1–50

1. (*c*)	6. (*b*)	11. (*b*)	16. (*d*)	21. (*d*)	26. (*a*)	31. (*d*)	36. (*c*)	41. (*c*)	46. (*c*)
2. (*a*)	7. (*b*)	12. (*a*)	17. (*d*)	22. (*a*)	27. (*b*)	32. (*b*)	37. (*a*)	42. (*c*)	47. (*c*)
3. (*c*)	8. (*d*)	13. (*d*)	18. (*b*)	23. (*c*)	28. (*d*)	33. (*b*)	38. (*d*)	43. (*d*)	48. (*b*)
4. (*c*)	9. (*a*)	14. (*b*)	19. (*a*)	24. (*c*)	29. (*d*)	34. (*b*)	39. (*b*)	44. (*b*)	49. (*d*)
5. (*b*)	10. (*c*)	15. (*a*)	20. (*a*)	25. (*b*)	30. (*c*)	35. (*a*)	40. (*a*)	45. (*d*)	50. (*a*)

INDEX